HERITAGE AND HOPE

HERITAGE AND HOPE

The African-American Presence in United Methodism

GRANT S. SHOCKLEY
GENERAL EDITOR

KAREN Y. COLLIER
WILLIAM B. McCLAIN
ASSOCIATE EDITORS

ABINGDON PRESS
Nashville, Tennessee

HERITAGE AND HOPE:
THE AFRICAN-AMERICAN PRESENCE IN UNITED METHODISM

Copyright © 1991 by Abingdon Press

This book is printed on recycled, acid-free paper.

Library of Congress Cataloging-in-Publication Data

SHOCKLEY, GRANT S., 1919-
    Heritage and hope : The African-American presence in United Methodism / Grant S. Shockley.
        p.   cm.
    Includes bibliographical references and index.
    ISBN 0-687-16898-8 (alk. paper)
    1. Afro-American Methodists—History. 2. Methodist Church—United States—History. 3. United Methodist Church (U.S.)—History.
I. Title.
BX8435.S56   1991
287′.6′08996073—dc20
                                                                          91-24090
                                                                          CIP

MANUFACTURED IN THE UNITED STATES OF AMERICA

C O N T E N T S

P R E F A C E

L. Scott Allen

The historical records of American Methodism are scarce and scattered when searching for the story of the participation of black people who remained in United Methodism and contributed to its growth, development, and witness.

This paucity of data is largely due to the difficulty historians have encountered in seeking publishers who were receptive to manuscripts in this field. The consequences of this situation have greatly impoverished American church history generally, and the field of black church history has been particularly affected.

Heritage and Hope represents a constructive effort to eliminate this deficiency and preserve the significant impact of black religious experience and developments within United Methodism upon the Methodist movement as a whole.

The comprehensive scope of the material presented in this volume is indicative of a broad range of in-depth research, analysis, and interpretation of black United Methodist history and the experience of black United Methodists in the long course of their more than two-hundred-year relationship to the church.

This study encompasses the past and present and a projected future as cardinal elements of a meaningful history. It has produced some illuminating insights that may serve to sensitize The United Methodist Church to some new directions in which it should move in preparation for a more effective witness and outreach to the black community, the nation, and the world in the coming century. The objectives of this project will not be concluded with this initial volume. It should be continuously updated and expanded in the future by historians who are interested in preserving the rich heritage of a people whose commitment to United Methodism has been, under diverse and adverse circumstances, genuine and exemplary.

ACKNOWLEDGMENTS

One of the principal needs of The United Methodist Church has been to recover and make known the history of its racial/ethnic membership.

During the fall of 1984 and the winter of 1985 the General Commission on Archives and History of The United Methodist Church sponsored a series of four two-day consultations that brought together historians and leaders from United Methodism's Asian American, black, Hispanic, and Native American communities. Each of these consultations reviewed and assessed what had been done regarding the history of its constituency and what needed to be done to recover its story. This volume, one of a series of four, is the result. We are confident that it makes a significant contribution to our denomination's history.

The General Commission on Archives and History is grateful to the General Conference, and especially to the General Council on Ministries, for the financial support that has made this and the other volumes possible. We also express our appreciation to the authors and editors whose expert labors now broaden our knowledge of the history of the church, and to the United Methodist Publishing House, without whose cooperation there would be no series. A special word of appreciation goes to Rebecca Marnhout, who skillfully copyedited all four volumes.

Present and former members of the General Commission's staff, Carolyn DeSwarte Gifford, Susan M. Eltscher, and C. Jarrett Gray, Jr., have made important contributions to this project.

MAJOR J. JONES, *Chairperson (1980–1988)*
Ethnic Heritage and History Committee

CHARLES YRIGOYEN, JR., *General Secretary*
General Commission on Archives and History

9

EDITOR'S INTRODUCTION

Grant S. Shockley

People in the United States who call themselves Methodist follow in the tradition of the religious movement that began in the eighteenth century with the evangelistic work of John Wesley and his brother, Charles Wesley. Historically, black people have been a part of that movement. Many thousands have been converted to it, participated in it, shaped its policies and plans, and made rich contributions to its life. Since its inception in this country in the 1760s, a black presence has influenced every decade and development of its more than two-hundred-year history. This in turn has indelibly influenced the secular as well as the religious life of the nation.

Whence this impact from a black presence? Basically, it has come from four major traditions: black United Methodists, those who remained in the Methodist Episcopal Church (1784–1939) through its change to The Methodist Church (1940–1968) and The United Methodist Church (1968–present); the African Methodist Episcopal (AME) Church, whose original black membership left the Methodist Episcopal Church under the leadership of Richard Allen in 1816; the African Methodist Episcopal Zion (AMEZ) Church, whose membership similarly left the Methodist Episcopal Church in 1820–1821, led by James Varick; and the Christian Methodist Episcopal (CME) Church, whose membership desired and secured a separate identification from the Methodist Episcopal Church, South, in 1870.

This volume is concerned particularly with those black Methodists who chose to remain in the United Methodist tradition. It is this segment of black Methodism that has most critically influenced the denomination and, through the denomination, the moral and social conscience of the churches and society in the United States.

Given this background, the purposes of this volume are five: (1) to provide a clarifying record of the historical development of the black community within The United Methodist Church; (2) to critically explore and examine the role and status of black people in United Methodism; (3) to highlight the aspirations, achievements, and contributions of black people in the church; (4) to assess United Methodism's faithfulness to its historic mission, and (5) to suggest guidelines for a liberating, reforming, and empowering black United Methodists now and in the future.

This is not the first attempt to produce a history of black people in the Episcopal Methodist tradition. Several writers (black and white) have published general book-length treatments of the topic covering general and special concerns. As early as 1890 L. M. Hagood published *The Colored Man in the Methodist Episcopal Church*. In 1910 *Methodism and the Negro* was written by I. L. Thomas. Almost fifty years then elapsed before the publication of J. Beverly F. Shaw's *The Negro in the History of Methodism*. In that same year (1954) the Board of Missions of the Church released Mason Crum's *The Negro in the Methodist Church*. An edited volume by James S. Gadsden resulted from the National United Methodist Convocation on the Black Church in Atlanta, Georgia, *Experience, Struggles and Hopes of the Black Church*. John H. Graham wrote *Black United Methodists: Retrospect and Prospect* in 1979, and William B. McClain published *Black People in the Methodist Church: Whither Goest Thou?* in 1984. In 1978 a Task Group on the History of the Central Jurisdiction Women's Organization published *To a Higher Glory: The Growth and Development of Black Women Organized for Mission in the Methodist Church, 1940–1968*.

Heritage and Hope, while not pretending to be complete, comprehensive, or in any way "official," will hopefully deal responsibly with the meager and scattered resources available and represent fairly the many opinions of our highly pluralistic constituency, both black and white.

Many individuals have contributed to the completion of this book. The General Editor is especially grateful to Charles Yrigoyen, Jr. and the staff of the General Commission on Archives and History for the initiation and support of the unique project of which this volume is a part. The black Bishops of The United Methodist Church, active and retired, have been encouraging and have responded whenever requested, with vital information.

Other persons who provided counsel and assistance were: Theressa Hoover, Board of Global Ministries (Retired, 1990); Major J. Jones, Chairperson, Ethnic Heritage and History Committee (1980–1988); Thomas Langford, the Divinity School, Duke University; Allen M. Mayes, Board of Pensions (Retired, 1990); C. Leonard Miller, General Council on Ministries (Deceased, 1991); Randolph Nugent, Board of Global Ministries; Barbara R. Thompson, Commission on Religion and Race, and Robert W. Wilson, Duke University Divinity School (Deceased, 1991). Ronald P. Patterson, Senior Editor, Abingdon Press, has rendered guidance and assistance throughout the publication process. Dean, Dennis M. Campbell, The Divinity School, Duke University, was encouraging and highly considerate of the time and priority given to this project.

Cooperation was received from many United Methodist boards and agency staff persons: M. Garlinda Burton, Barbara E. Campbell, Paul Extrum-Fernandez, Richard R. Hicks, Robert W. Huston, Marilyn Magee, Chiquita G. Smith, and Cherryetta Williams.

Source materials, documents, and manuscripts used and cited in compiling this book were located in libraries, archival collections and annual conference centers. Librarians and archivists who have made these materials available and helped in their use were: William C. Beal, Archives and History Center; Don M. Farris, Duke Divinity School Library; Wilson N. Flemister and Dovie Touchstone Patrick, Atlanta University Center Library; Channing R. Jeschke, Candler School of Theology Library, Emory University; and Kenneth E. Rowe, Drew University Library.

Specialized materials and information were often difficult to obtain. The following persons have been helpful in accessing this data: Peggy Billings (historical materials); Elwood G. Davis (Southern New Jersey Conference research); Dennis R. Fletcher (Eastern Pennsylvania Conference data); Ralph H. Jones (C. A. Tindley research); and Alfred L. Norris (Gammon Theological Seminary.)

A word of special appreciation is in order for the contributors to this volume and for the assistance of Associate Editors, Karen Y. Collier and William B. McClain. Also, a word of gratitude is offered for the typing and word-processing expertise of Reta L. Bigham. Finally, inspiration, support and assistance with manuscript preparation details have come from my wife, Doris T. Shockley.

CONTRIBUTORS

Lewis V. Baldwin, Ph.D., Northwestern University. Associate Professor, Religious Studies, Vanderbilt University. Author of *"Invisible" Strands in African Methodism: A History of the African Union Methodist Protestant and Union American Methodist Episcopal Churches, 1805–1980*. Recent publication: *There Is a Balm in Gilead: The Cultural Roots of Martin Luther King, Jr.*

Karen Y. Collier, Ph.D., Duke University. Minister, Seay Hubbard United Methodist Church, Nashville, Tennessee. Her 1984 Dissertation: "An Examination of Varied Aspects of Race and Episcopacy in American Methodism 1844–1939."

Major J. Jones, Th.D., Boston University. Former President-Dean, Gammon Theological Seminary, Interdenominational Theological Center. Present position: Chaplain to the Atlanta University Center. Recent publication: *The Color of God: The Concept of God in Afro-American Thought.*

C. Eric Lincoln, Ph.D., Boston University. Professor, Religion and Culture, Duke University. Recent publications: *The Avenue, Clayton City* (novel); *This Road Since Freedom; The Black Church in the African American Religious Experience.*

William B. McClain, D.Min., Boston University. D.D. Professor of Preaching and Worship, Wesley Theological Seminary. Recent publications: *Black People in the Methodist Church; Travelling Light: Christian Perspectives on Pilgrimage and Pluralism; Come Sunday: The Liturgy of Zion.*

Grant S. Shockley, Ed.D., Columbia University. Professor Emeritus of Christian Education, the Divinity School, Duke University. Contributor to *Ethnicity in the Education of the Church;* Advisory Editor of and Contributor to *Encyclopedia of Religious Education;* Co-Editor of *Working with Black Youth.*

F O R E W O R D

C. Eric Lincoln

In 1791 Richard Allen, one of the earliest church fathers in black Methodism, was asked by his fellows in the Free African Society of Philadelphia to lead them in founding an African Episcopal Church. Allen graciously acknowledged the grave honor extended him by his Christian friends and neighbors who had so recently found their communion with St. George's Methodist no longer tenable, and who were in consequence urgently in need of more reliable spiritual groundings. However, even though he (with Absalom Jones), had been a founder and a leader of the Free African Society, which bridged their departure from St. George's, Allen's demurrer, painful as it must have been, was nonetheless candid, clear, and classic: "As for me, I could never be anything but a Methodist . . . and I am thankful that ever I heard a Methodist preacher!"

Allen's staunch fidelity to Methodism, even in the face of the demeaning unpleasantness of segregation he and his friends had experienced at St. George's, is an early dramatization of the extraordinary bond that has characterized the African American devotion to the Methodist Church from its inception. The whole history of Methodism witnesses to Richard Allen's poignant confession. From the eighteenth century on to this present day, the blacks who heard the Methodist preachers on their lonely itinerations from frontier to frontier and from town to town have been mighty impressed with what they heard. They took it to heart and made it the organizing principle of their lives, directing their critical relations with God and man. Methodism is richer and infinitely more potent in spirit and in outreach because they did.

John Wesley himself authenticated the tradition of black involvement by baptizing two black Methodists in 1758. In Maryland in the 1760s, Anne Sweitzer, a black woman, confirmed Wesley's open door protocol when she became a founding member of the first Methodist society in Maryland. Two years later in New York City, another black woman, known to us only as

Bettye, was one of five persons to attend the Methodist services inaugurated by Philip Embury. And when the John Street Church—the first meeting house for the nascent communion, was built in New York City in 1768, the names of several black subscribers appeared on its roster of membership. Similarly, there was an African presence at the Christmas Conference of 1784, which marked the formal organization of the Methodist Church, just as there was an African presence at the celebration of Pentecost, which launched the Christian church two thousand years earlier, half a world away. In Methodism as in Christianity, the serious involvement of a black constituency dates from its initiation, and when the Civil War split the Methodist communion into Northern and Southern fragments seventy-five years after its formation, African membership in The Methodist Church had reached approximately 207,000, the overwhelming majority of them in what was to become the Methodist Episcopal Church, South.

The war took its inevitable toll on black membership in the southern church. Tens of thousands of black Methodists sought to express their new sense of freedom by becoming a part of the Africanization movement symbolized by the African Methodist Episcopal (AME) and AME Zion churches, and by the self-confident African Baptist churches that antedated the founding of the black Methodist communions. Others transferred their membership to the Northern branch of the riven Mother Church. But some stayed put, and because they did the history of Methodism took on a distinguishing patina that could hardly have been anticipated. Methodism went on to develop a church within a church, a curious phenomenon designed as a *modus vivendi* for addressing the difficulties white Methodists had long experienced with black acceptability despite the obvious conflict of these difficulties with the fundamental principles upon which the faith was alleged to rest.

This development was exaggerated by the exigencies of war. Previously, the slave status of Africans in The Methodist Church was sufficient justification to some, though certainly not to all, white Methodists for the institutionalization of differential treatment in the church consistent with that in the society at large. The end of the Civil War abruptly changed the civil status of African Americans, though it scarcely affected their social location, so the church was faced with the problem of redefining its social polity for a black minority who were now citizens instead of slaves. What was to be the new African American's access to spiritual community and fellowship? And what was to be the new rationale upon which the quality of that access would rest? It was not a problem The Methodist Church was eager to engage. The problem was mitigated for a time by the aggressive crusading of the preachers and evangelists from African Methodism who came south in the wake of the Union armies. The black evangels challenged their black brothers and sisters to leave the segregated galleries of the white man's churches and find dignity and spiritual comfort in a church of their own, an *African* church. Such a challenge was not to be ignored. Freedom included among other things the freedom to leave: to leave the plantation, to leave the South, to leave the church that had been part of the machinery of bondage. So many Africans opted for the new challenge and possibilities they saw in this vision of freedom that by the end of the Civil War there were only 78,742 African Americans left in the Methodist Episcopal Church, South.

But some stayed where they were, effectively resisting the challenge to slough off their debased status in their birthright churches via the strategy of renouncement. They weathered the disgust, the pity, and the ridicule of their well-meaning friends in African Methodism, but ironically, they were welded by the same sentiments expressed by the founder of African Methodism almost a hundred years earlier, when he confessed to the world that he "could never be anything but a Methodist." For his spiritual counterparts in the southern church, Richard Allen's dictum that "no religious sect or denomination would suit the capacity of the Colored people as well as the Methodist" was as sound and as sacred to them as it had been to him when he put his church above his personal consideration. For them as for him, Methodism was a birthright not lightly to be eschewed.

But a war had been fought, and black freedom, however qualified, was a reality. Responsibility is ever the corollary of freedom, and to some minds responsibility implied the ability to cope with life in all its dimensions, including the spiritual. Inevitably, there were black Methodists remaining in the southern church whose loyalties to Methodism were unimpeachable, yet whose sense of personal and racial responsibility called them to a mission and a destiny on terms more responsive to their own determinations. They wanted to be and to remain Methodists, but Methodists free to pursue their peculiar responses to life's challenges, exempt, insofar as possible, from the prejudgments of the slavocracy from which they had so recently been liberated. It was such a group of black Methodists who petitioned the General Conference meeting in New Orleans in 1866 for their orderly dismissal from the Methodist Episcopal Church, South, without prejudice. Their petition was received benignly and effected with dispatch. Four years later the Colored Methodist Episcopal Church (CME) in America was born at Jackson, Tennessee.

The elation of the petitioners that they had been able to leave the fellowship without summarily leaving the church was properly sobered by the realization that they were their own keepers in Christ from that day forward. But this was what they had said they wanted, and now their independence was a reality. While they could take comfort from the fact that they had not been hastily and hostilely severed, severed they were. There was a discreet remorse among some in the Mother Church who watched them go, and the Mother Church itself assisted them with goods and services, consultation and advice. The ordination of their bishops and the regularization of their episcopal polity was carefully

17

attended by officers of the General Conference of the Methodist Episcopal Church, South, appointed for that purpose. And above all, the promise of a continuing relationship of good will and community as brothers and sisters in Christian Methodism (albeit in separate communions) gave this newest adventure in black Methodism a distinctly different cast from that of the African churches. The CME Church in America was its own peculiar expression of the will to Christian responsibility in a society where clear choices were not always viable. They were *independent* Methodists, but they still had strong bonds of mutual sentiment and informal oversight with the Southern Methodist Episcopal Church. They were black Methodists, but by their own self-perception they were not *African* Methodists. They were by their own designation the *Colored* Methodist Episcopal Church in America, and under that carefully constructed denominational ensign, they served notice on the world, and more particularly on themselves, of their distinctive approach to the challenge of Christian responsibility.

The departure of the Colored Methodists was not one of the more innocuous incidents of Methodist church history. To some degree the CME exodus bought time for an institution that still had to come to terms with the consequences of the late unpleasantness it recognized as the War Between the States. But it was clear to all concerned that Southern Methodism was scarcely prepared to modify substantially the traditions and the conventions of slavery that had long clouded the witness of the church to suddenly accommodate the new and improbable implications of black freedom. The war was over, but the resistance to the implications of that war has not, even to this day, fully dissipated. There was ambivalence, as indeed there always is, in the challenge of causes men set great store upon. Such ambivalence was clearly pronounced in the peculiar stratagems of CME withdrawal. But there was ambivalence in the Mother Church as well. There were in many cases strong emotional ties to the black individuals who separated themselves from the fellowship of the church, but there were also some feelings of dismay at the impending threat to the institutionalized patterns of behavior that depended substantially upon the socializing and monitoring roles of the church. Beyond that, the CME exodus represented one more episode of fragmentation of the Methodist community, and the first to strike directly at the Southern constituency since it parted company with its Northern counterpart.

The miracle of Methodism finds its most remarkable expression not so much in the fact that those who left the original church were so inflexible in their determination to continue to pursue Methodism under whatever rubric or designation as in the fact that a significant remnant declined to leave the Mother Church under any circumstances. The enticements and the provocations for blacks in The Methodist Church to seek spiritual peace and personal dignity elsewhere are an indelible part of Methodist history. Yet the Black Remnant that weathered those provocations and enticements not only survived and flowered but also turned out to be a determinative force in the shaping of Methodist history ever since. It is these committed Christians who in their commitment "could never be anything but Methodists" *in the citadel of Methodism,* who here seek to share their identity and their historic commitment more meaningfully with the church they love and serve. They are the black loyalists who long ago chose to make their witness where they were. In face of inscrutable fate, they made their stand by faith: faith in God and faith in the certain triumph of his church. They "could never be anything but Methodists," because Methodism can never be anything more than the people who comprise it.

Why did the black Methodists stay on in The Methodist Church where they were undervalued as persons, and where their spiritual consideration was generally less than enthusiastic? First of all, in true freedom the option to stay is as viable as the option to leave. To stay with the Mother Church was the expression of freedom and the challenge of responsibility the Black Remnant decided to pursue. They had a different vision. The African churches and the CME churches had demonstrated the courage of their most compelling convictions through the instrumentality of new and independent black communions. In so doing they had an immutable guarantee that the determinations of their churches would always be their own. Their destinies and polity would be of their own making, and in their own hands. Black United Methodists had no such consolation, but they had a vision of a church that would in time transcend the accidents of race and the ephemerality of station. In their church they were a small minority, and in the eyes of some a troublesome, pejorative minority at that. But where there is the gravest doubt, there is also the greatest opportunity for faith to be relevant, and for sacrifice to be productive. The Black Remnant stayed to witness because witnessing under stress is the oldest and most significant tradition of the faith. And while no mortal is ever completely inured to stress, these black men and women were well equipped by previous experience to endure it until their change should come.

The Black Methodist Remnant is the historical critical mass that persistently urges the church toward the development of a social consciousness more consistent with its spiritual ideals. Although the notion of The United Methodist Church as a white communion still persists in the shorthand of popular identification, that appellation is no longer strictly creditable. The church does have an overwhelmingly white constituency, and in consequence its ambience, style, and critical determinations tend to reflect that fact. But the underlying reality is that United Methodism today is multiracial, and its perceived racial characterization will wither of its own inutility when image and substance are finally in agreement. The Black Remnant is the primordial conscience of United Methodism, and its peculiar witness is to be faithful to its commitment to help the church find that elusive place that comes when

19

spiritual rhetoric and human awareness are in compliance with each other. From the beginning they accepted reality and worked and prayed for change.

Change did come, but not quickly, and not much. The reunification of The Methodist Church in 1939 brought North and South together again in a single communion, but ironically, the sectional healing did not have an effective carryover regarding the racial issues that had precipitated the breach in the first place. Unquestionably, the African Americans who had faithfully maintained their identification with both sides of the divided church for three quarters of a century had a right to expect that if North and South could forgive and forget the manmade grievances for which they had gone to war, surely the artificial grievances of racialism would be wiped out in the process.

Such was not to be. The racial climate of the country has usually found its most painful expression in the church, and in 1939 the Great American Dilemma was all-pervasive in American society. The Methodist Church was unprepared to put conscience above convention, however the implications of reunification might have been perceived. But the church did address the problem, devising in the process an institutionalized machinery called the Central Jurisdiction that gave candid, official recognition to segregation in the church. The Central Jurisdiction created, in effect, a captive black church, complete with a junto of black bishops restricted to the oversight of black Methodists. In terms of spiritual responsibility and religious comity, the Central Jurisdiction was hardly an exemplary arrangement. It gave official approval to the unwillingness or the incapacity of Methodist Christians to be Christian Methodists, and it offered the church instead a pernicious and demeaning contrivance unworthy of Machiavelli, to say nothing of Jesus Christ. Even so, the "Methodist Solution" was probably considerably ahead of the efforts of its counterpart communions of the American mainline churches, who generally refrained from addressing "the problem" at all.

In 1968 the Methodist Church was merged with the Evangelical United Brethren, an ethnic (German) communion, to form The United Methodist Church. This merger produced a church of many million members worldwide, and it also relieved Methodism of its awkward and unflattering Central Jurisdiction. Since that time the Methodist status in the religious community has appreciated significantly, and The United Methodist Church has attained increased distinctiveness for its outreach to racial and ethnic minorities, and for its acceptance of women clergy. But the millennium is not yet. The local congregations of the church are still essentially segregated, and the church-within-a-church syndrome persists despite the unrestricted deployment of a multiracial episcopacy. At the congregational level, tacit racialism remains the rule, and eleven o'clock Sunday morning is still the most segregated hour in America.

Black Methodists are aware of their church's failings, but they are also proud of its accomplishments. They have kept the faith that kept them Methodists, and they concede that their spiritual destiny and that of their church are irretrievably intertwined. When freedom came, they were the ones whom freedom called to witness where they were. Methodism was their heritage, a patrimony peculiarly suited to their needs and responsive to their commitment to forward the kingdom of God and the dignity of man wherever the need was apparent. This volume is the chronicle of that commitment.

C H A P T E R   1

EARLY AFRICAN
AMERICAN METHODISM

Founders and Foundations

Lewis V. Baldwin

The contributions of Negroes to the early rise and development of Episcopal Methodism in America have suffered from scholarly neglect. In the main, general historical interpretations of American Methodism and the emergence of Episcopal Methodism in the late eighteenth and nineteenth centuries are treated as if they bear only a casual connection to people of African descent.[1] One explanation for this is the scarcity of detailed information. A more important factor is an ingrained tendency to overlook ways in which the African American experience has informed and enriched Episcopal Methodism. Recognizing these problems, some Methodist scholars have emphasized the need for a serious effort to include Negroes more fully in the accounts related to the Methodist Episcopal tradition.[2]

The purpose of this chapter is threefold. First, attention is devoted to those events and circumstances that made Negro Methodists a vital part of the Methodist Episcopal tradition. Second, some consideration is given to how African Americans have influenced Episcopal Methodism, and in turn been influenced by it. Finally, the dynamics that gave Negro Methodist churches a unique expression within the larger framework of Episcopal Methodism in America are underscored.[3] The years within which this chapter is focused, 1784–1864, were chosen because they represent that time frame when Negro and white Methodist founders emerged to give shape, character, direction, influence, and institutional identity to Episcopal Methodism in this country.

EARLY NEGRO SOCIETIES AND CLASSES

Methodism began in America in the 1760s with the work of independent laypersons. Figures such as Barbara Heck, Philip Embury, and Robert

Strawbridge have been widely recognized as pioneers in this effort, but there were also Negro laypersons involved. When Strawbridge formed the first American Methodist Society near Sam's Creek in the northern part of Maryland in 1764, an African slave named Anne Sweitzer was said to have been among the charter members.[4] A slave woman called Bettye was one of the five persons present when the John Street Society was organized in Philip Embury's home in New York two years later.[5] The names of Margaret, Rachel, and several other African servants appeared among the list of contributors to the fund for building the first Methodist meeting house in New York.[6] The active participation of Negro women in these developments is particularly noteworthy. During this time Negro women and men were accepted into Methodism with whites irrespective of their race or slave status, but this was never meant to suggest full equality of the races.[7] Joseph Pilmore, Richard Boardman, Francis Asbury, Richard Whatcoat, and other Methodist itinerants encountered Negro members during their travels through Delaware, Maryland, Virginia, New Jersey, Pennsylvania, and New York, and they marveled at the tremendous enthusiasm with which these slaves and free Negroes responded to the Methodist appeal and shared in its promotion, despite the laws and customs imposed by a racist society. Their testimony is vital for understanding the importance of Negro lay initiative in the planting and early development of Methodism in America.[8]

Another side of the story of American Methodist beginnings has to do with the significant contributions of Negro preachers. These figures had appeared in considerable numbers in Methodist circles by the 1780s and were wielding influence among both Negroes and whites despite restrictions on their movement, function, and opportunities for leadership. As Harry V. Richardson has observed, we do not know the names of many of these early Negro preachers, "to say nothing of the story of their lives."[9] We do know that they had no warrant from John Wesley, that they were deprived of the benefit of ordination, and that they were often not allowed to address their hearers from the pulpit. Nevertheless, Negro preachers made rich and lasting contributions to Methodist beginnings on these shores. Often endowed with natural ability and eloquence, they proclaimed a simple, Bible-based gospel that moved and humbled Negro and white, male and female, slave and free. They inspired their people to join Methodist societies, classes, and Sunday schools, thus accounting in large measure for the popularity of Methodism among blacks.[10] Indeed, these preachers symbolized the spiritual power of Negroes, as well as their capacity for leadership in the church and in their own lives.[11]

The first Negro preacher to establish a wide reputation in Methodism was Harry Hosier. Born a slave in North Carolina around 1750, Hosier was converted under the preaching of the eminent bishop Francis Asbury, and though unable to read or write, he became a circuit-riding preacher with a reputation almost as great as that of the bishop. His powerful evangelical preaching at Methodist society meetings from New England to Maryland resulted in the conversion of many whites and Negroes.[12] The *New York Packet* referred to Hosier as one of the most gifted preachers in the world, a characterization echoed by Freeborn Garrettson, the Oxford-educated bishop Thomas Coke, the Philadelphia Quaker Benjamin Rush, and others among his contemporaries.[13] Hosier traveled extensively on circuits with Garrettson, Coke, Francis Asbury, Richard Whatcoat, Jesse Lee, and other appointees of John Wesley, and he should be included among that illustrious group of preachers/missionaries who conducted American Methodist work until the Christmas Conference of 1784.[14] The most memorable tribute to Hosier, who died in 1806, was paid by Bishop Coke, who insisted that "any story of the beginning of Methodism in America which does not give a prominent place to Harry Hosier, familiarly called 'Black Harry,' is inadequate. Surely he deserves a place in Methodism's Hall of Fame."[15]

Other Negro preachers who were active in the early Methodist movement included Richard Allen, Daniel Coker, Henry Evans, Absalom Jones, Christopher Rush, Abraham Thompson, and James Varick. All of these men shared with Wesley's appointed preachers a concept of ministry and a missionary urgency and compassion that was rooted in the Evangelical Revival in England and the Great Awakening in colonial America.[16] They traveled on circuits, preached at Methodist meetings, and provided spiritual leadership for their people. The most notable among them was Richard Allen, a Delaware ex-slave who traveled with Richard Whatcoat, Peter Morratte, and Irie Ellis on various circuits in Delaware, Maryland, and New Jersey.[17] When segregated practices became increasingly evident in the Methodist Episcopal Church in the late 1780s and 1790s, Allen, Daniel Coker, Christopher Rush, Abraham Thompson, and James Varick withdrew and became pioneers in the independent African Methodist movement, and Absalom Jones broke away and became the first African Episcopal priest in America. Henry Evans was the only one in the group to remain with the predominantly white Methodist Episcopal Church.[18]

There is no way to determine the exact number of Negroes who joined Methodist societies in America in the 1760s, 1770s, and 1780s. Thomas Rankin estimated that by 1777 "many hundreds of Negroes" had joined the Methodists, a figure that appears impressive in view of Marcus Jernegan's claim of a low incidence of conversion among Africans generally throughout the colonies.[19] The vast majority of Negro Methodists to whom Rankin referred were laypersons, and some undoubtedly were recognized as lay preachers. By 1784 the Methodist membership was approximately 15,000, with Negroes constituting about 10 percent of that number. Many were slaves who were not permitted to attend meetings on a regular basis because of the demands of the plantation work schedule.[20] The following letter written to

Joseph Pilmore by a slave in November 1771 illustrates the problem confronted by slaves who affiliated with the Methodists:

> Dear Sir,—these are to acquaint you, that my bondage is such I cannot possibly attend with the rest of the Class to receive my ticket, therefore beg you will send it. I wanted much to come to the Church at the Watchnight, but could not get leave; but, I bless God that night, I was greatly favoured with the spirit of prayer, and enjoyed much of His Divine Presence. I find the enemy of my soul continually striving to throw me off the foundation, but I have that within me which bids defiance to his delusive snares. I beg an interest in your prayers that I may be enabled to bear up under all my difficulties with patient resignation to the will of God.[21]

EARLY NEGRO RESPONSE TO METHODISM

Several reasons account for the strong support given by Negroes to Methodism in those early years. First, the Methodist style and ethos of revivalism allowed for a freedom of expression that was similar to what many Negroes had experienced in African traditional religions. They were free to sing, pray, preach, testify, groan, weep, shout, and dance with an intensity of emotion that was unacceptable in many religious communions in America at that time. Methodist preachers frequently commented in their diaries about the "uncommon manner" in which Negroes expressed themselves at Methodist meetings, and some noted how Negro emotional effervescence inspired similar behavior among white Methodists.[22] This kind of emotional outlet provided a context of meaning for Negroes in the Methodist movement as they sought to satisfy their spiritual thirst as well as to make sense of their existence as an abused and exploited people. In a strange way, Methodist meetings provided an atmosphere for Negroes to preserve some of the religious values and traditions they had brought from Africa.

Second, the simplicity of the Methodist teachings struck responsive chords in the hearts of Negroes. The teachings they heard and accepted with enthusiasm from Methodist evangelists focused upon experiential religion rather than creed and doctrine. The emphasis on conversion, holiness, assurance, Christian perfection, and God's enduring parental love for all creatures tinkled sweetly on their ears, particularly since an ethos of love, acceptance, and personal growth and maturity was so immediately existentially vital in the sociopolitical context in which they were forced to live. The lessons of the Bible were presented in such a way that God's eschatological hope was revealed to even the most untutored slaves and free Negroes. Richard Allen spoke for the early Negro Methodists when he wrote:

26

> I was confident there was no religious sect or denomination that would suit the capacity of the colored people as well as the Methodists, for the plain and simple Gospel suits best for any people, for the unlearned can understand, and the learned are sure to understand; and the reason that the Methodists are so successful in the awakening and conversion of the colored people is the plain doctrine and having a good discipline.[23]

The egalitarian impulse of Methodism was also a significant feature attracting Negroes. Methodist doctrine affirmed their right to share equally with whites in the experience of conversion and as recipients of God's saving grace. This kind of Christian egalitarianism made the Methodist faith accessible to illiterate slaves and slave-owners alike. It occasionally transcended the spiritual realm to evidence a concern for the physical freedom of Negroes, despite the efforts of many white Methodists to maintain a rigid separation between spiritual and temporal equality.[24] Methodist preachers such as Francis Asbury, Thomas Rankin, Freeborn Garrettson, and Thomas Coke, inspired by the moral claims of John Wesley against slavery, found the Methodist mandate "to reform the nation and spread scriptural holiness throughout the land" inconsistent with slaveholding principles.[25] Pointing to this inconsistency on one occasion, Asbury declared that "the Lord will certainly hear the cries of the oppressed, naked, starving creatures."[26] During his many conversations with whites in the Philadelphia area in 1775, Rankin not only attacked slavery on moral grounds but also expressed amazement at the paradox of whites agitating for freedom from British colonial domination while holding thousands of Africans in bondage.[27] Garrettson was verbally abused for inculcating "the doctrine of freedom" in his sermons "in a private way" in Virginia and North Carolina in 1775, and Coke was threatened with bodily harm and indicted for disturbing the peace while preaching against slavery in Virginia a few years later.[28] The antislavery ideas of these men accounted to some degree for the condemnation of the slave system by Methodist Conferences in 1780, 1783, and 1784. Francis Asbury complained that Methodists often had serious problems gaining access to slaves because "their masters are afraid of the influence of our principles."[29] Many Negroes were highly encouraged by this opposition to slavery, as indicated by their support for the Methodist cause. For them, Methodist antislavery activity in those early years provided a semblance of hope in a society that seemed determined to destroy every vestige of their humanity.

Another reason for the popularity of Methodism among Negroes was the fact that the early Methodist preachers actively evangelized them and accepted them into the societies. This was in keeping with the spirit and example of John Wesley, who had offered spiritual guidance to Negroes in South Carolina as early as 1737, and who baptized two African Methodists in 1758. Stirred by the sight of the large number of unevangelized Negroes without a shepherd,

Methodist preachers traveled on horseback to towns, plantations, and small farms, urging slaveholders to grant their slaves permission to attend public worship. The dedication of Methodist preachers to this task was such that it became a proverbial saying on cold winter days that "there is nothing out today but crows and Methodist preachers."[30]

Finally, Negro converts themselves were a dynamic force in attracting their own people to Methodism. The image of Negro Methodists as passive pawns receiving Christian teachings from white Methodists is grossly misleading. Negro Methodist pioneers freely and enthusiastically shared their faith with the unsaved, causing many Negroes as well as whites to submit to the power of the Methodist faith. The tremendous service Negro Methodists rendered in converting and nurturing the faith of others in their community is perhaps the best example of the vitality and diversity of the early Methodist witness in America.

By 1780 the number of Negroes in Methodist societies was such that special provisions were deemed necessary to control them. Question 25 of the Methodist minutes for that year reads as follows: "Ought not the assistant to meet the coloured people himself, and appoint as helpers in his absence proper white persons, and not suffer them to stay late and meet by themselves? Ans. Yes."[31] This effort to ensure white control and supervision over black Methodist gatherings was obviously rooted in paternalism and in a need to circumscribe Negro religious authority and autonomy. Such an oppressive system within Methodism developed inevitably as a product of the social realities of that period. Many white Methodists simply doubted that Negroes had the capacity to take charge of their own spiritual welfare and destiny.

THE NEGRO IN THE ORGANIZATION
OF THE METHODIST EPISCOPAL CHURCH

The involvement of Negroes in the organization of the Methodist Episcopal Church in 1784 was evident at many levels. Hundreds in Methodist societies were automatically a part of this new development. Harry Hosier was among those sent out to call the circuit-riding preachers together for the Christmas Conference in Baltimore, which was the focal point of this historic event.[32] Hosier and Richard Allen are said to have represented blacks at the Conference, and their presence was symbolic of what would become a long-standing, mutually enriching, and sometimes precarious relationship between black Americans and Episcopal Methodism.

The place of Negroes in Methodism and in American society as a whole proved to be a critical issue at the Christmas Conference. The Methodists had raised this question in various ways since the 1760s, but the birth of the Methodist Episcopal Church and the new nation caused it to surface anew.

28

Question 41 of the *Book of Discipline,* which was put before the delegates in Baltimore, was stated in these terms: "Are there any directions to be given concerning the Negroes?" The answer given was essentially the same as that provided by the Methodist Conference in 1780, four years earlier: "Let every preacher, as often as possible, meet them in Class, and let the assistant always appoint a proper white person as their leader. Let the assistants also make a regular return to the Conference on the number of Negroes in Society in their respective circuits."[33]

One nineteenth-century Methodist historian concludes that it was "the reluctance of some to accept the situation of Negro equality in the church that led to the discussion of the question, 'What shall we do with the Negro?' "[34] Despite an atmosphere charged with the sounds of the Enlightenment principles of reason, freedom, social progress, and the natural rights of man, the delegates at the Christmas Conference simply were not prepared to eliminate patterns of racial inequality that were already deeply embedded in the church and in society generally. However, they did pass a resolution calling for the abolition of slavery, denouncing it as "contrary to the golden laws of God, on which hang all the law and the prophets; and the inalienable rights of mankind, as well as every principle of the revolution." The Annual Conferences were encouraged to "address themselves to the legislatures of those states in which no general laws had been passed for that purpose, urging the gradual emancipation of the slaves."[35] The delegates also adopted rules for the expulsion of members of Methodist societies who persisted in owning, buying, and selling slaves. The rules of 1784 were bitterly opposed by many Methodists, and they were never enforced to the letter.[36]

Unfortunately, the newly formed Methodist Episcopal Church took no steps to curtail patterns of segregation that were developing increasingly within its ranks. The segregation of Negroes in worship had appeared in the "earliest days when Methodism consisted mainly of preaching services in loosely organized societies," and that practice "not only continued but crystallized" with the organization of the Methodist Episcopal Church.[37] According to Dwight W. Culver, the Cumberland Street Methodist Episcopal Church in Charleston, South Carolina, was first to introduce a segregated gallery in 1787. In time, segregated galleries, "nigger pews," and "African corners" became quite generally the custom in Methodist Episcopal churches in the North and South. In cases where separate services were held by black Methodists, they were almost always controlled and supervised by whites.[38]

The Christmas Conference had few redeeming features as far as the future progress of Negroes in Episcopal Methodism was concerned. The number present at the Conference was amazingly small, and the idea that white Methodists were eminently capable of determining what was best for their Negro counterparts prevailed. The failure of the delegates to grant real freedom and equality of ecclesiastical status to Negro Methodists set the stage for two important developments. First, it ensured that questions about the place of Negroes in the predominantly white Methodist Episcopal Church would continue to surface for years to come. Second, it created an atmosphere that would eventually lead to the rise of movements for independence among African Methodists. In short, all prospects for a united Episcopal Methodism in America seemed to disperse into the winds.[39]

OTHER INDEPENDENT METHODIST EPISCOPAL CHURCHES

The year 1786 was quite significant for Negroes in Methodism. For the first time the Methodist Episcopal Church made a distinction between black and white members in its records, noting that there were 1,890 blacks of a total membership of 18,791.[40] More important, it was in that year that the idea of a separate organization for African Methodists was conceived in the mind of Richard Allen, who had been licensed to preach by the Methodist Episcopal Church in 1784. Recalling that experience, Allen wrote:

> I thought I would stop in Philadelphia a week or two. I preached at different places in the city. My labor was much blessed. I soon saw a large field open in seeking and instructing my African brethren, who had been a long and forgotten people and few of them attended public worship. . . . I established prayer meetings; I raised a society in 1786 for forty-two members.[41]

The small society Allen started represented a first step in the direction of a separate church for his people. Another step was taken in April 1787 when Allen took the lead in forming the Free African Society, "a self-improvement association which was designed to provide mutual aid in times of misfortune, and to exercise a kind of moral oversight over its membership by visitation and prayer."[42] A short time later the movement began in full swing when Allen and a small group of Negroes walked out of St. George's Methodist Episcopal Church in Philadelphia after being pulled from their knees during prayer, apparently because they violated that church's racial policies. This event culminated in the organization of the Bethel African Methodist Episcopal Church under Allen's leadership in 1794. Although Bethel functioned in relationship to the Methodist Episcopal Conference for some two decades, it was here that the preliminary work for an independent African Methodism in the United States was advanced to a new and significant level.[43]

The Allenite protest at St. George's served as a model for other Negro Methodists who resented the indignity of segregation and the lack of opportunity for advancement in the Methodist Episcopal Church.[44] In 1794 African Zoar was started in Philadelphia by other Negro dissidents who left St. George's. This church remained in connection with the Methodist Episcopal

Church. In 1796 Negroes walked out of the John Street Methodist Episcopal Church in New York and eventually built the "African" or Zion Chapel. Similar movements sprouted in Baltimore, Wilmington (Delaware), Attleborough (Pennsylvania), Salem (New Jersey), and Charleston between 1796 and 1816. The separate churches that stemmed from all of these movements operated under the tutelage of the Methodist Episcopal Church from their beginnings. In time, the Negroes in these churches, in addition to those at Bethel in Philadelphia and Zion Chapel in New York, completely severed ties with the Methodist Episcopal Conference.

The separatists in Wilmington were the first group to establish their unconditional independence from white Methodism. This movement started in 1805 when some forty Negroes followed Peter Spencer and William Anderson out of the Asbury Methodist Episcopal Church because of discrimination in worship. Spencer and Anderson were lay preachers, which means that the Wilmington movement was essentially a lay movement. In May 1805 the group erected Ezion African Methodist Episcopal Church but were forced to surrender the building to the Methodist Episcopal Conference seven years later because of a dispute with a white elder over church property and the method of selecting preachers to preach there. In 1813 Spencer, Anderson, and their followers secured another building not far from Ezion, and the Union Church of Africans was organized "with due forms and ceremonies." Spencer and Anderson were "set apart" as elder ministers with general oversight of this body, which was also called the Union Church, the African Union Church, the Union Church of African Members, the African Union Methodist Church, and the Union Methodist Connexion. The separatists from Salem, New Jersey, united with this church, and by 1815 it had established denominational connections with other congregations in Delaware, New York, and Pennsylvania.

In April 1816 Richard Allen's followers formed a completely separate and independent ecclesiastical compact in Philadelphia with the dissenters from Baltimore and Attleborough, Pennsylvania. This body became the African Methodist Episcopal (AME) Church but was also known as the Bethel Methodist Connexion. Peter Spencer and a delegate from Salem, New Jersey, represented the African Unionists at the AME organizing Conferences, but disagreements between them and Allen concerning matters of church discipline, style, and organization kept them from uniting with the AMEs. Furthermore, the African Unionists had already organized, formed a connection, and settled on a *Book of Discipline,* and they "had no intention of unshipping matters a second time."[45] The separatists from Charleston were not present in Philadelphia, but they, under the leadership of Morris Brown, were later organized into the AME denomination. Richard Allen, who had been ordained a deacon by the Methodist Episcopal bishop Francis Asbury in 1799, was ordained by an elder and elected the first AME bishop at the organizing Conference.

The members of Zion Chapel in New York were the third group of African Methodists to achieve denominational status. The Zionists, as they were called, launched their movement under the guidance of Francis Jacob, Thomas Miller, Christopher Rush, June Scott, Abraham Thompson, James Varick, and Peter Williams. Miller, Rush, Scott, Thompson, and Varick were licensed preachers. On June 21, 1821, they united with Negro representatives from churches in Long Island (New York), New Haven (Connecticut), and Philadelphia to form the AME Zion Church in America. The next year the process was completed at another Conference when Rush, Thompson, and Varick were formally ordained as elders. Varick was elected the first general superintendent of the AME Zion Church.[46] The body had not progressed far when conflicts began to interfere with its pattern of development. In addition to its conflicts with white Methodists, it engaged in fierce competition with the AME Church. The Zionists also suffered internal dissension and several schisms before settling down to a relatively calm existence.[47]

In 1837 *Colored American,* a black newspaper based in New York, issued a report that revealed similar and dissimilar patterns in the development of the African Union, AME, and AME Zion churches. The backgrounds of these churches reflected a common pattern that extended from segregated practices in the Methodist Episcopal Church to separate meeting times, separate meeting places, autonomous local churches, and independent denominations. Their leaders had to engage in protracted legal struggles with white Methodists before gaining their full independence. Despite the many problems they had encountered with the Methodist Episcopal Conference, the African Unionists, Bethelites, and Zionists adopted articles of religion, general rules, and discipline in conformity with the Wesleyan and Methodist model. An editor of *Colored American* described "the tenets and discipline" of the Union Church of Africans as being "substantially the same as that of the Bethel and Zion Connexions."[48]

Clear differences emerge when these denominations are compared at the level of style, organization, and polity. The AMEs and Zionists adopted virtually all aspects of traditional Methodist polity, but the African Unionists chose a more simplified organization. Rejecting both the episcopacy and the presiding eldership, they elected five laymen in each congregation to serve as ruling elders and gave them authority to ordain ministers and to license local preachers. They retained the ordination of deacons, who could preach and baptize but not administer the Lord's Supper or church discipline. The elder ministers, whose position was similar to that of the AME bishop and the general superintendent of the AME Zion Church, had complete authority in these matters.[49] Also unlike the AME and AME Zion communions, the Union Church of Africans emphasized the stationed pastorate more than the itinerancy and emphasized local autonomy while weakening connectional authority and control. The latter policy "made it possible for other congregations to organize, to own their own property, and to participate in every level of church government in a congregational or 'associated' polity.' "[50] According to one nineteenth-century source, the Union Church of Africans was "not Presbyterian, Episcopal, nor Congregational, but from its origin *Associated.*"[51]

Several other features of the Union Church of Africans distinguished it from the AME and AME Zion denominations. First, the African Unionists developed a strong tradition of lay involvement, thus making lay representation possible at all Conferences and meetings. This feature also allowed for considerable participation on the part of women. Six women were among the signatories of the Union Church of Africans' Articles of Association, and the denomination took an early position in favor of women as local preachers.[52] The emphasis on lay participation was not an entirely unexpected development, since the Union Church of Africans was the only one among the three original African Methodist bodies to be organized exclusively by laymen and laywomen. The Zionists also emphasized lay involvement on a smaller scale.[53]

Second, the African Unionists did not embrace all elements of the Methodist multiple Conference system. This is another example of how they differed from the AMEs and the Zionists. They rejected the General Conference in the traditional Methodist sense. Aside from the Annual, District, and Quarterly Conferences, the African Unionists held one quarterly meeting annually on the last Sunday in August, at which time a general reunion and religious revival occurred at the Mother Union Church of Africans in Wilmington, Delaware. This meeting, widely known as the Big August Quarterly, normally attracted thousands from New York to Virginia for a day of feasting, family reunions, and religious celebration. No such celebration was held by the AMEs and Zionists.

NEGRO METHODISM: A UNIQUE EXPRESSION

Although the early independent African Methodist churches had much in common with the Wesleyan and Methodist tradition, there were ways in which they found a special or unique expression. The sociopolitical realities that made their existence necessary set them apart from white Methodism. More specifically, Negro Methodist churches originated and developed as separate and independent structures because worshiping with white Methodists in terms of equality was not a viable option for them. Because of the unique circumstances that led to their formation, the existence of Negro Methodist denominations cannot be explained simply on the basis of the principle of voluntarism, which established the separation of church and state and the equality of all churches under the law. When the early black Methodists called for religious freedom, they did not mean *only* what the white Methodists meant, namely, the freedom to support their churches and ecclesiastical activity apart from any interference or financial support from the state. For the Negro Methodists, religious freedom also meant the privilege to worship God without being called "niggers," and without the restraining effects of white presence, encroachment, and control. It involved the freedom to exercise independent responsibilities—to elect as well as be elected to church offices, to ordain and be ordained, to discipline as well as to be disciplined, and to preach and administer the sacraments. Because this freedom was not allowed in white Methodist churches, Negro Methodists withdrew and started their own movements for denominational formation and autonomy.

Negro Methodist denominations also developed a distinctive life of their own in the areas of worship and theology. Their constituents had special spiritual and ritualistic needs that could only be fulfilled in a Negro church situation. Many were illiterate and did not feel comfortable with hymnals, prayer books, disciplines, and theology books. The early Negro Methodists were an emotional people who needed a context in which to express their joys and sorrows freely and collectively. To meet these needs, the Negro Methodist churches featured a variety of liturgical innovations that suited the untutored mind and that allowed for freedom of expression and group involvement. The preaching, prayers, singing, testimony, shouting, and religious dance were products of communal creativity, with elements that reflected the influence of both African traditional religions and Euro-American evangelical Protestantism. The West African–based ring dance was quite common in Negro Methodist circles, despite the opposition of leaders like Richard Allen and Daniel A. Payne.[54] That ceremony, which Sterling Stuckey calls "the most important African ritual in antebellum America,"[55] was a prominent feature at the annual Big Quarterly religious festivals of the African Unionists, which also drew support and participation from AMEs, Zionists, United AMEs, Colored Methodist Protestants, African Wesleyans, and Negroes in largely white Methodist churches. Newspapers in Wilmington, Delaware, carried descriptions of ring dance performances at Big Quarterly throughout the nineteenth century, leaving little doubt as to the importance of that ritual for Negro Methodists in the Delmarva peninsula area:

> In the basement of the church a hundred or more men formed a circle and swayed to and fro, sometimes fast and sometimes slow, according to the metre of the hymn sung. Those who formed the inner line of the human ring were the most violent in their movements and most of the time perspired so freely that they could not have been more wet if a hose had been turned upon them. Frantically, they urged one another to more violent feats of gymnastic devotion, clapping their hands, jumping and shouting, and occasionally groaning. When they grew weary they dropped upon their knees and prayers were offered.[56]

The theological focus of Negro Methodists found perhaps its fullest expression in the folk sermon and the spirituals, which evidenced a close relationship between a this-worldly concern for liberation and an other-worldly concern for salvation. James H. Cone characterizes the early Negro Methodist churches as "visible manifestations of Black Theology."[57]

The distinctiveness of Negro Methodist churches went beyond the strictly ecclesiastical. They took a strong stance against slavery and racism in their doctrine and by the moral example they set, thereby becoming institutional symbols of Black Power and human liberation. While it was not always publicly known or reported, Negroes in traditionally Negro Methodist churches and in the predominantly white Methodist churches were involved in the continual struggle of their people for liberation and survival. They attacked colonization, boycotted slave-made goods, assisted runaway slaves on the Underground Railroad, exposed the hypocrisy of white Christianity, and challenged the nation with a new vision of freedom and democracy. They also advocated sobriety and temperance, industry and thrift, the sacredness of the home and family, the sanctity of the marriage vow, black pride and identity, and self-help.[58] Negro Methodist churches provided their constituents with opportunities for self-expression, recognition, leadership, and group cohesion. Unlike free, individualistic white church persons in the prospering American civilization, who could afford to preach personal salvation and rugged individualism in business enterprise, Negro Methodist churches had no choice but to be involved in the struggle of Negroes as a community, because their own independence and integrity as religious institutions were inextricably linked to the liberation of their people.

NEGRO METHODISTS IN MISSION

Early Negro Methodist denominations viewed missionary outreach as a vital and integral part of their task as agents of God. Their sense of mission included the development of strong church leadership and the urgency of preaching and seeking actively the conversion of sinners to Jesus Christ. Their primary focus was on home missionary activity, but their success in this area up to 1864 was severely limited because of a scarcity of resources and a racial climate that restricted their movement in certain areas of the country. This was particularly true in the case of Negroes in the Methodist Episcopal Church. Many of them had a real number of "unsaved" as missionaries, but the white Methodists refused to offer them the opportunities and resources for such efforts. Whites in Methodist Episcopal congregations, North and South, rarely thought of their Negro counterparts as effective and responsible missionaries, despite the many instances where even illiterate slaves influenced the conversion of masters. Their need to use Christianity as a tool to control precluded any possibility of employing them widely as missionaries, especially since religion-inspired resistance to white oppression was known to occur. Thus the largest number of missionaries sponsored by the Methodist Episcopal Church prior to 1864 were white, even in cases where mission activity was conducted among slaves. John Stewart, born of free parents in Virginia in 1786, was the first Negro in the Methodist Episcopal Church to gain a considerable reputation for outstanding contributions to domestic missions. From the time of his conversion in 1816 until his death seven years later, Stewart was highly effective as a missionary to the Wyandot Indians in Upper Sandusky, Ohio. He succeeded in converting many of the Wyandots in the face of bitter opposition from white traders and Roman Catholics who had tried unsuccessfully to evangelize the Indians. He was probably the first Methodist preacher to achieve great success among the Wyandots. Stewart also moved many whites to repentance in Marietta, Ohio. His work inspired the organization of a missionary society in the Methodist Episcopal Church, "the first of a long series of institutional adventures which made Methodism mighty."[59] Because of his great work, Stewart should be ranked with James H. Mallard, James E. Glenn, and other pioneers in Methodist missions.

THE CONTINUING NEGRO DRAMA IN THE METHODIST EPISCOPAL CHURCH

The history of Negroes in the Methodist Episcopal Church did not end with the formation of separate and independent Negro denominations. A relatively large number of Negro preachers and laypersons remained in the Methodist Episcopal Church despite its discriminatory policies and practices. Between 1797 and 1827, when movements for independence among African Methodists were in full swing, the number of Negroes in the Methodist Episcopal Church increased from 12,215 to 54,065. By 1840 this number had reached 87,197, chiefly due to an elaborate program of "plantation missions" among the slaves in the South. Others remained because of their belief in the potential of the Methodist Episcopal Church as an advocate of Negro rights and freedom. This opinion was based on the well-known opposition of Francis Asbury, Thomas Coke, and other Methodist leaders to slavery.

The departure of Richard Allen and other Negro separatists from the Methodist Episcopal Church did not lead that institution to radically change its racial policies. In 1800 a "Regulation Respecting the Ordination of Colored People to the Office of Deacon" was approved by the Methodist Episcopal Church, but this did not give Negroes full access to ministry and leadership in the church.[60] Segregated practices continued to exist in local congregations throughout the country. Furthermore, between 1800 and 1828 the printed minutes of the Methodist Episcopal Church did not reveal a single action taken against slavery. Apparently the church had receded from the radicality of its earlier antislavery positions in order to appease its Southern wing and to maintain unity within the general body.[61]

As a compensation for its moral failure regarding the slavery issue, the Methodist Episcopal Church turned its attention to active missionary work among Negroes. The first major organized effort was launched in 1809 when the South Carolina Conference sent James H. Mallard and James E. Glenn to evangelize slaves from the Ashley to the Savannah rivers, and from the Santee to the Cooper rivers. By 1829 the efforts of Mallard and Glenn had been expanded under William Capers, a pioneer in Methodist plantation missions, who was named superintendent of a separate agency for the evangelization of slaves by the South Carolina Conference. In 1840 Capers became the secretary of the Southern Department of Missionary work, and from that position he inspired much enthusiasm, support, and activity on behalf of Negro missions throughout the South.[62]

In the latter 1820s and 1830s a militant phase of abolitionism engulfed parts of the country, and the Methodist Episcopal Church found that it could no longer ignore the slavery controversy and all its tragic implications. Orange Scott, LeRoy Sunderland, and other rising abolitionists in the church began to raise the slavery issue with great regularity and vigor. Convinced that slavery was "unscriptural," these men led a small band of preachers and laypersons out of the Methodist Episcopal Church in 1842 and formed the Wesleyan Methodist Connection. Once again blacks had become a major issue at a critical stage in Methodist Episcopal Church history.[63] This development occurred at a time when Frederick Douglass, Harriet Tubman, Jermain Loguen, Henry McNeal Turner, and others in the Negro Methodist denominations were attacking slavery on moral grounds. These Negro Methodists undoubtedly presented a strong moral challenge to white Methodists with respect to slavery and racism.[64]

The 1844 General Conference of the Methodist Episcopal Church witnessed a resurfacing of tensions over slavery. Two cases took center stage at this Conference. First, the delegates refused to honor the appeal of Francis A. Harding, a Baltimore preacher who had been suspended by his Annual Conference for refusing to free several slaves acquired by marriage. The second case involved Bishop James O. Andrew of Georgia, who was told to desist from the exercise of his office until he freed slaves passed down from his first wife's estate.[65] The Southern delegates were outraged by these actions, and furious debates and disputes occurred with Northern delegates. An official break along sectional lines took place in May 1845 when the Southern delegates met in Louisville, Kentucky, and organized the Methodist Episcopal Church, South.[66] The tensions that caused this major rupture in Episcopal Methodism were exacerbated by the presence of thousands of Negro members in the Methodist Episcopal Church.

Between 1845 and 1864 the Methodist Episcopal Church and the Methodist Episcopal Church, South, continued to approach the slavery issue and the whole question of what to do with Negro Methodists in somewhat different ways. Most in the Methodist Episcopal Church seemed to be opposed to slavery in principle, but they did little to support militant abolitionism and projects for the spiritual welfare and social uplift of Negroes. Furthermore, Negro members in the Methodist Episcopal Church were still being denied privileges and responsibilities on an equal basis with white members. The Methodist Episcopal Church, South, was essentially proslavery, and it sought to minimize the impact of abolitionist rhetoric by devoting thousands of dollars and other resources to plantation missions. From 1845 to 1861 that institution alone raised $1.5 million for the evangelization of slaves. More than $93,000 was set aside for this purpose in 1862.[67] Slave owners and non–slave owners contributed freely to the effort, and so did Negroes in the Methodist Episcopal Church, South. Milton C. Sernett is right in saying that "Negro missions had become a great moral cause . . . the balm applied to the Southern conscience."[68] Much of this activity among slaves had its roots not just in a concern for the spiritual state of the slave community but also in a sense of guilt and in a need to justify and safeguard the institution of human bondage in the South.

The firing on Fort Sumter in 1861 and the coming of the Civil War had little impact on attitudes of white Methodists toward Negroes and slavery. Northern Methodists tended to view the war as a crusade to save the Union, and Southern Methodists generally saw it as an attack on their values and institutions. Neither viewed it as a crusade to lift Negroes from slavery to freedom and equality on a level with whites. Different perceptions loomed in Negro Methodist denominations. For black Methodists, "the Civil War was God's vehicle of deliverance. Internecine strife, they believed, would purge the nation of the sin of slavery and eradicate those barriers which had prevented them from entering the mainstream of American life."[69]

C H A P T E R 2

THE METHODIST EPISCOPAL CHURCH
Promise and Peril
1784–1939

Grant S. Shockley

The presence, participation, and perspectives of black Methodists who remained within the organizational structure of the Methodist Episcopal Church (1784–1939) and its successor bodies, the Methodist Church (1940–1968) and The United Methodist Church (since 1968), can best be understood when viewed in individually distinct periods. They should also be viewed in relation to the conditions, issues, and opportunities present in each era.

The black condition during the formative years of Methodism in America was essentially one of oppression. Black people endured slavery until Emancipation, color discrimination when legally free, and segregation in the South, North, and West by custom or law or both in the general society and the church. It is crucially important to understand this condition and the limitations on participation and achievement it imposed on black people in this early period as well as in the periods that followed. Equally important in understanding the continuing black presence in Episcopal Methodism is the black perspective. Black people who remained within the Methodist Episcopal Church had a reason for doing so. They had heard, believed, and claimed the gospel of salvation from the hands of the Methodists, and despite only a "token" invitation they decided to stay in the "church of the Wesleys." They refused to be "defined out" of Methodism on racial grounds.

This chapter is an attempt to relate how black Methodists—like their white counterparts—having been converted, saw the world as their parish and sought "to reform the Continent, and spread scriptural Holiness over these lands."[1]

CONVERSIONS, MEMBERSHIP, AND CHURCHES

Conversions to Methodism

Methodist evangelization among black people in colonial America and well into the national period was one of the most phenomenal accomplishments in

United States Christian mission history. The thousands of black converts who accepted Christianity as their religion and Methodism as their denomination represented one of the largest nonwhite accessions to the Christian church in North America.

Lay preachers including Philip Embury and Robert Strawbridge, Francis Asbury, and British Methodist missionaries following Wesley's "world parish" approach proclaimed a universal gospel of love, judgment, and salvation. Black slaves and free black persons alike responded quickly to the Wesleyan message. One wonders how many thousands more black people would have responded to the gospel if it had not been proclaimed by Christians engaged in slavery practices.

There is a second dimension to this mission story. From the earliest times in American Methodist history, black people themselves have evangelized. Slaves, ex-slaves, and indentured servants preached and converted whenever and wherever it was possible for them to do so. Many of these black evangelists are nameless, and facts about others are scarce. John Wesley recognized the willingness, as well as the eagerness, of black people to receive and share the gospel.

Church Membership

From Wesley's time until the North-South division of the Methodist Episcopal Church (1844–1846), evangelistic efforts among the "unsaved," black or white, were pursued with vigor and generally on a somewhat nonracial basis. Seldom, however, was equality of treatment accorded to black converts. From the beginning of Methodism, they were admitted to membership in the societies. As their numbers grew, however, and the societies became churches, racial discrimination increased, and full fellowship was withheld by some white disciples of Wesley from other black disciples of that same Wesley. Edwin S. Gaustad found this to be a general principle in his study of the period and stated it as follows: "As the number of Negroes increased to the point where they became the dominant group in a community or a church, both Negro and White groped for new solutions."[2]

In consequence of this principle, Methodism in its church life from the middle 1760s to the middle 1780s practiced and explored every possible pattern of contractual relationship between blacks and whites in churches: simultaneous corporate worship in the same church building, simultaneous segregated worship in the same church building, separate worship at different times in the same church building, separate worship in separate churches under white "supervision," separate worship in separate churches without "supervision," and, finally, separate denominations organized by blacks.

What is unique about the black constituency of the Methodist Episcopal Church that remained after other black members separated to form new denominations is the fact that while deeply resenting the discriminatory treatment that all of the blacks received, they chose not to leave. In so doing their continuing presence in separate congregations became not only a protest but also a witness to the ineffectiveness of such treatment in dissuading them from their bonding to Christ and the church through Wesleyan, as well as Episcopal, Methodism. This attitude was not a fleeting one or limited to that generation. It has persisted since the late 1700s to the present.

Church Growth and Development

Given the caste distinctions and indignities experienced by black members in Methodist Episcopal churches in the North and/or the South between the Revolutionary War and the Civil War, blacks in the North had to make a decision about the location of their church membership. The decision of black Methodists outside of the slave South prior to Emancipation to remain within the denomination gave them little alternative but withdrawal from their white churches and the establishment of "separate" black congregations. This process, which probably began in the early 1780s, soon took the form of "house church meetings." Often they also functioned as mutual aid societies. African Zoar Church, Methodism's first organized black church (1794), evolved from this form in the late 1780s. It is also highly plausible to believe that of the thirty-six or so societies (of fifty-one) reporting black members at the Christmas Conference (1784), many in the North followed this pattern.

Black members in the Methodist Episcopal Church, South, did not have the option of withdrawal. Prior to Emancipation they remained a part of the churches of their masters, if affiliated with the church at all. From about the 1820s to the Civil War, plantation missions were initiated to care for the spiritual needs of the slaves. Following Emancipation, thousands of black Methodists chose to leave the Methodist Episcopal Church, South, for membership in the eagerly missionizing Methodist Episcopal Church or the Christian (Colored) Methodist Episcopal Church (established cooperatively with former slaves of the Methodist Episcopal Church, South, in 1870). Many also chose to unite with other black denominations, such as the African Methodist Episcopal and the African Methodist Episcopal Zion churches or Baptist churches.

PREACHING, WORSHIP, AND MUSIC, 1784–1939

Preaching, worship, and music were central and distinctive characteristics of black congregations in the Methodist Episcopal Church. A review of this development to 1939 falls naturally into three periods, based on the free or slave status of black people and their location in slavery or nonslavery states.

41

Prior to Emancipation free blacks in nonslavery states were churched in two patterns. In the earliest days of Methodism, they attended and worshiped in white Methodist Episcopal churches. The fervent preaching, experiential religious beliefs, and evangelistic singing of many of these Methodist churches appealed to them, including some of the hymns of Isaac Watts and the Wesleys. Following the Revolutionary War and the development of independent (though not separatist) black congregations such as African Zoar, black Methodists continued this mode of worship and adapted it to their own needs. J. Jefferson Cleveland states, "When Blacks began to establish their own churches, they did not discard the sophisticated hymns learned from their experiences in white Christian worship; rather many of these hymns were adopted and converted into original Black songs."[3]

A similar situation developed in the South, as Northern Methodist Episcopal missionaries established churches there after the Civil War. Characteristically, Methodist evangelistic preaching, expressive worship, and Wesleyan hymn singing found moderately wide acceptance among thousands of ex-slaves. Hundreds united with Methodist Episcopal churches for this reason, and also for the opportunity to attend the schools that were related to Methodist Episcopal churches. In due course, Negro folk religion and spirituals merged with a somewhat more restrained Methodist Episcopal worship tradition to produce a unique black Methodist Episcopal religious ethos. Wendell P. Whalum describes this development:

> The Black Methodists and Baptists endorsed Watt's hymns, but the Baptists "blackened" them. They virtually threw out the meter signature and rhythm and before 1875 had begun a new system which, though based on the style of singing coming from England to America in the eighteenth century, was drastically different from it. It was congregational singing much like the spiritual had been in which the text was retained.[4]

Waves of black urban migrations from the South to the North, Midwest, Southwest, and eventually the West Coast from the turn of the century (1900) to World War II brought other changes. As increased economic and educational opportunities became available to black people in their new environments in urban centers outside the South, social class differentiation began to reflect itself. E. Franklin Frazier stated that "on the basis of the occupational differentiation of the Negro population, a new system of social stratification or socioeconomic classes came into existence."[5] This new social phenomenon in the black community had a significant impact on black Methodist Episcopal churches. A unique composite of evangelical but "dignified" worship, together with an excellent Christian education program and community-sensitive approach, appealed to a burgeoning black middle class. Conversely, black Methodist Episcopal churches were not as attractive to many of the far more numerous but less advantaged migrants to the cities from southern black churches that tended to be emotionally more highly expressive in their religious behavior.

Several things should be mentioned before leaving this section on Methodist Episcopal preaching, worship, and music. Though the Negro spiritual was a significant part of the religious culture of the entire black membership of the Methodist Episcopal Church, no recognition of it is found in any of the General Conference–authorized hymnals produced from 1790 to 1935. Second, the pulpit and music ministry of Charles A. Tindley introduced what became known as the "gospel hymn" into the Methodist Episcopal Church and into the black church between 1905 and 1925.[6] This musical form is the recognized predecessor of the later gospel music developed by Thomas O. Dorsey in the 1920s and 1930s.

Exemplary preachers of the period covered in this chapter include Harry Hosier (1750–1806) and Henry Evans (d. 1810). Since 1864 Charles A. Tindley (1851–1933), Walter H. Brooks (1859–1923), Lorenzo H. King (1878–1946), W. A. C. Hughes (1877–1940), and John W. Haywood (1883–1933).

HISTORIC CHURCHES

Black Methodist Episcopal churches that are historic—namely, earliest in the denomination, established before the Annual Conferences of which they later became a part, first black congregations in a region, or otherwise significantly notable—should be noted.

Churches in the Northeast

In the Northeast, African Zoar, Philadelphia, is the oldest congregation of black Methodist Episcopalians in the denomination.[7] Zoar symbolizes the Black Remnant that remained in the Methodist Episcopal Church as a matter of choice, integrity, and positive protest following the walk-out of Richard Allen, Absalom Jones, and their followers due to discrimination against them in St. George's Methodist Episcopal Church. Mt. Hope (extinct), Salem, New Jersey (1801), was the first black Methodist Episcopal church in New Jersey.[8] Sharp Street in Baltimore (1802), the mother church of several black Methodist Episcopal churches in Maryland, resulted from the secession of black members from Lovely Lane Methodist Episcopal Church.[9] Ezion, Wilmington, Delaware (1805), appeared as the first black Methodist Episcopal congregation in Delaware,[10] having separated from the white Asbury Church for reasons similar to those of Zoar, Mt. Hope, and Sharp Street.

One of the first black churches in New England and the first black church in Boston was Fourth Street Methodist Episcopal Church.[11] In 1949 it was renamed Union. Asbury in Washington, D.C. (1836), was founded by a group of black members related to the prestigious Foundry Methodist Episcopal Church of that city.[12] Concluding this brief chronicle of the earliest beginnings of black Methodist Episcopal churches in the Northeast, including New England, is Logan Memorial, Parkersburg, West Virginia (1866). Probably an outgrowth of the First (white) Methodist Episcopal Church, it was built for "persons of African descent."

Churches in the Southeast

Black Methodist Episcopal origins in the Southeast fall into several patterns. Some few antebellum black Methodists who were slaves remained in Southern Methodist churches throughout their lives. Some remained until Emancipation and united with churches organized for them by Methodist Episcopal missionaries from the North. Many left the Methodist Episcopal Church, South, which cooperated with its former black members in establishing the Colored (since 1954, "Christian") Methodist Episcopal (CME) Church (1870). Still others transferred their memberships to the avidly missionizing black Methodist denominations that literally invaded the South following the Civil War, namely, the African Methodist Episcopal (AME) Church and the African Methodist Episcopal Zion (AMEZ) Church.

The story of the rise of black Methodist Episcopal churches in the Southeast begins in North Carolina. Methodism was introduced there by a black local preacher named Henry Evans about 1800. The church he built was called the "African Meeting House." It was dedicated as Evans Chapel in 1802 and visited by Francis Asbury in 1805. For some time this church was biracial. At some before the North-South schism in the Methodist Church (1844–1846), the white members apparently withdrew. Evans Chapel eventually became (in the late 1860s) an AMEZ Church.[13] The earliest black Methodist Episcopal Church in the Southeast and in North Carolina that was established and continued was the Gum Swamp Methodist Episcopal Church in the small town of Bolton (near Wilmington). Organized in 1803, it was moved to another location in 1899 and again in 1941, at which time it became Smith Chapel.[14] In an effort to establish the Methodist Episcopal Church in the South after the Civil War, Wilson Temple Church in Raleigh and Red Bank Church near Winston-Salem were established as early as 1865.

There is some evidence to suggest that the earliest black Methodist Episcopal Church in Georgia was Newnan Chapel in Newnan. This congregation may have existed since 1840.[15] It is more certainly known that Central Church in Atlanta, successively named Clark Chapel and Lloyd Street, is among the oldest black churches begun by Methodist Episcopal missionaries from the North after the Civil War. It was organized in 1866.[16] Clark College was founded in Central Church (1872), and the organizing session of the former Atlanta Annual Conference was held there.

Asbury Church in Lexington, Kentucky, is considered to be the mother church, if not the oldest, among black Methodist Episcopal churches in the state. It was "founded" in 1844 with the appointment of a white Kentucky Conference minister for its 835-member congregation.[17] Rivaling Asbury for historical preeminence is Jones Temple in Louisville. Formerly Jackson Street Methodist Episcopal Church, Jones Temple holds the distinction of having hosted the first session of the Lexington Annual Conference in 1870.

Mt. Zion Church at Leesburg, Virginia, appears to have been the oldest black Methodist Episcopal Church in that state. It originated in the Old Stone Methodist Episcopal Church, claimed to be the oldest known piece of Methodist property in America (1776). About 1848 the white members of the church withdrew to adhere to the Methodist Episcopal Church, South. Following the Civil War (about 1865) a black congregation was formed in the Old Stone Church building, taking the name Mt. Zion.[18]

Black Methodist Episcopal Church beginnings in Mississippi center at Holly Springs, where Asbury Church was organized in 1866. Asbury Church was closely related to and involved in the establishment of Rust College later that same year. The Upper Mississippi Conference was organized in Asbury Church in 1891.[19]

Four black Methodist Episcopal congregations in South Carolina lay claim to being among the oldest black Methodist Episcopal churches in the state. Warren M. Jenkins contends that "Old Bethel" in Charleston is probably the oldest Negro Methodist Church in the Conference. It was an outgrowth of Bethel Methodist Episcopal Church, South, in 1854. Centenary, also in Charleston, was organized in 1866 by northern missionary A. W. Lewis, who led a black congregation en mass out of Trinity Methodist Episcopal Church, South. Wesley, again in Charleston, was a third congregation to organize about this same time (1866). Its members were formerly related to the St. James Methodist Episcopal Church, South. Trinity Church in Orangeburg also claims a founding date of 1866 and asserts its historical seniority on this basis.[20]

Clark Memorial Methodist Episcopal Church in Nashville, Tennessee, was named to commemorate the outstanding educational accomplishments of Bishop Davis W. Clark, the first president of the denomination's Freedmen's Aid Society. Organized in 1866, Clark Church represents one of the earliest if not the earliest black Methodist Church organization in the state. It was in this church that Central Tennessee College, later Walden University (including Meharry Medical School) was organized.[21]

Following earlier efforts in the 1820s to establish a black Methodist Episcopal church presence in Mobile, Alabama, a black congregation was firmly established in Birmingham in 1869, St. Paul.[22] (Among the outstanding pastors of this stellar congregation in contemporary times was J. Echols Lowery, president of the Southern Christian Leadership Conference and acknowledged as one of the nation's most influential religious and civil rights leaders.)

Concluding this review of black church development by the Methodist Episcopal Church in nine southeastern states is a brief look at Florida. Methodist Episcopal work among black people in Florida can best be viewed in three periods. Before the Civil War, fairly extensive missionary work was done among black people. After the Civil War, Florida lost thousands of black members to crusading missionaries from other denominations, especially black ones. Later, the Methodist Episcopal Conference organization, biracial but with a particular concern for black people, made a real effort to reach as many black people as possible, with only moderate success. When the Florida Annual Conference first convened in 1873, several black churches were charter members. Probably the oldest of these was Trinity (later Ebenezer) in Jacksonville. Its founding date was possibly between 1865 and 1870.[23]

Churches in the Midwest

The story of black Methodist Episcopal Church organization in Ohio begins in Wesley Chapel (Old Stone Church), Cincinnati, shortly after it was founded in 1805. The white members of Wesley objected to the emotional expressiveness of its black worshipers and proceeded to segregate them. In response to this, the black membership withdrew and established a separate church service at Deer Creek about 1815. While at Deer Creek, Wesley Chapel members unduly dominated the affairs of the black church, to the extent that a group withdrew in 1823 and later became an African Methodist church. In the 1800s, the Deer Creek remnant secured a slave preacher from Kentucky to serve them, James King. Still later in the 1800s, they became Union Chapel. The activity of this small congregation, until it was received by the Lexington Conference, is unclear. It is known that they moved to several locations before becoming Calvary Methodist Episcopal Church. The founding date for Calvary could be as early as 1824.[24]

The Iowa Annual Conference, organized in 1844, had twelve black lay members out of 5,403. Given an 1839 Iowa Territory law requiring black people entering the territory to prove their freedom or post a bond guaranteeing "good behavior," it can be assumed that the twelve were free blacks. Further, it is reasonable to assume that black people were not sought as settlers in the "free" Northwest. In any event, by 1860 there were only 1,069 black people there. Burns Chapel Methodist Episcopal Church, named for the first black Methodist Episcopal missionary, Bishop Francis Burns (1809–1863), was probably established soon after his death or in the early 1870s.[25]

The first black Methodist Episcopal presence that can be documented in Indiana is at Indianapolis. Matthew Simpson's *Cyclopedia of Methodism* refers to the existence of "Coke's Chapel (colored)" between 1874 and 1876, making this the oldest black Methodist Episcopal church in Indianapolis as well as in the state and the predecessor of the outstanding Simpson Memorial.[26]

St. Mark Methodist Episcopal Church in Chicago, one of the outstanding churches in Methodism and for decades the largest black Methodist church west of the Allegheny Mountains, began as a mission led by several families of laypeople. With the leadership of able pastors and laypeople, it soon became the leading appointment of the former Lexington Annual Conference. Bishop Matthew W. Clair, Jr., was elected to the episcopacy from the pastorate of this church in 1952.[27]

The dates of origin of black Methodist Episcopal churches in Michigan, Minnesota, Wisconsin, and the Dakotas have been difficult to ascertain. This problem will necessitate year approximations. It is reasonably certain that Scott Memorial Church in Detroit, named for the third black Methodist Episcopal missionary bishop, Isaiah B. Scott (1854–1931), is the oldest black Methodist Episcopal church in Detroit and in the state. Its founding date is assumed to be 1912. Camphor Memorial Church in St. Paul, Minnesota, similarly named for a black Methodist Episcopal missionary bishop, Alexander P. Camphor (1865–1919), was probably organized about the time of World War I. The same is likely to be true for the two churches in Wisconsin: St. James in Milwaukee and St. Matthias in Beloit. A 1923 district superintendent's report by P. T. Gorham, Chicago District, Lexington Conference, refers to a "preaching place" in Grand Forks, North Dakota, but it is not mentioned in future reports. There is no reference anywhere to a black Methodist Episcopal church in South Dakota.

Churches in the Southwest

Methodist Episcopal outreach among black people in the Southwest began in the 1820s in and around New Orleans. It eventuated in the organization of what has come to be widely known as Mother Wesley Church, New Orleans, 1838.[28] In 1842 "Wesley" appears as a black appointment in the Louisiana Conference of the Methodist Episcopal Church. Three events give Wesley a unique place in the history of black Methodism: It was the site of (1) the first reading of the Emancipation Proclamation in Louisiana; (2) the organization of the Mississippi Mission Conference, which would eventually "birth" four black Annual Conferences—Texas (1867), Mississippi and Louisiana (1869), and Upper Mississippi (1891); and (3) the organization of the Louisiana Annual Conference.

Union Memorial Methodist Episcopal Church, St. Louis, Missouri (1846),[29] the oldest black Methodist Episcopal Church in Missouri, has been in continuous existence since its founding. The contemporary design of its new (1961) edifice is a regional attraction. Wesley Chapel, Little Rock, Arkansas (1863),[30] "founded" several major churches in Little Rock. Philander Smith College was born there. Two of the earliest black Methodist Episcopal churches in Texas are Trinity, Houston (1865), and Wesley Chapel, Austin (1865).[31] These flagship churches were prominent in the founding of Texas Southern University and Huston-Tillotson College, respectively. Quayle Memorial Methodist Episcopal Church, Oklahoma City, Oklahoma, represents the earliest black Methodist Episcopal work in that state.[32] From mission status in 1881 to full status in 1889 and Conference admission in 1890, it has also become an exemplary inclusive congregation. Asbury Church in Topeka, Kansas, appears to be the first black Methodist Episcopal church there. While conclusive dates are unavailable, it did exist by 1908.[33] There are only scant traces of the origin of Clair Chapel, Omaha, Nebraska, but there has been an active congregation there since the early decades of this century.

Churches on the West Coast

Black Methodist Episcopal Church organization in California and the far western states dates from a black mission established in Sacramento in 1850. Largely due to the lack of black leadership, that mission was a failure, and in 1851 the church, which had taken the name First Colored Methodist Church, petitioned the AME Church, which was active in the region, for membership in that body. Little was done by the then California Annual Conference until 1910, when some black employees of the Pullman Company and Southern Pacific Railroad urged and aided in effecting the establishment of what became the William Taylor Memorial Methodist Episcopal Church in Oakland, California. Earlier in the southern part of the state, however, there had been other activity. In 1888 the first permanent California Methodist Episcopal church organization was founded through the missionary outreach of the Southern California Conference, the establishment of Wesley Chapel Methodist Episcopal Church in Los Angeles. By 1939 at least four more churches had been organized by the Southern California Conference. With unification in 1939 and the uniting of the work in Arizona, several more black churches were added. The same process was true in the California-Nevada Conference.[34]

EVANGELISTS, LOCAL PREACHERS, DEACONS, ELDERS, AND WOMEN

The black minister was indispensable in the establishment, growth, and spread of black Methodist Episcopal churches. As the General Conferences gave authorization, local preachers, deacons, and elders were the ones who exhorted, converted, and organized classes and societies. The fruits of their labor gave Methodism what, until very recently, was the largest black constituency of any major Protestant denomination in the nation. Justifying, claiming, and struggling to exercise the prerogatives of these ministerial offices has been a long, difficult task for black ministers. Our attention will now focus on that struggle. After describing the need to extend the itinerancy system to include black Methodists, an attempt will be made to trace their tortuously slow inclusion into the components of that system: local preachers, deacons, and elders.

Between 1800 and 1875 thousands of black members in white Methodist churches in the North and South left the Methodist Episcopal Church to establish their own "Methodist" denominations—for example, the Union AME Church (1813), the AME Church (1816), the AMEZ Church (1820), and CME Church (1870). The major reasons for these mass defections were increased racial tension between blacks and whites at the local church level and the denial of full clergy rights at the denominational level in the parent denomination.

Small groups of black members in many Methodist Episcopal churches did not leave the parent body, notably the remnant black members of St. George's Methodist Episcopal Church in Philadelphia, who in 1794 became African Zoar Church. This remnant group had the same complaints and joined in the same protests as those who did leave, but they chose to resolve their problems internally rather than leave. This group and groups like them in Philadelphia, Baltimore, Washington, D.C., and throughout the Delmarva peninsula advanced the following kinds of reasons for wanting ministers of their own color and congregations under their control while still remaining in the Methodist Episcopal denomination:

- rejection by fellow white Methodists, causing feelings of inferiority based on their color and their low status as slaves or former slaves
- discrimination in seating during worship, sacramental administration, and burial places
- restrictions upon emotional expression in worship, including responses to praying, preaching, and singing
- clear perceptions of excessive dominance of black church affairs by white church and denominational officials
- an autocratic, insensitive, and often abusive manner of supervision on the part of white presiding elders
- the endless taunting by other all-black denominations about the necessity of having to have white pastors and elders

With this background, let us review what occurred to black persons in the Methodist itinerant system from about 1784 to 1939.

Evangelists

Francis Asbury was persuaded that a converted black man was prepared by God "for peculiar usefulness to the people of his own colour." J. B. Finley reports that a Negro servant named Cuff frequently led religious devotions when no white preacher was available. In 1785 Asbury met a slave named Punch who "became a great light among his people, leading many to Christ." Punch later converted his overseer, who became a Methodist preacher. Abel Stevens relates the story of a black class leader in the Western District between 1796 and 1804 who was a highly effective exhorter.

W. W. Wightman, in his *Life of William Capers,* recalls "several extraordinary colored men" who served as evangelists in South Carolina. Still another black evangelist was John Charleston, a gifted preacher who had been ordained by Bishop William McKendree. Charleston, a convert of the Sunday school organized by Thomas Crenshaw in his home in Virginia, was reputed to have converted "thousands." Eventually, Charleston, failing to receive full ordination, left the Methodist Episcopal Church and united with the AME denomination.

A clear instance of licensing an exhorter occurred in 1833, when on the recommendation of Foundry Church in Washington, D.C., Eli Neugent was made an exhorter.[35]

Local Preachers

The next group of critical importance in evangelizing and church building were the black local preachers. Often gifted in spiritual matters, but mostly illiterate slaves or ex-slaves, this group performed yeoman service to the denomination from its earliest beginnings to the formation of Annual Conferences among black Methodists in the 1860s and beyond.

The status of these local (unordained) preachers was almost universally deplorable. W. C. Jason, Sr., points out that most of them received little or no pay, had very low status, were often ignored by their white presiding elders, and because of slave status, age, and domestic responsibilities, were unable to "travel" or seek an Annual Conference relationship. However, they were the most common source of the black ministers who eventually formed the mission Annual Conference.

The earliest black local preacher in the Methodist Episcopal Church of which we have any knowledge is Harry Hosier (ca. 1750–1806). Probably licensed to preach by St. George's Methodist Episcopal Church (Philadelphia) in the 1780s, he was acknowledged as one of the truly great preachers of his century. His famous sermon, "Barren Fig Tree" (Adams Chapel, Fairfax County, Virginia, 1781) was the first one preached by a Negro to a Methodist church in America. Likewise, his sermon in Thomas Chapel (Chapeltown,

Delaware, 1784) was the first one preached by a Negro to a white congregation. Another early black local preacher in Episcopal Methodism was the renowned Richard Allen (1760–1831). Later to become the founder of the AME Church (1861), Allen was licensed to preach in 1784. Henry Evans (ca. 1740–1810) is probably the third-best-known black licensed local preacher of note in Methodist history. A remarkable evangelist, indefatigable itinerant, and church builder, Evans was licensed in Virginia and introduced Methodism into Fayetteville, North Carolina, about 1800.

Other early licensed black local preachers include Jacob Tapisco and James Champion (1809); Perry Tilghman, lay preacher and first black pastor in charge assigned to African Zoar (1835); and Spencer Taylor, licensed to preach by the Methodist Episcopal Church, South, in the 1850s.[36] In 1852 the black local preachers in the area of what later became the Delaware and Washington Annual Conferences began to hold periodic Conferences on matters pertaining to their welfare and concern. These Conferences eventuated in the founding of the Delaware and Washington black Annual Conferences.

Deacons

Historically, deacons in the Methodist Episcopal Church were those who looked toward the ordained ministry. They were preparing for that ministry and were able to "travel"—meaning, take an appointment as probationary members of an Annual Conference. The slave status of most Southern black local preachers in the antebellum South and the quasi-free status of most Northern blacks, together with their limited opportunities for preparation for ministry, severely limited their eligibility to qualify as deacons. The complementary status of local deacons or nontraveling deacons seems to have been substituted to care for situations such as black local preachers dealt with in this period.

The first black local deacon ordained by Asbury was Richard Allen (1799). Presumably elected by the Philadelphia Conference, Allen, who had also been licensed as a local preacher at St. George's, was selected exclusively to promote and care for the "black work" of that particular church. This fact is clarified by the action of the General Conference, which met in 1800:

The bishops have obtained leave by the suffrages of this General Conference to ordain local deacons of our African brethren, in places where they have built a house or houses for the worship of God; provided that they have a person among them qualified for that office, and he can obtain an election of two-thirds of the male members of the society to which he belongs, and a recommendation from the minister who has the charge, and his fellow-laborers in the city or circuit.[37]

It is noteworthy that Asbury did not mention his 1799 ordination of Allen, nor did the 1800 General Conference publish their authorization to ordain black local deacons in the *Discipline*.[38]

Harry Hosier's ordination as a local deacon poses a question. W. Thomas Smith relates the situation as follows:

> William Calbert and other officials of St. George's Methodist Episcopal Church in Philadelphia drew a formal request for Hosier's ordination for presentation to the 1805 meeting of the Philadelphia Conference. While ministerial orders are not mentioned it can be assumed that since he was a local preacher, he was being proposed for Deacons' orders. From the record the request was not approved and Harry Hosier was never ordained a Deacon.[39]

In 1806 Asbury mentions in his journal that on May 16 he ordained "three Africans as Deacons."[40] Six years later (1812) a fuller journal entry adds, "A charge has been brought against me for ordaining a slave, but there was no further pursuit of the case when it was discovered that I was ready with my certificates to prove that he had been granted his freedom."[41] James Varick, one of the three, later left John Street Methodist Episcopal Church, joined with a dissenting group, and eventually established the AMEZ Church.

Daniel Coker (1780–ca. 1846) and William Miller were Francis Asbury's two final ordinands (1808). Coker,[42] an outstanding example of initiative and leadership, soon freed himself from slavery, succeeded in getting a basic education, started a school, was called to the ministry, and was ordained a local deacon by Asbury in 1808. Following this he became active in the AME Church. Coker, an excellent preacher, rose rapidly in his denomination, even to the point of being elected its first bishop, but he declined to serve. William Miller affiliated with the Methodist Episcopal Church briefly and then united with the AME Church.

Elders

The ministerial order or office of elder in the Methodist Episcopal Church was composed of ministers with three qualifications: certain academic training, probationary membership in an Annual Conference, and deacons' orders. They were those who had to devote their full time to the practice of ministry and accept annual appointments from a bishop.

Eldership and full Conference membership came to black pastors relatively late, and then first to those who were to serve in Africa. The General Conference of 1832 authorized the bishops of the church to appoint preachers to "people of color," but without the privilege of Conference membership.[43] This "limited itinerancy" applied to black ministers until the establishment of Annual Conferences to accommodate the "unique" circumstances of black preachers. The chronology begins with the opening of Methodist Episcopal work in Liberia, allowing bishops to appoint agents for African colonization when asked by an Annual Conference. In consequence of this, bishops could also appoint for more than two years preachers to people of color.

John Graham relates that the first black preacher admitted into full membership in an Annual Conference of the Methodist Episcopal Church was John H. Mars (1804–1889). Mars was licensed to preach around 1828, ordained a deacon by the New York Conference in the 1830s, received "on trial" in the New England Conference, and shortly thereafter (1864) ordained an elder and admitted into full connection.[44] Others early ordained as elders include Spencer Taylor (1866), Missouri Conference;[45] Samuel Weston, W. O. Weston, J. A. Sasportas, Francis Smith (1866), South Carolina Conference;[46] and Frost Pullett (1872), Delaware Conference.[47]

Women in Ministry

Before going further in this section tracing black access to the unordained and ordained ministry, a word about the availability of these opportunities to women is in order. John H. Graham recalls the long struggle that women have had gaining clergy rights. This effort climaxed in the 1920 General Conference Episcopal Address, which gave the first really positive indication of the recognition and acceptance of women for ministry in more than a century. The address said, in part, "Boards and institutions that directly touch youth in the years it is making its life decision ought to have coordinated systematized plans, not for . . . an occasional . . . recruiting but for a continuous . . . regard for *gathering men and women for the ministry.*"[48] Following this address the General Conference authorized the granting of licenses for women who desired to be local preachers.

The first black Annual Conference to grant a local preacher's license under this new ruling was the Upper Mississippi. That same year (1920), the Greenwood District approved a license for Mrs. Mary E. Jones.[49] In 1926 there was further action toward equal clergy rights for women. Laura J. Lange was ordained a local deacon in 1926 and a local elder in 1936.[50] This made her the first black woman to be so ordained in any black Annual Conference. Both of these ordinations had been voted by the Lexington Conference. Bishop Theodore S. Henderson (1868–1929) and Bishop Matthew W. Clair, Sr. (1865–1943), presided over these ordinations. Further advances in clergy rights for women would not be made until 1956.

PRESIDING ELDERS/DISTRICT SUPERINTENDENTS

Black presiding elders emerged as a "new" class of black leadership with the organization of the Black Annual Conference (1864). Usually they were selected by the bishops from among the most literate, articulate, and effective ministers in the Conferences. A cross-sectional view of the first black ministers appointed to this office in what were then biracial Mission Conferences can be obtained by noting these early selections.

Actually, the first black American minister appointed to a presiding eldership was Francis Burns (1809–1863). Burns, later (1858) to become the first black missionary bishop, was appointed for work in Liberia in 1849.[51]

The first black presiding elders in a domestic Annual Conference were those in the Delaware Mission Conference (July 1864). Their names and districts were as follows: Isaac Henson, Delaware River District; James Davis, Odessa District; Wilmore S. Elzey, Choptank District.[52] The second group of black presiding elders appointed were in the Washington Mission Conference (October 1864): Benjamin Brown, Sr., Chesapeake-Baltimore-North Baltimore District; James Harper, Potomac-Washington District.[53]

In the Southwest, the first black presiding elder appears in the Mississippi Mission Conference, organized in 1865 and originally including Mississippi, Louisiana, and Texas. In 1867 James D. Lynch was appointed to the South Mississippi District.[54] The South Carolina Mission Conference in the Southeast, which initially (since 1866) had all white presiding elders, appointed its first black presiding elder in 1870. Warren Jenkins indicates that J. A. Sasportas became the presiding elder for the Summerville District.[55] The first black presiding elder appointment in the Midwest was in the Lexington Mission Conference (1869). This Conference originated in Kentucky but eventually extended its borders to include the entire Midwest. The appointments were Henry Lytle, Louisville District, and David P. Jones, Lexington District.[56]

By 1870 there were eighteen black presiding elders in the Methodist Episcopal Church representing each of the five black Annual Conferences that had been organized to that date. In addition to these, four Liberian presiding elders were serving under Bishop John W. Roberts (1812–1875) in Liberia. A word of commendation in the *New York Christian Advocate* (February 11, 1869) evaluated the work of these early presiding elders: "Thus far the colored Presiding Elders have done their work well. Their administration has been prudent, active, and successful." By 1939 there were eighty-four black district superintendents.

CONFERENCE GROWTH AND EXPANSION

It has already been noted that Negroes participated in every phase of the growth of early Methodism in America. They were members of its first societies, circuits, and Conferences. Given the problematic nature of the racially circumscribed relationship that Negroes had in white churches and

Conferences, however, it was only a matter of time before they needed and desired their own Annual Conferences. Advocacy for these began almost immediately after the North-South division of the Methodist Episcopal Church in 1844. The reasons for this fell into two categories: credibility and advancement potential. First, in the urban North, where most of the Negro Methodist Episcopal churches were located prior to the Civil War, Negroes belonging to these churches were taunted by members of the AME and AMEZ churches for belonging to the "white man's church." They were reminded that they were disallowed ordained elders, presiding elders, bishops, Annual Conferences, and representation in their General Conferences. This caused Negro Methodist Episcopal churches to lose members, with many defecting to other Negro Methodist bodies and some to non-Methodist Negro churches. Second, only Annual Conferences could provide the necessary status, security, and opportunity for ordination, Conference membership, eligibility for appointments as district superintendents and bishops, General Conference representation, and special appointments.

Protesting this situation, Negro preachers and laypeople petitioned their Annual Conferences. In 1848 John P. Durbin presented to the General Conference memorials (petitions) from the Negro local preachers of the Philadelphia and New Jersey Conferences, requesting supervision. (Similar resolutions were presented from Negro preachers and laypeople in the Washington-Baltimore area.) The 1852 General Conference received similar memorials and responded by advising "that the Negro local preachers . . . be assembled annually by the presiding bishop for the purpose of conferring on means for promoting their work and for assignment."[57] Memorials were sent to the 1856 General Conference, but the 1852 action was reaffirmed. A bold venture was made in 1860 to request a "provisional" Annual Conference for Negro preachers. This was rejected because it could not be done "without doing violence to [the Church's] regulations."[58] Finally, in 1864 the General Conference created the Committee on the State of the Work Among People of Color. This committee recommended the legislation that the General Conference voted, that "Negro Mission Conferences be organized."[59] Opposed by Gilbert Haven (1821–1880), a Negro rights activist, as "discriminatory," this step was nevertheless a small one in the right direction in a tortuously slow effort to advance Negro clergy rights. Incidentally, Haven was white but represented a significant community of advocacy, principally in the North but also in the West and to some degree in the South.[60]

The period 1864–1925 witnessed the rise, spread, and growth of twenty-five Negro Annual Conferences. The majority of these organizations experienced uninterrupted growth from the dates of their founding to the advent of the Central Jurisdiction (1940).

The life of two of them (Delaware and Washington) spanned the entire period. Several Conferences continued in successor bodies through mergers or reconstitution. Some few disappeared after having lasted for a number of years. This section of this chapter will recount briefly the origins, growth, and major changes in the life of these bodies, which represented the first efforts of Negroes in the Methodist Episcopal Church to initiate mission and self-direction. This review will be accomplished by identifying and tracing the individual histories of these Conferences that originated in six regional centers across the country.

Philadelphia/Eastern Shore/Northeast/New England

The largely urban Northeast, the initial source of agitation for Negro Annual Conferences and the location of the bulk of Episcopal Methodism's Negro membership prior to the Civil War, was the site of the first two Annual Conferences among Negroes in the United States. The Delaware Conference was authorized by the 1864 General Conference and organized on July 28 in John Wesley Church (later Tindley Temple), Philadelphia, Pennsylvania, by Bishop Edmund S. James (1807–1876). (W. S. Elzey was elected secretary.) The boundaries of this pioneering Mission Conference were set to include Delaware, New Jersey (eastern), Maryland, Pennsylvania, Virginia, and the Northeast. Tributary Conferences in its formation (1865) were Philadelphia, New Jersey, New York, and Newark. Delaware was the state from which it took its name.

Eleven members (racially mixed) charted the Conference and are considered its founders: Joshua Brinkley, Isaiah Broughton, Samuel Dale, James Davis, Wilmore S. Elzey, Isaac Hinson, John G. Manluff, Jehu H. Pearce, Frost Pullett, Harrison Smith, and Nathan Young. Periodic missionary and evangelistic efforts extended the work of the Delaware Conference from its center in Philadelphia to New Jersey, the Eastern Shore (Maryland and Delaware), New York, and New England. In 1868 the Delaware Conference achieved full Annual Conference status and immediately elected one of its founding members, James Davis, to the 1868 General Conference. Davis thus became the first Negro delegate to that body.

The first work of the newly organized Conference was distributed across three districts: Delaware River, under Isaac Henson, presiding elder; Odessa, under James David, presiding elder; and Choptank under Wilmore S. Elzey, presiding elder. (The term "presiding elder" was used until 1908, when it was replaced by the term "district superintendent.") It consisted of nineteen founding appointments extending from the Philadelphia area through southern New Jersey to the southern part of the eastern shore of Maryland-Virginia.[61]

Alexander P. Camphor was a member of the Delaware Conference. Noah W. Moore of the Delaware Conference was elected to the episcopacy in 1960.

Baltimore/Potomac/Virginia and South

Authorization for the establishment of the Washington Conference was granted by the same 1864 General Conference that brought the Delaware Conference into existence. It met for organization on October 27 in Sharp Street Church in Baltimore. Bishop Levi Scott (1802–1882) was the presiding bishop, and Benjamin Brown was secretary. The boundaries of this second Negro Mission Conference embraced western Pennsylvania, western Maryland (including Baltimore), the District of Columbia, Virginia (west of the Potomac River), and portions of West Virginia. Contributing Conferences to the new territory and membership of the Washington Conference were Baltimore, East Baltimore, Philadelphia, Pittsburgh, Virginia, and Western Virginia. Washington Conference founders include Benjamin Brown, Elijah Grissem, James H. Harper, and James Peck. There were two original districts in the Washington Conference: Chesapeake, under Benjamin Brown, presiding elder, and Potomac, under James H. Harper, presiding elder. The first appointments made in the new Conference covered the territory from Baltimore east to Annapolis, west to Hagerstown, Maryland, and Cincinnati, Ohio, and south through Washington, D.C., to Alexandria, Richmond, and Norfolk, Virginia. In 1868 the Washington Conference (together with the Delaware) was admitted to the status of a full Annual Conference and elected its first General Conference delegate, Benjamin Brown, that year. In 1872 the Conference attained another "first," the eligibility to elect its first lay delegate to the General Conference, James O. Harris. By 1875 Washington Conference work required six districts and extended to the boundaries of each state of its assigned responsibility, including West Virginia.[62]

Members of the Washington Conference elected to the episcopacy were Matthew W. Clair, Sr. (1865–1943), W. A. C. Hughes (1877–1940), and Edgar A. Love (1891–1974).

New Orleans/Gulf Coast/Texas

The third major thrust in Negro Conference organization after the Civil War and a first effort to actually reenter the Southwest grew out of the organization of the Mississippi Mission Conference. Following Union Army occupation forces on their southward march, Methodist Episcopal missionaries evangelized, missionized, and recruited ex-slaves for membership in the denomination. Churching them in Army-confiscated Methodist Episcopal, South, churches or improvised buildings, within a relatively short period of time there was the need for some type of Conference organization. Accordingly, under the 1864 General Conference authorization to develop "mission conferences," Bishop Edward Thomson (1810–1870) organized the Mississippi Mission Conference in Wesley Chapel Church, New Orleans, on Christmas Day, December 25, 1864. Negro probationary members lacking the skill to write necessitated the election of a white minister as secretary, John P. Newman (1826–1899), an advocate for the rights of the Negro in the church and later one of its distinguished bishops.

The original territory of the Mission Conference included Mississippi, Louisiana, and Texas. The leadership for the vast expanse of work came from the following Negro and white missionaries to that region:

William Murrell	J. M. Bryant
Emperor Williams	S. M. Small
Henry Green	J. Goodwyn
Hardy Ryan	Anthony Ross
Scott Chinn	David Ennis
Samuel Osborne	Thomas Kennedy
H. G. Jackson	R. K. Diossey
N. L. Brakeman	W. M. Henry

Their fields of labor and service were across a three-state territory subdivided into four Mission Districts: New Orleans, Opelousas (Louisiana), Mississippi, and Texas. The work of the Conference progressed rapidly in the months after its establishment. Beginning with the formation of the Texas Mission District into a Mission Conference in 1867 and the formation of the Louisiana Mission District into a Conference in 1869, the Mississippi Mission Conference was no longer necessary, and it was terminated.[63]

The Texas Conference

The Texas Conference (biracial) was organized by Bishop Matthew Simpson (1811–1884) in Trinity Church, Houston, on January 3, 1867. Geographically, it comprised the state of Texas, including stations of work on three districts: Texas Mission, Houston, and German Mission. Its founders were basically Mississippi Mission Conference ministers: Joseph Welch, elected secretary of the new Conference; Samuel Osborne; David E. Dibble; J. Davis; and G. E. Brooks.

In 1869 the Texas Mission Conference became a full-fledged body and took the name Texas Annual Conference. In 1874 it was divided to form the West Texas Conference (authorized by the 1872 General Conference). This body was formally organized in Wesley Chapel Church on January 22–26. The presiding bishop was Thomas Bowman (1817–1914).

Included in its boundaries was all Negro work in West Texas, not included in the work of the Texas Conference. With the formation of the Southern German Conference in 1874 to include all German-speaking Methodists in Texas and the organization of the white ministers to form the Austin Conference in 1877, the Texas and West Texas Conferences became exclusively Negro and remained so until 1939 and beyond. (Isaiah B. Scott

(1852–1931), the first United States Negro missionary bishop elected for Liberia (1904), was a member of the Texas Conference. In 1944 Willis J. King, (1886–1976), also of the Texas Conference, was elected to the episcopacy).[64]

The Louisiana Conference

The Louisiana Conference, a division of the Mississippi Mission Conference, was organized in Wesley Chapel Church (built by its members while still slaves) on January 13, 1869. The presiding bishop for the historic occasion was again Matthew Simpson, and the secretary, John P. Newman. According to its charter it was to include the entire state of Louisiana. The work of the Conference extended over circuits and stations on five districts. In 1893 the Conference divided on the matter of race. The white work in the Louisiana and Texas Conferences was consolidated into the Gulf Mission. In 1897 this mission became a Mission Conference, and in 1904 the Gulf Annual Conference. Thus after being a biracial Conference for twenty-four years, the Louisiana Conference became an all-Negro body and continued as such for the remainder of the Methodist Episcopal era.[65]

South Atlantic Coast/Mississippi

South Carolina was a major reentry point for Methodist Episcopal missionary work among Negroes in the Deep South. Building on foundations laid by W. T. Lewis and others as early as 1862 and taking advantage of Negro Methodist Episcopal work that had already been established in Charleston and elsewhere, South Carolina was ready for the establishment of a mission shortly after the Civil War. Accordingly, Bishop Osman C. Baker (1812–1871) organized the South Carolina Mission Conference on April 2, 1866, in Charleston. Missionary Alonzo Webster of the Vermont Conference was elected secretary. Founder-members of what was to become the largest and one of the strongest Negro Conferences were T. Willard Lewis, Alonzo Webster, J. A. Sasportas, H. D. Owens, F. Smith, T. Phillips, W. J. Cole. W. J. E. Tripp, Mansfield French, D. D. Leavitt, H. J. C. Emerson, Jack Grimke, J. C. Nixson, and L. Anders.

The boundaries set at the organizing Conference gave responsibility to the Conference for the work of the church in South Carolina, Florida, and eastern Georgia. Two districts of work were established: Charleston for the South Carolina work, under T. Willard Lewis, presiding elder (white), and Florida for mission work in Florida and eastern Georgia, under D. D. Leavitt, presiding elder (white). In 1868 the General Conference limited the boundaries of the Conference to South Carolina and Florida. In 1872 it restricted them to South Carolina. From the time when South Carolina became a full-status Annual Conference (1868) until the end of the Methodist Episcopal period, the work of this Conference exhibited solid growth and progress in all departments of its program.[66] Not the least of this progress was the contribution of one of its native sons to the episcopacy (1964), Bishop James S. Thomas, for whom a street is named in Sumter.

Holston Valley and Deep South Developments

The pioneering missionary work done in South Carolina was the first phase of a three-pronged thrust in Negro Conference organization in the Southeast. By 1925 this territory could claim the largest number of churches and Conferences of any region of the denomination. The following chronological review will briefly describe this remarkable progress in the Holston Valley, Tennessee; southwestern Virginia; western North Carolina; northeastern South Carolina; Alabama; Mississippi; North Carolina; Georgia; and Florida.

In the western region of this assigned territory, the Tennessee Mission Conference, organized on October 11, 1866, by Bishop Davis W. Clark (1812–1871), began its work in the Holston Valley. The 1876 General Conference enacted permissive legislation allowing it to separate its Negro and white work, as requested by some. In consequence of this the Tennessee Conference became exclusively Negro. In 1880 it divided its work on a geographical basis and with the permission of the General Conference formed the East Tennessee Conference (October 25, 1880). Bishop Erastus O. Haven (1820–1881) presided at its organization. Following this division both Conferences continued until Union in 1939.

The Central Alabama Conference was organized on October 18, 1876, by Bishop Levi Scott (1802–1882). Formerly a part of the Alabama Mission Conference (1867), it divided its work along North-South lines in 1900, creating the Mobile Conference in the southern part of the state. In 1908 the two Conferences reunited and continued as the Central Alabama Conference until 1939.

A final Negro Conference organization occurred in the "Old South." The Mississippi Conference, originally a part of the 1865 Mississippi Mission Conference, became a separate body in 1869. It was constituted on January 7, 1869, in Asbury Church, Holly Springs. Bishop Matthew W. Simpson was the presiding bishop. (John H. Graham relates that Bishop Simpson was delayed for this Conference. In his absence, the Conference elected James Lynch (1839–1872) as chairman pro tempore.) In 1891 the Mississippi Conference divided its work geographically. Having been granted their request for division, the Upper Mississippi Conference (northern section of the state) was duly organized on February 5, 1891, with Bishop Edward G. Andrews (1825–1907) presiding. Both of these Conferences continued until 1939.[67]

During the second phase of Negro Conference organization, Methodist Episcopal missionaries moved to the eastern Atlantic Coast area. In Portsmouth, Virginia, Bishop Levi Scott (1802–1882) organized the Virginia and North Carolina Mission Conference in 1867. In 1869 Bishop Edward R.

Ames (1806–1879) established the North Carolina Conference at Union Chapel, Alexander County, North Carolina, on January 14. This key Conference, which continued until 1939, was the Annual Conference home of bishops Robert E. Jones (1872–1960), Robert N. Brooks (1888–1953), and Prince A. Taylor (b. 1907).[68]

The third and final phase of Negro Conference development occurred in the Deep South states of Georgia and Florida. The Georgia Mission Conference established in 1867 by Bishop Davis W. Clark (1812–1871) in Atlanta set off its Negro work in the Savannah Conference organized by Bishop Levi Scott on November 1, 1876, in Augusta. Two decades later in 1896, the Savannah Conference divided its work, creating the Atlanta Conference for the northern part of the state. The presiding bishop at the organization of this Conference held in Lloyd Street Church (Central) in Atlanta on January 21, 1897, was Bishop Cyrus D. Foss (1834–1910). Both of these strong Conferences continued throughout the Methodist Episcopal period.[69] L. Scott Allen (b. 1918) was a member of the Georgia Conference, which elected him a bishop in 1967.

The last Negro Conferences were formed in Florida. As a result of the work of the Freedmen's Aid Society, a biracial Conference was begun there in Ebenezer Church, Jacksonville, on January 19, 1873. Bishop Edward R. Ames was the presiding officer. The boundaries of this Conference included all of the state with the exception of an extreme western portion of it. With the organization of the St. John's River Conference (white), the Florida Conference became an exclusively Negro body. Later (1905) the continuing Florida Conference set off its work in the southern part of the state in a South Florida Mission. This became a Mission Conference in 1921, and in 1925 Bishop Ernest G. Richardson (1874–1947) organized the South Florida Conference.[70] Both Florida Conferences continued until Unification in 1939.

Lexington/Northwest

The Lexington Conference, destined to carry Negro Methodists into the Midwest, Northwest, and the Rocky Mountains area, took its rise from the humble Colored Mission District in the Kentucky Conference of the Methodist Episcopal Church. Organized in 1866, this district had churches whose histories and roots could be traced to members, societies, and churches dating to 1832. When constituted as a district, it had churches and preaching points in practically every part of the state, such as Covington, Lexington, Louisville, and Harrodsburg. Lexington's formal Conference organization followed a familiar pattern. Early in 1868 the Negro preachers in the Kentucky Conference met separately from the whites and requested the Conference to petition the General Conference for an Annual Conference of their own. The Kentucky Annual Conference responded positively and sought from the General Conference the authorization for a separate Conference. Shortly after a favorable response from the 1868 General Conference, Bishop Levi Scott (1810–1870) organized the Lexington Conference on March 2, 1869, at Harrodsburg. (The name "Lexington" was taken from Lexington, Kentucky, one of the early growth centers of Negro Methodism in the state.) Initially, the boundaries set for the Lexington Conference included Kentucky. These limits were extended by succeeding General Conferences to include Ohio and Indiana (1872), eastern Illinois (1876), and later Michigan, Minnesota, and Wisconsin. Lexington Conference founders, among the earliest Negro Methodist ex-slave preachers to venture beyond the southern region, were Henry H. Lytle, Israel Sims, Zail Ross, William H. Lawrence, Marcus McCoomer, Peter Booth, Hanson Talbot, Nelson Saunders, Andrew Bryant, Adam Nunn, George Downing, Willis L. Muir, Elisha C. Moore, and Scott Ward.

Building on the solid foundation of the earlier pioneer missionaries and church builders of the past, the Lexington Conference followed the trend of Negro migration from the South in the 1920s and established missions and churches in practically every major metropolitan center in the Midwest, including Chicago, Cincinnati, Cleveland, Columbus, Dayton, Des Moines, Detroit, Ft. Wayne, Indianapolis, Kansas City, Louisville, Milwaukee, Minneapolis, St. Louis, and Toledo.[71] Elected to the episcopacy from Lexington were Matthew W. Clair, Jr. (1952); Charles F. Golden (1960); and M. Lafayette Harris (1960). The life of the Lexington Conference ran its course in the Methodist Episcopal Church until 1939.

Westward Expansion

Two other Negro Annual Conferences aided in extending Methodism westward, Central Missouri and Central West. An Enabling Act of the 1884 General Conference allowed the Negro members of the St. Louis and Missouri Conferences to form a separate body. In keeping with this permission, these Conferences, meeting at Glasgow and Warrensburg, Missouri, in 1887, voted to allow the creation of a Negro Conference. Accordingly, the Central Missouri Conference was formed on March 24, 1887, at Sedalia, Missouri. The presiding bishop was Wilbur F. Mallalieu (1828–1911). Its first boundaries embraced Negro work in Missouri. The General Conference of 1890 changed these original boundaries to include Negro work in Kansas, Iowa, Nebraska, and western Illinois. In 1900 the boundaries were again changed to include Negro work in the Oklahoma Territory. These boundaries remained in force until 1902, at which time a new "Okaneb" Conference was organized, and all Negro work in Oklahoma, Kansas, and Nebraska was placed in it. For reasons not altogether clear, the Okaneb experiment was impractical, and it was dissolved in 1903. Replacing it was the Lincoln Conference, including Oklahoma, Missouri, Kansas, and Nebraska. The Lincoln

Conference persisted for twenty-four years (1903–1927) until a 1928 General Conference Enabling Act set a new boundary for the Central Mission Conference. This new boundary included these parts of the Lincoln Conference in Kansas, Colorado, and Nebraska, as well as the work in Iowa, North and South Dakota, Montana, and western Illinois. The new designation for this Conference organized in Kansas City April 15, 1929, by Bishop Matthew W. Clair, Sr., was Central West.[72] This body continued until 1939.

The extension of the boundaries of the Lincoln Conference (1903–1927) to include Colorado represented the farthest western outreach of any Negro Conference. Likewise, the organization of Scott Memorial Church in Denver (1904) represented the western most church established under any Negro Conference auspices.

Little Rock/Southwest

The 1876 General Conference anticipating what it termed the necessity of organizing "a conference in the bounds of the Arkansas Conference especially adapted to the Colored work" developed an Enabling Act which provided that as soon as there could be found twenty Negro Traveling Preachers in the Conference, it would be legal, by majority vote, "to organize a Colored Conference." . . . At the Conference Session of 1878 division was voted, although there were then only four Negro ministers in full connection.[73]

Against this background the Little Rock Conference was organized and held its first session February 21–24, 1879, at Van Buren, Arkansas, with Bishop Edward G. Andrews (1825–1907) presiding. Since that time it has played a key role in extending the missional thrust of Negro church and Conference development in the Southwest.

Founders of the Little Rock Conference were Harry Brock, A. C. Crawley, Eli Dye, J. D. Gibson, Tarlton Harden, J. H. Henry, John H. Johnson, W. S. Langford, Henry McDonald, Oscar G. Moss, Ezra Qualls, Albert Tate, George W. Taylor, Brooks Washington, and J. W. Williamson. The first appointments of this fledgling Conference were made to two districts, Little Rock and White River. Although there were some Negro preachers in this racially mixed Conference, the presiding elders and pastoral appointments were white.

The Little Rock Conference was biracial in character until about 1900 or 1904, at which time the General Conference ordered boundary changes that literally displaced most of the white people from the Little Rock Conference. The first Negro presiding elder was G. N. Johnson. The first Negro secretary of the Conference was W. W. Duncan.

The period 1904–1917 in the Little Rock Conference has been referred to as its progressive years. Pulpit and lay leadership, including women leaders, emerged. (Anne T. Sticklin became the first Negro woman and perhaps the first woman elected to the General Conference [1904]). The Conference gave yeoman support to its college, Philander Smith, the only institution of its kind in the region west of the Mississippi River. Finally, in cooperation with the Central Missouri Conference (1886–1928), Negro Methodist expansion strategy was redesigned. Mission churches and districts of its work were assigned briefly to the Okaneb Conference (1902–1903), and Oklahoma work was opened. From 1902–1927 the Lincoln Conference, which had superseded the Okaneb, was extended and strengthened. In 1928 the Little Rock Conference absorbed the Oklahoma work, and the new configuration was designated the Southwest Conference (1929); it continued until 1939.[74]

Summarizing, by 1929, a decade prior to Unification (1939), twenty-five Negro Conferences had been formed, covering two thirds of the nation from New York (Brooklyn and Jamaica, Long Island) to Colorado (Denver). Also, excepting in New England and on the West Coast, the Methodist Episcopal Church was completely divided along racial lines. Inclusiveness had become a moot issue. Negro Conferences, though organically related to the Methodist Episcopal Church, were in actuality separate and apart from it in significant ways. In any event, at the time of Unification, the twenty-five Conferences, in response to population shifts, membership increases and decreases, and General Conference direction, had been consolidated into nineteen.

MISSIONS, EVANGELISM, AND COMMUNITY OUTREACH

It is important to note that with the emergence of evangelists, preachers, and pastors among black people in the Methodist Episcopal Church, there grew a vital interest in community outreach and home and overseas missions. Black Methodists have contributed a valuable presence to and significant support for the missionary and evangelistic work of Methodism from its beginning. Faithful to the word and witness of its founder John Wesley, they have gone forth personally through their churches and in community efforts to reach "the lost, the least and the last," whoever they are and wherever they may be found.

It was mentioned earlier that the first black churches were not only religious societies but mutual aid societies as well. This dual function can be clearly traced in the historical development of black Methodist Episcopal Churches, such as Zoar in Philadelphia (1794), Sharp Street in Baltimore (1802), Calvary in Cincinnati (1824), and Wesley in New Orleans (1838). These mutual aid societies were not only for the benefit of the families and friends of the members of these churches. They attempted to meet the needs of the unchurched on a "need" basis. Together with the preaching of Charles A. Tindley (1851–1933), this kind of mutual aid program was perhaps the genius of the phenomenal growth of many of our early black Methodist Episcopal churches. Another mission outreach function of the early black Methodist Episcopal Church was that of affording asylum to fugitive slaves. An example of this would be Zoar, which stood out as an asylum for escaping slaves.

Bishop Matthew W. Clair, Jr., reveals yet another facet of the early contribution of black people to mission when he claims that the unusual evangelistic and missionary ministry of Henry Evans "helped lay the foundation for the work of William Capers, who later . . . gave himself unreservedly to the task of the evangelization of the slave."[75] It is well known that Black John Stewart (ca. 1766–1823) was among the first Methodists to reach out to the Native American population between 1817 and 1819. It was Stewart who founded Methodism's first successful mission to the Wyandot Indian tribe in Ohio. This eventually led to the formation of the Missionary and Bible Society of the Methodist Episcopal Church (1820).[76]

Home Missions After Emancipation

The abolition of slavery in the South in 1863 and the emancipation that it brought to millions of black people presented the church and the nation with the most serious and complex problem that either had ever faced. Following a brief period of cooperation through federal reconstruction agencies such as the Freedmen's Aid Bureau, many church denominations developed their own programs to aid and educate the ex-slaves.

The Methodist Episcopal Church created the Freedmen's Aid Society for this purpose in 1866, one of the boldest ventures in mission to be undertaken at that time. At the outset, it seemed that this effort by the church would be initiated, managed, and controlled by both men and women. When women were finally refused what they considered to be significant status and control in the Freedmen's Aid Society, they wisely considered other options to accomplish their objective, "to enlist and organize the interest of Christian women in behalf of the needy and destitute in all sections of the country." After an unsuccessful attempt to accomplish their goals through the already established Woman's Foreign Missionary Society, the Woman's Home Mission Society (WHMS) was organized in 1880. An interesting historical fact behind the formal organization of the Woman's Home Missionary Society is its conception in the heart and mind of Jennie Culver Hartzell, while working in Mother Wesley Chapel Methodist Church in the 1870s. The wife of Joseph C. Hartzell, pastor of Ames Chapel Methodist Episcopal Church in New Orleans, Jennie Hartzell, had a burning conviction that something had to be done to help the needy, destitute, and unconverted young women and children in New Orleans.

It is from this beginning that the Woman's Home Missionary Society and its many schools, homes, orphanages, deaconess training ventures, and other projects evolved. In the years between 1880 and 1939, the Woman's Home

Missionary Society cooperated with other boards, agencies, and institutions of the church to organize, support, and manage the following groups of facilities: nineteen community centers (known as Bethlehem Centers in the South), which still exist in many cities; six residential homes for children and youth; five residential homes for working women; a deaconess training institution; and two homes for the aged. Bessie M. Garrison was the first black National Woman's Home Missionary Society field secretary (1907).

In addition to the various institutional services and programs that have assisted black Methodists, they have been involved in mission themselves. In 1900 W. H. Riley and his wife, both of the Lexington Conference, initiated a deaconess Training School in Cincinnati "to answer the cries of the suffering and the needy." In 1904 Shelly J. Gale of Zoar Church in Philadelphia, Pennsylvania, became one of the first black women in the denomination to receive consecration as a deaconess. In 1923 Bishop Robert E. Jones founded Gulfside Assembly at Waveland, Mississippi. Its purpose was "to serve the needs of black people in the Southern regions of the church" through leadership conferences, skill training, and spiritual renewal activities. In 1924 the Board of Home Missions and Church Extension established a Bureau of Negro Work to conduct and promote rural pastors' schools that were to reach people with programs that would improve the overall performance of church programming.[77]

Overseas Ministries

Black Methodists have been involved in missions overseas since the early 1830s. Matthew W. Clair, Jr., reminds us of Solomon Cartwright, a black man who was selected for missionary service in Africa in 1831. A young black teacher, Eunice Sharp, together with Francis Burns, sailed for service in Liberia in 1834. Three of the four black missionary bishops elected by the General Conference between 1858 and 1916 were themselves former missionaries. Alexander P. Camphor (1865–1919), the last black missionary bishop to be elected, was also the first regularly appointed black missionary of the Methodist Episcopal Church. Around 1884 three additional black missionaries went to Liberia for service: Lavinia Johnson; John Morris, "a slave whose freedom was bought on approval of the Foreign Mission Board for $700"; and Sarah Simpson, a black teacher.

Anna E. Hall should be remembered: The first black graduate deaconess of the Methodist Episcopal Church (1899), "Mother Hall," as she was called, spent twenty-four years in Liberia. As a result of her outstanding work, she was awarded a citation (1956) by the Liberian president, William V. S. Tubman. Other black missionaries who served in Liberia during the Methodist Episcopal Church era include the Reverend and Mrs. J. A. Simpson, 1899–1921; the Reverend and Mrs. Frederick A. Price, 1905–1946; the

Reverend and Mrs. R. G. Embree, 1914–1944; and Hattie T. Hooks, 1930–1937.

Turning briefly to missions and missionaries in other parts of Africa, before returning to Liberia Susan Collins served in Angola under the Woman's Foreign Missionary Society (WFMS) from 1901 until her retirement in 1920. Martha Drummer joined Collins in 1906 and served in Angola until her retirement in 1923.

In closing this brief survey of black workers who served in overseas missions prior to 1940, it should be noted that two black women, registered nurses, were assigned to three-year terms in Bolivia in 1931.[78]

Missionary Bishops

Four black American Methodist Episcopal ministers were elected by the General Conference to superintend the work in Liberia between 1858 and 1916. Francis Burns (1809–1863), a native of Albany, New York, and a missionary to Liberia for twenty-four years, was elected a missionary bishop by the Liberia Conference in 1858 under a provision of the General Conference of 1856. Bishop Burns was the first missionary bishop to be elected by the Methodist Episcopal Church. John W. Roberts (1812–1875), a native of Petersburg, Virginia, was also elected a missionary bishop by the Liberia Conference in 1866. It is noteworthy that Bishop Roberts was the brother of Joseph J. Roberts, a Methodist local preacher and the four-time elected governor of Liberia. Isaiah B. Scott (1854–1931), a native of Midway, Kentucky (near Frankfort), was elected a missionary bishop for service in Liberia by the 1904 General Conference. From 1896 to 1904 Scott was the editor of the *Southwestern Christian Advocate* (1876–1940), forerunner of the *Central Christian Advocate* (1941–1968). Alexander P. Camphor (1865–1919), a native of New Orleans and a missionary to Liberia from 1897–1908, was elected a missionary bishop for service in Liberia in 1916. This recognition climaxed his distinguished career as a professor of mathematics, pastor, college president, and for a period, United States vice-counsel in Liberia.[79]

Sunday Schools, Epworth League, and Christian Education

The rise of the Methodist Episcopal Church in America coincided with the growing Sunday school movement. Francis Asbury greatly encouraged this, viewing it as a method of evangelism as well as religious instruction. Two examples illustrate this early Methodist concern for the religious education of Negroes. William Elliot, a Methodist layman, started a Sunday school in his home in the vicinity of Oak Grove, Virginia, in 1785. One session was held for his family and another for his "young" slaves and "bound-out white boys."

Asbury himself started a Sunday school for the instruction of slaves in the home of Thomas Crenshaw in Hanover County, Virginia, in 1786. An earlier reference has been made to the fact that one of the students of this Sunday school was John Charleston, who later became a renowned preacher-missionary in the AME Church. Around this same time, the Methodist Episcopal Church adopted a requirement that every Methodist preacher minister to the religious needs of the Negroes within the bounds of his charge. In 1790 the Annual Conference approved for inclusion in the *Discipline* the required establishment of a Sunday school "to instruct poor children, White and Black, to read."

During the 1790s and the early 1800s, as the church moved deeper into the South and plantation country, the wisdom of teaching slaves to read was increasingly questioned. The suspicion was that literacy would make slaves less manageable and perhaps even rebellious. As a result of this, the Sunday school movement was replaced in the South by the "Plantation Mission" approach. This method provided oral religious instruction that did not require literacy. It also provided a truncated version of the biblical material that was used in other parts of the country, and it was taught by carefully selected white preachers. William Capers (1790–1855) of South Carolina was the innovator of this plan, which persisted from about 1829 to the beginning of North-South hostilities in 1861.

Following Emancipation, religious education in black Methodist Episcopal churches followed the conventional Sunday school pattern. Since the founding of African Zoar Church, however, these Sunday schools, like their parent churches, were segregated. A few may have initially been biracial, but as the white "separatist" pattern prevailed, these were eliminated. The Sunday school literature was that of the Methodist Episcopal denomination without modification for use in black Sunday schools. It consisted of lesson books, hymnals, catechisms, creeds, and confessions.

Summarily, the Sunday school remained the principal source of Christian education in black Methodist Episcopal churches until the advent of the Epworth League Movement for youth.[80]

Epworth Leagues

Youth work in most mainstream Protestant denominations in the United States traces its origin to the Christian Endeavour Movement, organized in 1881. This is true for both black and white churches. In some ways, the Christian Endeavour concept represented an outgrowth of the Sunday school idea, adapted to adolescents. Its membership requirements were commitment to the Christian faith, constancy in attendance, and serious Bible study and prayer.

The Christian Endeavour design was the most influential model in youth work for at least a decade. Following this design, denominations, beginning with the Methodist Episcopal Church, began to develop their own youth programs. The Methodist Episcopal program was the "Epworth League," organized in 1889 as the result of a merger of several youth groups and societies of Methodist youth in various parts of the denomination.

In 1896 I. Garland Penn, a young black layman, was elected assistant general secretary of Epworth Leagues, with responsibility for promoting the Epworth League in the "Negro" Conferences. By 1910 Penn's remarkable report indicated 2,670 senior and junior chapters in twenty Annual Conferences. In 1912 W. W. Lucas succeeded Penn in Epworth League work.

World War I interrupted youth work in American churches. This had its effect on the Epworth League in black Methodist Episcopal churches. In the 1920s, youth work took on new vigor. Several black Annual Conferences discontinued the practice of holding Sunday school and Epworth League Conventions in tandem, thus freeing the summer for youth institutes. In 1927 the West Texas Conference became the first to exploit this opportunity and led the way among the nineteen black Annual Conferences in developing exciting summer youth programs.

The 1930s were the ecumenical years in youth work. Under the guiding influence of the United Christian Youth Movement, the Methodist Episcopal Church became involved in cooperative forms of youth work and ecumenical Conferences here and abroad. In 1934 Juanita Jackson Mitchell, a lay youth member of the Washington Conference (Sharp Street Church) who was involved in these movements, was elected vice president of the National Council of Methodist Youth, becoming the first black person elected to a national Methodist Episcopal youth office. During this same period, Karl Downs, president of Samuel Huston College at the time of his untimely death in 1948, was also active in Methodist youth affairs, as was civil rights activist James L. Farmer, Jr., the son of the late J. Leonard Farmer, Sr., prominent black Methodist scholar and educator for several decades.

CHRISTIAN EDUCATION TO THE 1930s

From 1900 to 1920, Christian education, including Epworth League work in black Methodist Episcopal churches, was in a state of high transition. Black churches generally were seeking to assist families that had recently migrated to northern, midwestern, and western cities in adjusting to the rigors and complexities of metropolitan living. Rural evangelism and Sunday school socials were hardly adequate to compete with the secular amusements of the city and the sudden increase in leisure time. Reports and reflections such as these continued to come from black Sunday school and Epworth League field executives.

Among those carrying these responsibilities in this period were Robert E.

Jones (1901–1904), later (1920) elected the first black general superintendent (bishop) in the Methodist Episcopal Church; C. C. Jacobs; E. M. Jones; J. W. E. Bowen, later (1948) elected a bishop; Robert N. Brooks, also later (1944) elected a bishop; and F. H. Butler.

Generally speaking, with the exception of the comments noted, these men's reports were positive. There were indications of growth in the number of Sunday schools and Epworth Leagues and in attendance at these activities. New Sunday schools were being established, and teachers were being recruited and trained. Methodist Episcopal materials were being used, and youth were uniting with the church on profession of faith. Vacation Bible schools were flourishing, and youth summer institutes were catching on.

The situation became more somber in the mid-1920s and 1930s. Veteran Christian educator Timothy B. Echols remarked about this period, "It was not only true in the West Texas Conference but throughout Methodism that the Sunday School and Epworth League Movements were at their lowest ebb. The name Epworth League no longer attracted young people."[81]

Echols not only posed the problem but also proposed a solution. Assuming that leadership training was the key solution, he developed two crucial strategies. First, he organized youth institutes for the training of youth and adult leaders who work with youth. These institutes, to be held primarily during the summer months, became the base on which the Christian education programs of the entire four-Conference New Orleans Area was rejuvenated. Echols's second plan was college related. It proposed deploying college teachers of religious education as teachers of Sunday school and as Epworth League teachers and leaders. The plan was eminently successful. Eventually it became something of a model and was adopted by other black Annual Conferences.

A second important development in this period was the emergence and employment of persons professionally trained in Christian education. In 1934 the former New Orleans area became the first black episcopal area to appoint an executive secretary of Christian education, Timothy B. Echols. In 1934 the former Delaware Annual Conference became the first black Conference to appoint an Executive Secretary of Christian Education, Frederick J. Handy. By the end of the 1930s, several black local churches had also employed directors of Christian education in part- or full-time positions. An example would be the late Arsania M. Williams at Union Memorial Methodist Episcopal Church, St. Louis, Missouri.[82]

Schools, Colleges, and Higher Education

It would be difficult to overestimate the contribution of the Methodist Episcopal Church to the educational advancement of black people in the South following the Civil War. With the help of well-wishers in the Methodist

Episcopal Church, South, various women's missionary organizations, benefactors, and philanthropic foundations, something of a miracle was accomplished in the last quarter of the nineteenth century in the area of education among a significant number of the millions of recently freed slaves. Equally inspiring was the response of these freed persons and their early involvement in their own religious, educational, and social elevation.

The activity and achievement of this mission in the Methodist Episcopal era ending in 1939 covers almost a century of effort. From about 1844 until the Emancipation Act of 1863, Methodist Episcopal work among black people was largely restricted to the Delaware and Washington Conferences. There was some activity in the Midwest and South, however. In 1853 the Cincinnati Conference of the Methodist Episcopal Church explored the possibility of a college for black youth. This inquiry materialized in 1856 with the establishment of Wilberforce University in Xenia, Ohio. Named for the English Emancipation advocate William Wilberforce (1759–1833), this fledgling institution did not survive and was sold to the AME Church in 1863.[83] During the same period, other Methodist Episcopal work was going on in the South, despite the Civil War. Missionaries were attempting to organize schools and churches, albeit with the assistance and encouragement of Union armies.

Perceiving the need to advocate for the Negro, the General Conference of 1864 requested that the United States Congress create a national Bureau of Freedmen's Affairs to minister to the needs of the newly freed slaves. This action had grown out of much prior work done by the Methodists in cooperation with various Freedmen's Aid commissions of other Protestant denominations. Especially prominent in this work was the effort of the American Missionary Association, eventually the missionary agency of the Congregationalists, Baptists, Episcopalians, and northern Presbyterians.

Freedmen's Aid Society Schools

The Methodist Episcopal Church cooperated with both government and church agencies in educating freed slaves. In the government sector, it worked through the various Freedmen's Aid commissions and in the churches through their various channels for this purpose. Shortly after the war, Willis J. King points out that "there soon developed a tendency on the part of the several church bodies to set up their own denominational schools."[84] It was for this purpose that the Freedmen's Aid Society of the Methodist Episcopal Church was organized in 1866.

In 1864 the General Conference noted and approved the "humane work" that was then being done on behalf of the freedmen by an assortment of groups, including church organizations, and commended their causes as worthy of support. On August 7, 1866, a group of Methodist Episcopal ministers and laymen, desiring to pursue this work more intentionally as

Methodists, organized the Freedmen's Aid Society in Trinity Methodist Episcopal Church, Cincinnati, Ohio. The society began its work in the fall of 1866, establishing schools in ten southern states, enrolling about three thousand students, and recruiting forty teachers. The General Conference of 1865 officially recognized the society and authorized it to "labor for the relief and the education of the freedmen . . . in cooperation with the Missionary and Extension Societies of the Methodist Episcopal Church." Following legal incorporation in 1870, the bishops sent out their first church-wide appeal for general support. In 1872 the General Conference took the crucial step of making the society a "benevolent association" of the church and asking each pastor to request an offering on its behalf. It is worth noting that in 1870 William H. Crogman, later to become a renowned classical scholar and the first black president of Clark University, was the first Negro teacher employed by the Freedmen's Aid Society. Between 1872 and 1939 the society was renamed several times to accommodate changing objectives and functions: Freedmen's Aid and Southern Education Society (1888–1904); Board of Education, Freedmen's Aid and Sunday Schools (1904–1908); Freedmen's Aid Society (1908–1920); Board of Education for Negroes, General Board of Education (1920–1924); Department of Education for Negroes, General Board of Education (1924–1939).

The heart of this almost matchless venture in educational mission was the effort of the Freedmen's Aid Society to establish institutions of higher learning for ex-slaves, free black people, and needy white youth. This thrilling episode can best be understood by looking at its early developments, changing emphases, and consolidations until Unification (1939).

Early Institutions

In three decades (1866–1896) the Freedmen's Aid Society, in cooperation with the Board of Missions and Church Extension and the Woman's Home Missionary Society, laid the foundation for the present system of secondary schools, senior and junior colleges, and professional schools supported by the denomination today. (Several schools were initiated by the Freedmen's Aid Society and/or Annual Conferences and individuals but were discontinued or merged, including Central Alabama College, Huntsville, Alabama [1866–1923]; Richmond Normal School, Richmond, Virginia [1867–1875]; Haven Normal School, Waynesboro, Georgia [1868–ca.1915]; LaGrange Seminary, LaGrange, Georgia [1870–ca. 1915]; Haven Institute, Meridian, Mississippi [1879–1928] Key West Academy, Key West, Florida [1889–ca. 1990] and George R. Smith College, Sedalia, Missouri [1894–1925].)

The story begins in 1865 with Central Tennessee (Walden) College in Nashville. From a humble beginning in a building formerly used by a Methodist Episcopal Church, South, congregation (Andrew Chapel), John Seys, former missionary to Africa, started a Methodist Episcopal church and missionary school. In 1866 the school was formally organized in what is now Clark Memorial Methodist Episcopal Church. Following years of sacrificial service by pastors, missionary teachers, and especially President John Braden, Central Tennessee College became a flagship institution in the denomination. It was this college that gave birth to Meharry Medical School. In 1897 its academic strength was such that it could offer departmental programs. At this point it became Walden University. Several circumstances in the early 1900s contributed to the decline of Walden University, which reverted to a preparatory school in the 1920s and closed in 1935.[85]

Rust College, founded as Shaw University, began as a school for "Negro children" in Asbury Methodist Episcopal Church, Holly Springs, Mississippi. It was organized by a white Methodist Episcopal pastor, A. C. McDonald, and an ex-slave, Moses Adams. In 1868 the Freedmen's Aid Society assumed management of the school, and by 1870 it was ready for incorporation by the state of Mississippi. After granting its first two college degrees in 1878, Shaw University, renamed Rust University in 1891, proceeded to establish an enviable record as a strong and progressive institution through the outstanding careers of many of its graduates. The administration of the first black president, Matthew S. Davage (1920–1924), brought new vitality to the institution. Focusing on the teaching mission of the school, Davage sought improvement in faculty, facilities, and support. President L. M. McCoy, who succeeded Davage, continued to emphasize the teaching function of the college and was instrumental in its accreditation by the Mississippi State Department of Education and the American Medical Association in the 1930s. McCoy retired in 1957. He was followed by Ernest A. Smith, an alumnus, who provided a decade of effective leadership.

Even a thumbnail sketch of the background history of Rust College is incomplete without some comment about the helpful cooperative relationship between the Board of Education and the Woman's Home Missionary Society. The Board of Education oversaw the administration of the academic work, and the Woman's Home Missionary Society supervised dormitory life and home economics work. This separation of responsibilities, accomplished through the pressure of E. L. Rust Hall, was a financially helpful and mutually beneficial relationship.[86]

Morgan College in Baltimore, the third black Methodist Episcopal school organized in 1866, was founded in December of that year. Its earliest name was Centenary Biblical Institute, in celebration of the centennial of American Methodism. Chartered in 1867 and opened formally in 1872, Morgan was literally a creature of the Delaware and Washington Annual Conferences. In 1890 its name was changed to Morgan College to honor a Baltimore Conference minister. Beginning as an embryonic theological school, the curriculum successively included other disciplines. Women were admitted in 1874, and a "feeder school," Princess Anne Academy, was established in 1890 by the Delaware Conference. (A similar preparatory school, Virginia Collegiate and Industrial Institute, was organized at Lynchburg, Virginia in 1892). Three of the most prominent educator-ministers of the Methodist Episcopal Church led this academy: Frank Trigg, Pezavia O'Connell, and Thomas H. Kiah. During the administration of John O. Spencer, an endowment fund was started, buildings erected, and faculty and curriculum enriched. In 1925 Morgan College was accredited by the Middle States Association of Colleges and Secondary Schools. By 1939, during the administration of Morgan's first black president, Dwight O. W. Holmes—the son of a Washington Conference minister, John O. Holmes—Morgan College became a Maryland State institution, taking the name Morgan State College. Its Methodist presence was continued in the establishment of Morgan Christian Center.[87]

The South Carolina Conference (1866) initiated Claflin University in 1869, essentially to prepare persons for the ministry and teaching. It originated from the union of Baker Biblical Institute at Charleston and a training school at Camden, effected by the Freedmen's Aid Society. The new school was relocated to Orangeburg at the time of its founding. Other benefactors and founders of Claflin include E. A. Webster, T. W. Lewis, and Lee Claflin of Massachusetts, in whose honor the college was named. The college experienced solid growth in organization, curriculum, enrollment, and faculty development throughout the 1870s. Despite the perennial lack of adequate funds and a disastrous fire in 1876, it offered its first baccalaureate degree in 1883. Having achieved degree-granting status, Claflin began to attract both state appropriations and philanthropic foundation funds, in addition to Freedmen's Aid Society and Woman's Home Missionary assistance for an industrial home for girls. The unique and close relationship between the state of South Carolina and Claflin was abruptly terminated by an action of the 1892 General Conference. By 1912, however, it had taken its place as one of the most progressive and effective Negro colleges in the South. World War I somewhat affected the progress of Claflin, but the long and brilliant administration of President L. M. Dunton (1884–1922) laid an excellent foundation for his successor, Dr. J. B. Randolph, the university's first black chief administrator. During the Randolph administration, high school work was discontinued and college-level studies emphasized.[88]

The year 1869 also witnessed the rise of Clark University. Named for the first president of the Freedmen's Aid Society, Bishop Davis W. Clark, it has since become one of the nation's outstanding small universities. Beginning as an elementary school in Atlanta, prior to the existence of any public school system, Clark found housing in its early days in what is now Central United Methodist Church. The university successively evolved from a preparatory normal and theological school into a strong senior college. Clark's academic emphasis began as early as 1876–1877 with the appointment of its first black faculty member, William H. Crogman, a classical scholar. Clark was chartered as a university in 1877. In 1883 its theological department became a separate institution, Gammon Theological Seminary. Several landmark developments occurred in the development of the university. Industrial education, partially funded by the John F. Slater Fund, dominated the curriculum during the administration of E. O. Thayer (1891–1899). Thayer Hall was established at Clark in 1883 by the Woman's Home Missionary Society "to train Negro girls in homemaking under Christian auspices." Following the Thayer administration, the industrial education emphasis peaked about 1900. In 1903 Professor William H. Crogman became acting president, and in 1904 he was named president of Clark College. The first black person to hold that post, Dr. Crogman greatly strengthened the academic as well as the industrial and agricultural aspects of the college's program. A new era in Clark's history begins in 1924 with the coming of Matthew S. Davage to the presidency. Industrial education having become obsolete, Davage sought, with the assistance of a brilliant young academic dean, James P. Brawley, to standardize an academic curriculum, upgrade the faculty, revise the curriculum, and secure accreditation from the Georgia Association of Colleges and certification of its teacher education program from the State Department of Education.[89]

Bethune-Cookman College, one of three Methodist Episcopal black colleges representing a merger, began as Cookman Institute in Jacksonville, Florida, in 1872. It was the result of the efforts of two Methodist Episcopal ministers, W. B. Osborn and S. B. Darnell. Originally funded by the Freedmen's Aid Society, Cookman was closely related to the Florida Conferences. It offered a junior college level program until the 1940s. During this time it progressed from elementary studies to classical and theological disciplines. By 1890 industrial studies were also included, having been provided for by John F. Slater funds. Following the resignation of S. B. Darnell, who had done a remarkable job as the founding president (1872–1894), Cookman Institute experienced difficult times. Much of its momentum was recovered, however, by the strong leadership of G. Barts Stone (1909–1919). When Stone retired, Cookman affiliated with Clark University in Atlanta, where many Cookman students had elected to complete their senior college years. In 1923 the Board of Education voted to merge Cookman with Daytona Normal and Industrial Institute for Negro Girls in Daytona Beach, Florida. It was headed by the indomitable Mary McLeod Bethune, who had founded Daytona Normal in 1904 and had had it chartered in 1920. The new institution, consolidated in Daytona Beach, merged in 1923 as a coed vocational senior college of the Methodist Episcopal Church. In 1929 it was fittingly renamed Bethune-Cookman. After weathering the financial reverses of the Great Depression, Bethune-Cookman moved steadily forward.[90]

Dillard University, founded in 1930, was the result of a merger of Straight University (1869), an American Missionary Association (AMA) school of the Congregationalist Church (United Church of Christ), and New Orleans University (1869), a Methodist Episcopal and Freedmen's Aid Society school.

New Orleans University, the predecessor of Dillard, emerged from the life of several institutions in and around New Orleans. Prominent in its development was Thomson Biblical Institute in New Orleans (1866), originally founded to train ministers for the Mississippi Mission Conference. By 1873, after merging with and/or absorbing several smaller institutions, it became firmly established as New Orleans University. In 1924 the General Conference of the Methodist Episcopal Church recommended the merger of New Orleans and Straight Universities. By 1930 this was accomplished, producing one of the strongest Negro colleges in the nation.

Flint-Goodridge Hospital is so intimately related to the history of Dillard University that it should be mentioned here. Its history involved four institutions: Flint Medical College (1889–1911), Sara Goodridge Hospital (1901–1916), the Nurse Training School (1901–1934), and Flint-Goodridge Hospital. From 1889 to 1911, Straight University had sponsored Flint Medical College. From about that same time, New Orleans University had sponsored Flint-Goodridge Hospital. In 1928 several foundations, church boards, and city fathers met together to do something significant about a college for Negroes in New Orleans. The plan included Flint-Goodridge Hospital. After aborting rumored plans to transfer Flint-Goodridge's assets to Meharry Medical School for the support of Flint Medical College's students who transferred there when the medical school in New Orleans was closed in 1911, a new Flint-Goodridge Hospital was projected as a part of the new Dillard University. Upon the completion of this new complex, Dillard became a flagship institution in the combined fields of higher education, nursing education, and hospital administration. Much of this was possible due to the yeoman leadership of Albert W. Dent (1904–1983), president of Dillard from 1940–1969.[91]

The historical development of Bennett College falls into three periods: Bennett Seminary, Bennett College, and Bennett College for Women. The Bennett story begins with its founding in St. Matthews Methodist Episcopal Church in Greensboro, North Carolina, in 1873. The Freedmen's Aid Society took control of the seedling institution in 1874. Named for Lyman Bennett—a Troy, New York, donor—it existed until 1883 as a theological seminary. Within a few years, seminary subjects were supplemented with college preparatory, normal school, and classical courses. In 1886 the Woman's Home Missionary Society introduced industrial work for women at Bennett College and constructed living accommodations for them, Kent Hall. The election of Charles M. Grandison to the presidency of Bennett College in 1889 was significant. He was Bennett's first black head, and indeed the first black president of any Freedmen's Aid Society school. Following several presidential administrations at the college indicating progress, Bennett fell upon difficult days. In response to then newer trends of higher education among women, the Board of Education of the church in cooperation with the Woman's Home Missionary Society elected to develop Bennett as a college for women. This unique and exciting venture was launched in 1926 under the extraordinary, able leadership of David Dallas Jones (1887–1956). Working together with his wife, Susie Williams Jones, he helped Bennett College become one of the nation's finest and most distinctive small colleges for women.[92]

Wiley College in Marshall, Texas, was established as Wiley University in 1873. A Freedmen's Aid Society school, it was chartered in 1882, making it the first black chartered college west of the Mississippi River. Wiley College bears the name of Bishop Isaac W. Wiley (1825–1889), a charter member and former president of the Freedmen's Aid Society. Wiley graduated its first class in 1888, and by 1893 it was a firmly established institution. About 1890 the Woman's Home Missionary Society erected the King Home for Girls to complement its industrial program for women. In 1893 the first black president in the history of the institution was elected, Isaiah B. Scott (1854–1931). Scott served three years as president before leaving to become editor of the *Southwestern Christian Advocate*. Later he became the fourth and last black missionary bishop of the Methodist Episcopal Church (1904). Matthew W. Dogan (d. 1947) succeeded to the presidency of Wiley in 1896 and began a legendary tenure lasting almost fifty years. During this time he developed the "Wiley Method," a higher education philosophy that combined classical learning with industrial education. Physically, the campus grew tremendously; academically, its curriculum was enriched and its faculty increased. Alumnus Emmett J. Scott, secretary to Booker T. Washington, was instrumental in securing a Carnegie grant for a library building at Wiley. In summary, the Dogan administration was one of the most exemplary in black higher education up to that time.[93] Egbert C. McLeod was Dogan's successor as president. In 1948 he resigned that post to accept the pastorate of Boston's historic Union Memorial Church.

Philander Smith College, the second institution founded west of the Mississippi River, opened as a school for freedmen in Little Rock, Arkansas, in 1877. Its first name was Walden Seminary in honor of Bishop John M. Walden (1831–1914), a leader in the Freedmen's Aid Society. In 1879 Walden Seminary was moved into Wesley Chapel Methodist Episcopal Church (Little Rock), the first church built by black people in Arkansas. Chartered as a college in 1883, it received a large gift of money in the same year for two purposes: the erection of an administration building and, in cooperation with the Woman's Home Missionary Society, the construction of a building to be known as the Adeline M. Smith Industrial Home. As a result of these gifts, the college was renamed for the major donor, Philander Smith of Oak Park, Illinois. The college awarded its first degree in 1888. In 1896 James M. Cox became the first black president of Philander Smith. During his administration the physical plant was enlarged and the academic program restructured. The George C. Taylor administration witnessed further expansion of the physical facilities, the standardization of the academic program, and the incorporation of George R. Smith College. Philander Smith's landmark administration was that of M. Lafayette Harris (1936–1960). Among his many accomplishments were the acquisition of the Little Rock Junior College site, the launching of a major capital campaign, urban renewal involvement, and accreditation by the North Central Association of Colleges.[94] Roosevelt D. Crockett succeeded Harris as president. After a notable four-year administration, he resigned to accept a State Department position in El Salvadore (1965).

Samuel Huston/Huston-Tillotson College in Austin, Texas, was founded in September 1878 in the Wesley Chapel Episcopal Church. Its historical roots go back to the first session of the West Texas Annual Conference in 1874, where a deep interest was expressed in a college "to provide the benefits of education for its members." In 1875 George W. Richardson, a former Civil War chaplain living in Minnesota, visited Austin, recognized the need for a school, and opened one with six students in a rented Methodist church. Following the destruction of this church by fire in 1876 and its immediate rebuilding, the Conference adopted the "orphaned" school as its own, taking the name Andrews Normal School, for Bishop Edward G. Andrews (1825–1907), the presiding bishop who had done so much to bring the school to fruition. Dallas was proposed as its location. In 1877 the Conference decided to relocate the school more centrally in Austin and appointed a financial agent to solicit funds within the West Texas Conference.

Shortly after its opening (1879), Andrews Normal College became the West Texas Conference Seminary and placed its property and future in the hands of the Freedmen's Aid Society. In 1887 a large gift of money had been given by a Samuel Huston of Iowa for buildings at the seminary. The name was changed to Samuel Huston College, and construction began. Financial reverses, including the financial panic of 1893, delayed the actual opening of the college for more than ten years. It finally began instruction in 1900. Its first president was Reuben S. Lovinggood, also the first black president to inaugurate a Freedmen's Aid Society enterprise. By 1904, largely due to the astute leadership of its president, an excellent faculty, and a strong board of trustees, the college was pointed in the direction of a bright future. Some of that future was the coming of the Eliza Dee Home to the campus. Through the influence of the women of the West Texas Conference, funds were raised and solicited from the Woman's Home Missionary Society, which eventually (1904) brought the home and a home economics program to Samuel Huston.

James P. Brawley reports in his *Two Centuries of Methodist Concern: Bondage, Freedom, and Education of Black People* that "amazing progress was made during the first twelve years (1900–1912) of the life of Samuel Huston College." More specifically, funds were secured, a faculty developed, and a curriculum outlined and articulated. Lovinggood's administration (1917–1943) was by any standard the apex of Samuel Huston's achievement.[95]

Administrations following Lovinggood from 1917 to 1943 were those of

M. S. Davage (1917–1920); J. B. Randolph (1920–1922), R. N. Brooks (1922–1926), Thomas R. Davis (1926–1930), Willis J. King (1930–1932), and Stanley E. Grannum (1932–1943), K. E. Downs, J. T. King, and the incumbent J. T. McMillan.

Other Schools and Academies

The Methodist Episcopal Church established several schools and colleges other than those that eventually became four-year degree-granting institutions. Morristown Junior College in Morristown, Tennessee, was founded and chartered in 1881. It was organized primarily to meet the educational needs of black youth in the Holston Valley area. Between 1888 and 1931 the late president Judson S. Hill led Morristown to become one of the most unique schools of its kind in the region, providing "work-study" assistance to hundreds of Negro youth. Miller W. Boyd (1897–1952), president of the institution during the 1930s, gave strong leadership to the college during very difficult times.

Between 1885 and 1921, a total of six secondary schools were founded to serve in places where there was little or no educational opportunity. In addition to sound high school programs, these schools provided health, home training, and religious salvation to their students. Listed with their dates of founding and years of service before merging or closing, they were as follows:

1. Haven Home (1885–1932), originally located in Savannah, Georgia, and merged with Boylan School in Jacksonville, Florida.
2. Boylan Home (1886–1932), located in Jacksonville, Florida, which became Boylan-Haven in 1932 and a junior and senior high in 1933.
3. Allen Home in Asheville, North Carolina, a graded industrial school donated to the Woman's Home Missionary Society for that purpose. It has rendered outstanding service as a boarding school for Negro girls.
4. Browning Home/Mather Academy (1887) built in Camden, South Carolina, with funds from a New England legacy. In 1890 the Woman's Home Missionary Society took charge of this academy, which became an exemplary girl's boarding school.
5. Gilbert Academy, from 1918 to 1935 the high school department of New Orleans University (Louisiana). This school became a private high school with the initiation of the then new Dillard University. It was maintained by the Woman's Home Missionary Society until 1940. It then became an institution under the Women's Division of Christian Service until its close in 1949.
6. Sager-Brown Home in Baldwin, Louisiana, initiated by the Woman's Home Missionary Society in 1921 in the vacated property of Gilbert Academy, following its transfer to New Orleans.

Brawley notes the interesting fact that the homes established by the Woman's Home Missionary Society on the campuses of black colleges were eventually integrated with the home economics programs of those schools, with continuing support from the Women's Society of Christian Service.[96]

Professional Schools

The Methodist Episcopal Church has made and is making a major contribution to professional education in America through the training of black ministers, physicians, dentists, nurses, public health practitioners, and medical researchers in two institutions it founded in the 1870s.

Gammon Theological Seminary, to be discussed later, had its beginning in 1872 as the Theological School of Clark University, which had been founded in 1869. Gifts from Elijah H. Gammon enabled the separate development of the theological work of Clark beginning in 1883. Called by many of its graduates "the school of the Prophets," Gammon Seminary since the 1920s has been one of two theological schools providing accredited theological education primarily for Negro ministers of the denomination and beyond. Many of the most outstanding black scholar-theologians have taught its hundreds of alumni, who have rendered outstanding service to the church as pastors, district superintendents, bishops, college presidents, church editors, missionaries, and church board executives.

Meharry Medical College, established in 1876, originally the Medical Department of Central Tennessee College (later Walden University), was, for more than half a century, one of the few medical schools in the nation preparing black men and women for the medical professions. Until the 1980s it was one of only two traditionally black accredited medical schools.[97] Meharry's first black president was Harold D. West [1952].

Higher Education Executives

Black laypeople and ministers were significantly involved in the executive decision-making process in higher education in the Methodist Episcopal Church in each period of its structural development. During the early stages of the growth of the Freedmen's Aid Society, black involvement was found at the mission and later the Annual Conference level. Almost without exception, black and white members would jointly determine their educational needs and prioritize them. The society would respond by evaluating requests, often modifying them and sometimes denying them. The society itself would sometimes identify opportunities for educational mission and fund them in consultation with the black and white constituencies of the Conferences. A second area of consultative decision making was financing and fundraising. Educational initiatives were required to have local, community, and/or

Conference endorsement, if possible. Given this, and some effort to be responsible in fundraising, most projects that were considered worthy usually received some assistance.

A third area of cooperative planning revolved around the site of the institutions. Largely determined by the local people who were involved, it was on occasion influenced by the supervisor of the society.

Still another area was curriculum development. More often than not, the courses of study of these embryonic institutions were determined by the elemental needs of ex-slaves to learn to read, write, and do the simplest of arithmetic functions. Next, the need to teach the barely literate how to teach the illiterate was important. Last but not least, a simple, basic training in the Bible was necessary in these schools or "academies," because it was crucial that candidates for the ministry be literate enough to preach and practice some pastoral skills.

The second period in Methodist Episcopal development in higher education among Negroes may be referred to as the Freedmen's Aid and Southern Education Society period (1888–1904). Several things occurred during this time. The work of the society was expanded to include the organization of schools for white youths in the South. The society proposed a reorganization of its departments, and a black minister was brought to the staff. M. C. B. Mason (1859–1912), the first black person to hold a staff position in the denomination, held first the position of field secretary (1891–1893) and then the position of assistant corresponding secretary (1893–1896). In 1896 he was elected one of the two corresponding secretaries of the society with responsibility for Negro schools. In 1908 Mason was elevated to the position of senior corresponding secretary of the Freedmen's Aid Society, a position that he kept until his death in 1912.

I. Garland Penn (1897–1930), a brilliant black educator, elected ten successive times as a lay delegate to the General Conference, succeeded Mason in 1912. When the name of the Freedmen's Aid Society was changed to the Department of Educational Institutions for Negroes in 1920, Penn continued as a secretary of the board until 1924, at which time he was appointed secretary for Endowment and Field Promotion for Negro Schools.[98]

Pioneer Scholars, Presidents, and Executives

In less than a decade after the cessation of slavery, a young black scholar was in preparation for educational leadership in the Methodist Episcopal Church. In 1865 orphaned William H. Crogman, at the age of twenty-seven years, entered Pierce Academy in Middleboro, Massachusetts. As a student there, he demonstrated exemplary scholarship and was graduated in 1870. Upon graduation, he was immediately employed by the Freedmen's Aid Society as their first Negro teacher at Claflin University. Later he pursued further study at Atlanta University in Atlanta, earning a bachelor of arts degree in 1876 and a master of arts degree in 1879.

William H. Crogman was a pioneer for a long line of black scholars and teachers in the Methodist Episcopal Church. In the succeeding years, thousands of aspiring young black students would study in Freedmen's Aid schools, hundreds would teach in these schools, and scores would attain coveted degrees in academe. Witness the record of some of those who achieved doctoral degrees from the 1880s to the 1930s:

- J. W. E. Bowen, Sr. (1855–1933), Ph.D., Boston University (systematic theology), 1886
- Pezavia O'Connell (1861–1930), Ph.D., University of Pennsylvania (biblical languages), 1898
- J. Leonard Farmer, Sr. (b. 1885), Ph.D., Boston University (Old Testament), 1918
- Willis J. King (1886–1976), Ph.D., Boston University (Old Testament), 1921
- M. Lafayette Harris (1907–1966), Ph.D., Ohio State University (philosophy), 1933
- Dwight O. W. Holmes, Ph.D., Columbia University (education), 1935
- Flemmie P. Kittrell, Ph.D., Cornell University (family life), 1936.[99]

Early Black College Presidents

The avowed philosophy and policy of the Freedmen's Aid Society, and later of the Board of Education of the Methodist Episcopal Church, in its educational mission among black people was not only to assist them in building schools but also to prepare them for the leadership of these institutions. In due time this happened. The following review of the transfer of college presidential leadership from white to black administrations from 1890 to 1938 is inspiring:

- C. N. Grandison became the first black president of Bennett College and the first black president of any Freedmen's Aid Society school in 1889.
- Isaiah B. Scott succeeded to the presidency of Wiley College as its first black head in 1893. Later Scott became a missionary bishop.
- J. M. Cox became the first black president of Philander Smith College in 1899 and remained in that position until 1924, laying a strong foundation for its future growth.
- R. S. Lovinggood assumed the presidency of Huston–Tillotson as its first black leader in 1900, rendering outstanding service until 1916.

- W. H. Crogman, the first black teacher employed by the Freedmen's Aid Society in 1870, became the first black president of Clark University in 1906. He had been a leading faculty member there since 1880.
- The venerable J. W. E. Bowen, Sr., was the first person of color to hold the presidency of Gammon Theological Seminary, from 1906–1910.
- The first black president of Claflin College was the legendary J. B. Randolph, whose tenure lasted almost a quarter of a century.
- In 1923 Mary McLeod Bethune became the first woman to head any Methodist Episcopal college and the first black to head the merged Cookman Institute and Daytona Industrial School for Girls, which soon became Bethune-Cookman College.
- Dwight O. W. Holmes assumed the presidency of Morgan College in 1938 just as it was in the process of becoming affiliated with the state of Maryland system of higher education. He was the son of John A. Holmes of the former Washington Conference.

It should be added that the first black president of Delaware State College, not Methodist Episcopal related, was W. C. Jason, Sr., of the former Delaware Conference. Jason's presidency lasted twenty-seven years, from 1896–1923.[100]

MINISTERIAL EDUCATION

Ministerial education for black clergy in the Methodist Episcopal Church passed through several stages to reach its present formation. This section will follow that evolution through to the establishment of Gammon Theological Seminary.

One of the most persistent themes to be found throughout the period in which soon-to-become black Annual Conferences were being organized was the desperately urgent need to educate ministers for rapidly growing black churches. That story begins with the schools, academies, and colleges organized by the early Methodist Episcopal churches and the Freedmen's Aid Society in the South from 1865 to about 1875. During that period, one of the important purposes of the society—namely, to provide training for ministers—was pursued with unusual dedication and vigor.

The schools founded by the society in each of the mission Conferences, without exception, included biblical and/or theological subjects in their curricula. Central Tennessee College (later Walden University) had a theological department by 1889. Rust College in 1871 (then Shaw University) had a biblical studies department. Morgan College actually began as Centenary Biblical Institute in 1867. One of the two schools that merged to form Claflin University (later Claflin College) was Baker Biblical Institute, referred to as the "crown of glory" of the university. Cookman Institute (later a merging constituent of Bethune-Cookman College) reported its need to help train ministers and teachers. New Orleans University (later to merge with Straight University to form Dillard University) grew out of several schools, one of which was Thomson Biblical Institute. Bennett College was originally organized as Bennett Seminary. In 1879 it reported a full theological course of study in addition to normal, college, and preparatory work. Philander Smith College was first organized as Walden Seminary, "where our young men may be educated for the ministry and our people may have the benefit of a first class seminary education." Samuel Huston College (later Huston-Tillotson) was initiated as a West Texas Conference school on the basis of the following statement made at its third Annual Conference: "We value an educated ministry, and declare it to be our purpose to raise the standard of ministerial qualification . . . and . . . open the way for the establishment of a Conference Seminary."[101] Clark University (later Clark College), originally established "for the special training of colored people for teachers and the work of the ministry," played an especially critical and unique role in the development of theological education in the Methodist Episcopal Church. Later it will be observed that its program became the basic model of a full-fledged theological department among the society schools. Finally, early courses in the Wiley curriculum reflect the concern of the college for ministerial education. In summary, biblical, theological, or religious subjects and/or departments were integral parts of many of the schools founded by the Freedmen's Aid Society prior to 1875.

The emergence of a strong and unique theological department at Clark University marked a new stage in the education of ministers. Inspired by the zeal and generosity of Bishop D. W. Clark, whose death in 1821 left a bequest for the strengthening of theological education at Clark, a theological seminary named to honor him was created there. Within less than two years, the seminary was operative. A student body had been enrolled, a faculty and dean selected, and the classes moved to a new site. During the decade that followed, Clark Theological School, which Brawley points out "was really a department of Clark University," became an exemplary model of theological education for its time.[102] Its faculty, curriculum, and enrollment as well as financial support from the Freedmen's Aid Society and Methodist benefactors, put it in the forefront in its field.

The next major advance in ministerial education began with the election of Wilbur P. Thirkield to the deanship of the seminary by the Freedmen's Aid Society in 1883. Under Thirkield the faculty was increased, physical facilities provided, and, of utmost importance, Elijah H. Gammon (1819–1891) of Batavia, Illinois, a retired Methodist Episcopal minister who became a wealthy businessman, became deeply interested in the ministerial education of Negroes. This interest eventuated in gifts of more than half a million dollars. Late in 1883, upon its completion, the theological seminary building was fittingly named the Gammon School of Theology.

Several crucial decisions were made in the early years of the life of Gammon Theological Seminary that definitively changed its future. In 1887 Mr. Gammon proposed that Gammon become an independent institution under the Freedmen's Aid Society and that the society pay most faculty salaries and make land available for expansion. These proposals were agreed to, and Gammon increased the endowment with a large gift and willed to the school an equally large sum.

There are some further important developments related to ministerial education among Negro Methodists before 1939 that should be mentioned. In 1888 Gammon School of Theology became an autonomous Methodist Episcopal school, independent of Clark University. It took the name Gammon Theological Seminary, and its board of trustees, chaired by Bishop J. M. Walden (1831–1914), elected the incumbent dean, Wilbur P. Thirkield, as its first president. Also in 1888, the presidents of the Freedmen's Aid Society colleges transferred their theological epartments to Gammon, making it the most noted Negro institution of its kind in the nation. In 1906 J. W. E. Bowen, Sr., who in 1893 had become the first Negro professor at Gammon, was elected the first black president of the seminary. In 1932 Bishop Willis J. King (1886–1976), former professor of Old Testament at Gammon (1918–1930), became the second black president. Still later, in the 1930s, the Woman's Home Missionary Society provided funding for the Department of Religious Education at Gammon. Finally, the Home Department of the Board of Missions of the Methodist Episcopal Church, South, established several scholarships.[103]

THE SOUTHWESTERN CHRISTIAN ADVOCATE

Excepting its church pulpits and college classrooms, no institution in the denomination has had more impact upon black education, opinion, and public issues than the *Southwestern Christian Advocate*. Created "to give enlightenment to the constituency of the Methodist Episcopal Church," it has done so with courage and fairness.

"The Southwestern," as it was popularly called by black Methodists before unification, has an interesting background. Initially a weekly news journal for circulation among the black membership of the church, it began as the *New Orleans Advocate*. It was edited and published privately from 1866–1869 by John P. Newman (1826–1899), a Northern white missionary, later (1888) to be elected a bishop. From 1873–1876, Joseph C. Hartzell (1842–1929), a white presiding elder of the New Orleans District, also later elected to the episcopacy (1896), edited and published the *Southwestern Christian Advocate* privately. His intent in this publication was to "advocate" in "no uncertain sound on the great question of equality between the races."[104] The General

Conference of 1876 authorized the publication of a "southern" edition of the
Christian Advocate, with the tacit understanding that it was to be read primarily
by black people, and promised to subsidize it. Hiram R. Revels (1822–1901),
then a member of the Mississippi Conference, was elected to the editorship of
"The Southwestern" but declined to accept the position. Hartzell was elected
and served as editor from 1876–1882, followed by Lewis P. Cushman, who
was editor from 1882–1884.

The first black editor of "The Southwestern" was the well-known
preacher-scholar Marshall W. Taylor (1847–1887), a member of the
Lexington Annual Conference. Taylor was editor only three years before his
death in 1887. His successor was A. E. P. Albert of the Louisiana Conference,
a former member of the Book Committee of the General Conference of the
Methodist Episcopal Church. He served for four years. E. W. S. Hammon, an
outstanding leader and preacher, again of the Lexington Conference, followed
Albert and remained in the position four years (1892–1896). He was
succeeded by Isaiah B. Scott (1854–1931), who came to "The Southwestern"
from the presidency of Wiley College. After remaining eight years
(1896–1904) in the editorship, Scott was elected a missionary bishop by the
1904 General Conference for service in Liberia. Robert E. Jones (1872–
1960), who would become the first black bishop to serve in this country,
served the longest editorship, 1904–1920. Lorenzo H. King (1878–1940)
was editor of "The Southwestern" from 1920–1931, having come to that
position from the pastorate of the historic Central Church in Atlanta. The last
editor of "The Southwestern" to serve a full term as editor before Unification
in 1939 was Alexander P. Shaw (1879–1966). Shaw, elected from the
pastorate of Wesley Church in Los Angeles, was the first and only editor not
chosen from a historically black Annual Conference. King served from
1931–1936 before being elected to the episcopacy in 1936. Gammon's church
history professor, Robert N. Brooks (1888–1953), served four years
(1936–1940) as editor of the *Southwestern Christian Advocate* and four years
(1940–1944) as editor of the *Central Christian Advocate,* as it was renamed in
the Methodist Church following Unification (1939).[105]

GENERAL SUPERINTENDENTS

Agitation for the election of black episcopal leadership began in 1868
among the first black delegates elected to that General Conference. Henry N.
Oakes points out that their case rested on the earlier elections of Francis Burns
and John W. Roberts. These 1868 delegates introduced a new requirement,
however—namely, that "the General Conference . . . elect persons of 'African
descent' to provide episcopal supervision for the Negro conferences being
formed in the South."[106] Several arguments were advanced to support this

urgent request. First, the Methodist Episcopal Church had promised its black membership equality of treatment as well as equality of opportunity. Second, the black Annual Conferences were in need of closer episcopal supervision, and this could best be done by black bishops. Third, it was felt that, in the interest of keeping and recruiting black people for the Methodist Episcopal Church, black bishops were needed. Fourth, it was felt almost universally among the black membership of the church that a black episcopal presence "would provide inspiration and stimulate race pride."[107]

The first formal request for a black general superintendent or bishop to be elected by the General Conference and assigned for service in the United States came in 1872. At that time, black ministers in the church were declared eligible, but none were considered qualified. The response to the resolution presented to the General Conference by James D. Lynch on behalf of the leadership of the black Annual Conferences and black General Conference delegates essentially said, "There is nothing in race, color or former condition that is a bar to an election to the Episcopacy."[108] A renewal of this demand was made at the 1876 General Conference. This was futile, because the General Conference decided not to elect bishops at that time. The General Conference of 1880 made a progressive, though dubious, step in the direction of electing a black bishop by recommending the election of a black bishop for black people. Despite this introduction of a "limited episcopacy," quadrennially until 1900 the most highly qualified black candidates failed to be elected. This default of intentionality was especially noted in the failure of the General Conference of 1896 to elect J. W. E. Bowen, Sr., the first black scholar to earn a Ph.D. from Boston University, a distinguished educator, former pastor, and then professor of historical theology at Gammon Theological Seminary.

Black Bishops Elected

Despite the covert compromise of a "limited episcopacy" restricting black bishops to black episcopal areas, the decision of the 1920 General Conference to elect a black bishop meant a new day for black people in the Methodist Episcopal Church. Briefly, this is how it occurred. W. W. Lucas, a Mississippi delegate to that historic Conference, presented a resolution calling for a committee to survey and validate the desperate need of black people for black episcopal leadership. The General Conference, rather than creating the requested committee, referred the resolution directly to the Committee on Episcopacy. The epochal recommendation of that committee to the General Conference was the selection of two Negro general superintendents and their election on a separate ballot.[109] This report was highly acclaimed, widely supported, and adopted by the General Conference, assuring for the first time in the history of the denomination the election of Negro episcopal leadership with all the privileges and rights pertaining to that office. While the "limited episcopacy" feature was a compromise, the action moved the church further ahead toward equality of treatment and opportunity than it had ever been or ever thought possible.

Elected to assume these historic leadership positions were two distinguished ministers—Robert E. Jones and Matthew W. Clair, Sr. Robert E. Jones (1872–1960) had risen to the episcopacy from a brilliant career in the church as a pastor, Sunday school field secretary, *Southwestern Christian Advocate* editor, member of the Joint Commission to draft the Plan of Union, and outspoken leader for the church and civil rights. No less outstanding was Matthew W. Clair, Sr. An eloquent preacher, eminently successful pastor and administrator, and presiding elder, Bishop Matthew W. Clair, Sr., was also the father of a bishop, Matthew W. Clair, Jr. (1890–1968).

The retirement of Bishop Matthew W. Clair, Sr., in 1936 necessitated the election of a replacement. A lengthy and contentious power struggle developed on the floor of the General Conference between two rival candidates for the coveted position. The end result was a political statement that eventuated in the withdrawal of both candidates, Willis J. King, president of Gammon Theological Seminary, and W. A. C. Hughes, director of the influential Department of Negro Work, Board of Missions and Church Extension. On May 13, 1936, Alexander P. Shaw (1879–1966), editor of the *Southwestern Christian Advocate,* a noncontender for the episcopacy, was elected as a compromise candidate. Shaw's outstanding preaching ability, pastoral skills, and administrative experience contributed much to a highly effective episcopal career of almost two decades. Both W. A. C. Hughes and Willis J. King were later elected to the episcopacy, Hughes in 1940 and King in 1944.[110]

ECUMENICAL RELATIONS

Black members of the Methodist Episcopal Church have been ecumenically involved through historical ties, denominational representation, and cooperative relations since the 1880s. The nature and extent of that involvement has varied according to the needs and circumstances of denominational selection, the levels of ecumenical engagements, or the types of programs involved. As a matter of general principle, it has not been the policy of the denomination to intentionally regard race or color in policy, programmatic, or representational designations.

Historical Ties

Practically all black people in the United States who claim to be Methodists acknowledge the historical ties that bind them with other churches in the

Wesleyan tradition. There are especially significant family ties with three historically black traditions: the AME Church, the AMEZ Church, and the CME Church.

The AME Church had its origin in Richard Allen's 1787 withdrawal from St. George's Methodist Episcopal Church in Philadelphia, Pennsylvania, (1816). Similarly, the AMEZ Church was founded in 1821 by Methodist Episcopal local deacons who withdrew "temporarily" from John Street Methodist Episcopal Church in New York City. The CME Church, whose black members were a part of the Methodist Episcopal Church, South, prior to the Civil War, requested separation from their existing denomination in 1870 on the basis of what has been referred to as "incompatibility."

Denominational Representation

The black ecumenical profile of the Methodist Episcopal Church prior to 1939 stands out most clearly in the record of their participation in denominational, interdenominational, and international Conferences and agencies.

Black clergy and laypersons have represented American Methodist Annual Conferences at every Methodist ecumenical Conference since the denomination's inception in America. A sampling of the list of delegates to three decennial events is noteworthy. In 1881 V. H. Bukley (South Carolina) and E. W. S. Peck (Washington, D.C.) were representatives at London, England. The church was represented by A. E. P. Albert (Louisiana); J. W. E. Bowen, Sr. (Washington); C. N. Grandison (North Carolina); H. R. Revels (Mississippi); and others at Washington, D.C., in 1891. In London again in 1901, M. C. B. Mason (Florida), I. B. Scott (Texas), and J. M. Shumper (Mississippi) were delegates. In 1911 W. C. Thompson of the Delaware Conference was a delegate to the Toronto, Canada, Conference. The record of black attendance at the 1921 London gathering is not available, but in 1931 Mary McLeod Bethune (Florida), M. S. Davage (Louisiana), M. W. Dogan (Texas), D. H. Hargis (Delaware), D. D. Jones (North Carolina), and S. H. Sweeney (Lexington) were delegates at Atlanta.

On the interdenominational front, there has been black representation on the field staff of the American Bible Society since J. P. Wragg of the Atlanta Conference was elected to superintend the society's "colored" work. Wragg was succeeded in this post by D. H. Stanton of the Florida Conference, who served in the position until his death in 1957. In a similar position in the state of Arkansas, R. C. Childress, an eminent public school teacher and college professor at Philander Smith, was employed for several years (1905–1908) as a field staff person in Arkansas by the International Sunday School Association. I. Garland Penn, assistant general secretary of the Epworth League, was a member of the Executive Committee of the International Sunday School Association. In 1922 Mary McLeod Bethune, a representative of the Methodist Episcopal Church to the Federal Council of Churches (1908–1949), was chosen to serve on its executive committee.

At the World Council of Churches level of the ecumenical movement, the policy and structure of the denomination prior to 1940 accounted for the absence of black representatives from the Methodist Episcopal Church from seven critical planning meetings preceding the formation of the World Council: Edinburgh, Scotland, World Missionary Conference, 1910; Stockholm, Sweden, Conference on Life and Work, 1925; Lausanne, Switzerland, Conference on Faith and Order, 1927; Jerusalem, World Missionary Conference, 1928; Oxford, England, Conference on Life and Work, 1937; Edinburgh, Scotland, Conference on Faith and Order, 1937; and Madras, India, World Missionary Conference, 1938.

A final ecumenical activity that falls within the pre–Central Jurisdiction years under discussion is the relation that black Methodist Episcopalians had through their affiliation with the National Fraternal Council of Churches. Founded as the Negro Fraternal Council of Churches in Chicago (1934), it eventually included twelve all-black denominations. It had three main purposes: to foster cooperation among its member black denominations, to be a coordinating center for cooperation, and to cooperate with nonchurch groups. A. P. Shaw and J. W. Golden (1883–1961) were associated with this ecumenical effort from its inception.[111]

NOTABLE LEADERS AND PERSONALITIES

This chapter on institutional origins and developments between 1784 and 1939 concludes with an overview of singular contributions made by individuals who remained in Episcopal Methodism, who in their time won church, community, and national acclaim.

Harry Hosier (1750–1806), who traveled with Francis Asbury, Thomas Coke, Freeborn Garrettson, and Richard Whatcoat, was an exemplary circuit rider. The sermon that he preached at Adam's Chapel in Fairfax County, Virginia (1781), accords him a place in history as the first black preacher to deliver a sermon to a Methodist congregation in America. Hosier also pioneered preaching the gospel to slaves. His preaching offered them hope of freedom in Christ and the fellowship of the Methodists. Recognized as one of the great preachers of his time, he joined Freeborn Garrettson and Jesse Lee in spreading Methodism through the Hudson Valley, down the Delmarva Peninsula, and into New England. Asbury assigned Harry Hosier the responsibility of showing Thomas Coke the work the Methodists were doing in America prior to the historical Christmas Conference in 1784. While he was not physically present in Philadelphia in 1787 when Richard Allen and other black members left St. George's Church, he sympathized with their action. When the Free African Society was organized, John Street Church assisted him in gathering funds to travel to the meeting in Philadelphia.[112]

It is a little known fact that Prince Hall (1735–1807), the founder of the oldest black social fraternal organization in the United States, was a Methodist. Born of racially mixed parentage in Barbados, West Indies, he was apprenticed to a leather merchant at twelve years of age. As a young man he migrated to Boston, Massachusetts, in 1765, where he found employment, gathered sufficient funds to buy property, and educated himself. Hall was attracted to the Methodists in the Boston vicinity, united with them, and probably became a local preacher. For a brief time, he may have pastored a small congregation. At the outset of the Revolutionary War, Hall joined the Continental Army and served in it for the duration of the conflict. Following the war, Hall's interest was redirected to Free Masonry. Together with other black Free Masons, he established African Lodge 459 in Boston in 1791, as well as lodges in Pennsylvania and Rhode Island. After his death, the lodge was renamed the Prince Hall Grand Lodge. Black Harry Hosier met Prince Hall while on his New England evangelistic tour. It could have been this connection that initiated Hall's interest in the Methodist Episcopal Church.[113]

A third remarkable personality emerges in black Methodist history prior to the Civil War, John Stewart (ca. 1786–1823), Methodism's first evangelist-missionary to Native Americans. Stewart was a reformed drunkard who had been converted at a Methodist campmeeting near Marietta, Ohio. A native Virginian of French-Indian-Negro lineage, he was fond of singing hymns with "a sweet tenor voice." The Wyandot Tribe in the vicinity of Upper Sandusky, Ohio, heard John Stewart and invited him to speak with them. With the assistance of an interpreter, Jonathan Pointer, a black who had been reared among the Wyandots, Stewart preached to the Wyandots, and many of them were converted. After John Stewart's death in 1823 and following their relocation by treaty to Kansas, the Wyandots requested that a mission church be built for them by the Methodists, whom they knew about through John Stewart. This church has become one of Methodism's official shrines.[114]

Between 1864 and 1920 a number of black Methodist Episcopal leaders, ministers, and laypersons emerged. Some were eminent firsts in their positions within church structures, others were committed to making the church socially and politically relevant, and still others to evangelizing in the midst of inner city populations.

William H. Crogman deserves more visibility than either black history or higher education has accorded him. Born and orphaned in the West Indies Islands (Saint Martin) at a young age, Crogman made his early livelihood as a mariner. Eventually he attended and graduated from Pierce Academy in Middleboro, Massachusetts (1870). He immediately became the first black teacher to be engaged by the Freedmen's Aid Society to teach at Claflin University. Following graduation from Atlanta University with baccalaureate and master's degrees, Crogman embarked on a teaching and later administrative career at Clark University that was to span forty-five years, as described above.

Crogman was a churchman as well as a Christian scholar. A member of three General Conferences (1880–1888), he was the first person of color to serve as an assistant secretary of that body as well as of the University Senate, a body of the General Conference that then determined degree requirements for all Methodist Episcopal colleges. In the larger Georgia community, Dr. Crogman served as Chief Exposition Commissioner for the 1895 International Exposition. He made an enduring contribution to higher education among black people in another venture in which he participated, the American Negro Academy. This group of Negro intellectuals, including its founder Alexander Crummell, W. E. B. DuBois, F. J. Grimke, Crogman, and others, brought focus and clarity to the famous Washington-DuBois "debate" over classical versus industrial education. The mediating position of Crogman on this issue brought a needed and valued balance to this critical discussion.[115]

A contemporary of William Crogman in higher education in Atlanta in the last quarter of the nineteenth century and the first quarter of the twentieth century was the scholar-minister J. W. E. Bowen, Sr. Possessor of a New Orleans University baccalaureate and a Boston University doctorate, Bowen was considered one of the most mature scholars of his race and one of its most trusted leaders. Bowen was the first person of color to teach at Gammon Theological Seminary and the first to become its president (1906). In 1904 Bowen founded and edited a magazine, *The Voice of the Negro*, which became something of a weathervane for his thinking and that of a fairly large segment of the black middle class in Atlanta and in the South. *The Voice of the Negro*, while less radical than some would have desired, nevertheless pursued public and race issues, particularly mob violence, vigorously.

On the matter of classical versus industrial education, Bowen tended to be a classicist. At the same time, he was almost invariably a personal and public supporter of Booker T. Washington. Bowen, together with persons like Crogman, John Hope, R. R. Wright, Sr., and, of course, W. E. B. DuBois, greatly influenced the thinking of the period.[116]

Other influential black Methodist leaders of the period in the South and North also had their impact. James D. Lynch (1839–1872) was a black reconstruction minister-politician who united with the Methodist episcopal Church in 1867. William B. Gravely, who has written extensively about Lynch, indicates that he was highly instrumental and effective in organizing Methodist Episcopal work in Mississippi. Gravely also pointed out that Lynch joined the Methodist Episcopal Church largely because he felt that that church offered the best opportunity to combine religion and political uplift in the service of the newly freed women and men of the South.[117]

Hiram R. Revels (1822–1901), the first black person ever to serve in the United States Senate, was influenced to become a Methodist on somewhat the same grounds as Lynch. Politically a moderate, Revels brought a judicious balance to his public life and work that won wide respect for his leadership. After serving in the Senate (1870–1871), he returned to the active ministry and served intermittently as an educator, political activist, and presiding elder in the Mississippi Conference until his death.[118]

Before leaving the southern scene, Emmett J. Scott (1873–1957) should be mentioned. Scott, a prominent lay member of Asbury Methodist Episcopal Church in Washington, D.C., was highly influential in the early part of this century. As the personal secretary to Booker T. Washington and executive secretary at Tuskegee Institute, he had direct access not only to Washington but also, through him, to the White House. Scott received two presidential appointments between 1901 and 1913: special assistant to the secretary of war, under President Theodore Roosevelt, and membership on the United States Commission to Liberia, under President Howard Taft. Additionally, Scott was a founding member of the National Negro Business League. Considered an able and astute administrator and diplomat, this native Texan and Wiley College graduate routinely handled some of the most complicated issues in church, state, and educational matters in his time with integrity and aplomb.[119]

There are three other notable black Methodists in this period: two northern black ministers and a minister-diplomat. William H. Brooks (1859–1923), who still holds the distinction of being the longest tenured pastor of St. Mark's Church in New York City (1897–1923), introduced a comprehensive style of ministry during his pastorate of what was then called the "Cathedral of Negro Methodism." Though young, several characteristics endeared this Morgan College and Howard University graduate to the congregation: strong, prophetic preaching; caring and constant pastoral work; and excellent administration; and community involvement. Brooks was highly regarded in the New York Conference and became the first black minister elected a delegate to the General Conference from a predominantly white Conference (1920). He was instrumental in the organization of Newman and Butler Memorial churches in Brooklyn and in the Bronx, and he was responsible for the revitalization of the floundering Salem Mission in Harlem. Dr. Brooks was not only active in the life of the Harlem community but also a prime mover in its affairs. He was involved in the Niagara Movement, predecessor of the National Association for the Advancement of Colored People (NAACP), and a member of its first executive committee.[120] Until the time of his retirement, St. Mark's had more than a thousand members, a comprehensive weekday program that reached across Harlem, and a total ministry impact that defined it as a model institutional church.

The remarkable and inspiring ministry of W. H. Brooks at St. Mark's continued in the growth and development of the Salem Mission and the forty-two-year pastorate of Frederick A. Cullen (d. 1946). Young Cullen, a member of the former Delaware Conference and a graduate of Morgan College and Drew Theological School (1908), was requested by the New York Conference through W. H. Brooks to transfer there and to pastor the Salem Mission (1902). The small congregation quickly outgrew its first three meeting places and eventually (1924) purchased the Calvary Methodist Episcopal Church edifice. The membership had decided to relocate rather than integrate as the population of the community became increasingly black. The phenomenal growth of Salem in the next two decades is legendary. Under Cullen's community-oriented leadership, the membership of this first black congregation actually organized in Harlem increased dramatically to become one of the fastest growing churches in New York City.[121]

The ministerial career of Louisiana native Ernest W. Lyon (ca. 1850–1938) is in some way similar to the careers of both Hiram Revels and James Lynch. While basically committed to pastoral ministry, all three sought to articulate their gifts for ministry in nontraditional ways. Following excellent academic training and ordination, Lyon was appointed to several distinguished pulpits, including New Orleans, New York City (St. Mark's, 1891–1897), and Baltimore. Shortly thereafter and early in the presidential administration of Theodore Roosevelt (1901–1909), he accepted an appointment as the United States Minister-Resident and Consul General in Liberia. Apparently a condition in this acceptance would be the freedom to teach theology in the College of West Africa. Lyon's contribution during his term of office in Liberia might be summed up in saying that he faced the issue of black immigration to West Africa realistically, basing a United States policy on the principle that those who go to Liberia for permanent residence there should be able to support themselves and in addition make some meaningful contribution to the host country. Following his term of service in Liberia, Lyon returned to the United States and the active ministry. He was elected to the General Conference of 1920, 1924, and 1928 before retiring from the Washington Conference.[122]

Tindley Temple Church in Philadelphia, Pennsylvania, as its name indicates, honors its most distinguished and nationally acclaimed pastor, the Reverend Charles Albert Tindley (1851–1933). It was built in 1924 during his lifetime and pastorate as a tribute to his phenomenally effective ministry of more than three decades (1902–1933). The story of his rise from the menial job of sexton to the leadership of one of American Methodism's largest and best-attended churches is awe-inspiring. Tindley was born on a farm near Berlin, Maryland, on the eastern shore of the peninsula in the very humble home of his Methodist parents. His mother's death when he was two years old led to his being "hired out" as soon as possible. He developed a thirst for the knowledge to read, which he taught himself to do. Upon becoming a young man, Tindley married Daisey Henry, and the couple went to Philadelphia. They found lodging with a former Berlin family who invited them to attend the church that he would one day pastor, John Wesley. He immediately sought and found work as a hod carrier and later served as sexton for the church he attended. Young Tindley, albeit with a wife and child to support, pursued an education in night school, day school, from friends, even from strangers. A call to the ministry soon came to Tindley. Self-prepared, he studied and passed his exams for ordination. He had several appointments before becoming the presiding elder of the Wilmington (Delaware) District, after which he began a memorable pastorate at Bainbridge Street Methodist Episcopal Church in South Philadelphia in 1902.

Tindley's effectiveness as a minister was the result of several things: his ability to identify with the common people, of which he was one; his gifted preaching; his ability to use music in worship and preaching; and his tireless pastoral work and deep compassion for the unfortunate.

These "gifts and graces," so well-suited to the needs of the parish community of Bainbridge Street Church, began to evidence themselves in record-breaking attendance. In 1906 Bainbridge Street Church bought a vacated white church on the now famous site of Broad and Fitzwater streets to accommodate their preacher's audience. The "new" edifice was named East Calvary Methodist Episcopal Church.

As Tindley became increasingly outstanding as a preacher, he became a political force but was scrupulous in his dealings with members and politicians alike. East Calvary also became an educational and cultural center for South Philadelphia, without serious rival. Its forums debated civil rights issues, and its pastor advocated justice for the oppressed. As the undisputed leader of the Delaware Conference, he was called "Prince of Preachers" and elected to a seat in the General Conference delegation from 1908 until his death.

The crowning joy of Tindley's ministry was the erection of a new church in 1924 to accommodate the more than two thousand members who came to hear him preach and the thousands more who received other ministries from the bounty of this faithful congregational pastor through the church's renown "street ministry." Tindley died in his seventies, not without failures and regrets, but it is hoped with the full knowledge that his leadership pioneered a style of church life that foreshadowed much of what is done today.[123]

William H. Crogman often referred to Lorenzo Houston King as the most brilliant student ever to be graduated from Clark University. This high estimation was to be validated in King's remarkable career in the Methodist Episcopal Church as a scholar, teacher, pastor, editor, civil leader, activist, and bishop. Born in Macon, Mississippi, in 1878, Lorenzo King graduated with honors from Clark College and with distinction from Gammon Theological Seminary. He earned a second B.D. degree from Union Theological Seminary and pursued post graduate studies at Columbia University in New York. Ordained in the Atlanta Conference, King pastored churches in Georgia, climaxed by his appointment to Central Church in Atlanta and a professorship at Clark University. At the 1920 General Conference, he was elected editor of the *Southwest Christian Advocate*. In that position, his formulation of Negro rights and issues and his unmatched oratory won for him the distinction of national religious leadership.

Called to the pastorate of St. Mark's Church in New York City in 1931, he came to be known as one of the denomination's most eloquent preachers and leaders. He ran unsuccessfully for Congress in 1938 before being elected to the episcopacy in the Methodist Church in 1940. L. H. King exemplified in his almost half-century career in ministry achievement, excellence, integrity, and race leadership of the highest caliber. He died in 1946.[124]

W. A. C. Hughes (1877–1940) was the son of a Methodist Episcopal minister and the grandson of a Methodist "slave preacher," responsible for building the first Methodist Episcopal church used by black people in Maryland. The experience of being raised in a rural community in the state of his forebears significantly influenced Hughes's ministerial practice. Hughes prepared for his ministry that was to cover over forty years (1897–1940) by graduating from Morgan College and continuing studies at Gammon Theological Seminary in Atlanta and Union Theological Seminary in New York City. After serving several leading appointments, including one to the historic Sharp Street Church in Baltimore, and a district superintendency, he was appointed to the directorship of Negro work in the Board of Home Missions and Church Extension in Philadelphia, Pennsylvania.

The newly created position had grown out of studies and field investigative work done by black staff persons who previously held positions similar to that of Hughes: G. G. Logan, field agent, 1903–1910; W. W. Lucas, field agent, 1910–1912; and I. L. Thomas, field agent, 1912–1917. The major finding of these investigations was the necessity of practical help in workshop-type experiences for black pastors without seminary or even college training and/or for graduates assigned to rural and small congregation appointments. Between 1917 and 1940, Hughes developed such a program, called Schools of Practical Methods. The program sessions were usually held on the campuses of Methodist colleges and adapted to meet the pastoral needs of undereducated black ministers. This program placed Hughes in strategic settings across the church and attracted national attention. It doubtless assisted Hughes in making a strong bid for election to the episcopacy, which he achieved shortly before his death in 1940. An exceptionally gifted preacher and undaunted advocate for the less privileged, he would have doubtless made an outstanding contribution to the episcopacy had he lived.[125]

The life sketch of Mary McLeod Bethune (1875–1955) appropriately climaxes this section about black Methodists who made singular contributions during the Methodist Episcopal era. Mary Bethune was born in a humble sharecropper's home on a rice and cotton farm in South Carolina to parents who were freed slaves. She and her fourteen sisters and brothers were taught about God as a "friend and guide." From her earliest years, she sought knowledge in order to help others. Graduating from Scotia Seminary, a Presbyterian school in Concord, North Carolina, she sought an even deeper understanding of her faith and further preparation to serve as a missionary in Africa. With this purpose in mind, she attended Moody Bible Institute in Chicago. Upon graduating, she unsuccessfully sought an opportunity to go to Africa as a missionary. When this failed to materialize, she sought to work with young black women and girls in her own country.

The remainder of the Mary McLeod story is legendary. She founded several schools for girls. The one bearing her name, Bethune-Cookman College, has educated thousands of black youths. She has advised United States presidents about the needs, hopes, and problems of youth. She established the major voice and platform for black women in America, the National Council of Negro Women. She consulted with the heads of nations as they framed the United Nations' Declaration of Human Rights. She proudly claimed her Methodist identification and represented the South Florida Conference at four quadrennial General Conferences between 1928 and 1940. Considered one of the most influential persons in black American history, she was the recipient of innumerable honors, including the NAACP's Spingarn Medal. The first monument-memorial to a black American and a woman has been erected in her memory in Washington, D.C.'s, National Park.[126]

C H A P T E R 3

A UNION THAT DIVIDES
Development of a Church
Within a Church

Karen Y. Collier

REUNION AND THE ROLE OF RACE

The proposal to segregate Negroes in the reorganization of The Methodist Church in 1939 was not a new arrangement. Most white Protestant churches in America had been bastions of segregation and racism throughout their histories.[1] Every major white denomination in the United States had, at some point in time, organizationally partitioned its Negro membership.[2] The period following the Civil War was particularly notable as a time when most Protestant denominations established all-Negro congregations, presbyteries, synods, Conferences, or dioceses.

Although in many ways the Central Jurisdiction of The Methodist Church was an extension of the patterns of segregation and racism in American Protestantism, to analyze the jurisdiction solely in these terms is simplistic and somewhat shortsighted. Most church historians have since agreed that the origin and development of the Central Jurisdiction was racist and that it represented segregation. There are more fundamental issues involved in the constitutional sanctioning of segregation in Methodism. Though racism and segregation explain the "what" in the developing of a Central Jurisdiction, they do not begin to suggest the "how" and the "why" of the Central Jurisdiction. The reasons and means by which an ecclesiastical structure, namely, The Methodist Church, could allow this kind of organization to come into existence are the subjects of this chapter.

In a church that has historically claimed the doctrines and traditions of Christianity, the heritage of Anglicanism, and the ideals of American democracy, the issue of a structure that sets forth equality of persons with "special" categories or mechanisms for a segment of its membership seems abnormal. And yet "special" provisions have consistently been made for Negro Methodists. The veracity of this assessment is borne out by several factors.

99

First, the framers of the Plan of Union who created the jurisdiction consciously recommended that Negroes be separated in the new church. They predetermined the expedience of unification in preference to the integrity of the total constituency of the church. During the discussions of union by members of the Joint Commission on Unification, the Reverend Edwin B. Chappell of the Methodist Episcopal Church, South, stated:

> For the plan, as I understand it, simply provides for separating Methodism into closely related and cooperating sections on the basis of racial differences and needs. . . . The plan makes it possible to provide for cooperation without involving those dangers of friction and misunderstanding which are involved in the preferential plan. . . . The plan can be modified as to leave each race free to develop its racial traits and fulfill its racial destiny without being hampered by the other.[3]

Later in the same discussions, Bishop Earl Cranston of the Methodist Episcopal Church said:

> Now, if you ask me if the proposed Associate General Conference puts the colored people outside of our Church, I say No. The establishment of an Afro-American Associate General Conference is not pushing these brethren beyond our Church. It is not a segregated relation. It is an ecclesiastical fellowship representing but one spiritual communion, which has its beginning in the heart of God and as its bond the spirit of divine love communicated to all human hearts which are born of the Spirit. Christian fellowship is spiritual. It does not inhere in ecclesiastical scheme, nor can it be given or taken away by any human authority.[4]

Another factor supporting the existence of "special" treatment is the history of the Negro in Methodism. As mentioned above, segregation was not a new experience for Negro Methodists. Although the Methodists made significant pronouncements relative to the eradication of slavery and later racism, the status of Negroes within the church had primarily been one of "separate and different." An example of one of the earliest distinctions can be found in the *Minutes* of the first Methodist Episcopal Church Conference, 1784, where the following answer was given to the question, "Are there any directions to be given concerning the Negroes?"

> Let every Preacher, as often as possible, meet them in Class. And let the Assistant always appoint a proper white Person as their Leader. Let the Assistants also make a regular Return to the Conference, of the number of Negroes in Society in their respective Circuits.[5]

100

In this instance, specific instructions and supervision were deemed necessary for Negroes. There would also be particular notice taken of the number of Negroes in a certain group.

It also is instructive to examine the situation of Negroes in the Methodist Episcopal Church in view of one other observation about the period before the Civil War. There were opportunities for Negroes and whites to worship together in the same service, but this arrangement was not designed to indicate that there was equality among worshipers. There were more practical reasons—that is, whites wanting to prevent insurrections. As Gayraud Wilmore points out:

> White Christians did not assume that the equality which was denied in civil society should be available within the Church. As a matter of fact, the pattern of relationship between Black and White in the household of God made it difficult for Americans to presume that there was anything immoral about inequality in the household of Caesar.[6]

The incidents resulting in the withdrawal of Negroes from the St. George's Methodist Episcopal Church in Philadelphia and the John Street Methodist Episcopal Church in New York are reminiscent of such situations. Although Negroes worshiped in the same setting, there was special seating and sermonizing. When churches were eventually built to accommodate Negro congregations, whites continued to be present in order to supervise and monitor the services and meetings.

The Negro situation, therefore, has to be viewed differently. It has to be analyzed from within the construct of the meaning of Methodism and its structure. It is necessary to examine the uniqueness of the Negro Methodist experience in America and the way in which it was used to facilitate the process of unification.

IMPEDIMENTS TO REUNION

The complexity of issues related to the place of the Negro in Methodism is uncovered by examining the background of the plans for the reunion of Methodism. Union and the subsequent establishment of the Central Jurisdiction in 1939 has often been viewed as the result of continuous negotiations among the three groups involved. As John Moore points out, this was not the case.[7] There were many internal as well as external factors that caused disruptions during the sixty-three years that it took to develop and finalize a plan. Both Northern and Southern Methodists incurred substantial losses as a result of the Civil War and its aftermath. There were heavy declines in church membership, property, and influence, particularly in the South.

Northern and Southern Methodists competed for Methodists' memberships and property.[8] Losses were due not only to competition among white Methodists but also to the mass exodus of Negroes from predominantly white denominations (including Methodists) to independent Negro churches and denominations.[9]

The two branches were also impeded by problems that stemmed from the period of the 1844 split. Each of them had strong feelings relative to the question of slavery. Although the immediate conflicts had been settled by the schism of the church and the later Civil War, the Methodist Episcopal Church, South, sustained a preference for exclusion of Negroes from the church. It continued to support the idea that there should be a separate church for Negroes, even though there were still a few Negro members in the Methodist Episcopal Church, South. The Methodist Episcopal Church (despite its own segregating practices) maintained that its Negro constituency should continue its membership. Also, both groups had to renegotiate their identities as Methodist denominations of equal status.[10] The particulars of power and authority in the machinery of a new, "united" church had to be determined. Ultimately, they had to find a way to preserve their regional individuality within a redefined national structure.

When the Methodist Episcopal Church, South, and the Methodist Episcopal Church severed their ecclesiastical ties, there was much controversy around the particulars of the separation. The Methodist Episcopal Church claimed that the Southern church had broken from it. The Southern church never agreed with this interpretation. They considered that the actions taken at the General Conference of 1844 left them little choice except to leave.

There are several elements in the response of the Southerners and their sympathizers that related to the union negotiations. Their departure from the Methodist Episcopal Church was the result of a number of issues, including an immediate reaction to the stance taken by the church on slavery. (The 1844 General Conference voted to suspend a minister and bishop who were involved in slavery from active service in the church.) However, the Southern faction was more incensed by the power and authority assumed by the General Conference, to the detriment of the episcopacy.[11] Contrary to the majority opinion of the Methodist Episcopal Church, the Southern group viewed the episcopacy as

> a co-ordinate branch, the executive department proper of the government. A bishop of the Methodist Episcopal Church is not a mere creature—is in no prominent sense an officer of the General Conference. . . . In a sense by no means unimportant, the General Conference is as much the creature of the episcopacy as the Bishops are the creatures of the General Conference. . . . Because Bishops are in part constituted by the General Conference is not a mere appointment to labor. It is an official consecrated station, under the protection of law, and can only be dangerous as the law is bad or the Church corrupt.[12]

Despite a decision rendered by the United States Supreme Court that the two bodies were legally separated, the Methodist Episcopal Church, South, remained adamant in its position. This was one of the factors that helped to create tension in the connection. The irritating points for the Methodist Episcopal Church, South, were in the implied notions (1) that they had initiated the movement to separate and (2) that the Methodist Episcopal Church was the main body of Methodism and that the General Conference was the *ultimate* power in the church instead of coequal with the episcopacy. Southern Methodists and their supporters felt that both churches were equal inheritors of the tradition of John Wesley and American Methodism.[13]

NEGRO METHODISTS AND REUNION: CONSIDERATION WITHOUT CONSULTATION

Initial attempts to reconcile the differences between the two groups failed. It was not until 1876 that the efforts to begin reunion talks were successful. In that year, representatives of the two churches met at Cape May, New Jersey, August 17–23, and developed a document that recognized the legitimacy of both Methodist branches. According to Bishop Edwin H. Hughes of the Methodist Episcopal Church:

> This document laid the only possible basis for reunion. It did away with all talk about the homeward "return of the wandering daughter," and used the word "branch" in the domestic sense rather than in the horticultural sense. Henceforth neither Church was represented by a limb torn by anger from the one recognized tree, but was "a legitimate branch" of the "one Methodist family." The unified hearthstone was distant, but it had become assured. The solid wall was making ready to become an open door.[14]

Between 1898 and 1910, the pros and cons of union were continually debated, particularly in the church press. The major concerns of the two denominations were eventually concretized: How would the churches be organized so as to protect property, sectional and racial integrity, and the episcopacy as the Methodist Episcopal Church, South, perceived them? In what ways would the authority of the General Conference and the probity of Negro members of the Methodist Episcopal Church be secured, in keeping with the perspective of the Methodist Episcopal Church?[15] How could a reunion of churches be achieved between the churches without the larger Methodist Episcopal Church absorbing the smaller Methodist Episcopal Church, South, and the Methodist Protestant Church?

In 1908 the Methodist Episcopal Church approved a plan that had originated with the Methodist Episcopal Church, South, to establish the

Federal Council of Methodism. The council, composed of three bishops, three ministers, and three laypersons from each church, was given the task of reducing friction between the two bodies by 1910. At the local level, points of tension were to be handled in Annual Conferences by commissions with joint representation also.

Initially, the questions relative to identity and authority were to be settled by plans that called for a federal rather than an organic union. Both churches would remain essentially separate entities, but they would participate in programs of mutual interest and benefit similar to the projects undertaken by the Joint Commission on Federation in 1898. A federation mode would, it was hoped, allow for ministry in the same territory without tension. How this would be accomplished varied in accordance with the many proposals that were devised. As early as 1891, a jurisdictional approach was advanced by Dr. W. P. Harrison, the book editor of the Methodist Episcopal Church, South:

> Let there be one Methodist Episcopal Church in America under four General Conference Jurisdictions: (1) The Methodist Episcopal Church, North, comprising New England and the Central States to the Mississippi River, (2) the Methodist Episcopal Church, South, comprising the territory of the slavehold-ing states as they existed in 1860, or, if preferred, the boundary established by the Plan of Separation in 1844; (3) the Methodist Episcopal Church, West, comprising all the territory west of the Mississippi River; (4) the Colored Methodist Episcopal Church, comprising the African, the African Zion, and the Colored Methodist Episcopal Churches. These four divisions would be held in one church organization by a nexus of a Methodist Church Council meeting once in four years. The Council is to have no legislative or judicial function, but to be an advisory body only.[16]

Given the terms of this proposal, all parties would be able to maintain their individual churches and yet consider themselves a part of a total community of Methodists. Note the fourth jurisdiction, which suggests a union of the Negro Methodists in independent Negro denominations and churches, as well as those in the Methodist Episcopal Church. There was a strong movement to have all of Negro Methodism united into one body during the period.[17] A workable proposal that called for structural changes in the two predominantly white denominations was not accepted until 1910.

The years between 1908 and 1910 were significant for union in that they represented the point at which the Methodist Protestant Church entered the discussions, changing the focus of union. Methodist Protestants' input is sometimes considered negligible. However, it was probably their entry into the talks that turned the tide of the discussions from a federated to an organic union.

The Methodist Protestant churches were located in both the North and the South. By and large, those in the North were supportive of the Northern church, and those in the South sympathized with the Southern church. It was more advantageous to work for a basically united Methodism in order that Methodist Protestants would not suffer another schism.

The president of the Methodist Protestant Church, Thomas H. Lewis (1852–1929), engaged in many of the conversations on union. He was privileged to address the General Conferences of both the Methodist Episcopal Church and the Methodist Episcopal Church, South, in 1908 and 1910, respectively. He also spoke to the members of the Federal Council of Methodism on July 6, 1910. At that time, he impressed upon the delegates the need for a systemic reformulation of Methodism:

> The United Methodist Protestant Church was as much separated by a North and South line prior to 1877 as the two Methodist Episcopal Churches are now. You may think this demonstration is not big enough to be regarded as any more than a model; but it is a working model—anyhow, it goes all right. The fact is, the union of our two sections is so complete that it constitutes almost the only barrier to our union with these larger bodies separately.[18]

His appeal resulted in the creation of three commissions that represented each of the particular denominations. The commissions met in Baltimore in December 1910. From this meeting, a Committee of Nine was selected to thoroughly examine the implications of union. The commissions explicitly cautioned the committee to leave the basic structure of Methodism intact: "There was, therefore, to be no radical change in organic laws and fundamental principles. . . . It was to be a union whereby the outstanding characteristics of each of the three Methodisms should find a place within a United Methodism."[19] Subsequently, they reported back to the Joint Commission on Federation at a meeting held May 10, 1911, in Chattanooga, Tennessee.

The statement by the Committee of Nine offered a choice of two names for the new church, the Methodist Episcopal Church in America or the Methodist Church in America. It cited points of commonality such as Articles of Faith, conditions for membership, and ritual. The proposal recommended that authority in the church be specified in the constitution and given to one General Conference and three or four Quadrennial Conferences. Everything that was considered "connectional" would be governed by the General Conference, while the Quadrennial Conference would deal with local affairs. It further advised that representation should be equally distributed among the laity and clergy in "two houses." Members of the "two houses" would be chosen from the Quadrennial Conferences and the Annual Conferences:

> The delegates in the first house shall be apportioned equally among the Quadrennial Conferences and elected under equitable rules to be provided therefor. The ministerial delegates in the second house shall be elected by the

ministerial members of the Annual Conferences, and the lay delegates by the laity within the Annual Conferences under equitable rules provided therefor. Each Annual Conference shall have at least one ministerial and one lay delegate. . . . All legislation of the General Conference shall require the concurrent action of the two houses.[20]

Bishops would be designated by the Quadrennial Conferences. The Annual Conferences would be placed in areas determined by the Quadrennial Conference. The plan especially indicated that lay representation was important and that the interpretation of constitutional issues should not be given to any of the Conferences.

The report of the committee included key elements from several papers that had been presented during the meeting. There was considerable evidence of the particular groups represented. Among the seven basic suggestions of the report, there was a significant omission. The status of Negro Methodists was not mentioned. This may have been purposeful, but Bishop Moore did not acknowledge this point in his writing. Earlier discussions in the Cincinnati meeting of the committee approached the subject of Negro Methodism. For example, in one of two papers, which also mentioned bishops specifically, the following recommendation was made:

8. The Colored Methodists would best be served through a union of all the colored churches and members with the active financial and personal interests of the unified Church. . . . If the union of all colored churches cannot be secured, try to plan for the union of the Colored Methodist Episcopal Church and the colored membership of the Methodist Episcopal Church. If that is not practicable, make another General Conference District for the colored membership, giving them the additional power to elect their bishops (with authority limited to their own district), and, as a fair offset, their delegates would not have voting power in the General Conference.[21]

This statement was a provision supported by clergy and laity from the Chattanooga area and each of the churches. Another recommendation was made in a paper by Bishop Earl Cranston (1840–1932) of the Methodist Episcopal Church, which suggested five Jurisdictional Conferences, "one of these jurisdictions [to] include the Negro membership now related to our several existing organizations."[22] He also commented on possible relations between the Episcopacy and jurisdictions: "We would allow to each jurisdiction the right to suggest legislative action, to nominate its pro rata representation in Board of Bishops."[23]

The Joint Commission on Federation eventually adopted the study by the Committee of Nine. They amended the report, however, to include a statement on Negroes and representation in Quadrennial Conferences. In reference to Negro Methodists, they added "that the colored membership of the Methodist Episcopal Church, the Methodist Protestant Church, and such organizations of colored Methodists as may enter into agreement with them, may be constituted and recognized as one of the Quadrennial or Jurisdictional Conferences of the proposed organization."[24]

Between 1912 and 1914, the Joint Commission submitted the proposal to the three General Conferences. Both the Methodist Protestant Church and the Methodist Episcopal Church, South, accepted the report in substance. Each of them recognized its limitations, but they affirmed its basic principle of union by reorganization. For example, when the General Conference of the Methodist Episcopal Church, South, met in 1914, the report of the commission was assigned to a study committee. The result of the committee's work was summarized in a declaration that later became the Oklahoma Declaration. The only addition that the committee made to the Joint Commission's proposal was a statement that reemphasized the Southern church's stance on the role of Negro Methodists in the church: "However, we recommend that the colored membership of the various Methodist bodies be formed into an independent organization holding fraternal relations with the reorganized and United Church."[25]

The Methodist Episcopal Church decided not to review the report of the commission at its 1912 General Conference. Instead, it received the findings and waited until 1916 before taking action. Its unreadiness stemmed from the fact that the proposal was considered incomplete. Additionally, members of the Conference had reservations concerning the suggested status of the General Conference. From their vantage point, its authority was significantly weakened by the recommendation of the commission. All three of the denominations overwhelmingly maintained concerns for unification. They voted to continue participating in a Joint Commission and took steps to officially create a Joint Commission on Unification.

NEGRO METHODISTS AND REUNION: CONSULTATION WITHOUT CONSIDERATION

By 1916 the Methodist Episcopal Church and Methodist Episcopal Church, South, had made provisions to establish their Joint Commissions. The Methodist Protestant Church became silent in the negotiations after 1912. Their most vocal spokesperson for union, Thomas Lewis, failed to be reelected to the presidency of the church. They further recognized the need for the two Episcopal Methodisms to resolve their fundamental questions concerning regional autonomy, the powers of the General Conference, and Negro participation in the church. The basic issue for the Methodist Protestants had been equal lay representation, although they had indicated other concerns.[26] They registered an acceptance of the substance of the proposal in regard to this issue and discontinued their active role in union talks until 1928.

Between December 29, 1916, and August 16, 1939, the dates of the first and last meetings of the Joint Commission, there were two additional plans that were presented to General Conferences of the two Methodist Episcopal denominations.

The commissioners began the second phase of their work by establishing four individual committees: a committee to deal with General and Jurisdictional Conferences, a Judicial Council committee, a Status of the Negro Membership committee, and a General Reference committee. Each committee established the primary issues relating to its particular concern. In the case of Conferences (which consumed most of the discussion at Traverse City, Michigan), familiar questions emerged with reference to the distinguishing powers of the General and Jurisdictional Conferences and the ways in which the general itinerancy of the bishops would be preserved if regional Conferences had the power to elect them.

The Methodist Episcopal Church, South, was adamant in the position that these would be regional or Jurisdictional Conferences and that they would have necessary powers of administration, election, and legislation. Conversely, the General Conference would have limited and designated powers. Members of the committee representing the Methodist Episcopal Church were firm in their criticism of a jurisdictional scheme. They interpreted the regions or jurisdictions as "separate churches," introducing a "diocesan" episcopacy and destroying the general episcopacy. From the perspective of Northern Methodists, "connectional officers would have to be elected by a national forum, the General Conference, in order to have support from the total church."[27]

The Judicial Council, so named by John Moore, was discussed at the Savannah meeting on January 23, 1918.[28] There was little dissension on this topic. The important concerns were that there be a Judicial Council that would interpret the constitution of the church and render judgments on matters pertaining to the *Discipline*. This was to be a safeguard against either the General or Jurisdictional Conferences making ultimate judgments in the church.

The "status of the Negro membership" preoccupied the agenda of one of the longest meetings of the commission. While the Judicial Council took only two days of the Savannah meeting, the topic of Negro involvement in the church continued for about thirteen days until February 6, 1919.[29] In the *Proceedings* of the aforementioned meeting as well as other church and larger community periodicals written throughout the period of union talks, the issue of Negro Methodists was indicated to be a determinative element.[30] This was, in fact, the essential element that forced both Episcopal Methodisms and the Methodist Protestants to agree to a jurisdictional approach to union. This thesis is partially suggested by the fact that the problem was more than deciding the kind of role that Negro Methodists would have, even though that was a key issue. The more crucial question was how Negro Methodist leadership, particularly in the person of Negro bishops, would function in the new church. As indicated above, the machinery for the election of Negro bishops had already been devised by the 1912 General Conference of the Methodist Episcopal Church. Moreover, two Negro bishops were elected at the 1920 General Conference.

In the Savannah meeting, members of the Methodist Episcopal Church expressed their support for a Negro membership within the church, even if it meant having a single region for them.[31] The opposite perspective was held by representatives of the Methodist Episcopal Church, South.[32] In essence, they wanted Negro Methodists out of the united church and continued in a separate ecclesiastical structure, which would govern its own actions. As John Moore indicated, "The Southern people were fully convinced that this [separate] state of things was best for both races, and best for Southern civilization and that it [separation] should continue."[33] The committee on the status of Negro membership had difficulty in bringing an acceptable report. Its initial presentation at Traverse City had included two reports. A majority of the committee had affirmed "an African Associate General Conference," in which the makeup of black Conferences would include all the persons of "African descent in the United States and Africa" that were organized in Annual and Mission Conferences and missions.[34] The status of these individuals was likened to that of those who were related to American Methodism in foreign countries. Several commissioners disagreed with the proposal and asked that it not be accepted in lieu of a separate and distinct organization, rather than a jurisdiction.[35] A subcommittee was appointed to rethink the issue. They said in part, "Your Committees have found it impossible to present their conclusions . . . without stating the same in a form which relates this subject to questions already reported upon or to be reported upon by coordinate committees and tentatively adopted by the Joint Commission."[36] They further offered another possibility:

1. Create an Associate General Conference which shall comprise within its jurisdiction the Negro membership of the church in the United States and Africa, and which shall have complete legislative, judicial, and executive powers in the ecclesiastical government of said Negro membership in harmony with and subject to the Constitution of the unified Church. Said Associate General Conference shall have the power to elect the bishops, constitute the boards, and elect their general administrative officers, for the said Negro conferences and memberships.[37]

In the above offering, several factors are explicit. Negroes would be organized separately. They would have fundamental authority and power over their affairs, whether legislative, executive, or judicial. Contact with the united church would be unnecessary and unlikely, except for purposes of fellowship. There would be a similarity and yet a distinction between a Negro "region" and a foreign "region." Representation in the work of the General Conference of the new church would be minimal. The status of Negroes would not be the same as that for white people. Needless to say, persons from the Methodist Episcopal Church, South, supported the idea of an Associate General Conference rather than an Associate Regional or Jurisdictional Conference. Northern members were more inclined to affirm the Associate Regional or Jurisdictional Conference plan. Issues concerning the status of the Negro membership remained unresolved at the close of the Savannah meeting.

There was a degree of progress, however. The committee had been able to appoint another subcommittee of eight, which developed a formula for jurisdictions that was eventually adopted by the churches. Nevertheless, members of the Savannah meeting did not give final approval to this report. Even so, the April 10, 1918, meeting of the commission in St. Louis continued the discussions. The commission report was inconclusive. For this reason, the commissioners decided to announce temporary findings to the General Conference of the Methodist Episcopal Church, South, which would meet shortly. At this point, there was some consensus that neither the restrictive rules nor the general itinerant system for bishops should be weakened, regardless of the regional Conference.[38] The Southern church in its May 2–8, 1918, Conference reaffirmed its positive concern for union and its desire that Negro Methodists not be a part of the reorganized church.

PROPOSED STATUS FOR THE NEGRO

At the next session of the Joint Commission on Unification in Cleveland, Ohio, July 7–10, 1919, the role of the Negro Methodist constituency was the total agenda for the meeting. Two differing perspectives were immediately apparent in the Methodist Episcopal Church's call for a Quadrennial or Regional Conference for Negroes with proportional representation essentially equal to that of white people, and the insistence of the Methodist Episcopal Church, South, upon a Regional or Quadrennial Conference for Negroes equal to those located outside the United States (e.g., Latin America), with predetermined and limited representation in the General Conference. Also, the Methodist Episcopal Church, South, added a provision that would make it possible for Negroes to set up a separate church: "Whenever the membership in full standing of any of those Regional Conferences shall exceed four hundred thousand, upon request of said Conference the General Conference shall organize the membership of the said Conference into an Associate General Conference."[39] The Southern church was unmoving in its stance on

Negro membership in the church. They were unable to agree with the suggestion of equality between Negro and white Quadrennial or Jurisdictional Conferences. In reflecting on the perspective of the Methodist Episcopal Church, South, Moore says:

> They [the Southern Commissioners] believed that the strength of the Church must and would be measured always by the strength and authority of its white membership in the United States. They believed that the spread of control would weaken the force and effectiveness of the denomination in itself and in its ministrations.[40]

The commissioners continued to be unable to resolve their problems. On January 15, 1920, they reconvened in Louisville, Kentucky. In preparation for the meeting a subcommittee had been elected to take another look at union in its totality.[41] Without the full support of any of the factions in the commission, the subcommittee devised a constitution that they presented to the respective General Conferences.[42]

The proposed constitution contained specific provisions for each segment of its membership: (1) white membership in the United States, (2) "colored" membership in the United States, and (3) membership in foreign countries.[43] There were to be seven jurisdictions under one General Conference. The white jurisdictional membership was not specified. In contrast, the "colored" membership was listed as one clergy and one layperson for each two thousand full church members, or two thirds of that number. The General Conference had the final word on changes in this jurisdiction. The total membership of this region was not to exceed four hundred. These provisions were similar to those for the constituency of the church located outside of the United States. Persons, including bishops, were elected to serve in the region and not in the church at large. The General Conference was given the authority to assign bishops to any jurisdiction, "except as herein otherwise provided."[44]

Negro participation in the General Conference was also limited. White Regional Conference representation could not exceed 20 percent of the total membership, nor could they have fewer than 100 delegates. Negroes were limited to 5 percent of its total membership, with no more than 30 to 42 delegates. The constitution also made provisions for an Associate General Conference among its foreign and "colored" community.[45]

Neither of the General Conferences was able to achieve a full endorsement of the suggested constitution. Methodist Episcopal Church delegates agreed to the proposal, despite some dissension. Members of the Methodist Episcopal Church, South, Conference approved the plan in principle. At both General Conferences there were futile attempts to open the discussions on union and the constitution to the total membership of the churches. Both of the churches were unready to approve any plan of union.

In the period that followed 1922, there was a change in the makeup of the commission. Many of the original members had died. Others resigned their positions on the commission to assume different responsibilities in the church. When the commission reconvened, the Methodist Episcopal Church had replaced many of their number, including one of its Negro representatives, Robert E. Jones. The Methodist Episcopal Church, South, however, was able to retain several persons from its former commission.

The debates continued at the next meeting of the Joint Commission at Cincinnati, Ohio, January 18–19, 1923. Despite the development of another plan, which was presented to both General Conferences and the Annual Conferences of the Southern church, little was accomplished in the way of formalizing union. Discussions in the Methodist Episcopal Church, South, intensified to the point that by the time its next General Conference met in 1926, a four-year moratorium on unification negotiations was declared. The talks were not totally disrupted because the Methodist Episcopal Church, South, appointed a small Research and Investigation committee to reexamine all aspects of unification. They also met with the Methodist Episcopal Church on matters pertaining to property. When the General Conference of the Methodist Episcopal Church, South, reconvened in 1930, they received the findings of the Research and Investigation Committee, which cautiously affirmed union. Both the Methodist Episcopal Church and the Methodist Protestant Church had maintained their interests, and in 1928 each appointed a Committee on Interdenominational Relations. The Methodist Episcopal Church, South, selected a similar committee in 1930 to promote fraternal relations with the Methodist Episcopal Church.

Informal deliberations on limited topics were started between the Methodist Episcopal and Methodist Protestant churches in 1930. Members of the Methodist Episcopal Church, South, were consulted on occasion to determine their disposition toward unification. A Joint Commission of the three branches finally convened August 27–29, 1934, in Chicago, Illinois. After reviewing their long history and considering achievements and failures, they set up a small committee that determined the parameters for a union. There were two additional meetings of the Joint Commission, in Louisville, Kentucky, March 13–14, 1935, and Evanston, Illinois, August 14–16, 1938.

THE PLAN OF UNION

On May 10, 1939, the Methodist Episcopal Church, the Methodist Episcopal Church, South, and the Methodist Protestant Church became the Methodist Church.

Administration in the new church was a function of four Conference structures and two councils. In addition to the General, Annual, and Central Conferences,[46] there were six Jurisdictional Conferences. The episcopacy was represented in the Council of Bishops, and the interpretation of church law and legislation was assigned to a Judicial Council.

The Plan of Union, which ultimately became the constitution for the Methodist Church in America, authorized one General Conference with equal suffrage and representation for clergy and laity of the total church. The General Conference was made the legislative branch and given supervision of all matters pertaining to the connection, except where specific limitations were stipulated by the constitution. Division II, Article IV, of the constitution explained the fourteen duties of the General Conference. These included the powers

To define and fix the conditions, privileges, and duties of church membership.

To define and fix the qualifications and duties of Elders, Deacons, Supply Preachers, Local Preachers, Exhorters, and Deaconesses.

To define and fix the powers, duties, and privileges of the Episcopacy; to adopt a plan for the support of the Bishops, to provide a uniform rule for their superannuation and to provide for the discontinuance of a Bishop because of inefficiency or unacceptability.

To initiate and to direct all connectional enterprises of the Church, such as publishing, evangelistic, educational, missionary, and benevolent, and to provide boards for their promotion and administration.

To fix a uniform basis upon which Bishops shall be elected by the Jurisdictional Conferences and to determine the number of Bishops that may be elected by Central Conferences.

To change the number and the boundaries of Jurisdictional Conferences upon the consent of a majority of the Annual Conferences in each Jurisdictional Conference involved.[47]

Jurisdictions would control regional affairs, the election of bishops, and matters of promotion in the united church. Of the jurisdictions, five were determined by geographic location and one by race. The General Conference established conditions for membership that included persons from among the clergy and laity. Representatives to the Jurisdictional Conference were chosen by Annual Conferences. There were six functions of the Jurisdictional Conferences designated by the constitution:

1. To promote the evangelistic, educational, missionary, and benevolent interests of the Church, and to provide for interests and institutions within their boundaries.

2. To elect Bishops and to co-operate in carrying out such plans for their support as may be determined by the General Conferences.

3. To establish and constitute Jurisdictional Conference Boards as auxiliary to the General Boards of the Church as the need may appear, and to choose their representatives on the General Boards in such manner as the General Conference may determine.

4. To determine the boundaries of their Annual Conferences, provided that there shall be no Annual Conference with a membership of fewer than fifty ministers in full connection, except by the consent of the General Conference.

5. To make rules and regulations for the administration of the work of the Church within the Jurisdiction, subject to such powers as have been or shall be vested in the General Conference.

6. To appoint a Commission on Appeals to hear and determine the appeal of a traveling preacher of that Jurisdiction from the decision of a trial committee.[48]

The episcopacy was to be localized in the new church. Bishops would maintain their status as general superintendents in the church, but they would no longer be elected by a General Conference. Except in special cases, a bishop would live and govern within the jurisdiction that elected him. Each bishop was made a member of the Council of Bishops, which was to meet annually. Bishops would retain their power to station the preachers and preside over individual Annual Conferences.

RESIGNATION TO A COMPROMISE

Negroes continued to be a part of The Methodist Church, despite its dual jurisdictional system. They were, however, constitutionally segregated within the new structure. The episcopacy maintained its image as the central feature of Methodism in the United States. While some of its powers were relinquished to the General Conference and Judicial Council, the view of episcopacy as a basic element of the Methodist connection was retained. It (episcopacy) also continued to be identified in terms of a white general superintendency. Negroes who were elected to the episcopacy were elected to a Negro episcopacy that served the Central Jurisdiction and not the total church. This redefined the meaning of episcopacy, such that a Negro episcopacy was determined to be different and unequal.

In describing the final day of the Uniting Conference, James P. Brawley (1894–1985) states:

When the curtain fell on the closing session of the Uniting Conference, . . . the union had been consummated. The Methodist Church was a fact, and the proclamation was sounded forth: "The Methodists are one people!"

They were one people, but "all was not right with the world," nor with the Methodist Church. A membership of more than 320,000 Negroes had been legally segregated into the Central Jurisdiction.[49]

The above assessment differs somewhat from that of Bishop John Moore, who failed to consider the overwhelming, negative responses of Negro Methodists and some whites. In his analysis of the union plan, Moore was optimistic about its impact on the total constituency. His basis for interpretation was the majority vote that was given by the membership of the three churches in representative assemblies, and the continuous support that representative groups gave throughout the movement for union. Reactions to the plan were not overwhelmingly positive.[50]

Negroes repudiated the plan. The 1936 Methodist Episcopal Church General Conference voted 470 to 83 in favor of the plan. Negro delegates represented a substantial part of the opposition, with 36 voting decisive nos and 11 abstaining. They also declined to stand during the singing of the hymn "We're Marching to Zion" when the votes were finalized.[51] In Annual Conferences, seven of the nineteen Negro Annual Conferences voted against the plan. Of the remaining twelve, some voted favorably, and some refused to vote. The latter group decided that there was nothing that could be accomplished by their vote.

The final plan was totally unacceptable to a majority of Negro Methodists. Even though they had been supporters of union, the dualism incorporated in the jurisdictional system was considered opprobrious to them. Negro Methodists had been aware of the possibility of union throughout the negotiations. They had participated in a February 15–17, 1916, national forum on union held at Evanston, Illinois,[52] and discussed the implications of union at a meeting of Negro Methodists in Nashville, Tennessee, 1914. There was also Negro representation among the commissioners who worked on the unification of the three churches.

Negro members of the Methodist Episcopal Church affirmed the creation of a new church on the basis that they would continue within the mainstream of the predominantly white structure. Despite existing separate relations in the church, efforts to unify independent Negro Methodist denominations,[53] and attempts to put Negro Methodists out of the predominantly white Methodist Church, Negroes maintained a desire to be a part of the Methodist Episcopal Church.[54] In so doing, the arrangement was not envisioned as permanent. Among Negro Methodists, the plan was reinterpreted to reflect their racial pride—recognizing a degree of independence without being a part of a caste system or without being thrust out of the church.

C H A P T E R 4

A DIVISION THAT UNITES
Pride and Perseverance, 1940–1968

Grant S. Shockley

Two things were happening in America in 1939 that distracted The Methodist Church from contemplating the full implications of its actions in the creation of the Central Jurisdiction on May 10 at Kansas City, Missouri. Western Europe was on the verge of a world war that would almost certainly involve us as a nation in a matter of months. Second, the new church was experiencing the euphoria of having just become a denomination of seven million members, making it the second largest Protestant denomination in the country. There was dissatisfaction, however, with the Central Jurisdiction and all that it symbolized. Its institution had written segregation into the constitutional framework of the denomination. This singular act by a major church body in an egalitarian democracy was an affront to the foundations of Christian community and a flagrant violation of the inclusive principle inherent in Wesleyan Methodism. Yet despite this, Negro Methodists faced the Central Jurisdiction with a steadfast faith in the ultimate triumph of justice, even in The Methodist Church. They drew once again on the spiritual resources that had nurtured them in their families and churches and had sustained them through the ordeal of slavery, the compromise of Reconstruction, the degradation of Jim Crow laws, and the ravages of a devastating economic depression. They knew that the years ahead in the church would be problematic and difficult. Arbitrarily placed in a de jure as well as a de facto situation, they were determined that not even this would deter them from their appointed Christian mission and their Wesleyan vision of inclusive fellowship, world mission, and reconciliation. It is the purpose of this chapter, then, to begin recollecting how a remnant of Negro Methodists, who had remained in the Methodist Episcopal Church with integrity, contributed to it and at the same time protested its far from ideal situation, one that would inevitably self-destruct under the weight of its own contradiction.

POLITY AND STRUCTURAL CHANGES

The Central Jurisdiction concentrated, in a single regional structure, approximately 370,000 Negro Methodists. This number did not include about 15,000 Negro members in predominantly white Methodist churches in the North Central, Northeastern, and Western Jurisdictions or the very few Negro persons who may have been members of churches in the South Central and Southeastern Jurisdictions. Ostensibly, the Central Jurisdictional arrangement represented an effort to initiate contact and fellowship across racial lines while maintaining self-contained and self-governing black/white racial structures with "equality of treatment," representation, and participation. This arrangement was never approved by a majority of the Negro membership, and it was not considered to be a final solution to the racial issue in The Methodist Church. It was, rather, accepted only as a preliminary step toward a more inclusive fellowship.

J. Leonard Farmer makes this point very clear in an address to the first Central Jurisdictional Conference in St. Louis, Missouri (June 19, 1940): "Our task today and tomorrow is twofold. It is to strive that there will be no backsliding from the degree of Christian brotherhood which now obtains, and to labor toward the eventual realization of full Christian brotherhood for ourselves in this church and through ourselves for our entire race."[1]

There were both advantages and disadvantages in the Central Jurisdictional system for members, ministers, and ministry. J. B. F. Shaw and others have indicated that at the denominational, jurisdictional, and Annual Conference levels, theoretically at least, the jurisdictional plan offered political parity. The status, privileges, and prerogatives of the Central Jurisdiction were essentially the same as those of their counterparts in reference to matters of voting, delegate representation, and staff positions.[2] Following this interpretation of the legislation of the Uniting Conference (1939), the constitutional rights of the Central Jurisdiction to initiate, influence, or vote legislation were not infringed. The episcopal office was theoretically uncircumscribed. Second, Negro ministers and laypersons had the opportunity to develop their leadership gifts and creative potential within a framework of appreciative acceptance. Third, the Central Jurisdiction provided opportunities for a larger number of general and jurisdictional elective and executive staff positions than had ever existed.[3] There are illustrations of this from the record:

- Fourteen Negro bishops were elected by the Central Jurisdiction between 1940 and 1967 (Appendix H).
- Negro laypersons and clergy served on all major (and many minor) boards, commissions, and agencies of the denomination as elected representatives.
- There were Negro members on the influential 1952 Survey Commission to restructure the denomination, which in some sense became the predecessor of the Program Council (1968) and the General Council on Ministries (1972).[4]

Prior to the creation of the Central Jurisdiction, there were only a dozen Negro persons in executive-level staff positions across the denomination. By 1967 that number had more than doubled.[5] With the appointment of J. Ernest Wilkins (1895–1959) to the Judicial Council in 1948, there was a fairly significant Negro representation at every level of the new structure of The Methodist Church.[6]

The disadvantages of the Central Jurisdiction system somewhat paralleled the advantages. The basic negative feature of the system was the fact that it was a highly visible and indefensible symbol of a "separate and unequal" relationship between black and white members of the same church denomination. The obvious fact that substantiates this, critics said, began with the physical geography in the Plan of Union. Under this plan more than seventy Annual Conferences in the United States were divided on a geographic basis into five regions or "jurisdictions." Superimposed on these was the Central ("Negro") Jurisdiction, comprised of Negro Annual Conferences. Confirmed in a written constitution and validated by legal incorporation, such an arrangement required the most credulous mind to not strongly suspect that exclusiveness rather than inclusiveness was the belief and attitude of The Methodist Church. This stance, it was insisted, did little to enhance Methodism's image as an inviting and/or open fellowship. A second major disadvantage of the Central Jurisdiction was the imbalance of power it created for blacks in a predominantly white denomination. Despite the effort to equalize voting rights, delegate power, and Negro staff presence, it was still virtually impossible to neutralize the impact of the overwhelming odds of 375,000 versus 9 million in any legitimate way. The result of such a situation was, therefore, a continuing white dominance–Negro protest power struggle. A third disadvantage inherent in the Central Jurisdiction structure was the limited effect that its leadership could have in influencing, negotiating, or decision making on major issues. This constricted situation required Negro leadership to continuously spend excessive amounts of time and energy brokering power or accommodating opposition, rather than proactively engaging the issues and struggles of its own multiproblem minority. In conclusion, the bishops of the Central Jurisdiction suggested that even though the number of Negro executive and elective leaders may have increased during the Central Jurisdiction years, "not one Negro has been elected to the top administrative position of any of these General Boards nor has a non-white member been elected as President of one of the General Boards of the Church."[7]

The bishops went on to say, through their spokesperson, Bishop Charles F. Golden (1912–1984), that only one Negro person had ever chaired a major board or agency (referring to J. Ernest Wilkins's presidency of the Judicial Council, 1956–1957), and only one Negro bishop had ever led the Council of Bishops (Bishop Prince A. Taylor, Jr., 1965–1966). He also observed that "not one Negro from The Methodist Church was included among our visitors selected to attend the Second Vatican Council, nor was one included among the Methodist representatives to the Consultation on Church Union."[8]

MEMBERSHIP, CHURCHES, AND EVANGELISM

The Negro membership of The Methodist Church in 1940—resulting from the unification of the Methodist Episcopal; Methodist Episcopal, South; and Methodist Protestant branches—stood at approximately 375,000. The vast majority of this number (about 350,000) represented the membership of the nineteen Negro Annual Conferences of the Methodist Episcopal Church (1784–1939). The Negro membership of the Methodist Protestant Church (1830–1939) constituted a second component of that total, with about 10,000 members. These had been in six small (segregated) Conferences: Arkansas Mission, Georgia Mission, Baltimore Colored Mission, South Carolina Colored Mission, Colorado-Texas Colored Mission, and the Dallas Colored Mission.[9] Prior to Unification, they merged with contiguous Methodist Episcopal Negro Annual Conferences. The largest and strongest of these Conferences was the South Carolina Colored Mission Conference. A third Negro membership population of approximately 15,000 came from predominantly white Annual Conferences with black churches and white churches reporting black members. These churches and members were located in New England (Boston vicinity), New York State (New York City and suburbs and Buffalo), Wisconsin (Milwaukee); Minnesota (Minneapolis-St. Paul), the West Coast (Los Angeles, San Francisco, San Diego, Oakland, and Pasadena), Nevada, (Las Vegas), Oregon, (Portland), and Arizona (Phoenix).[10] Apparently, unless unreported, there were eight states without Negro Methodist congregations or members in 1940: Idaho, Montana, New Hampshire, North Dakota, South Dakota, Utah, Vermont, and Wyoming.

Membership and Population Increases

It was widely expected by lay members, ministers, and leaders that the new concept and shape of the black community within The Methodist Church would contribute to revitalization and a substantial membership increase. Later it will be seen that significant, relevant, and enriching programs were developed on local and Annual Conference levels and by the Central Jurisdiction as a whole. It will not be possible, however, to show any significant membership growth among Negro Methodists between 1940 and 1968. Despite the national Negro population increase, Negro Methodist membership not only failed to increase, it actually declined. A 1962 study reported that 69 percent of all Negro people lived in the historically southern states in 1940. In 1950 that percentage had declined to 60.2, and twenty years later (1970) only 52.2 percent of Negroes lived in the South.[11]

The net gain in membership for Negro Methodist churches as a result of the migration of Southern Negroes to northern and western cities, however, was small if any. Wilson, Davis, and Kipter spoke to the meaning of this trend:

> In recent years there has been a dramatic shift of Negro population to the North, but a comparable shift in "center of gravity" has not occurred in the Central Jurisdiction membership. In 1950, 38.1 percent of the members of the Central Jurisdiction belonged to the four annual conferences in the northern section of the country. Ten years later, in 1960, the percentage was 38.0. One of the greatest mission fields in the world is right on our doorstep, among Negro residents of the northern cities.[12]

The implication is the same for Central Jurisdiction church membership in the cities. Robert Wilson and Alan Waltz reporting for 1950–1960 write that "in every city there was a large increase in the number of Negro inhabitants. The increase ranged from 15,192 in Denver to 320,372 in Chicago. In all the cities except one, the church membership grew but the increase was very small when compared with the population increase."[13]

CENTRAL JURISDICTION CHURCHES

The number, location, and types of ministry offered by the churches of the Central Jurisdiction, which served Negro Methodists almost exclusively, are important indicators for a historical study. At the turn of the century there were 3,398 Negro churches in the denomination. These congregations served 239,274 members through the services of 1,705 pastors.[14] The number of churches increased to 3,743 by the First Central Jurisdictional Conference of The Methodist Church in 1940. Some of this increase included the fifty-plus Negro Methodist Protestant churches that merged with contiguous Negro Annual Conferences just before Union (1939). During the years 1940 to 1964, the final year for a full Central Jurisdiction statistic due to Evangelical United Brethren–Methodist unification activity, the number of churches in the Central Jurisdiction declined. In 1950 the number was 3,016. In 1960 this figure declined to 2,867, and by 1964 the report was 2,853. The cause or causes of declining Negro membership in this period are not specifically known. A plausible explanation, as will be seen later, is the measurable decline in Negro rural Methodist churches due to migration to the urban centers and the failure of the urban Negro churches to attract and hold these immigrants.

Turning to the different types of churches and the ministries offered, several observations can be made. Two major types of churches are observable in the rapidly urbanizing environment of the period. First, there were the historic churches (discussed in chapter 2) that were founded as Methodist Episcopal congregations between the establishment of African Zoar Church (1794) and the period of the organization of the early Methodist Episcopal Conferences in the South. These churches were essentially tradition oriented. The first social organization of any kind developed and controlled by people of color, they provided what E. Franklin Frazier believed to be "an organization and structuring of Negro life which has persisted until the present time."[15] Frazier refers here to the Negro church as an agency of social control and promoter of Christian sexual ethics and family stability. The reference is also to the Negro church as the place where people began to learn of the need for self-help, mutual aid, education, and economic cooperation. Examples of historic Negro Methodist churches that continued these critical functions and redefined them for their day are numerous. On a regional basis, they were Asbury, Washington, D.C.; St. Mark, Chicago; Wesley Chapel, New Orleans; Union Memorial, St. Louis; Jones Temple, Louisville; Centenary, Charleston; St. Paul, Birmingham; Central, Atlanta; and Wesley Chapel, Los Angeles.

The second type of church of the period 1940–1968 is the community-institutional church. These churches sought to provide—in addition to the ministries of the historic churches and in cooperation with various kinds of community agencies—a full range of services to help meet the needs of the thousands of Negro people who had migrated to the urban centers and were experiencing extreme frustration and dehumanization together with poverty, hunger, unemployment, and ever-present racial discrimination. Typical of many churches like these with highly intentional programs around these vital concerns were Tindley Temple, Philadelphia; St. Daniels, Chester, Pennsylvania; Salem (Harlem), Brooks Memorial (Jamaica), and Metropolitan Community, all in New York City; Cory, Cleveland, Ohio; Scott Memorial, Detroit; St. Matthews, Greensboro, North Carolina; Wesley Chapel, Charleston; Lennon-Seney, Knoxville, Tennessee; Quayle, Oklahoma City, Oklahoma; and Mt. Zion, New Orleans. In the West, among others that could be mentioned of this type, were Scott Memorial, Denver; Taylor Memorial, Oakland, California; Jones Memorial, San Francisco; and Holman, Los Angeles.

EVANGELISM AND OUTREACH

The apparent inability of many Negro Methodist churches, especially in the East and Midwest, to appeal to a broad spectrum of people in Negro urban communities in the post–World War II years was a serious one. Despite impassioned pleas and well-outlined programs by the Central Jurisdiction and its leadership, this trend persisted (and remains today). Bishop R. E. Jones reported to the Central Jurisdictional Conference in 1940 that 25 percent of its churches (442) had failed to add a single member to their rolls. In 1948 the jurisdiction's Committee on Evangelism indicated serious concern for the lack of effort in aggressively pursuing recent Negro migrants into the cities. Ironically, between 1948 and 1950 the jurisdiction did gain more than 8,000 members under an effectively organized "United Evangelistic Mission." In 1956, however, the Central Jurisdiction was again reminded that a gigantic effort would have to be made in membership recruitment if it was to not only hold its own but also grow faster than the population, or begin to match the phenomenal progress that the Roman Catholic Church had made in the Negro community.

Several factors may have been related to this declining syndrome and influenced it. The suggestion that The Methodist Church had been "less aggressive" than other Negro denominations in seeking "the younger, less traditionally oriented,"[16] seems to have had validity. Sociologist E. Franklin Frazier believes that at least three things may have accounted for Methodism's lack of appeal to Negro people in this period: lower toleration for recreational activities, such as dancing; less awareness of social injustices and church involvement; and a feeling that Negro churches were not managed efficiently.

The then growing trend among urban Negro churches toward bigness and formalization and the loss of a sense of intimacy, familiarity, and informality were undoubtedly other factors. The most important cause, however, seems to have been a growing class differentiation pattern. As comparable, though often segregated, educational opportunities became available to Negroes, class differentiation began to reflect itself in relation to occupational status, social roles, education, and income. This burgeoning social stratification had a significant impact in the Negro Methodist church community. It developed what C. Eric Lincoln has referred to as a "middle class mentality" separating them from the Negro masses that Methodism has perennially sought to serve and include in the church.[17] Succinctly, the question that the years 1940–1968 raised for Negro Methodists was how to maintain missional integrity as a fairly high-status church marooned in low-status neighborhoods.

PREACHING, WORSHIP, AND MUSIC

In an effort to describe what happened to preaching, worship, and music in Negro congregations of the Methodist Church from the 1940s through the 1960s, trends in the Negro community and its churches must be looked at and understood. It has already been mentioned that there was a decline in Negro Methodist Church membership precisely in those areas where there were large Negro population increases. In this connection it has been ventured that the traditionally white-oriented worship service that prevailed in many, if not most, Negro Methodist churches was a factor in that decline. Second, it was perceived by many in the Negro community that with some exceptions, Negro Methodist churches were not especially active in community affairs. This image prevailed when many other Negro churches were becoming increasingly active in poverty, hunger, drug, unemployment, and civil rights issues. This impression gained credibility as many so-called middle- and upper-income Negroes, including a large number of Methodists, left the central city for the suburbs in the late 1940s and early 1950s. Third, many of the Negro Methodist churches that did remain in the central city were not really inviting or inclusive of those who lived in its radius of potential attendance. The preaching, worship, and music they offered was often considered "bookish," ritualistic, and "non-Negro." It was not attuned to them culturally, nor was it something in which they could comfortably participate. Fourth, during this same period (1940–1968), The Methodist Church was in the process of presenting to its churches a *Book of Worship* that, if followed, suggested an even more enriched Sunday liturgy, not even remotely applicable or adaptable to the average Negro church in the typical Negro community. Nevertheless this liturgical renewal trend was followed by some Negro pastors in certain elitist Negro Methodist churches.

In concluding this litany of misgivings about the middle-classness of the Negro Methodist churches of the period 1940–1960, it has not been my intention to villainize Negro Methodists. There was often integrity in what they did and what they sought to accomplish. The objective of many of these mainstream Negro Methodist pastors and churches was to achieve a mix of the traditional and the indigenous in preaching, worship, and music that would appeal to Negroes of Methodist persuasion and, at the same time, attract others. How well this was done or even whether it is possible is certainly open to question.

Black Participation in Worship Planning

Black Methodists, by virtue of legislation at the time of the unification of the three branches of Methodism, were represented in all phases of worship planning at the denominational level of The Methodist Church. Charles W. Caldwell, layperson, and Edgar A. Love, minister and later a bishop, were Central Jurisdiction representatives to the Commission on Rituals and Orders of Worship from 1940–1952. Renamed the Commission on Worship and Arts in 1952 and again renamed the Commission on Worship in 1956, its black representatives from 1952 to 1968 were Frederick Hall, J. DeKoven Killingsworth, the Reverend Matthew D. McCollum, the Reverend Daniel L. Ridout, and Anna W. Robinson.

In 1960 the General Conference authorized a special committee to revise the 1935 hymnal. There were three Negro members in that group: J. DeKoven

Killingsworth, Daniel L. Ridout, and Bishop Noah W. Moore, Jr., who was appointed a consultant to this committee.

Historically, it is important to note two things in connection with the 1964 hymnal. For the first time in American Methodist history, Negroes served on a hymnal revision committee. Second, the 1964 Methodist hymnal was the first hymnal of a major United States denomination to include Negro spirituals: hymn 404, "Go Tell It on the Mountain"; hymn 330, "Let Us Break Bread Together;" hymn 286, "Lord, I Want to Be a Christian"; hymn 244, "When the Storms of Life Are Raging"; hymn 212, "There Is a Balm in Gilead"; hymn 287, "We Are Climbing Jacob's Ladder"; hymn 436, "Were You There When They Crucified My Lord?" Third, the hymn "When the Storms of Life Are Raging" was one of the many hymn-gospel songs written by the famed Negro preacher and founder-pastor of Tindley Temple Church in Philadelphia, Charles A. Tindley (1856–1933). It was arranged by Daniel L. Ridout (1898–1984), a distinguished church musician and member of the former Delaware Conference. Ridout also arranged "There Is a Balm in Gilead" and published *Twelve Negro Spirituals: Interpretations and Arrangements* (1950).

MISSION, MISSIONS, AND OUTREACH

The 1939 Plan of Union not only consolidated in one church the second largest Protestant body in the nation, it also created one of the largest church mission structures in the Protestant field. A merger of the several preexisting mission boards and agencies of the former Methodist Episcopal; Methodist Episcopal, South; and Methodist Protestant churches, the Board of Missions and Church Extension became the denomination's single executive, administrative, and missional planning authority for the worldwide as well as nationwide mission and outreach of The Methodist Church.

Elected Negro members of the initial Board of Missions and Church Extension were H. W. Bartley; Mrs. M. W. Clair, Jr.; James L. Farmer, Jr. (Youth); Mrs. D. H. Hargis; Irma G. Jackson; Mrs. D. G. Jones; Joy L. Mitchell (Youth); John A. Patton; and Julius S. Scott, Sr.

The remainder of this section of the chapter will briefly detail the role, status, and contribution of Methodists in and to the mission efforts of the church.

Division of Foreign Missions

The years 1940–1968 confronted the church and the Board of Missions with three tasks: helping to rebuild a world devastated by World War II, helping to prepare national leadership in overseas countries where the church was at work, and increasing the Negro presence in overseas mission situations. In responding to the task of coping with emergency relief for those left destitute and homeless by the war, the 1940 General Conference established the Methodist Committee on Overseas Relief (MCOR). Originally a temporary agency, it became a permanent committee in 1944 representing the church in the field of overseas relief and rehabilitation. From the beginning of MCOR, Negroes have been identified with it. Bishops Alexander P. Shaw and Lorenzo H. King gave it leadership in the early 1940s. From 1948 to 1968 James P. Brawley, John B. Cook, Claire C. Harvey. T. W. Kees, Dorothy E. McNorton, Arsania M. Williams, and Noah W. Moore, Jr. (later elected a bishop) served at various times on the committee.

In developing a follow-up missional thrust program to the Crusade for Christ during the 1944–1948 quadrennium, the Crusade Scholarship Program, initiated late in the 1944–1948 quadrennium, was strengthened and broadened during 1948–1952 to include Methodist racial minority students in the United States. This was done at the request of Bishop Edgar A. Love, the superintendent of Negro Work in the Board of Missions and others. It is noteworthy that the Negro Crusade Scholars who benefited from this program have become leaders in the church and beyond as pastors, teachers, missionaries, college presidents, and bishops.

The task of increasing a minority presence in the Division of Foreign Missions overseas staff, especially Negro, has been a formidable one for the Board of Missions. Beginning in the late 1950s, aroused missionaries regularly called attention to the scandalous scarcity of Negro (and other racial minority) missionaries, board decision makers, and executive staff members. These allegations were substantially correct. The race and gender profile of the Division of Foreign Missions in the 1940s was almost totally white and male dominated, making a contradictory, if not negative, witness about Methodism's racial stance. The few Negro missionaries that had served and were then serving through the division were deployed in Africa, chiefly in Liberia.

The earliest response to this status quo racial situation in the mission field was a series of seminars concluding with a conference, "Racism and World Order," initiated by the then recently appointed Ralph E. Diffendorfer (1879–1951), executive secretary of the Division of Foreign Missions. The report candidly stated the existence of racism across the world and the urgent necessity for the Methodist Church to deal with it.[18]

Diffendorfer in 1946 made a second effort to confront the situation indicated by the 1944 Conference in a plea to "go beyond the sending of Negro missionaries only to Africa to serve among Negro peoples."[19] Beginning in 1947, the Division of Foreign Missions staff in cooperation with the news magazine of the Central Jurisdiction, the *Central Christian Advocate,* editorialized on and featured the need for Negro youth to commit themselves to missionary careers, citing specific openings in African and Asian countries.[20] In 1948 special three-year programs were developed to attract youth, including minorities, to consider missionary careers overseas. At about this same time (1947), the Women's Division of Christian Service national seminar meeting at DePauw University urged their division to "lead out in race relations by recruiting, training and employment of more colored personnel in its staff and for service in its institutions at home and abroad without discrimination."[21]

In connection with this fairly extensive effort of the church to recruit Negroes for careers in mission, it is important to note some of the reasons Negro youth gave for not choosing such careers. Allen M. Mayes, then a Negro pastor in Texas and an elected member of the Board of Missions (1960–1964), summarizes this thinking in the Williams Report of 1978. Sensing frustration on the part of missionary recruiters, he explained that several things were restraining factors for Negro youth in reference to missionary careers: family responsibilities disallowing separation for long periods of time, a feeling of obligation to assist younger family members to obtain additional education, and the need to maximize the opportunities that college and graduate professional training can command in the Annual Conferences in the United States.

Negro Missionary Deployment

From Unification to Merger, a total of about thirty Negro missionaries served the church through the Division of Foreign Missions. They were in twelve countries on three continents. In Africa they were in Algeria, Angola, Congo, Belgian Congo, and Liberia. They could also be found in China (until 1949), India, Malaysia, Pakistan, and Sarawak. While modest, this record suggests an improvement on the church's previous situation.

Elected Negro members of the Division of Foreign Missions from 1940 to 1968 were Bishop Lorenzo H. King; Julius S. Scott, Sr.; James L. Farmer, Jr. (Youth); and Perry W. Howard.

Joint Committee on Missionary Personnel

Prior to 1964, the Joint Committee on Missionary Personnel (JCMP) had not been chaired by a Negro. Given the intensive effort that the church was then making to recruit Negro missionary personnel, the JCMP requested the assignment of Bishop Charles F. Golden to the committee. Once assigned, he was elected to chair it. In terms of staff, Negroes first held interim or acting minor staff positions in the World Division in the early 1960s. The first permanent executive staff persons were Rose M. Catchings (1966), Women's Division appointment as functional secretary, Ministry to Women; and Grant S. Shockley (1966), World Division, functional secretary for Christian Education. In 1967 Isaac H. Bivens became the first black staff member of the Missionary Personnel unit with the title associate secretary.

Division of Home Missions and Church Extension

The postwar environment in which the new Division of Home Missions and Church Extension would carry on its tasks of mission with and among Negroes in the 1940s through the 1960s would be crisis oriented. Negro communities in the cities, towns, and rural areas were to experience a second world war, with all of its dislocations. There would be a dramatic increase in the number and types of social problems incident to rural–urban–suburban migration. Discrimination and overt racism would escalate as Negroes sought legal justice and wider opportunities in housing, education, and employment. Before this period ends in the 1960s there would be an epochal and eruptive Negro civil rights movement that would climax in Black Revolution. Negro Methodist churches, together with all Negro churches, would be confronted with the responsibility to minister in such crises, including the problem of dealing with a constitutionally segregated Central Jurisdiction comprising almost three quarters of a million Negro members distributed over the entire nation.

Migration

Historically, the urbanization of black people has been the result of "push and pull" forces in the quest for a more adequate living situation and advancement opportunities. This movement may be traced in three successive periods. The first large-scale migration of blacks from the South began before World War I. It brought southern blacks to eastern, midwestern, and West Coast cities in large numbers. After World War I even larger numbers of black people found their way to the metropolitan centers. The Great Depression somewhat restrained further major black population increases in the cities. With the advent of World War II industrial job opportunities, black people were again attracted to the cities. This time they came in even larger numbers, again converging on the large urban centers of the North, Midwest, and West. At mid-century a demographic revolution was in progress. For the first time in American population history, the majority of the black people in the nation were city dwellers. Equally significant was the fact that the cities to which blacks had come were rapidly becoming non-white. This new profile, in the ensuing decades, was to become the source of another of the nation's and church's problems, inclusiveness. Further, it was to have far-reaching implications for employment practices, housing patterns, school populations, and church congregations.[22]

Urbanization made a significant two-way impact during the 1940s to 1960s. It affected the rural areas and churches from which the migrants had come, and it contributed to the growth of black suburbia, which would become the new location of some of the largest black churches in the country.

Harry V. Richardson, in the landmark study of the black rural church, *Dark Glory,* indicates several results of the migration of blacks from the rural and urban South to the North, Midwest, and West. First, black migrants decreased the population of cohesive southern rural black communities. Second, black landowners who left further decreased the number of a valuable but vanishing group. Third, black migrants decreased the membership of the southern churches left behind and the financial support they sorely needed. Fourth, in some communities if a number of family groups migrated, the church so affected was often forced to close.[23]

Black suburbia, as enclaves of housing for black domestic workers, had existed in the North and Midwest at least since the rise of white suburbia in the early 1920s. After World War II and into the 1950s and 1960s, middle-income black people sought occupancy and home ownership in suburbia, especially following the easing of discriminatory practices to keep them out and the availability of credit and mortgages.

The Response to Negro Migration from the South

With the foregoing social data in mind, we turn to a brief description of the program that the Division of Home Missions and Church Extension designed to meet the challenges and opportunities posed by this migration. Under the direction of the staff of the Section on Church Extension of the Board of Missions, technical assistance and guidance was made available to hundreds of black churches to meet such needs as church building repair, renovation, reconstruction, and new building. Complementary services were also offered in the area of insurance programs, loan application, architectural planning, fund raising, debt financing, and mortgaging. John T. Fletcher (1872–1956) was the first black staff executive in this office (1940–1945). He was succeeded in this position by his nephew, Dennis R. Fletcher, who served until 1974, the year of his retirement.

Several programs were initiated in the Section on Home Missions of the Board of Missions through the Department of Negro Work between 1940 and 1968 to meet the needs of rural and urban churches and pastors. Home Missions missionaries served in these programs between 1940 and 1968: Sallie A. Crenshaw, founder of Good Shepherd Fold, and June Carol McIntosh-Porter. It will be mentioned later that other field staff for this work were essentially provided by the Women's Division.

On John's Island, off the South Carolina coast, a pastor was supported to minister among a severely disadvantaged black community in an isolated location. Home living skills, community organization, church development, and leadership training models were shared with them in a manner that taught them to indigenize and continue this work.

In St. Mary's County Larger Parish in Maryland, the larger parish idea was instituted for the first time in the Central Jurisdiction. This demonstration project, involving seven churches in St. Mary's County, had as its objective to show what could be done if small rural churches had even moderately trained leadership and fairly adequate church buildings. As a consequence of observing this "model," other Conferences organized similar projects.

Edsel A. Ammons, later (1976) to become a bishop, was supported in an experimental urban ministry in Rockford, Illinois, where he helped the churches of that city to understand the nature and purpose of mission in disadvantaged communities.

In the mid-1960s the National Division of the Board of Missions initiated and partially financed the Metropolitan Ecumenical Urban Services Training (MUST) program. At that time it was an innovative approach to the mission of urban churches in the city, taking the church to city streets, apartments, businesses, and other centers of secular life. This first major cooperative venture in urban mission challenged the churches to work together on those projects that can best be done ecumenically. Randolph W. Nugent, later to become head of the Board of Global Ministries, served as the first program director of MUST.

Nineteen community centers and six homes (for children, young women, and older adults) were operated in the Central Jurisdiction. Many of these institutions were cooperatively administered and financed with the Women's Division. Their general objective was to carry the redemptive message of the churches to people in their communities through meeting at least some of their recreational, educational, and social needs. These programs did much to assist and stabilize urban migrants, students, and working parents in the 1940s and 1950s, as they struggled to survive in the difficult and often hostile environment of the metropolis.

Two training events sponsored by the Department of Negro Work in cooperation with other church agencies deserve particular mention. The annual Schools of Practical Methods, often held on the campuses of black colleges, with their offering of courses designated to meet the needs of the community, were of inestimable value to rural pastors with limited educational backgrounds, as well as to those who needed refresher work. The other outstanding training events in the missions area were the quadrennial Institutes for City Pastors and Workers. These institutes were planned to introduce urban pastors to practical ways and means of dealing with problems and opportunities for mission in their churches.

Gulfside Assembly in Waveland, Mississippi, founded by Bishop Robert E. Jones, was a unique Negro resource in the church; "it was the only institution in United Methodism founded by Negroes, supported mostly by Negroes and developed by Negroes."[24] A gathering center for Negro Methodists for generations and the burial place of Bishop Jones, Gulfside still represents a special place for women, men, and youth to gather for fellowship, information, and sharing.

A concluding word in this section should be spoken concerning the unique relationship that existed (and still exists) between The Methodist Church and the Christian Methodist Episcopal (CME) Church. The 1939 Plan of Union honored the long-standing and valued relationship that the Methodist Episcopal Church, South, had with the CME Church by assuring that it would continue in the Methodist Church. In response to several requests from the CME Church for financial support for church extension on the West Coast, mission work in Southern Africa, and maintenance funds for religious education, it seems to have been generally agreed that cooperative planning should continue through the Methodist Church with the CME Church, rather than primary or secondary funding of projects or programs. Further, from the minutes of the Joint Commission it appears that an earlier (1947) mentioning of an organic union of the CME Church and the Methodist Church was held in abeyance.

Negro Elected Board Members and Staff

The first elected Negro members to the Division of Home Missions and Church Extension were Bishop Alexander P. Shaw; the Reverend H. W. Bartley, Florida; John O. Patton, Lexington; Mrs. M. W. Clair, Jr., Lexington; Joy L. Mitchell (Youth), Washington, D. C.; and G. D. Rawlings, Washington, D. C.

Church Extension Negro staff have been referred to earlier. It is now necessary to identify Negro staff responsible for Home Missions programs from 1940–1968. From 1940–1952, practically all of the work in the area of Home Missions was accomplished through the Department of Negro Work, initially established by W. A. C. Hughes (1877–1940). When Hughes was elected to the episcopacy in 1940, Edgar A. Love (1891–1974) succeeded him. Love was elected to the bishopric in 1952. Charles F. Golden (1912–1984), who had been Love's assistant and director of Field Service in the Department, became an associate secretary in the National Division. The Department of Negro Work was closed in 1952 "since Negroes no longer wished to be designated as a group requiring special ministry," and its former programs included in the several departments of the division.[25] Golden became a director in the Division of National Missions in 1956. He was elected to the episcopacy from that position in 1960. Golden's successor in the national division in 1960 was John H. Graham. In 1967 Negail R. Riley (1930–1987) came to the National Division to fill a field staff position before becoming executive secretary for Urban Ministries in 1968.

The Women's Division of Christian Service

The Women's Division of Christian Service is the parent national organization of all local, district, Conference, and jurisdictional units of

United Methodist Women's work. The division is a unit of the Board of Global Ministries, where it relates to other national and world program divisions and departments.

When the Women's Division of Christian Service was authorized by the Uniting Conference in Kansas City, Missouri, in 1939, it became the first and largest national organization of Protestant women in the United States. In preparation for this event, The Methodist Church united the six previously existing missionary and "church aid" organizations of the three uniting denominations into a single new creation, the Women's Division of Christian Service.[26] This organization, built around the concept of church as mission and women as full participants in that mission under their own governance, went far beyond the then prevailing understanding of home missions, foreign missions, and "ladies aid." It also saw as integral to its mission assisting women to understand their Christian faith in holistic and global terms and sharing that expanded concept with all women (and others) everywhere, whatever their status or condition. Second, they devised a strategy to carry out this mission on three levels of church organization: local, national, and global. Additionally, they pledged to support that mission through prayer, service, and giving beyond their local church obligations. Third, the women developed a positive, constructive political style of relating organizationally in a male-centered and male-dominated denomination that resulted in equality of status, respect for their political competence and management skills, and recognition of their earned right to power. Fourth, from the outset, the Women's Division of Christian Service, its local units (known from 1940–1968 as Women's Society of Christian Service), and its complementary auxiliary, the Wesleyan Service Guild, challenged the basic assumptions of any racial separatism that might have been implicit or imposed by the jurisdictional structure. They derived their own operational style, one that was without inseparable barriers and that encouraged uniting Methodist women of varied racial backgrounds around the larger mission of the church and the essential purpose of the organization. They covenanted to do this, and when necessary they honored that covenant in visible and tangible acts of solidarity.

As members of this same fellowship and servants of this same mission, the women of the Central Jurisdiction together with all Methodist women anticipated—though with some apprehension—the first quadrennium of the Methodist Church.

Central Jurisdiction of the Women's Division of Christian Service

Through the Women's Society of Christian Service, black Methodist women were an integral part of the origin, formation, growth, and development of the Women's Division of Christian Service, just as they were a part of the earliest beginnings of Methodism in America. The following highlights of the Women's Society of Christian Service in the Central

Jurisdiction years hopefully offers a faithful cross-sectional view of the role and contribution of black Methodist women from 1940–1968.

The organizing period for the Central Jurisdiction Women's Society of Christian Service preceded the ratification of the Plan of Union. In 1938 Bishop Robert E. Jones convened a provisional committee to prepare for the transition to the new organization. Members of that early committee were Elizabeth Jones (Mrs. R. E. Jones, chair), Hattie H. Hargis (Mrs. D. H. Hargis), and Irma Green (later Mrs. L. A. Jackson). Susie Jones (Mrs. David D. Jones) was a consultant. Mission leaders from the nineteen black Annual Conferences met in 1939 to plan for Annual Conference orientation sessions. Concurrent with the first meeting of the Central Jurisdictional Conference in St. Louis, Missouri (June 1940), the Provisional Committee met with delegates from each of the Annual Conferences to perfect a provisional organization. The charter meeting was held on December 9, 1940, in historic Calvary Church, Cincinnati, Ohio. Margaret Davis Bowen (Mrs. J. W. E. Bowen, Jr.) was elected president. One of the featured speakers for the occasion was Mary McLeod Bethune.[27]

This fledgling organization made impressive progress over the next twenty-eight years. The number of societies in local churches grew from about 1,500 in the 1940s to more than 2,000 in the 1960s. Membership growth reflected a similar increase, rising from about 30,000 to a one-time high of more than 50,000 (1956), while averaging 45,000 during 1940–1968.[28] If it is considered that there were approximately 3,000 local churches in the Central Jurisdiction at this time, this means that the society organized about two thirds of the jurisdiction. This was a remarkable job of administration.

The main and memorable strength of the Woman's Society of Christian Service was the programmatic contribution it made to the life of the church and particularly to the Central Jurisdiction. Carrying out its purpose with black women in the context of the black church and the black community, its objectives became to "(1) unite all women of the Church in Christian living and service; (2) help develop and support Christian work among women and children around the world; (3) develop the spiritual life; (4) study the needs of the world; (5) take part in . . . service activities as will strengthen the local church, improve civic, community and world conditions."[29] In the remainder of this section of the chapter, a brief summary of the involvement of the Central Jurisdiction women in implementing the objectives mentioned above will be made in the three program categories of the organization: home fields, foreign fields, and Christian social relations and local church activity.

Home Fields

The Women's Division of Christian Service supported work in four areas of home missions between 1940 and 1968: community centers, schools and colleges, and homes and hospitals.

1. Nineteen community centers, sometimes housed in churches, provided typical programs of child day care, youth activities, home/school community liaison assistance, and youth employment to children and youth in black communities.
2. Until the 1960s the division gave moderately strong financial support to Bennett College and Clark College through their home economics programs. Since the 1960s their funds have been directed to special projects at these schools.
3. Children's homes such as Sager-Brown, Friendship Homes for young black business women living in large cities, dormitories on black college campuses, and homes for the elderly continued to serve during this period despite severely limited budgets.
4. Brewster Hospital in Jacksonville, Florida, Flint-Goodridge Hospital in New Orleans, and Hubbard Hospital in Nashville served with distinction as Methodist institutions until closed or merged with other units.

The following are those who served as deaconesses and home missionaries under the Women's Division of Christian Service during the Central Jurisdiction years. They were located in churches, community centers, schools, children's homes, college campuses, and hospitals in fourteen states: Olive Alston (deaconess) (1963–1975); Josephine Beckwith (1942–1973); Daisy M. Cabean (deaconess) (1965–1973); Flora Clipper (deaconess) (1952–present); Rosie Ann Cobb (deaconess) (1935–1971); Lelia M. Robinson Cox (deaconess) (1954–1966); DeLaris Johnson (deaconess) (1955–1960); Isabella R. Jones (1906–1949); Phoebe Reynolds (deaconess) (1956–1961 and 1963–1969); Edna Mae Ridley (deaconess) (1964); Willa Stewart (deaconess) (1924–1951); Marian Wooten (deaconess) (1962–1972).[30]

Foreign Fields
The Women's Division of Christian Service sponsored ten missionaries in Africa, Asia, and South America between 1940 and 1968. Three of those were full term and seven were special term. Full-termers were Ellen Barnette, India (1950–1953) and West Pakistan (1958–1964); Pearl Bellinger, India (1950–1953 and 1956–1957); and Janet Evans, Lima, Peru (1954–1968). Special-termers were Burnetta Armstrong, Liberia (1957–1964); Charlotte Brown, Liberia (dates of service undetermined); Barbara Patterson, Liberia (1956–1958); June G. Pembroke, Zaire (1957–1960); Rose Thomas, Angola, (1957–1961); Alberteen Ware, Angola (1956–1960); and Doris J. Wilson, Malaysia (1958–1961).[31]

Christian Social Relations/Local Church Activities
Christian Social Relations and Local Church Activities (CSR/LCA), the third department of work in the Women's Society of Christian Service, won a

place for itself in the annals of Christian social action of the Methodist Church in the same years embraced by the Central Jurisdiction. During these years the entire organization waged a full-scale assault against racism, sexism, injustice, and war. Much of the success of this effort was due to the outstanding leadership of a committed and fearless Christian, Thelma Stevens; much credit is also due to the leadership that she inspired, especially among the Women's Society leadership in the Central Jurisdiction. Taking seriously their slogan born in the 1940s, "All action is local," Women's Society for Christian Service units in the Central Jurisdiction joined with other kindred spirits in their organization, denomination, and communities to work on a number of projects.[32] Together, both attitudinal and behavioral changes were accomplished:

1. Attitudinal
   - Black women in the Women's Society came to a new sense of personal and racial identity, causing them to refuse "to be invisible in a multiracial society."[33]
   - Black women in the Women's Society took seriously their own guidelines: "to be alert to social issues and needs in the changing times; to attempt to be a voice within the church to bring facts, understanding and clear challenge to action."[34]
   - Black women in the Women's Society became proactive, refusing any longer to react to policies and programs without their input and shaping resources and materials to meet the needs of their black constituencies as much as possible.

2. Behavioral
   - In the early 1940s black and white women urged the division and the church to support antilynching legislation.
   - On several occasions in the 1940s and 1950s, black women who had experienced discrimination at division meeting sites protested until changes were made rather than leave the site.
   - Working within the division for change, blacks and whites urged more than token representation in the missionary community, on board committees and division committees, and in staff positions.
   - In 1943 black and white women successfully urged the Board of Missions to assign staff people to work with women in localities having difficult problems of adjustment in churches and communities.
   - Black and white Women's Division members urged and obtained "a series of regional workshops on the family and [war] demobilization."[35]
   - In the middle and late 1940s the division, upon protests from black members, boycotted eating places that segregated black people at meeting sites of their national seminars.

- The division pioneered in the use of group dynamics in conducting human relations workshops at annual meetings. Out of such experiences came the division-sponsored *State Laws on Race and Color* (1951).
- At the urging of black and white members, the division eventually presented the General Conference with its landmark document, "Charter of Racial Policies" (1952).
- Division schools of missions became nationally outstanding forums on Christian social action almost from their inception.
- The Women's Division led the denomination in affirming the epochal decision rendered by the United States Supreme Court outlawing segregation in the nation's public schools.
- Resourced, inspired, and encouraged by its Section of Christian Social Relations and Local Church Activity, thousands of black and white women supported and participated in any number of phases of the civil rights movement of the 1960s. In so doing, endorsing the nonviolent approach of Martin Luther King, Jr. and specifically protesting the expulsion of James Lawson from the Vanderbilt School of Religion because of his civil rights participation.
- Finally, the Department of Christian Social Relations and Local Church Activities was instrumental in raising bond money for youth arrested in the Jackson Street Church incident (1961) in Mississippi, in supporting the 1963 March on Washington, and in requesting Congress to pass the Voting Rights Act of 1965.[36]

Women's Division Elected Members and Officers, 1940–1968

The first black women elected to represent the Woman's Society of the Central Jurisdiction to the Women's Division and the Board of Missions were Mrs. Ethel Clair, Kentucky; Mrs. Hattie R. Hargis, Delaware; Mrs. Irma G. Jackson, Louisiana; and Mrs. Susie Jones, North Carolina. First advisory members were Mrs. Pimella King, Mrs. Mayme Gordon, Mrs. Thelma McCallum, and Mrs. Claude A. Wade. Subsequently elected to division membership in various categories before 1968 were Mrs. Frances Badgett, Mrs. Margaret D. Bowen, Mrs. Jewel Caldwell, Mrs. Ruth Carter, Mrs. Marie Copher, Mrs. Mary Drake, Mrs. L. B. Felder, Mrs. Anita Fields, Mrs. S. L. Griffin, Miss Doris Handy, Mrs. Cleo Henry, Mrs. J. W. Jewett, Mrs. R. E. Jones, Mrs. Alice McLeod, Mrs. Gertrude Rivers, Mrs. Emma W. Strother, Mrs. Fannie Turner, and Mrs. Lucille Wilkins.

Black women elected to offices in the Women's Division (1940–1968) were Mrs. Lucile Wilkins, recording secretary; Mrs. Thelma McCallum, vice president (1960–1964); and Miss Doris M. Handy, vice president (1964–1968). Committee chairpersons during that same period were Mrs. Mamye Gordon, Missionary Personnel (1948–1952); Mrs. Gertrude Rivers, Student Work (1956–1960); Mrs. Thelma McCallum, Library Services

(1956–1960); and Mrs. Emma W. Strother, Missionary Education for Children (1960–1964). Presidents of the Central Jurisdiction Woman's Society during 1940–1968 were Mrs. Margaret D. Bowen (1940–1948); Mrs. Ruth Carter (1948–1956); Mrs. Anita Fields (1956–1964); and Mrs. Mary Drake (1964–1968).[37]

Women's Division Black Staff, 1940–1968

During the Central Jurisdiction years the Women's Division of Christian Service staff related to the Central Jurisdiction through a field work model—for example, employing a professional church worker "for field assistance in promoting and interpreting the purpose and program of the WSCS."[38] Four black professional persons were employed by the division to do this. From 1941 to 1943 Lillian Warrick (later Lillian W. Pope) held this position. She visited the black conferences and cultivated good will for the Women's Society, interpreting its program and helping to train local leaders. Warrick was followed by Vivienne Newton (Gray) who had come to the staff from the Home Missions Council of North America. Theressa Hoover, who would later (1968) hold the highest executive post in the division, followed Vivienne Gray, who resigned her position with the division to accept a missionary post in Liberia with her new husband-missionary, Ulysses Gray. Dorothy Barnette followed Theressa Hoover, remaining in the position until 1964.

Other persons served in professional staff capacities in the Women's Division of Christian Service. (Incidentally, they were all in the Christian Social Relations Section.) Ethel Watkins joined the staff and remained until 1957. In 1958 Theressa Hoover began a seven-year tenure in the Section on Christian Social Relations and Local Church Activities, which would climax with her election as assistant general secretary for Program and Education for Mission (1965). This advancement made her, at that time, the highest black executive administrator in The Methodist Church.

CHRISTIAN EDUCATION AND
THE METHODIST YOUTH FELLOWSHIP

When the Committee on Education of the First Central Jurisdictional Conference met in St. Louis, Missouri, in June 1940, two formidable tasks awaited it: (1) the development of an educational program within the guidelines of the newly created Board of Education and (2) the melding of this first goal with the problems and opportunities of the Central Jurisdiction. The size and critical importance of this task can be assessed by looking at a composite profile of the educational tasks confronting the Conferences:

- 150,000 church school students to be taught
- 20,000 church school teachers and leaders to be trained

- 50,000 youth to be united to Christ's church as full members (i.e., confirmed)
- 10,000 college (and other) students to be guided in Christian social living and career choices
- 2,000 pastors to be imbued with a more viable vision of the church's ministry through education

This section of the chapter will trace some of the developments that took place in the Central Jurisdiction to exploit these opportunities, as well as the problems mentioned in the above profile.

Church Schools

Attentive to the principle that the church school "has a total program and equipment that eventuates in the development of Christian knowledge, attitudes, appreciations and behavior which go to make up Christian character and Christian society,"[39] Christian education leaders in the 1940–1944 quadrennium set several objectives. A primary one was the election of an executive secretary whose duty it was "to organize and promote Christian education in our local churches."[40] A secondary objective was to promote financial assistance to black Annual Conferences to help defray the cost of employing age-level workers and/or Annual Conference executive secretaries of education. In 1944 the Education Committee of the Central Jurisdictional Conference observed with great concern a decline in church school enrollment, causing it to comment, "This ebbing tide of Religious Education . . . must be turned."[41] Further, the committee recommended "a strong department of Christian Education on each [black] college campus for training leadership in the local church."[42] At this same Conference the Editorial Division of the General Board of Education was commended for their use of Negro writers and pictures. Jurisdiction churches were also encouraged to use Methodist church school literature. The 1948 Jurisdictional Conference indicated church school enrollment increases in a few Conferences but pointed to weaknesses in the low level of adult involvement in teaching support. Pursuing an Editorial Division concern, the lack of any black staff writers, it was recommended to that division that it explore the issue as promptly as possible. The 1952 Jurisdictional Conference broke new ground in Christian education thinking. For the first time it related the educational process to the process of forming disciples. A notable statement on this issue was "A part of the training program should have for its purpose the training of all members in . . . churchmanship."[43] Other new ground had also been broken in the holding of a Family Life Conference in Chicago in 1951. The Central Jurisdiction was well represented there and left the meeting resolved to activate family life programs.

The Jurisdictional Conference of 1960 was memorable for Christian educators and evangelists. It confronted its more than three thousand churches with the fact that "we are reaching only half of our membership through our training agencies, which includes the Church School."[44] The episcopal address went on to say, "We need to strengthen and extend the function of the Conference Boards of Education in these seventeen conferences so that bolder and more realistic approaches may be made to these needs."[45] The last "full-strength" Central Jurisdictional Conference was held in 1964. In relation to Christian education, it urged the churches to exercise wisdom and care in recruiting the teaching staff of the church, the key to greater faithfulness and more effective service.

Methodist Youth Fellowship

A relatively brief statement can be made about work with youth in the Central Jurisdiction. This is not because of its nonimportance. Practically every message of the College of Bishops since 1940 exhorted the churches to "protect and enfold" them. Unfortunately, however, scant hard data exists about what they were actually doing in the local churches. Numbering about fifty thousand, distributed across more than three thousand churches in the jurisdiction, their attendance between 1940 and 1968 seems to have been only 50 percent of their membership. The size of their groups was small, and generally they were identical with the Sunday morning church school youth class. They were usually represented, as the *Discipline* required, at all levels of the denomination. Several gave outstanding leadership. (It is highly interesting to note that the youth group in the church has consistently given the jurisdiction a good percentage of its ministers.)

Leadership Education

Leadership education in the Central Jurisdiction was largely associated with the name of Timothy B. Echols (b. 1894) of the West Texas Conference. More than any other single person, he was responsible for developing the first leadership education program in the jurisdiction. Echols felt the acute need for more expertly trained professional leaders and their accreditation by the General Board of Education. As director of religious education in the New Orleans area, he developed and demonstrated a highly effective model of leadership education that interested the Leadership Department of the Board of Education. The plan was simple and educationally sound. Annually, a selected group of ministers and laypersons were to be invited to participate in an intensive week-long leadership education event. This Leadership Training School, which would rotate in the episcopal areas of the jurisdiction during the quadrennium, had two objectives: the preparation of (1) potential Conference executive secretaries of Christian education and (2) age-level workers for churches, districts, or the Annual Conference. The General Board of

Education Leadership Department provided the teaching faculty from their staff. The bishop of the area and the district superintendents served as consultants and resource persons as needed. The rotating host Annual Conference was responsible for the meals and lodging of the group.

The remarkable result of this project was the increase in the number of Conference executive secretaries from three in 1944 to twelve in 1948.[46] Additionally, a number of part-time and many volunteer certified workers in Christian Education were made available to the Conferences of the jurisdiction.

SCHOOLS, COLLEGES, AND STUDENT WORK

The profile of higher education in the Central Jurisdiction at its inception (1940) displayed eight senior colleges, two junior colleges, five secondary schools, three professional schools, around five hundred faculty members, and around five thousand students. Just prior to the dissolution of the Central Jurisdiction in 1966, there were nine senior colleges, one junior college (Morristown), one medical school (Meharry), one theological school (Gammon), around seven hundred faculty members, and more than eight thousand students.[47] The situations in which these institutions had to work to achieve their goals of Christian higher education in this period had grown out of three major contexts: (1) World War II, (2) United States Supreme Court desegregation decisions, and (3) affirmative action enforcement efforts. The student-campus situation had another background with which to cope, the free speech movement and the civil rights movement. Several things are to be learned by taking a closer look at changes in institutions between 1940 and 1968 as they struggled for survival and dealt with fermenting feelings that would erupt in the 1970s.

The mobilization of World War II led to decreasing enrollments, resulting in fewer students and faculty, especially male. More serious, however, was the decline in financial support for black colleges generally and black colleges related to The Methodist Church in particular.[48] The Central Jurisdiction made several constructive responses to this situation. In anticipation of the war and its probable impact, it determined at its first session in 1940 that "great sacrifice must be made in our giving for the religious nurture of our children and youth."[49] The Jurisdictional Conference went on to say, "Such a program is impossible without an adequate field staff."[50] In keeping with this, the Committee on Education requested the General Board of Education "to elect from the Central Jurisdiction an executive secretary of Education for these schools."[51] The request of the committee was approved by the General Board of Education, and in 1941 a veteran educator and school administrator, Matthew S. Davage, was elected associate secretary of the board. One of his first efforts was the revitalization of the Race Relations Day offering for black schools and colleges. Under his effective leadership that offering was increased from about $25,000 in the 1940s to almost $250,000 at the time of his retirement in 1952.[52] Additionally, each institution was alerted to review and strengthen its program in preparation for review and fund solicitation.

The period following World War II was more positive for black colleges. Returning veterans increased enrollments via government aid. A postwar economic boom enabled still other black youth to attend college. Younger black faculty, especially veterans, were able to complete graduate studies and degrees, often at government expense. A second positive aspect of the postwar period was the continuing desegregation of public higher education. This dynamic provided both black students and faculty with wider access to educational opportunities in the South and other regions. The Methodist Church and its black colleges responded to these opportunities and challenges by seeking to have all of their institutions regionally accredited as well as accredited by the University Senate of the church. (The University Senate was established by the General Conference of 1892. At that time its main functions were examination, standardization, and accreditation. Recently, its role has somewhat changed. While continuing to classify and list approved Methodist schools, it also offers assistance in institutional management and church relations. W. H. Crogman was the first black minister of this body.)

As soon as the southern Association of Colleges and Schools declared an open membership policy for black members (1957), two Methodist schools applied and were admitted—Bennett College and Clark College. James P. Brawley reports that "by 1961 all but one held membership in the Southern Association of Colleges and Schools and in the North Central Association. By 1974 all United Methodist black colleges were fully accredited."[53] It should be noted here that Philander Smith College had been a full member of the North Central Association since 1949. In 1948 Board of Missions executive Edgar A. Love was instrumental in having the Crusade Scholarship Program for overseas students to study in the United States extended to "minority and bilingual groups in the United States."[54] Under the dynamic leadership of James S. Thomas, Davage's successor, who would be elevated to the episcopacy, the church made a third response to the precarious plight of the black colleges. Race Relations Day offerings and goals were increased, bringing a half million dollars from that source by 1964. A gigantic funds campaign was initiated in 1960, which provided more than $2 million to the colleges for capital needs.[55]

The final developmental period of the black colleges in the Central Jurisdiction era has been referred to by Brawley in his *Two Centuries of Methodist Concern* as the "Black Student Revolution" period. Several forces in this period had a profound impact on all black colleges, including Methodist ones. Politically sensitized students demanded a larger voice in the management of college affairs. The black consciousness movement influenced curricular and teaching changes. The courts desegregated the last vestiges of legal segregation across the nation. The Higher Education Act (HEA) of 1965, with its massive program of development and student financial aid plans, made "colleges of choice" viable options for many heretofore excluded. Brawley correctly indicates that this totally new situation had serious implications for the colleges of The Methodist Church in three areas: competition for students, competition for faculty, and competition for finances.[56] An even more difficult question arose in this period, the answer to which was to be far more complex than it first appeared—namely, given access to all of the nation's colleges and financial aid to attend them, is there a reason to continue black colleges, especially in The Methodist Church? This question will be partially answered in chapter 6, which will discuss the effect of merger (or its noneffect) on denominational structural desegregation and merger.

Student Religious Work

The black senior colleges of the Methodist Church, in cooperation with the Division of Educational Institutions of the General Board of Education, sponsored two basic programs to promote the religious and social life of students. Students who wished to participate were provided with programs of "religious life and activities," including Sunday worship opportunities, Sunday school classes, religious emphasis weeks, exchange visits to neighboring colleges, leadership training in worship, and service in the local community. Methodist students on state and independent college and university campuses were provided for through Wesley Foundations, a Methodist presence on or near state and independent institutions, which sought to lead students to Christ, develop support communities for them, and work with them in creating "a new world order." The aim was to accomplish this through public worship opportunities, pastoral work including visitation, counseling, conferences, social recreation, and Christian service.

The chronology of these college programs and Wesley Foundations—which have been such a rich resource in the recruitment of leadership for the ministry, laywork in the church, mission work, and teaching—dates from the early 1920s. Timothy B. Echols (b. 1894) probably organized the first student religious work in the Central Jursidicion in connection with his position as Dean of Men and Director of Religious Activities at Wiley College in 1923. The earliest Wesley Foundation work was organized at Morgan State College (Baltimore, Maryland) in 1939 as Morgan Christian Center under the leadership of Howard L. Cornish (b. 1906). The work at Morgan had been made possible by the residual endowment from the liquidated assets of Morgan College. Following these two establishments, dates, places, and personalities became unclear. During the 1940s and 1950s, departments of

Bible, religion, philosophy, and religious education were activated on the campuses of each of the black Methodist senior colleges. In 1953 J. Otis Irwin was instrumental in establishing the Wesley Foundation at Lincoln University in Jefferson City, Missouri, in cooperation with University Community Chapel. Julius S. Scott organized the Wesley Foundation on the campus of Texas Southern University in Houston, Texas, in 1961 and served as its first director. Between 1940 and 1964 Wesley Foundations or Methodist Student Movement units appeared on the following campuses: Agricultural/Technical University, Greensboro, North Carolina; Bluefield State College, Bluefield, West Virginia; Florida Agricultural and Mechanical College, Tallahassee, Florida; Howard University, Washington, D.C.; Lincoln University, Jefferson City, Missouri; Maryland State College, Princess Anne, Maryland; West Virginia State College, Institute, West Virginia; Delaware State College, Dover, Delaware; Southern University, Baton Rouge, Louisiana; Jackson State University, Jackson, Mississippi; Tenessee State University, Nashville, Tennessee; and Kentucky State University, Frankfort, Kentucky.

The structural organization of the Methodist Church under the jurisdictional plan allowed for equality of representation at all levels of church organization. In reference to the General Board of Education, this meant that its membership consisted of all active bishops serving within the United States, one minister, one layperson, one youth, and additionally one minister and one layperson "for every 300,000 members or major fraction thereof within the jurisdiction."[57] During the years of the Central Jurisdiction, approximately fifty ministers, laypersons, and youth served on this board. In the 1940–1964 period, M. L. Harris; R. M. Williams; T. B. Echols; W. T. Handy, Sr.; W. M. Jenkins; M. J. Jones; W. M. James; G. S. Shockley; and E. A. Smith were ministers who served at least one quadrennial term. Laypersons who served during this period were M. M. Bethune; D. D. Jones; Miss. A. Williams; Mrs. F. G. Johnson; M. W. Boyd; H. L. Dickerson; J. R. Webb, Sr.; J. C. Hardcastle; J. Q. T. King; and Miss E. R. Johnson. Youth members for the period were Marcella C. James; T. P. Grisson, Jr.; Gladys Anderson; and C. Miller. Black bishops during the period were R. E. Jones; L. H. King; A. P. Shaw; W. J. King; R. N. Brooks; J. W. E. Bowen; M. W. Clair; M. L. Harris; N. W. Moore, Jr.; P. A. Taylor; and J. S. Thomas. University Senate members between 1940 and 1964 were S. E. Grannum (1940–1944); J. P. Brawley (1944–1964); and Willa B. Player (1964–1968). Elected executive staff from 1940–1967 in the Division of Educational Institutions were M. S. Davage (1940–1952), J. S. Thomas (1952–1964), and D. W. Wynn. Elected staff in the Division of the Local Church were T. B. Echols;[58] J. A. Greene (1943–1952); E. T. Dixon, Jr. (1952–1965); and W. J. Washington; and in the Editorial Division was James S. Gadsden. (Note: T. B. Echols was elected to the staff of the Division of the Local Church in 1943. He resigned in a policy issue crisis before ever formally taking office.)[59]

CHRISTIAN SOCIAL CONCERNS

Few would argue that a definitive and enduring contribution of Methodism to the early formation and development of religion in America was Wesleyan evangelicalism and the unique way in which it combined piety, evangelism, outreach, and social responsibility. For the followers of John Wesley, "entire sanctification" was the path to holiness, but likewise, "to reform the Continent and spread scriptural holiness over these lands"[60] was also a part of God's design for every Christian. The record of effort and achievement in this area is one of the most arresting chapters of American religious history.

From the beginning an important page of that chapter has been the Methodist witness in Christian interracial concerns. Despite H. Richard Niebuhr's detracting comment that "the socially beneficial results of Methodism were never 'designed,' but they accrued as mere by-products of the movement,"[61] several significant Methodist social involvements in certain periods of the life of the church are worth noting. The Methodist Episcopal Church was among the first national denominations to condemn slavery on moral grounds and to discipline members and ministers engaged in it. Few Christians were more active in the antislavery, abolition, and freedmen's aid movements than persons like Gilbert Haven (1821–1880).[62] While generally supportive of American participation in war efforts, Methodists were basically a "peace" denomination, with sometimes even pacifist leanings. Seldom were Methodists more united than in opposing the liquor traffic and supporting total abstinence. The earliest advocates of the labor movement among national Protestant church groups in the United States were Methodists. Through the *Western Advocate* (1876), Methodists pointed to the moral rather than the military implications of Custer's defeat in his battle against the Sioux Indians. In the twentieth century, individual Methodists and independent Methodist organizations such as the Methodist Federation for Social Welfare, founded in 1907, projected a bold Methodist social action image, although it was unofficial.

Race and Methodist Social Concerns

Easily the most difficult social issue that faced The Methodist Church in the decades following Unification was racism within its own fellowship. The Central Jurisdiction, which racially circumscribed the vast majority of the reunited denomination's almost 400,000 black members, had come to be regarded as an anomaly in the religious community and an embarrassment to the black membership and others who voted against it. The following brief narrative, rehearsing the highlights of that struggle in The Methodist Church (1940–1968), clearly demonstrates two things: the rise of a new, articulate, and militant leadership class of black Methodist ministers and laypersons and the key role of the racial issue in the work of the Board of Social and Economic Relations, later (1960) to become the Board of Christian Social Concerns.

Negro delegates and Annual Conferences voted against the Plan of Union in 1939. They perceived it to be blatantly segregationist. In the first Central Jurisdictional Conference (1940), it was made clear that in accepting the arrangement they were not accepting its widely perceived status of being separate and inferior. Rather, they were saying that black Methodists were placing loyalty to a united church above racial feelings and had faith that the denomination would move as fast as possible toward a nonsegregated fellowship.

At this point there was little to justify their optimism. The Social Creed adopted by the 1908 General Conference primarily spoke to exploitation of immigrants to the cities. Its only reference to race was the broad statement that "God is Father of all peoples and races . . . and all men [*sic*] are brothers."[63] This nebulous statement did not speak to the racism that black people then felt in church and the general society. In other words, separate and "as equal as possible" was the mood and messages of The Methodist Church in the 1940s and well into the 1950s. The 1944 General Conference went further. It repudiated white racial superiority. Its Committee on Race also envisioned the ultimate elimination of racial discrimination and requested the General Conference to appoint a commission "to consider afresh the relation of all races included in The Methodist Church."[64] The 1948 General Conference went even further. It condemned the Central Jurisdiction as a structure that "approves and tends to perpetuate . . . attitudes . . . attendant upon segregation" and renounced it as "evil" and "un-Christian."[65] In terms of action, the commission's recommendation to establish a permanent commission to handle racial, social, economic, and human relations issues was approved. The report of this commission to the 1952 General Conference created the denomination's first Board of Social and Economic Relations.

Beginning in 1952, a number of other positive changes occurred in race relations in the church. Black and white racial equality leaders and advocates were instrumental in initiating educational programs to combat racism and promote racial inclusiveness. The General Conference authorized a procedure for simplifying for black churches the process of voluntarily transferring from the Central Jurisdiction to another jurisdiction. It recommended full participation of all races in church activity, and equality of treatment for all races at national, regional, and other church meetings and the implementation of inclusive personnel and program policies in church institutions: schools, colleges, homes, and community centers.

A critical turning point in the thrust to desegregate The Methodist Church came in 1954 with the United States Supreme Court decision (*Brown* vs. *Topeka Board of Education*). This decision outlawing racial segregation in the nation's schools and the vigorous statements in support of it from the Council of Bishops (November 1954) and the Board of Social and Economic Relations (January 1955) refocused the church's strategy for desegregating the Central Jurisdiction from one of merely eliminating discrimination to one of eradicating the jurisdiction. As a consequence of this new approach, the first step to actually desegregate the jurisdictional system was taken at the 1956 General Conference. Amendment IX, providing a process whereby churches and Annual Conferences could transfer across jurisdictional lines, was voted. While this amendment technically was limited to transfers into a jurisdiction rather than the automatic abolition of segregated units within the jurisdiction to which the transfer would be made, it placed the issue in a larger context and raised the other critical issue of the timing of transfers. This would be the storm center of conflict for the next two quadrennia.

As the church moved toward the 1960 General Conference, it faced four major problems: (1) apprehension that the Commission on Interjurisdictional Relations would not go beyond a voluntaristic approach in eliminating the Central Jurisdiction, (2) concern that the residual Central Jurisdiction would be weakened due to attrition, (3) concern that "simple" transfers into white enclaves would promote isolation rather than inclusiveness, and (4) fear of the lack of time to adequately prepare host and/or "guest" Conferences for the major changes involved. When the 1960 General Conference took no significant action regarding the Central Jurisdiction beyond reaffirming the Amendment IX process, Central Jurisdiction leaders prepared and took their own corrective action. At their 1960 meeting (July 13–17) in Cleveland, Ohio, the Central Jurisdictional Conference created a Special Committee to Study Problems in Relation to the Status of the Central Jurisdiction. This highly select group, which came to be known as the Committee of Five, was comprised of James S. Thomas (later elected to the episcopacy), associate director, Division of Higher Education; Richard C. Erwin, prominent attorney-at-law; John H. Graham, director, Special Fields, National Division; John J. Hicks, pastor, Union Memorial Church, St. Louis; and W. Astor Kirk, director, Public Affairs, Board of Christian Social Concerns. Representing the entire Central Jurisdiction, the Committee of Five, in cooperation with the Commission on Interjurisdictional Relations and the Board of Christian Social Concerns, exhaustively analyzed and researched the Central Jurisdiction desegregation situation in a historic meeting at Cincinnati, Ohio (March 1962). Its findings, together with certain data from Interracial Leadership Conferences held across the church (1955–1959) and from the Second Conference on Human Relations (Chicago, August 30, 1963), definitively influenced the future course of desegregation in the denomination; the resulting report insisted on the following: (1) the realignment of Conferences to place all Central Jurisdiction Conferences in a regional jurisdiction, (2) the simultaneous transfer of the black Annual Conferences, (3) the immediate merger of the transferring Conferences, and (4) the merger of local churches. As expected, the Commission on Interjurisdictional Relations report was at variance with the Committee of Five report. While recommending the abolition of the Central Jurisdiction, they proposed that this be done voluntarily under Amendment IX, with no specific target date. Sensing this effort toward a continued voluntarism and gradualism, the Central Jurisdiction leadership, led by the Committee of Five, proposed the Kirk Amendment, which would eliminate the Central Jurisdiction and all references to it in the pending Plan of Union of The Methodist Church and the Evangelical United Brethren Church. The General Conference approved the Kirk Amendment, but it did not authorize the simultaneous transfer and immediate merger strategy recommended by the Committee of Five. Basically, they affirmed the report of the Interjurisdictional Relations Commission, urging the jurisdictions and Conferences to pursue the dissolution of the then remaining Central Jurisdiction as soon as possible. While this decisive and historic legislation dissolved the Central Jurisdiction, it left the important matter of the integration of the remaining segregated Conferences unresolved.

The leadership of the Central Jurisdiction responded to this turn of events with grave concern and apprehension. At the ensuing meeting of the Central Jurisdiction at Bethune-Cookman College, Daytona Beach, Florida (June 17–21, 1964), firm criteria were set for transferring the remaining black Annual Conferences into their regional jurisdictions. These included an integration plan with a target date for Annual Conference integration. This two-step plan of concurrent transfer and merger was opposed by the Southeastern Jurisdiction. Their approach was a "one-step-at-a-time" plan of transfer and then voluntary merger "when such merger is mutually agreeable."[66]

Still in keeping with the denomination's nonracial representation policy with reference to boards and agencies, more than two dozen Negro Methodists held membership on the Board of Christian Social Concerns between 1940 and 1968: Bishop Robert E. Jones, Edgar A. Love (later a bishop), Mrs. P. D. Johnson, and Francis N. Grant. Negro members on the commission were George W. Carter, Fannie D. Tyler, John W. Haywood, Robert T. Tatum, Bishop Alexander P. Shaw, and Virgil W. Hodges.

The 1952 General Conference, in an effort to focus a renewed sense of social mission, made a clear and positive response to the "Social Creed." Further, in an attempt to resolve the problem of the troublesome presence of the "unofficial" Methodist Federation for Social Action, it restructured its social action units, Temperance and World Peace, into a Board of Social and Economic Relations. The work of the new board was then redefined under three headings: Temperance, World Peace, and Social and Economic Relations. Negro members on these boards between 1952 and 1960, when further restructuring was to take place, were Bishop Edgar A. Love, Daniel M. Pleasants, Mrs. M. R. Bell, George W. Carter, Mrs. Mary Todd McKenzie, Bishop Willis J. King, Timothy B. Echols, James P. Brawley, Mrs. Claire C. Harvey, Rufus S. Abernathy (Youth), Sandra Morris (Youth), and Bishop Matthew W. Clair, Jr.

The 1960 General Conference, in seeking to still further integrate the three social action units of the church, authorized a Board of Christian Social Concerns with three divisions: Temperance and General Welfare, Peace and World Order, and Human Relations and Economic Affairs. Members of this board from 1960 to merger with the former Evangelical United Brethren Church included Claire C. Harvey, James P. Brawley, John T. King, John R. Washington, Charles S. Scott, Robert E. Hayes, Walter R. Hazzard, Bishop Prince A. Taylor, Bishop Edgar A. Love, Joseph B. Bethea, Sarah Clardy, Richard V. Moore, Bishop James S. Thomas, James M. Lawson, Richard E. Fields, Anna A. Hedgeman, Vivian W. Henderson, and Bishop Matthew W. Clair, Jr.

Elected staff executive leadership for the several units of the board since their inception (1940) were (1) Board of Temperance: A. R. Howard (1940–1956); Charles H. Dubra (1949–1955); and John L. Bryan (1956–1960); (2) Board of World Peace: John W. Haywood (1948–1955); and (3) Board of Christian Social Concerns: W. Alston Kirk (1961–1966); and Earnest A. Smith (1966–1980).

PUBLICATIONS AND COMMUNICATIONS

Some of the most vital moments of the Central Jurisdiction period had to do with writing, publishing, and communication activities. There are several highlights of this record that should not be lost to future generations of young Negro Methodists and the denomination.

Central Christian Advocate

The crown jewel of black Methodist writing and publishing in this period was the *Central Christian Advocate*. This connectional organ, called the *Southwestern Christian Advocate* until 1939, was unique not only in The Methodist Church but also in black church journalism. In every sense of the word, throughout its almost one-hundred-year history (1873–1968), it chronicled, encouraged, debated, and advocated—in the finest traditions of Christian journalism—the status and role of black people in Methodism and reflected Methodism through the eyes of its black constituents. In the words of the Central Jurisdiction's Committee on Publications, "We insist that there shall be free and untrammeled editorial expression so as to keep the Jurisdiction in constant touch with trends in world Christianity, and the Church in constant remembrance of the social implications of religion."[67] In keeping with this policy, the *Central Christian Advocate* provided a critically needed voice for the church to its people on the issues of the time. Editorials, news items, and feature stories recounted and critically appraised such issues as the desegregation of the armed forces, discriminatory employment practices, restricted voting rights for blacks, and public school segregation. The *Central Christian Advocate* did much more than advocate for black social, economic, and political rights. It informed the Central Jurisdiction about The Methodist Church's activities and programs. It imparted regional news about black churches obtainable nowhere else. It was also a necessary avenue of promotion for quadrennial emphases and programs. Bishop L. Scott Allen, while editor of the *Advocate*, well summarized its role: "Through it the Negro in The Methodist Church has had a chance to tell his story, express his hopes and aspirations and interpret his relationship to the Protestant movement in general and The Methodist Church in particular. In a very large way, it has been at once his basic resource journal of Christian opinion and his organ of expression."[68]

The editors of the *Central Christian Advocate* from 1940 until its demise and merger with the *Daily Christian Advocate* in 1968 were persons of stature, ability, and strength. Interestingly, each of them, similar to his predecessors in the Methodist Episcopal Church period, was elevated to the episcopacy from this editorship.

Robert N. Brooks (1888–1953) was elected editor of the former *Southwestern Christian Advocate* in 1936 from a church history professorship at Gammon Theological Seminary. He remained as editor following Union and became the first editor of the newly named *Central Christian Advocate*. Brooks served this position until 1944, when he was elected to the episcopacy. John W. E. Bowen, Jr. (1889–1962), came to the editorship of the *Central Christian Advocate* in 1944 from the pastorate of New Orleans's historic First Street Methodist Church. In 1948 he was elevated to the episcopacy at the Third Central Jurisdictional Conference. Dr. Prince A. Taylor, Jr., also a Gammon professor (religious education), followed Bishop Bowen. In 1956 he was elected to the episcopacy for service in Africa (Liberia). Succeeding Taylor was L. Scott Allen, pastor of Atlanta's prominent Central Methodist Church. Allen was the last editor of the *Central Christian Advocate* before the dissolution of the Central Jurisdiction.

The Central Jurisdiction Daily Christian Advocate

The General Conference of 1844 inaugurated the *Daily Christian Advocate*. This daily newspaper provided the Conference with "a daily report of its business."[69] With the institution of the Jurisdictional Plan in 1940, the *Daily Christian Advocate* idea was incorporated into that system. The names of the editors of the Central Jurisdiction *Daily Christian Advocate* deserve mentioning for their careful work of recording and publishing daily the minutes of Conferences for the expedition of the work of the Conferences and their delegates.

Wiley College faculty member Henry J. Mason, an alternate lay delegate from the Texas Conference, edited the *Daily Christian Advocate* in 1940 and 1944. He was ably assisted in this pioneering venture by Daniel L. Ridout and Adolphus S. Dickerson. Daniel L. Ridout edited and published the *Daily Christian Advocate* for the Conferences of the next five quadrennia, 1948–1964. He was assisted in this task at various times by W. T. Handy, Sr.; Frances C. Badgett; Virgil W. Hodges; Inez Christentery; Alvin S Bynum; and Clarence T. R. Nelson. The *Daily Christian Advocate* for the final session of the Central Jurisdictional Conference (1967) was edited by H. Walter Willis, Jr., under the editorial direction of the secretary of the Jurisdictional Conference, Allen M. Mayes.

Central Jurisdiction Area Publications

In addition to the *Central Christian Advocate* and its national coverage of news and features among black Methodists and the jurisdictional *Daily Christian Advocate*, there were newspapers in each episcopal area of the jurisdiction. Through the Commission on Public Information known as "Methodist Information," Daniel L. Ridout coordinated Methodist news-gathering through area correspondents in each episcopal area of the jurisdiction. The areas were covered as follows: Atlantic Coast, A. S. Dickerson; Baltimore, D. L. Ridout; New Orleans, W. T. Handy; and St. Louis, C. T. R. Nelson. In addition to this coverage, the bishops of most of the episcopal areas had their own official area publications. For example, Daniel Ridout edited and published *The Baltimore Area Messenger* from 1952–1964, and H. Walter Willis edited and published *The Voice*.

Church School Publications

Black Methodists, ministers, and laypersons have been writing for our church school publications at least since the 1920s. Editorial Division staff writers for our curriculum resources are only of recent origin. During the Central Jurisdiction period one appointment of a black editor was made. James S. Gadsden of the South Carolina Conference was appointed an assistant editor in the Department of Youth Publications, Editorial Division, Board of Education, in 1967.

Other Editorial Appointments

In concluding this section on publications and communications during the 1940–1968 period, it should be recognized that the Joint Commission on Education and Cultivation, related to the General Board of Missions, appointed three black staff persons in the early 1960s. George H. Daniels became associate director of the board's department of News Service. David W. Briddell became associate director of the Department of Visual Education, and Dorothy L. Barnette was elected to the position of associate director, Department of Studies and Schools of Missions.

In an appointment indirectly related to The Methodist Church, Methodist John L. Bryan (1913–1983) was elected the first black editor of the renowned Boston Methodist Church periodical *Zion's Herald* and served in that position from 1961–1971.

Black Board of Publications Membership

Central Jurisdiction membership on the Board of Publications from 1940 to 1968 was held by a total of six different people: Matthew S. Davage (1940–1956); Arthur R. Howard (1940–1956); L. H. Lightner (1940–1952); C. Anderson Davis (1956–1960); C. M. Winchester (1956–1968); and Joseph E. Lowery (1960–1968).

LAY ACTIVITIES IN THE CENTRAL JURISDICTION

Lay activity in the nineteen black Annual Conferences of The Methodist Episcopal Church had traditionally included little more than adult Bible study classes in the Sunday church school and perhaps membership in the Methodist Men's Brotherhood. While work among Methodist men existed since 1908, there was little or no formal organization until the 1920s.[70] It must also be mentioned that lay activities, though technically including women, were not really inclusive of them until the issues of women's rights and laymen's rights to be annual, jurisdictional, and general Conference delegates arose.

Following Union in 1939, women's work was consolidated in the Women's Division of Christian Service. At the level of the local church the Women's Division program operated through local Woman's Societies of Christian Service. Individual women were active in church-wide lay activities, and the Woman's Societies of Christian Service as an organization gave strong and critical support to local churches through departments of Christian Social Relations and Local Church Activities.

Methodist work among laymen after Union became exclusively identified with men, and structurally it was placed under the newly created General Board of Lay Activities.

The first Central Jurisdictional Conference meeting in St. Louis in June 1940 emphasized the importance of this new movement. The message of the College of Bishops conveyed that "our local churches will be strengthened in proportion as we bring to active leadership men and women who find joy in the service of the Lord."[71] Early in that first quadrennium, James H. Touchstone (1894–1974), later to become the first black staff executive with the new General Board of Lay Activities, reported that "a demand arose from ministers and laymen of the Central Jurisdiction for an Associate Secretary of the General Board." This recommendation was unanimously approved, and the position was created in August 1942.[72]

Lay Activities Elected Members

Members from the Central Jurisdiction serving by election of the Jurisdictional Conferences and/or by appointment from the early 1940s to 1968 were Bishops Lorenzo H. King, Robert N. Brooks, M. Lafayette Harris, and Matthew W. Clair, Jr. Ordained ministerial members were J. D. Wheaton, J. E. Brower, Emanuel M. Johnson, Dennis R. Fletcher, and John F. Norwood. Lay members were Charles W. Caldwell, Hally P. Johns, Samuel T. Middleton, John R. Patterson, Charles H. Johnson, and Ransom S. Durr.

Lay Activities Elected Staff

From 1942 to 1968 two black staff members served the General Board of Lay Activities. James H. Touchstone (1892–1974) was elected Associate Secretary for Promotion in 1942 and served until his retirement in 1964. Touchstone was succeeded by Charles P. Kellogg, who assumed the position in 1964. His title became associate director of Leadership Development. Kellogg remained with the Board of Lay Activities until 1976, at which time he resigned to accept an executive position on the Board of Global Ministries staff.

MINISTERIAL EDUCATION, RECRUITMENT, AND SUPPORT

Several of the eight quadrennial Episcopal Messages of the College of Bishops of the Central Jurisdiction from 1940 to 1964 devoted major space to the ministerial personnel situation. Taken together, excerpts from these pronouncements clearly indicate two things: (1) the indispensable role of the well-trained local pastor in executing the mission and program of Methodism, managing its temporal affairs, and conserving its polity; and (2) the ominous specter of a continual shortage of Negro ministers entering the ranks of the ministry either on trial or full connection. This section of the chapter will briefly review several aspects of what was undoubtedly one of the most serious problems of the Central Jurisdiction.

Ministerial Supply

A succinct summary of the grave situation in the supply of ministers for pastoral and other appointments is found in the Seventh Central Jurisdictional Conference Episcopal Message:

> A cursory examination of the ministerial manpower [*sic*] for the Jurisdiction for the last decade (1954–1964) reveals an unprecedented shortage. Only 304 . . . were admitted into full connection in all [17] conferences. For the same period, these conferences lost 522 ministers by death, withdrawal, expulsion, voluntary or involuntary location. This fact reveals a net loss of 218 ministers. To translate this statistic . . . the Jurisdiction had a net loss of 41.8 percent during the decade. . . . In addition to this appalling fact, 275 men were retired in the last ten years. . . . The median age of the ministers . . . is 53.3 years. Half . . . will retire within 18 years.[73]

Recruitment

Murray H. Leiffer, Garrett Theological Seminary's social research director, presented to the 1944 General Conference "the first scientific study of the Methodist Ministry in America." The alarmingly high age and retirement profile from that study highlighted the serious problem faced by the Central Jurisdiction in recruitment. The situation had not improved by 1948, causing Leiffer to report, "In the Central Jurisdiction . . . the age spread presents a serious problem. . . . For one reason or another it has been unsuccessful in receiving many young men for its work. . . . There is no sign of a build-up in the younger age group—a matter which should be of general concern to the entire Church."[74]

In 1952 Leiffer's continuing study and report to the General Conference indicated an even greater decline in the number of effective ministers, "dropping from 1,349 to 1,244, 7.8 percent in 4 years."[75]

The low number of Negro students in preparation for the ministry in accredited United States theological seminaries was another indicator of the critical recruitment problem of the Central Jurisdiction. The 1948 Episcopal Message stated that "according to the report of the Howard [University] School of Religion made in 1946, there were only 327 Negroes in preparation for the ministry in 41 theological schools. These 327 must fill the pulpits of all faiths and denominations."[76] The precarious situation in Central Jurisdiction ministerial recruitment during 1940–1964 may be summarized in a single phrase—in steady decline.

Ministerial Education

Equally as serious and in some ways even more difficult to resolve than the recruitment dilemma was the problem of maintaining an adequately educated ministry in the Central Jurisdiction years. Several factors were responsible. Related to the recruitment issue, relatively fewer college-educated Negro youth seemed interested in the ministry in the post–World War II years than in the 1920s and 1930s. Escalating academic qualifications to enter the Methodist ministry were also a factor. Following Union, a college degree requirement for admission on trial into an Annual Conference (1944) and, as of 1956, requirement of a seminary degree for admission to full connection, caused Negro youth to increasingly question their offering comparable educational credentials for much less income than their peers would receive with comparable training (or less) in other vocations. These and similar reasons resulted in a decreasing number of adequately educated ministers being available to serve an increasing number of congregations with a rapidly rising educational level.[77]

Pastoral Support

Pastoral support, which would normally include such items as salary, pension, medical care, housing and utility allowance, and travel, was generally limited to salary compensation and pension benefit payments in the early 1940s. During the 1950s and later some of the items noted above were provided through Annual Conferences that were able to fund their members through the Methodist Reserve Pension Plan. Timothy B. Echols, (1894–1983), who served as a secretary of the Board of Pensions, was given the specific task of cultivating the Methodist Reserve Pension Plan in the Central Jurisdiction.[78] It should be noted that pension rates in the Central Jurisdiction Conferences rose slowly but steadily from Conference averages of about $3 per service year to about $35 in 1964.[79]

Basic salaries in Central Jurisdiction churches rose from an average of about $1,500 annually in 1940 to about $2,500 in the middle 1960s.[80] Actually, this hardly represented a real increase beyond a token cost of living adjustment.

Women in Ministry

Black women in the Central Jurisdiction did not figure largely in the itinerant ministry of Methodism. There were at least two reasons for this. First, the General Conference did not authorize women to execute the clergy office until 1956. Second, the jurisdiction and lay and clergy members required time to adjust to the presence of women in this particular leadership role. While in several black Annual Conferences women had served as lay speakers, lay leaders, local preachers, local elders, and not infrequently as "accepted supply pastors," there was still hesitancy to fully include them in the traveling ministry. In retrospect, this seems to have been quite unnecessary. The invigorating, caring, and competent leadership and skills they brought to the church and its ministry in the last decade of the Central Jurisdiction years were highly positive and constructive.

A total of seven Central Jurisdiction women served the church in the traveling ministry between 1956 and 1968. Sallie A. Crenshaw of the former East Tennessee Conference was the first black woman to be ordained an elder and admitted into full connection in an Annual Conference. Emma P. H. Burrell of the former Washington Conference was the second black woman to receive the order of elder and Conference membership in 1959. Following these, Julia M. Walker, Central Alabama (1960); Elvernice Davis, Upper Mississippi (1965); and Muriel C. Hickman, East Tennessee (1967), were ordained elders and admitted into full connection in Annual Conferences. Pauline Cary and Muriel Q. Gilmore became associate ministers of Annual Conferences in the late 1960s.[81]

Commission on Ministerial Training

Several elected members from the Central Jurisdiction served on the Commission on Ministerial Training from 1948 to 1968. There is no record of representation from 1940 to 1948. Matthew W. Clair, Jr., seems to have been the first and only clergyman to have ever served this commission. Bishops Willis J. King; Matthew W. Clair, Jr.; J. W. E. Bowen, Jr.; M. L. Harris; and James S. Thomas were members of the commission until the former Evangelical United Brethren Church and The Methodist Church merged in 1968. It is of interest to note that neither the executive staff of the Commission on Courses of Study or the Commission on Ministerial Training ever had a Negro presence during the Central Jurisdiction years.

Board of Pensions

The work of the Board of Pensions was so closely related to that of the Commission on Ministerial Training that its Central Jurisdiction personnel and staff will be discussed together. Elected members from 1940 to 1968 included ministerial members D. W. Henry, Clarence F. Ferguson, Robert S. Mosby, and Allen H. L. Randolph. Lay members were Robert B. Hayes, Theodore L. Miller, W. Harold Flowers, Elmer T. Hawkins, and Harry L. Burney.

Members of the Central Jurisdiction Board of Pensions staff have been J. N. Crolley (1933–1948); Timothy B. Echols (1948–1963); and Allen M. Mayes (1963–1990).

Crolley rendered yeoman service in initiating a much needed pension program in the jurisdiction. Echols pioneered in interpreting and promoting the Reserve Pension Plan. Mayes, who attained the position of associate general secretary of the Board of Pensions, was one of the key designers of several of the intricate programs that attempted to equalize black clergy benefits in relation to the orderly dissolution of the Central Jurisdiction and the merger of The Methodist Church and the Evangelical United Brethren Church.

Gammon Theological Seminary

At the zenith of its renown in the 1920s and 1930s, Gammon Theological Seminary claimed the unique distinction of being one of only two nationally accredited Negro seminaries in the nation. Certain destabilizing situations in the late 1920s and the 1930s, however, changed this. The Great Depression of 1929 weakened its modest endowment. Student enrollment declined. Valued and scholarly professors retired. Lack of funds for adequate student scholarships and attractive faculty salaries mitigated against its remaining competitiveness. These factors considered, it was not surprising that a 1947 survey of theological education in The Methodist Church suggested that Gammon should close temporarily and plan for an alternative future in cooperation with Clark College and/or some of the other Negro seminaries in the Atlanta area.

Other more positive events were taking place in the Gammon situation in the 1940s, however, that would resolve the very serious problems of this historic institution. Residual funds for Gammon that had been raised in connection with the 1944–1948 Crusade for Christ were being held "in escrow" until the seminary could develop a plan for its future. The 1948 General Conference authorized stronger financial support for all of its theological schools, including Gammon. The election of Harry V. Richardson to the presidency of the troubled school assured it of young, vigorous, brilliant, and astute leadership. There was another factor. Three other Negro seminaries with problems similar to those of Gammon—Morehouse School of Religion (Baptist), Turner Theological Seminary (African Methodist Episcopal), and Phillips School of Theology (CME)—were interested in a cooperative, ecumenical arrangement.

The Richardson administration years proved to be a critical and positive turning point in the life of Gammon and a landmark of achievement in theological education for Negroes. In 1947 a contemplated move to the west side of Atlanta adjacent to Clark's new site was investigated. Richardson made a proposal for an interdenominational venture in theological education that was well received by philanthropic foundations and commended by the Gammon Board of Trustees and the church's Division of Educational Institutions. In 1957 the trustees of Gammon "approved in principle the plan of cooperation in an Interdenominational Theological Center."[82] When the center was chartered in 1958 and opened soon thereafter, it became one of the most singular experiments in theological education in North America. Some characteristics of the fledgling seminary were an autonomous board of trustees, a centralized campus administration and a central faculty, academic program, and student body. In addition, the Interdenominational Theological Center became a member of the Atlanta University Center. Through it, participation in the higher education programs of the many other colleges and universities in the metropolitan Atlanta area became possible.

Methodist members of the Gammon faculty during the 1940–1958 period were: F. W. Clelland (New Testament); C. B. Copher (Old Testament); E. T. Dixon (Rural Church); R. A. Felton (rural Church); S. E. Grannum (Theology); R. S. Guptill (Missions); J. W. Haywood (President); J. D. Killingsworth (Church Music); W. J. King (Old Testament); H. V. Richardson (President); G. S. Shockley (Christian Education); C. A. Talbert (Church History); P. A. Taylor (Christian Education); J. S. Thomas (Rural Church).

Methodist members of the Gammon faculty who became members of the first faculty of the Interdenominational Theological Center in 1958–1959 were: C. P. Copher (Old Testament); R. A. Felton (Rural Church); J. H. Graham (Sociology of Religion); R. S. Guptill (Missions); J. D. Killingsworth (Church Music); J. E. Lantz (Speech); E. H. Richards (Theology); H. V. Richardson (President); R. L. Williamson (Town and Country). Later in the 1960s W. T. Smith (Church History) came to the Gammon faculty.

DISTRICT SUPERINTENDENTS

Negro district superintendents had served only Negro districts from the inception of the organization of Negro Annual Conferences in 1864. At the time of the reunification of the three branches of Methodism in 1939, there were eighty-five such districts and superintendents in nineteen Annual Conferences. By 1952 there had been a reduction in the number of districts due to some redistricting and the consolidation of the two Annual Conferences in Georgia and Florida into state Conferences. The practice of racial leadership, however, continued.

The first known instance of a Negro being selected to superintend a predominantly white district in The Methodist Church was Bishop Lloyd C.

Wicke's (b. 1901) appointment of Samuel H. Sweeney (1888–1965) to serve
as the interim district superintendent of the New York District, New York
Annual Conference, from March 1 to May 27, 1962.[83] Harry B. Gibson, Jr.,
was the first Negro to become a member of the Rock River Annual Conference
cabinet in 1964. Gibson had been appointed by Bishop Matthew W. Clair, Jr.
1890–1968 to complete the unexpired term of John A. Greene, whose district
had been transferred into the Rock River Conference by the mutual action of
the 1964 Central and North Central Jurisdictions as a part of the process of
dissolving the Central Jurisdiction. The first Negro regularly appointed to
superintend a predominantly white district was Charles L. Warren
(1911–1971). Warren, pastor of St. Mark's Church in New York City, was
appointed by Bishop Lloyd C. Wicke to serve the metropolitan district of the
New York Annual Conference in 1964.[84]

In the Peninsula Conference in 1965, Bishop John Wesley Lord appointed
Edward G. Carroll (later elected to the episcopacy) to the superintendency of the
Washington-Northwest District and Richard H. Johnson to the Baltimore-
Northwest District of the Baltimore Conference. Immediately following the
untimely death of Richard Johnson in 1966, William E. Bishop succeeded
Johnson. In the Peninsula Conference, Bishop Lord appointed two Negro
district superintendents. Daniel L. Ridout (1899–1982), writer and renowned
church musician, was given the Chestertown District, and John R. Shockley
(1914–1982) was sent to the Wilmington District. In the Philadelphia
Conference, Bishop Fred P. Corson (b. 1896) appointed Tindley Temple's
Walter R. Hazzard superintendent of the South District. In the West Virginia
Conference, Bishop Fred G. Holloway (b. 1898) placed Ramsey M. Bridges
(b. 1912) in the Parkesburg District. In the Western Jurisdiction the one
appointment of a Negro to the district superintendency in 1965 was Robert D.
Hill. Pastor of the historic Taylor Memorial Church in Oakland, California, Hill
was brought into the cabinet of the California-Nevada Annual Conference by
Bishop Donald H. Tippett.

In reviewing the first appointments of Negro district superintendents across
the denomination, it is discovered that they were made in merging Annual
Conference sessions immediately following the 1964 General Conference.
Nine such appointments were made in the Northeastern Jurisdiction and one
each in the North Central and Western Jurisdictions.

EPISCOPAL LEADERSHIP

The episcopal office in American Methodism in relation to the Negro
historically has been compromised. From the beginning, the election of
Negroes to the episcopacy has been racial and limited. Negro missionary
bishops were limited to service in Liberia, West Africa. The first elected Negro

general superintendents (R. E. Jones and M. W. Clair, Sr.) were limited to the supervision of Negro Annual Conferences or the work in Liberia. Negroes elected to the episcopacy in The Methodist Church (1940) were limited to service in a jurisdiction, the structuring of which had been conceived in racial terms. In providing for bishops in the Plan of Union, for an example, "bishops were . . . to be elected by the Jurisdictional Conferences and by these alone, and . . . the supervisory powers of any bishop . . . were . . . to be confined to the particular jurisdiction which elected him or to which the Plan of Union assigned him."[85]

Despite the explicit racism of the "limited" episcopacy policy for Negroes in election, assignment, and supervision, the total situation was not unrelieved. A solitary feature of the Plan of Union was the measure of self-determination accorded the jurisdictions in the selection of their episcopal leadership. In the case of the Central Jurisdiction, this meant that Negro bishops would be elected by the Negro Annual Conferences and from among persons within it. The following paragraphs reflect upon those selected for this highest office of leadership in the denomination.

"A Cloud of Witnesses"

All of the Negro bishops who had ever been elected to the general superintendency in the former Methodist Episcopal Church were living and active when the First Central Jurisdictional Conference met at Union Methodist Church in St. Louis on June 18–23, 1940. Bishop Matthew W. Clair, Sr. (1865–1943), was there. Elected to the episcopacy in 1920 and the first Negro bishop to retire (1936), he had been recalled for active service in the Atlanta area before his death in 1943. Bishop Robert E. Jones (1872–1960) was there. The first elected Negro bishop (1920) had led the Columbus area. Bishop Alexander P. Shaw (1879–1966) was there. The last Negro general superintendent elected by the Methodist Episcopal Church in 1936, he supervised the New Orleans area.

1940–1956: Cultivation and Promotion

The tasks of the Central Jurisdiction in its early years were basically, though not exclusively, those of organization, election of bishops, program cultivation, and connectional promotion. The untimely death of Bishop W. A. C. Hughes (1877–1940) within a month following his consecration as the first bishop to have been elected in the Central Jurisdiction was a severe loss to the life and leadership of the church. His powerful and moving preaching, passionate advocacy for the poor and disadvantaged, and excellent administrative skills would have greatly strengthened the leadership of the jurisdiction. Hughes will be remembered, however, as the architect of the denomination's program of outreach and training through the Department of Negro Work.

In the brief span of his episcopal administration (1940–1946), Lorenzo H. King (1878–1946) widely influenced the work of the jurisdiction that elected him a bishop in 1940. Though chosen while pastor of New York City's St. Mark's Church, King's roots were deep in the soil of the South. His masterful pulpit oratory and presence, together with his concern that Methodism remain loyal to Wesley's social religious concerns, had a great impact on the developing identity and image of preachers and congregations.

Willis J. King (1886–1976) was the third episcopal leader elected by the Central Jurisdiction. His elevation to the bishopric for service in Liberia, West Africa, denoted the high priority given to this work entrusted to the care of the jurisdiction. An Old Testament scholar (Ph.D., Boston University), former seminary professor, college president, and president of Gammon Theological Seminary, Willis King, offered impeccable credentials for the leadership of the Liberian church, which he guided for twelve years. In 1956, upon returning to the United States, Bishop King supervised the New Orleans area following the death of Bishop Robert N. Brooks. King retired in 1960 and died in 1976.

Probably one of the most forceful and astute churchmen elected to the episcopacy in the course of Central Jurisdiction history was Robert Nathaniel Brooks (1888–1953). A Gammon Seminary and Northwestern University–trained church history professor, Brooks went to the episcopacy in 1944 from the editorship of the *Central Christian Advocate*, where he had served brilliantly since 1936. Under his episcopal leadership in the New Orleans area, a standard of excellent performance was achieved in all departments of the office of episcopal administration. His sudden death in 1953 was a real loss.

Eminent preacher and pastor Edward Wendall Kelly (1880–1964) was elected to the bishopric at the Second Central Jurisdiction Conference held at Bennett College in Greensboro, North Carolina, June 8–11, 1944. Kelly held the distinction of having pastored more large appointments than any in his generation. Kelly was an evangelist-preacher in every sense and a master of narrative preaching. The late Bishop Francis J. McConnell once said of him that he was one of four irreplaceable men.[86]

John Wesley Edward Bowen, Jr. (1889–1962)—the distinguished son of a minister, scholar, and seminary president, J. W. E. Bowen, Sr.—was born in Baltimore. He was educated at Philips Exeter Academy, Wesleyan University, and Harvard University. Admitted to the Atlanta Annual Conference in 1917, he served as a World War I chaplain, college teacher, Sunday School Board staff member, pastor, and district superintendent. Appointed to the editorship of the *Central Christian Advocate* (1944) from the pastorate of First Street Church, New Orleans, he remained there until his election to the episcopacy in 1948. Bowen was assigned to the Atlantic Coast area, where he served until retirement (1960). He died in 1962. Married to Margaret Davis Bowen, first

Central Jurisdiction Women's Society of Christian Service president, the world-traveled Bowens parented a son, John W. E. Bowen III. Christian character and intellectual strength together with a high sense of responsibility to encourage and enable an educated ministry were Bowen's marks.

Native Virginian Edgar Amos Love (1891–1974) was born at Harrisburg. His education was received at Morgan College Academy, Howard University, and Boston University. Love was admitted to the Washington Annual Conference in 1918, and following an army chaplaincy in World War I, he pastored churches in Maryland, Pennsylvania, West Virginia, and Baltimore (John Wesley). His pastorate at John Wesley was followed with a term as district superintendent. In 1940 he succeeded W. A. C. Hughes as superintendent of Negro Work in the Division of Home Missions. The 1952 Central Jurisdictional Conference elected Love a bishop of the Methodist Church. Assigned to the Baltimore area, Bishop Love presided over its Conferences until 1964, when he retired to his Baltimore residence where he died.

Edgar Love was married to Virginia Ross Love; they were the parents of Jon Edgar Love. Active in civic, social, and civil rights activities, Bishop Love may best be remembered for having organized black Methodists on the West Coast in the 1940s.

Matthew Wesley Clair, Jr. (1890–1968), and Bishop Matthew Wesley Clair, Sr. (1865–1943), were a rare father-bishop/son-bishop team in American Methodism. Born in Harper's Ferry, West Virginia, the junior Clair was educated at Syracuse University, Howard University, Boston University and the Iliff School of Theology. Clair was admitted to the Annual Conference in 1917. Before pastoring churches in Virginia, West Virginia, Florida, Colorado, and Indiana, he served as a chaplain in World War I. During 1936–1940 Clair was professor of practical theology at Gammon Theological Seminary. He was elected to the episcopacy in Philadelphia in 1952 from the pastorate of Chicago's St. Mark Church. Clair's episcopal ministry was spent in the St. Louis area, to which he had been assigned in 1952.

Bishop Clair married Ethel Christian Smith in 1920, and they were the parents of two daughters. He was a gifted preacher, liturgist, and writer. Known for his encouragement of young preachers and quality theological education, he died in retirement in 1968.

Educator-editor Prince Albert Taylor, Jr., was born in a Methodist Episcopal parsonage-home in Hennessey, Oklahoma, on January 27, 1907. He was a graduate of Samuel Huston College, Gammon Theological Seminary, and Columbia University. He also held the doctor of education degree from New York University. Taylor, who was ordained and admitted into full connection in the North Carolina Annual Conference in 1931, had pastored in North Carolina and New York. He taught at Bennett College before accepting a professorship in Christian education at Gammon Theological Seminary in 1943, where he remained until 1945. Shortly after the 1948 Jurisdictional Conference, he was elected to succeed J. W. E. Bowen, Jr., in the editor's position. In 1956 he was elected a bishop for service in Liberia, replacing Willis J. King, who had returned to the United States. Bishop Taylor was transferred back to the United States in 1964 and assigned to the New Jersey area. During 1965–1966 he became the first Negro to be elected president of the Council of Bishops. An active ecumenist, the bishop is married to Annie Belle Thaxton. They have a daughter, Isabella. He retired in 1976.

Charles Franklin Golden (1912–1984), another distinguished clergy son of a distinguished clergyman, J. W. Golden, was born in Holly Springs, Mississippi. Golden graduated from Clark College, Gammon Theological Seminary, and Boston University. He was admitted into full connection in the Annual Conference in 1936. His pastoral experience was obtained in Alabama, Georgia, Tennessee, Mississippi, and Arkansas. After teaching at Philander Smith College (1938–1941), Golden served the nation's armed forces as a chaplain (1942–1946). In 1947 he became director of field service in the Department of Negro Work at the Board of Missions. In 1952 and 1956 he became successively an associate secretary and divisional director. The Sixth Central Jurisdictional Conference (1960) elected him a bishop, assigning him to the Nashville-Birmingham area. In 1968 he became the first black bishop to be assigned in the Western Jurisdiction, from which he retired in 1980. Charles Golden will be remembered as an ardent social and civil rights leader as well as church statesman. He preceded his wife, Ida, in death.

Noah Watson Moore, Jr., the son of N. W. Moore, Sr., and his wife, Eliza, was born in Newark, New Jersey. Educated at Morgan College, Drew Theological and Drew University, Moore entered the Delaware Annual Conference in 1932. He served appointments in New York, Maryland, and Pennsylvania, including a district superintendency, before becoming pastor of Tindley Temple in Philadelphia. Also elected to the episcopacy at the 1960 Central Jurisdictional Conference, Moore was assigned to the New Orleans area. After the dissolution of the Central Jurisdiction (1968), Bishop Moore became the first black bishop to supervise a South Central Jurisdiction area (Nebraska). He retired to his Atlantic City home in 1972. Bishop Moore was married to Carolyn W. Lee Moore for more than fifty years. They have a daughter, Carolyn (Mrs. Arthur D. Weddington).

M. Lafayette Harris (1907–1966) was born in Armstrong, Alabama. His education was received from Clark College, Gammon Theological Seminary, and Boston University's School of Theology. Harris received a doctorate in philosophy at Ohio State University (1933). Admitted into full connection in the Lexington Conference (1932), he had extensive pastoral and teaching experience. At thirty-one he was elected to the presidency of Philander Smith College. His superb administration of the institution (1936–1960) transformed it from a dying enterprise to the first Negro institution accredited by the North Central Association of Colleges. An elected delegate to every General and Jurisdictional Conference from 1940 to 1960, he was elected to the episcopacy at the Sixth Session of the Central Jurisdictional Conference in Cleveland, Ohio (1960). After assignment to the Atlantic Coast area, he resided in Atlanta. He died in 1966, following a lingering illness. Married to Geneva M. Nelson in 1931, the Harrises had one son, M. Lafayette Harris, Jr. M. Lafayette Harris left the church a legacy of outstanding achievement in ministry, scholarship, administration, and service.

James Samuel Thomas, Jr., acquired the graces of a Christian upbringing in a parsonage home in Orangeburg, South Carolina. His higher education career was launched in response to a call to the ministry. He took degrees at Claflin College, Gammon Theological Seminary, and Drew University, and completed doctoral studies in sociology at Cornell University. Admitted to the South Carolina Conference in 1944, Thomas pastored in his native state before returning to Gammon as professor of rural church studies. Upon completing a doctorate, he was selected to succeed the venerable Matthew S. Davage in 1953, becoming associate director of the Department of Educational Institutions of the General Board of Education. His brilliant leadership of the Committee of Five, which strategized the desegregation of the denomination, is widely acknowledged to have influenced his election to the episcopacy in 1964. Just after his election, Bishop Thomas was transferred to the North Central Jurisdiction, becoming the first black bishop in that region. James Thomas retired in 1988. He married Ruth Naomi Wilson in 1945. The Thomases have four daughters: Claudia, Gloria, Margaret, and Patricia.

L. Scott Allen, the last bishop elected by the Central Jurisdiction, is a native Mississippian. He entered the ministry in 1938 and was admitted into full connection in the Atlanta Conference in 1940. He graduated from Clark College and Gammon Theological Seminary and holds a postgraduate degree from Northwestern University (M.A.). Allen served pastorates in Georgia from 1942 to 1956. He also taught at Clark College. His election to the editorship of the *Central Christian Advocate* came while he was minister at Central Church in Atlanta. When he was elevated to the episcopacy in 1967, he became the eighth *Central Christian Advocate* or *Southwestern Christian Advocate* editor to be so elevated. Allen was assigned for a brief time to the newly created Gulf Coast area (Central Alabama, Florida, Mississippi, and Upper Mississippi Conferences). In 1968 he was transferred to the Southeastern Jurisdiction and served the newly created Holston area as its first Negro bishop from 1968 to 1976. He was transferred to the Charlotte area in 1976, where he remained as resident bishop until his retirement in 1984.

Currently, he is directing the Center for Ministerial Exchange, Education, and Training for Inclusive Ministries and Open Itinerancy at Gammon Theological Seminary in Atlanta. He has been married to Sarah Charles Adams Allen since 1942.

ECUMENICAL RELATIONS

Participation in the ecumenical life and outreach of The Methodist Church during 1940–1968 varied in expression and activity. It happened in different ways: denominationally, interdenominationally, in church union conversation, and among women and black church bodies. It also occurred at various levels of institutional life, local and state, national and world.

World Methodist Council

The Methodist Church has a unique affiliation with the World Methodist Council (until 1951 the Ecumenical Methodist Council). An international organization and an interdenominational agency, it officially relates The Methodist Church in the United States to all other Methodist bodies in the world. Since 1947 it has met at five-year intervals and on a nationally delegated basis. In recent years, the decision was made that the council would become a world federation of Methodists enabling each unit "to preserve and extend [its] distinctive evangelical witness . . . and bring it as an invaluable spiritual contribution to the larger ecumenical movement in process of development."[87]

Negroes were elected delegates to meetings of the World Methodist Council held at Springfield, Massachusetts (1947); Oxford, England (1951); Lake Junaluska, North Carolina (1956); Oslo, Norway (1961); and London, England (1966).

From 1940 to 1964 Negro elected members of the Ecumenical Methodist Council (1888–1951) and the World Methodist Council since 1961 have been Bishops Robert N. Brooks, Willis J. King, Matthew W. Clair, Prince A. Taylor, M. Lafayette Harris, and Noah W. Moore. Several of the bishops were the ministerial elected members before their election as bishops. Elected lay members of the councils were Matthew S. Davage and J. Ernest Wilkins.

Interdenominational Involvements

Negro Methodists were meaningfully engaged in local, state, and regional ecumenical activities during the entire Central Jurisdiction period. For example, in the 1950s in Detroit, Michigan, representatives of the American Methodist Episcopal (AME), American Methodist Episcopal Zion (AMEZ), and CME churches, in cooperation with The Methodist Church, developed a Metropolitan Council of Methodism "to serve as a program clearinghouse and develop 'common strategies' pertinent to the church's witness to Metropolitan Detroit and Michigan."[88] In the late 1940s and 1960s, Bishop M. Lafayette Harris and Bishop Prince A. Taylor assumed leadership roles at the state level in ecumenical affairs in Arkansas and New Jersey, seeking to discover more viable approaches to urban problems. (Bishop Harris was then Dr. Harris, president of Philander Smith College in Little Rock, Arkansas.) There were few examples of cooperative, ecumenical projects that better witnessed to the gospel or more constructively influenced the civil rights movement than the National Council of Churches' Delta Ministry Project in Mississippi. This "church-funded mission agency that [drew] both its leadership and its agenda from the people themselves" was an exemplary model of church-communty development. Thelma Barnes, Dr. Aaron Henry, and other Methodists and EUBs were among those who gave sacrificial and courageous leadership to this historic project.[89]

National Ecumenical Activities

Three significant ecumenical activities involving Negro Methodists can be noted at the national level between 1940 and 1968: a bold new venture in theological education, a continuing ministry of Bible distribution, and a renewing structure for cooperative mission among national denominations.

Interdenominational Theological Center

In the 1950s the Interdenominational Theological Center (ITC) was an idea whose time had come. Four struggling Negro theological seminaries in the Southeast (three in Atlanta) were desperately seeking to resolve their financial dilemmas. Morehouse School of Religion (Baptist), Gammon Theological Seminary (the Methodist Church), Turner Theological Seminary (AME), all in Atlanta, and Phillips School of Theology (CME) in Jackson, Tennessee, confronted with few students, loss of faculty, little income, and very poor physical plants, faced a bleak future, if any at all. Harry V. Richardson, Gammon's Methodist president, Drew and Harvard University educated, proposed a response to the situation—the ITC concept. His plan was to create an accredited federation of autonomous denominational seminaries with one student body, faculty, curriculum, administration, and board of trustees. With the approval of the Gammon trustees and the support of Bishops J. W. E. Bowen and Bishop Matthew W. Clair, together with helpful financial contacts with Frederick D. Patterson, the United Negro College Fund president, ITC became a reality in 1958–1959. Referred to as "one of the most creative approaches in the nation to the needs and special opportunities found in the area of black theological education,"[90] it prepares a major percentage of all black recruits for the ministry of the black churches in the nation.

American Bible Society

Organized in 1816 "to encourage a wider circulation of the Holy Scriptures without note or comment," the American Bible Society pursued its mission of distributing Bibles on an ecumenical basis, especially to the disadvantaged, through local auxiliary societies. In 1820 its program was broadened to include distribution outside the United States. Generously supported by Protestant denominations, it is the world's largest Bible-distributing ministry. The Methodist Church has had a long and close relationship with the society. It shares in our Benevolence Program and influenced the institution of National Bible Sunday in The Methodist Church year. The American Bible Society has worked among Negroes since the Civil War. John P. Wragg (1855–1936), a member of the Atlanta Conference, was appointed a staff secretary in 1901. He continued in that position until his retirement in 1931 and was succeeded by another Atlanta Conference member, Daniel H. Stanton, who died in 1957.[91]

The National Council of Churches

The National Council of Churches of Christ in the USA, the national ecumenical agency through which The Methodist Church cooperated as a denomination with other Protestant member churches, was the successor organization to the Federal Council of Churches of Christ organized in 1908. Founded in 1950, it was the largest single ecumenical organization in the country. It has been well characterized by Dr. Gertrude B. Rivers, Howard University professor and a charter member of the Women's Society of Christian Service of the former Washington Annual Conference, as a "dramatic symbol of the unity which is coming slowly but surely to American Christianity."[92] Its objective, "to witness and serve in the world," was to be realized through a variety of services on behalf of the member-denominations:

1. representing a united Protestantism to the national government
2. representing the churches in programs of united service to human needs
3. providing Christian education resources on a cooperative basis
4. providing a united approach to evangelism
5. providing a vigorous program of Christian public relations on behalf of Protestantism
6. representing the churches in a united approach to the problems of society and international life
7 providing coordination and strategy for missions
8. representing the churches in ecumenical movements
9. strengthening Christian schools and colleges

10. coordinating the activities of the churches ministering to men and women in uniform

Central Jurisdiction bishops, ministers, laymen, and laywomen were elected to several categories of representation in the Federal Council of Churches and its successor, the National Council of Churches (1950–present): (1) representatives of The Methodist Church to the Federal Council (1940–1950) and (2) Methodist representatives to the General Board or General Assembly of the National Council. Those who served as representatives in either of these categories during 1940–1968 are listed here: Bishops A. P. Shaw, R. N. Brooks, W. J. King, E. W. Kelly, and M. W. Clair. Ministers who served included L. B. Felder; W. I. Gosnell; N. W. Greene; W. T. Handy, Jr.; W. T. Handy, Sr.; R. F. Harrington; M. L. Harris; J. W. Haywood; C. Henry; D. W. Henry; J. J. Hicks; O. B. Quick; G. S. Shockley; E. A. Smith; G. O. Tate; and J. D. Wheaton. Laypersons who served included J. W. E. Bowen III, J. P. Brawley, H. D. Brown, Mrs. R. K. Gordon, R. E. Hayes, R. E. Hunt, H. P. Johns, L. Lynn, T. McCallum, H. D. Smith, Mrs. L. C. Thomas, and H. C. Waters.

Anticipating the Evangelical United Brethren–Methodist merger, the 1964 General Conference appointed Theressa Hoover and Sumpter M. Riley, Jr., to membership on the Ad Hoc Committee on Union with the Evangelical United Brethren Church.[93]

World Council of Churches

The World Council of Churches is a Christian fellowship of member churches, denominations, or communions with a Protestant or Orthodox background. During the active years of the Central Jurisdiction, it had 171 member churches in 52 countries on every continent on the globe. The World Council of Churches, not formally organized until 1948 at its First General Assembly at Amsterdam, Holland, was the result of a consolidation of three previously existing ecumenical worldwide bodies: the International Missionary Council (1910), the Life and Work Movement (1925), and the Faith and Order Movement (1927). The World Council, organized into six geographic world regions, is governed by delegated assemblies of the member churches, which meet about every seven years. Its objective is to be an organization in which dialogue can occur around issues of creed, ministry, polity, mission, and program. Programmatically, it emphasizes "unity, witness, and service" expressed in practicing "Christian solidarity," uniting to meet human need, witnessing to the gospel, and seeking "unity and renewal" throughout the worldwide church.[94]

Central Jurisdiction members had low visibility as delegates in World Council affairs duing 1940–1968. This may have been due to the lack of direct interaction that Negroes in the Central Jurisdiction had with the larger church, beyond jurisdictional and national church activities. Negroes did attend the assemblies in Amsterdam (1948), Evanston (1954), New Delhi (1961), and Uppsala (1968). Their presence at these gatherings, however, was on a personal basis or related to a board, staff, or agency relationship. Excepting Bishop Alexander P. Shaw's election as an alternate delegate to the First Assembly of the World Council of Churches (Amsterdam, 1948) and Harry V. Richardson's election as a delegate to the Evanston (1954) and the New Delhi (1961) meetings and a member of the Assembly of the World Council of the Churches (1960–1964 and 1964–1968), there is no record of any other Negro participation until after 1965. This situation is alluded to by the late Bishop Charles F. Golden in reference to the lack of a Negro presence in the Visitor-Delegation to the Second Vatican Council: "It is also to be observed at the ecumenical level that not one Negro from The Methodist Church was included among our visitors selected to attend the Second Vatican Council, nor was one included among the Methodist representatives to the Consultation on Church Union."[95]

Negroes elected to the Commission on Church Union from 1940 to 1968 include bishops R. E. Jones, A. P. Shaw, W. J. King, P. A. Taylor, and M. W. Clair, Jr. Ministers were W. J. King, B. F. Smith, E. C. McLeod, M. L. Harris, O. B. Quick, S. M. Riley, and M. J. Wynn. Lay members were J. P. Burgess, Mrs. M. A. Camphor, M. S. Davage, V. E. Daniel, W. E. Wilson, and H. C. Waters.

Negroes and Ecumenical Relations

Thus far this discussion of Negroes and ecumenical relations in The Methodist Church has focused on their presence and participation in denominational activities. Little has been said about ecumenical relations between Negroes in the Central Jurisdiction and those in other Negro denominations. Efforts in the direction of such better understanding, cooperative action, and even union, while not numerous, are a part of the record.

The late Bishop Robert E. Jones, then (1940) senior bishop of the Central Jurisdiction College of Bishops, voiced the genuine interest of the jurisdiction in union with the AME, AMEZ, and CME churches in the first message from the college in 1940:

> In this connection it seems consistent that we should state that we would welcome into the Central Jurisdiction any of the distinctive Negro bodies if they so desire, especially the Colored Methodist Episcopal Church, provided the General Church extends the invitation and provided further, of course, that the plan as set up proves agreeable to them and to us. We do hope that the Central

Jurisdiction may not only be the means of a greater integration of Negroes in the Church, but may work toward ultimate adjustment of race relations along the lines of the highest, freest interpretation of Christianity and democracy, which must inevitably come if Christianity and democracy are to stand the test of the world.[96]

The Central Jurisdiction maintained an active relationship with the Negro Fraternal Council of Churches over the span of its more than three-decade existence (1934–1965). Dedicated to developing cooperative relations among its member churches, strengthening bonds of unity, and working together for racial and economic justice, the council was the most viable vehicle for ecumenical expression in the Negro community until the ascendency of the Southern Christian Leadership Conference in 1957.[97] Negro Methodist leaders identified with the Council were Bishop Alexander P. Shaw, J. W. Golden (1883–1961), and Bishop Edgar A. Love.[98]

Looking toward the possibility of a closer relationship with the Negro membership of The Methodist Church, the AME, AMEZ, and CME churches unofficially met in 1964 to discuss the implications of a union of their three denominations as a prelude to merger conversation with The Methodist Church. It was made clear by them, however, that no such "talks" would be possible with a "Central Jurisdiction."[99] The final session of the Central Jurisdictional Conference (1967) petitioned the 1968 General Conference "to invite and aggressively seek union with our brethren of similar doctrinal and historical background; namely, The Christian Methodist Episcopal Church, African Methodist Episcopal Church and the African Methodist Episcopal Zion Church, and the Council of Bishops set in motion any necessary Committees that will accomplish the above Union by the target date of 1976."[100]

NOTABLE NEGRO METHODISTS

Noteworthy and exceptional achievements and contributions were made by individual Negro Methodists to their communities, the nation, and the world during the Central Jurisdiction years. Citations of some of these accomplishments not only reflect personal credit but also witness to faith and the Christian stewardship of life.

In the fields of music, literature, and journalism, Union Memorial's (St. Louis) Grace Brumbry, Metropolitan Opera soprano, became the first of her race to sing at the famed Bayreuth Music Festival Theater (Germany). Leontyne Price, Metropolitan Opera star since her 1961 debut, made history again in her appearance in *Tosca*. Methodist Leslie Pinckney Hill's (1880–1960) blank verse drama *Toussaint L'Ouverture* remains a literary classic of its period.

In the area of church/religion, Harlem's Metropolitan Community Church pastor, William M. James, recruiter of more than fifty youth for ministry, was selected also to head the HARYOU Act, a multimillion dollar federal antipoverty program in the 1960s. C. Eric Lincoln, North Georgia Conference ministerial member, rose to prominence as a nationally and internationally acclaimed sociologist of religion with the publication of the classic case study *Black Muslims in America*.

During the civil rights period, several Methodists claimed major leadership roles. Gloster Current became national director of local branches of the National Association for the Advancement of Colored People (NAACP). Aaron Henry, a Clarksdale, Mississippi, Methodist, fearlessly led a voting rights campaign in the state and assisted in organizing the Freedom Democratic Party. Three members of the prominent Baltimore Mitchell family, Sharp Street Memorial members, were and are outstanding civil rights leaders. Lillie M. Jackson (1889–1975), national NAACP board member, led the Baltimore branch for almost three decades. Her son-in-law Clarence M. Mitchell (1911–1984) received the coveted NAACP Spingarn Medal in 1969 for a brilliant career as a civil rights lobbyist. Daughter Juanita Jackson Mitchell, first Negro National Methodist Youth Council vice president (1934), is currently an influential civil rights attorney. Youthful James M. Lawson, presently pastor of Holman Church (Los Angeles), stirred the South and the nation following his expulsion from Vanderbilt University Divinity School on the pretense that he advocated a campaign of civil disobedience.

Methodist luminaries in the education and human welfare fields include those in the health, social work, higher education, and sports fields. James P. Brawley (1894–1985), president of Clark College for more than two decades, was a rare combination of churchman and educator. During a brilliant presidency at Clark College (1940–1960), he and Clark College ventured to participate in what was to become one of the largest and most unique consortia in Negro higher education in the nation, the Atlanta University Center. The genius of this innovative model was conserving institutional identity and autonomy while sharing institutional strength for the common good of all. In the church, Brawley, many times a General and Jurisdictional Conference delegate, was instrumental in orchestrating much Central Jurisdiction opposition to Negro segregation in the church. A higher education scholar, he also wrote the definitive history of black higher education in Methodism, *Two Centuries of Methodist Concern: Bondage, Freedom and Education of Black People* (1974).

Dorothy L. Brown, M.D., was the first Negro woman physician to become a resident surgeon in the United States. She was also the first to be elected to the Tennessee State General Assembly.

Howard University's distinguished emeritus professor, Flemmie P. Kittrell

(Ph.D., Cornell University), holds membership in Asbury Church, Washington, D.C. A Fulbright scholar, Dr. Kittrell has done extensive nutrition research for the United States government in Liberia, Zaire, Congo, Morocco, India, and Bangladesh.

Two Negro Methodist educators contributed enormously to higher education in the second half of the twentieth century. Frederick D. Patterson (1901–1988), president emeritus, Tuskegee University and president of the Phelps-Stokes Fund, the oldest United States foundation in Africa, held consultant assignments for the federal government, was a consultant in higher education to Liberia, and was a Presidential Commission on Higher Education appointee (1947). As founder of the United Negro College Fund, the nation's first cooperative fund-raising organization for higher education, he helped strengthen more than forty historically Negro colleges for their educational mission.

Numerous recognitions and honorary degrees came to Willa B. Player, Ed.D., Columbia University, the first woman president of Bennett College (1955–1966). During her administration at Bennett, it became one of the first senior Negro colleges admitted to membership in the Southern Association of Colleges and Schools. A North Carolina state consultant for the 1950 White House Conference on Education, Dr. Player was selected in 1966 to direct the Division of College Support, United States Office of Education. In 1974 she was appointed executive administrator in the Office of Education, United States Department of Health, Education, and Welfare. She holds the prestigious Distinguished Service Award of the Department of Health, Education, and Welfare.

Jesse Owens (1913–1980), a Methodist, has been called the world's fastest human. Dominating the 1936 Olympic Games held in Berlin, Germany, he tied the world record for the 100-meter dash, set a broad jump record, a 200-meter record, and assisted in setting a 400-meter relay time. The winner of four gold medals, Owens became a charter member of the Track and Field Hall of Fame.

Several illustrious public servants in government and politics with Methodist backgrounds can be noted. J. Ernest Wilkins (1895–1959) was an active lay member of St. Mark Church (Chicago). After military service in World War I, he practiced law in Chicago. In 1953 President Dwight D. Eisenhower named Wilkins to the powerful Committee on Government Contracts. The following year (1954) he became the first Negro to occupy a subcabinet post when he was appointed assistant secretary of labor.

Vivian W. Henderson, Ph.D. (1923–1976), member of Warren Church, Atlanta, was president of Clark College at the time of his death. An outstanding economist, among his numerous board memberships were the National Bureau of Economic Research; Southern Regional Council (chair of the executive committee); Ford Foundation; Martin Luther King, Jr., Center for Social Change; and the Fund for Theological Education. In 1970 he was awarded the Medal for Distinguished Service by Teachers College, Columbia University.

St. Mark (New York City) claims Anna Arnold Hedgeman, Young Women's Christian Association executive and first consultant for New York City on racial problems. In 1943 she became executive director, the National Council for a Permanent Fair Employment Practices Committee. Later, Hedgeman was appointed a special consultant for the Department of State to India. In 1978 Hedgeman was named as one of fifty Extraordinary Women of Achievement in New York City by the National Conference of Christians and Jews.

African Zoar Church, Philadelphia, Pa.:
First Black Methodist Episcopal Church
1794

Harry Hosier (c. 1750–1806): Eloquent Pioneer Black Preacher

UPPER SANDUSKY, OHIO

Wyandotte Indian Mission Founded by John Stewart
c. 1819
First Methodist Episcopal Mission to Native Americans

Harry Hosier, the only person of color to see the ordination of Bishop Asbury (peeking from behind the pulpit).

(Painting by Thomas Coke Ruckle)

The Christmas Conference (1784): Harry Hosier Present

WILLIAM H. CROGMAN (1841–1931):
First Black Freedmen's Aid Society Teacher
1870

Gammon Theological Seminary, Atlanta, Ga.
First Accredited Black Theological School, Founded, 1883

J. W. E. BOWEN, SR. (1885–1933):
First Black President, Gammon Theological Seminary

MARSHALL W. TAYLOR
(1847–1887):
First Black Editor, Southwestern Christian Advocate
1884–1887

MARY McLEOD BETHUNE (1875–1955):
Educator, States woman, Churchwoman

Four presidents of Central Jurisdiction WSCS, from left to right: Mary Drake (Tennessee), 1964–68; Anita Fields (Kentucky), 1960–64; Ruth Carter (New Orleans), 1948–60; Margaret Bowen (New Orleans), 1940–1948

MATTHEW SIMPSON DAVAGE (1879–1976):
Higher Education Statesman

Associate Secretary General Board of Education
1940–1952

THERESSA HOOVER
Deputy General Secretary
Women's Program Division
Board of Global Ministries

CHARLES ALBERT TINDLEY (1851–1933):
"Prince of Preachers"
Pastor of Tindley Temple Methodist Episcopal Church, Philadelphia, Pa.
1901–1933

FIRST BLACK METHODIST EPISCOPAL BISHOPS SERVING IN THE UNITED STATES, 1920

BISHOP ROBERT E. JONES

Elected Bishop at Des Moines, Iowa, in 1920

Served New Orleans Area 1920–1936

Served Columbus Area 1936–1944
Retired 1944

Died May 18, 1960

BISHOP MATTHEW W. CLAIR, SR.

Elected Bishop at Des Moines, Iowa, in 1920,

Served Monrovia Area 1920–1924

Served Covington Area 1924–1936
Retired 1936

Served Atlanta Area 1939–1940
Died June 28, 1943

MISSIONARY BISHOPS

F. BURNS   J. ROBERTS   I. B. SCOTT   A. P. CAMPHOR

BISHOPS OF THE METHODIST EPISCOPAL CHURCH

R. E. JONES

M. W. CLAIR, SR.

A. P. SHAW

BISHOPS OF THE METHODIST CHURCH

W. A. C. HUGHES

L. H. KING

W. J. KING

R. N. BROOKS

E. W. KELLY

J. W. E. BOWEN

E. A. LOVE

M. W. CLAIR, JR.

P. A. TAYLOR, JR.

C. F. GOLDEN

N. W. MOORE, JR.

M. L. HARRIS

J. S. THOMAS, JR.

L. S. ALLEN

BISHOPS OF THE UNITED METHODIST CHURCH

R. C. NICHOLS

E. CARROLL

E. T. DIXION, JR.

E. A. AMMONS

M. TALBERT

W. T. HANDY, JR.

W. WHITE

F. E. MAY

F. C. STITH

E. W. NEWMAN

L. T. C. KELLEY

J. B. BETHEA

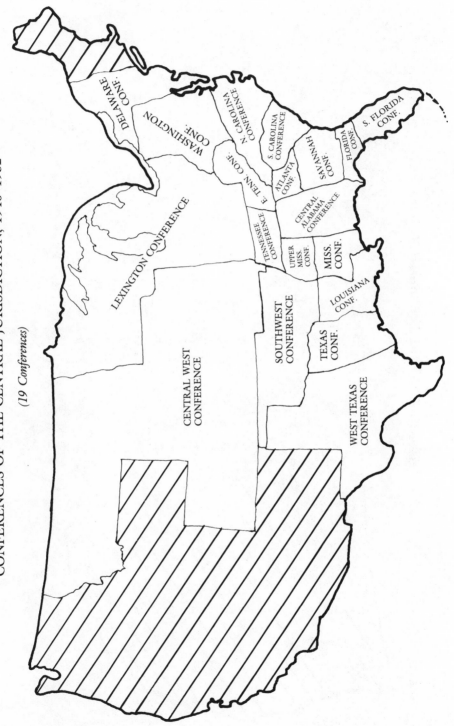

CONFERENCES OF THE CENTRAL JURISDICTION, 1940–1952

(19 Conferences)

DELAWARE CONF.

WASHINGTON CONF.

N. CAROLINA CONFERENCE

S. CAROLINA CONFERENCE

S. FLORIDA CONF.

FLORIDA CONF.

SAVANNAH CONF.

ATLANTA CONF.

E. TENN. CONF.

CENTRAL ALABAMA CONFERENCE

TENNESSEE CONFERENCE

UPPER MISS CONF.

MISS. CONF.

LEXINGTON CONFERENCE

LOUISIANA CONF.

SOUTHWEST CONFERENCE

TEXAS CONF.

CENTRAL WEST CONFERENCE

WEST TEXAS CONFERENCE

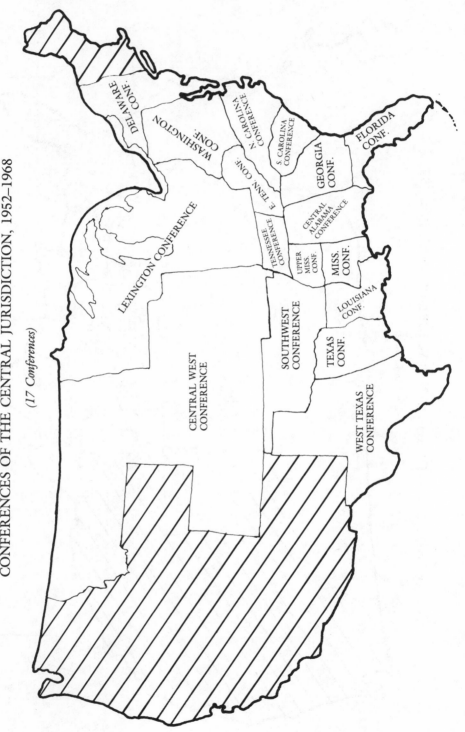

CONFERENCES OF THE CENTRAL JURISDICTION, 1952–1968

(17 Conferences)

DELAWARE CONF.

WASHINGTON CONF.

N. CAROLINA CONFERENCE

S. CAROLINA CONFERENCE

FLORIDA CONF.

GEORGIA CONF.

E. TENN. CONF.

CENTRAL ALABAMA CONFERENCE

LEXINGTON CONFERENCE

TENNESSEE CONFERENCE

UPPER MISS. CONF.

MISS. CONF.

LOUISIANA CONF.

CENTRAL WEST CONFERENCE

SOUTHWEST CONFERENCE

TEXAS CONF.

WEST TEXAS CONFERENCE

C H A P T E R 5

THE CENTRAL JURISDICTION
Passive Resistance

Major J. Jones

When legends are allowed to masquerade as history, truth gets distorted and checkered and sentimental memories operate as if they were facts. Such has been and is the case with the Central Jurisdiction—that contrived institutional machinery to handle the "black problem"—that signaled official and structural segregation in The Methodist Church for the first time in its history. The legends about its existence as being either the good old days or the old bad days are legion. The truth lies somewhere in between. But from whatever perspective one takes, no history of black people's membership in The United Methodist Church would be either adequate or complete without a comprehensive assessment of the Central Jurisdiction.

Many crucial decisions have had to be made by African Americans, whose presence on the North American continent by force has occasioned what sociologists have termed "the American dilemma." Perhaps one of the most critical decisions from the very beginning was whether to embrace at all what was presented as the Christian religion by slave masters and other white evangels whose practice of the religion belied the very essence of the faith proclaimed, let alone whether to join a Wesley-inspired Methodism and accept a perniciously concocted segregated Central Jurisdiction. The faith offered to the African indentured servants and slaves was certainly not the religion that those Africans had known who had been a part of launching the Christian church when it was born at Pentecost two thousand years earlier and thousands of miles across the ocean.

Understanding why black people elected to become Christians at all is a necessary part of an understanding of the Central Jurisdiction in particular and the presence of black people in United Methodism in general. The opinions of earlier historians have differed radically from the current and more informed opinions of contemporary thinkers as to why black people were moved to embrace the religion of the white Christian. Earlier thinkers led us to believe that black people who came to America, first as indentured servants, later as compelled slaves, and their American-born descendants were totally stripped of their original culture, especially of such intangible aspects of their being as world view and moral and religious values. Having had their cultural and religious heritage removed, these black slaves were a *tabula rasa* on which could be written a new religion, a new culture, a new world view, modified only by their limited conceptualized understanding. According to this view, black people are slightly different in culture and religion because they did not fully conceptualize the master's culture nor his Christianity.

A more informed and current view is offered by current black scholars such as Charles Long and Gayraud Wilmore, who contend that black people simply embraced that part of the religion of the master that was advantageous to their social, economic, and political well-being. They thought if it was good for the master and had given him such advantage, then it might well be prudent to identify with such a faith by *selective appropriation* and *prudent rejection* of the desirable and the undesirable, the useable and the unusable, aspects of white expressions of Christianity. In other words, they took what was useful; the rest they left.

In addition, let it suffice to say that the slaves were not unaware of the master's disdain, contempt, and debased views of black people. Indeed, they were mindful that they had been made slaves because many white people did not regard them as human, or, at best, as human as they were. Black people, therefore, were reluctant and selective embracers of any faith that even seemed to afford the master such an advantage; and yet Christianity was pragmatically attractive enough for a critical faith assessment. Thus with few exceptions, there was no totally uncritical assessment of the Christian faith as it was practiced by white people.

The slaves were highly selective of what they chose. They preserved the best of their own African heritage, and they selected those aspects of the master's Christianity relevant to their critical place in an alien culture. They understood the disparity between their own needs and aspirations and those that were evident wherever white Christians gathered. As C. Eric Lincoln aptly puts it:

> Blacks developed their own churches, but separate churches only relieved the physical impediments of the spiritual fulfillment of Black Christians. The prevailing doctrine of the white church was insidiously racist. It invited black people to believe in their inferiority as an act of God. . . . This was a slave-making, slave-keeping, ego-destroying doctrine which distorted the meaning of the black experience and consigned all who accepted it to an earthly life of ignominy and futility.[1]

Lincoln caught up in this statement the extreme, and yet the prevailing, intent of the religion of the white church, with few exceptions. During slavery, "the invisible institution," as E. Franklin Frazier called these secret religious gatherings, met at night, in secret, void of the white oversight. In the invisible church, away from the eyes and the ears of the slave masters and the overseers, there was the black pastor. Probably a carryover from the African religious past, a priest or at least a leader born of the indigenous cultural context of his time, this pastor was the leader and the interpreter of both religion and culture. My friend the late Daniel C. Thompson, a sociologist at Dillard University, used to say that this black preacher went to the white slave master's church on Sunday morning and heard the white preacher preach, and then he went to the invisible black church on Sunday night and preached the same sermon "as it ought to have been preached." Maybe the slaves were uneducated by Western standards, but they were not fools; they understood that the religion of the white church was the mere mortal creation of the white master and not the eternal creation of God. These African religionists were, as Wilmore puts it,

> fully aware that the God who demanded their devotion and the spirit that infused their secret meetings and possessed their souls and bodies in the ecstasy of worship, was not the God of the slave master, with whip and gun, nor the God of the plantation preacher, with his segregated services and unctuous injunction to humility and obedience.[2]

In addition to being a religious institution, the invisible church was the one central place where black people gathered to talk about freedom, conditions on other plantations, of slaves sold away to other locations, and of the larger world. The invisible church was a place, a very *special* place, where black people met to have *real* church, to enjoy free expression. Occasionally a traveler to freedom came by and told them of the journey. It was a place where personhood was preserved, where hope was kept alive, and where the dream of freedom could be nourished and kept viable.

We will miss the meaning of what happened in those bayous and swamps and wildernesses if we do not recall, above all, that the invisible church was related to the mainline denominational churches to which the slaves went with the master to worship on Sunday. So, from the arrival of the Dutch man-of-war ship at Jamestown in 1619 through the time of the formal organization of the Methodist Episcopal Church in 1784, and onward, black people have made critical decisions about their spiritual home on the American shores. And from the eighteenth century on to this present day, many have chosen to be Methodists. But the question remains—why?

WHY AFRICAN AMERICANS BECAME METHODISTS

With the possible exception of George Whitefield, who approved of slavery—even to the extent of owning slaves himself—early Methodists were generally against slavery. John Wesley and white members of Methodism, as exampled in the pronouncements of the Christmas Conference of 1784, were among the strongest voices against the institution of slavery. From the first General Conference and onward, resolutions against slavery were commonplace. However, there was always still a tendency to compromise when more resolute actions were needed. The late H. Richard Niebuhr rightly contends that the position that the Methodist Episcopal Church took against slavery and its efforts to exclude slaveholders from its membership attracted black people to the membership rolls of the invisible church and the visible black Methodist Episcopal churches of later years. The radical action by the General Conference of 1784 "to extirpate this abomination" was stated in the resolution that passed:

1. To expel all slaveholding members of Methodist Societies who would not in twelve months manumit their slaves after they reached a certain age (Methodists in Virginia "because of peculiar circumstances" were given two years of grace.)
2. To expel immediately all members who bought or sold slaves, except for the purpose of liberation.[3]

These were stronger words than could be made a reality. There were still ambiguities and grounds for interpretation that provided opportunity for escape. Yet as time passed and the new church acquired more members, and as slavery grew, moral and spiritual arguments were advanced in defense of slavery, even on the grounds of Scripture. Many Methodists, along with other white Christians, started to interpret the stance of the church so that it was not only compatible with but actually supportive of the institution of slavery, until the crisis of 1844, when Methodism split over the question of slavery.

There were some other reasons why black people embraced Methodism: First, early preachers actively sought out black people. Second, the message of early Methodism was a simple call for a conviction of sin, faith in Jesus Christ, a sense that God forgives sin, and that in that forgiveness salvation was assured. Third, there was the gospel message itself: the message of a just God who hated all expressions of evil, slavery among them. This God, they were assured, would in the end punish both evil masters and evil slaves. This just God who loved and cared for all gave his Son to die for salvation for all, including those who were poor and black. Finally, with few exceptions, the attitude of the Methodist preacher was against slavery.

The black slaves heard this message gladly and with great joy and thanksgiving. As one early convert expressed it, "I feel thankful that I ever heard a Methodist preacher. We are beholding to the Methodists, under God, for the light of the Gospel we enjoy; for all other denominations preached so high flown that we were not able to comprehend their doctrine."[4]

It must be noted, however, that in spite of early Methodism's liberal attitude and the radical resolutions against the institution of slavery, black people were still black people, whether they were slave or free. Neither religion nor the church had the power to break down rigid social customs. There were laws, social customs, and attitudes long antedating the coming of Methodism to America that drew a sharp line of distinction between black and white people within the societies and within the later churches.

CRUCIAL DECISIONS FOR BLACK METHODISTS: TO LEAVE OR TO STAY

Not all black churches were invisible, nor were all black Methodists in the galleries or balconies of white churches. When the numbers of black Methodists got larger and black people became a more demanding presence, things began to change. This was symbolized in the actions of Richard Allen at St. George's Methodist Episcopal Church in Philadelphia, when he, Darius Jinnings, Absalom Jones, and William White were pulled from their knees during a 1787 Sunday morning service: *They took a walk.* Their walk out of the church indicated that the black presence within the Methodist Episcopal Church had become too large to be contained within the white church. It was this painful walk out of St. George's Church that signaled the beginning of the independent black churches, the Methodist ones in particular.

Allen withdrew and formed the African Methodist Episcopal (AME) Church. Absalom Jones connected himself with the Episcopal Church and later became their first black priest at St. Thomas. These two choices, Allen to leave and Jones to stay within an organized white church, were symbolic of the dilemma facing black people in predominantly white churches. Other independent, free, and separate black churches were established as black people left to form their own communions. Some 1,066 black people withdrew with Allen, but approximately 42,304 black people elected to stay within the Methodist Episcopal Church. It is interesting to note that during this period the numbers of black people within the church outgrew those of all of the black-only churches. Until the split in 1844 over the issue of slavery, black people were mostly Methodist Episcopal. Two questions present themselves to us for answer, which may seem like the same question: Why did the black people who stayed not join Allen? Why did they remain?

In order, let us address these questions. First of all, in their beginning, the black denominations were small and unimpressive. So small was the AME Church that its first Annual Conference was held in homes. Daniel Payne, a historian of the early AME Church, puts it this way: "This then was the origin of the African Methodist Episcopal Church. Poor and lowly, an outcast and despised of men, it thus entered feebly into being."[5]

Second, black people themselves tended to look down on these beginning denominations that were so unimpressive, led by ex-slaves. Suddenly persons with whom they had had long association were calling themselves bishops and general superintendents, which many black people thought was ridiculous. Only men like Richard Allen made the difference and saved the new denomination from being deemed impossible. He was a well-respected, hard-working, frugal, and creative man with an impeccable character.

Third, meeting at separate places and at different times without white supervision was difficult and at times legally forbidden. The separate black churches were suspect and were often subjected to harassment and sometimes were unable to meet in certain locations.

Fourth, many black people felt that association with the white church provided them broader opportunities for interracial fellowship. It gave black people a better opportunity to know many more white people. Indeed, to belong to the same church with white people was considered an advantage.

In the fifth place, there were also economic advantages to be derived from the association with white people. It was seen as a great advantage for a people so economically weak, politically helpless, and legally defenseless, whether slave or free. The decision to remain within the Methodist Episcopal Church was a pragmatic one made in the interests of well-being, security, and advantage. Many of the white members of the Methodist Episcopal Church were friendly and politically helpful to the black members.

Finally, it must be pointed out that the Methodist Episcopal Church was enough concerned about the general welfare of the black members to provide educational and economic assistance. It should be noted that the Methodist Episcopal Church established more schools and places of learning and training for black people than any other denomination.

So Allen left with some, but many stayed and remained loyal to the Mother Church even though they were undervalued as persons and not truly accorded the rights and privileges of all other Methodists. There were both negative and positive reasons for staying.

If these were the reasons why many black people did not leave with Allen, what were the reasons why they stayed? First, there were those who considered it an honor to be in a white Methodist Episcopal Church. For that honor and privilege many black people were willing to compromise, to pay any price to belong, for in belonging they felt they were a part of the mainline Christian Church rehearsing here for the eschatological kingdom to come.

Second, there was a type of special recognition given to many black people because they were Methodist Episcopal members. Many would say they were of the better educated group of black people of the time. This was important to a people who knew illiteracy, oppression, poverty, and ignorance.

Third, there were many black people who felt that they could do more from within a large church that was majority white. They felt that the resources were more plentiful to help lift the race, and they were willing to suffer certain disadvantages to have the opportunity to have access to those resources for their families and their race.

Fourth, there were many who felt that if they stayed in the church they could change the attitudes and opinions of white people toward black people. They saw value in staying in the church, hoping as they associated with white people that they would be more willing to find all black people more acceptable.

One has to note that black Methodist Episcopal Church members were sometimes subjected to criticism and scorn and accused of a full and passive acceptance of white oppression and subjection. They were, at times, accused of being mere foils of white power structures, both within and outside the church. During Reconstruction and later, black members of the Methodist Episcopal Church were called the mere direct descendants of the house slaves of prior times, "Uncle Toms" accepting white rule while assuring white people that all was well in the black community and that black people could coexist with whites on an unequal basis.

That is somewhat the way it had been, and that is the way it was when the three branches of Methodism started talks that would eventually bring them back together in the historic Uniting Conference of 1939.

THE CENTRAL JURISDICTION IN HISTORIC PERSPECTIVE

When the Uniting Conference met in 1939 in Kansas City, the black delegates representing the nineteen black Annual Conferences into which most black members had been separated were some of the most distinguished black persons in American religion. The grandchildren of slaves, they were the unquestioned leadership within the Methodist Episcopal Church. They had been both targets of the criticisms discussed above and recipients of many of the benefits accruing from belonging to the Methodist Episcopal Church. Many of them had acquired their education in schools that had been founded and supported by the Methodist Episcopal Church. Many were close to and somewhat responsible to much of the white power structure of the Methodist Episcopal Church. The black people who were delegates to the Uniting Conference were the recognized leadership of the approximately 350,000 black people who had, for one reason or another, elected to join and remain in the majority white church. Surely they were aware of the fact that they were the primary reason that union of the three branches of Methodism had not taken place in all of the prior attempts.

The Plan of Union was clearly a contrivance to solve "the Negro Problem." It was a Machiavellian scheme to segregate the church officially for the first time, without calling it segregation, to appease the Southern church (and perhaps the Northern and Methodist Protestant churches, too). Placing all black Methodists in a central structure, while organizing the white members geographically, the plan clearly subordinated the black membership to the whites, stepping backward from the inclusiveness the black membership sought and the principles the gospel proclaims.

They were aware of their options, stated in the words of two of the delegates speaking on the floor of the Conference. Speaking in favor of the Plan of Union Daniel W. Shaw said:

> I am therefore prepared to ask the General Conference to appoint a Commission to draw up articles of separation and to draw a plebiscite on the question of setting the Negroes apart by themselves with all of their church and school property turned over to them in fee simple with an annual stipend of 120,000 reducible at the rate of 10,000 per quadrennium until the sum should be reduced to 50,000, which sum should be permanent or reducible only on the motion of the recipient, or on a ratio suggested above. . . . We shall want such separation as will really make the Negro the initiator and the leader in his own church.[6]

Speaking against the plan, David D. Jones, president of Bennett College, said:

> Everybody knows the plan is segregation and segregation in the ugliest way because it is couched in such pious terms. My friends, what does segregation do to people? It sets them aside. It labels them, it says that they are not fit to be treated as other people are treated.[7]

WHY DID THEY NOT WALK OUT?

Why did they not walk out of the 1939 Uniting Conference? Indeed, many answers have been offered, but none beyond the logic of the following: First of all, there were those who made the simple answer that black people had been a part of the Methodist movement since its inception in America and did not intend to withdraw or separate themselves from their religious heritage and history. Second, most of them were economically related to the church, and to withdraw from the Methodist Episcopal Church was to withdraw from their support. Third, there were many who felt that they could better address the issues of separation from within the church than from outside it. Fourth, there were many who reasoned that even though it would be divided constitutionally by race, there would still be broader leadership opportunities available within the new structure than were available in the church prior to Union. Indeed, they reasoned that the new Central Jurisdiction gave more opportunity for black leadership than had ever existed before. Though debatable, there were many who felt that the positives far outweighed the negatives. Within The Methodist Church, they reasoned, there would be opportunity for broader leadership of even white people.

196

Perhaps the late Bishop Willis J. King, then president of Gammon Theological Seminary, said it best:

> More important, however, than rights and prerogatives was the instinctive conviction evident from their earliest connection with the people called "Methodists" [that] this fellowship represented a communion that was seriously seeking to build a brotherhood among all men. They believed that their membership in such a fellowship would help in the achievement of world brotherhood.[8]

However, despite the hopeful convictions summed up in Dr. King's statement, there was still widespread debate among the nineteen black Conferences of the Methodist Episcopal Church as to whether they should accept the Plan of Union, and the plan failed to carry the vote in a majority of the Conferences. On the other hand, the plan was approved by a majority of the three uniting branches of Methodism, including the white membership of the Annual Conferences of the Methodist Episcopal Church. The die was cast; the fate of black Methodists was sealed: All black Methodists, except a small number in the far west and in the Boston and New York areas, were placed in a segregated Central Jurisdiction.

Although a few black leaders thought that it was somewhat unrealistic to hope for the elimination of all segregation at one time, it was with regret and disappointment that they arrived at the conclusion that it might be wise to accept unification with the Central Jurisdiction as a present condition, looking forward to a future time when the ideal of inclusiveness would prevail. The late Dr. James P. Brawley, president of Clark College and a delegate to the Uniting Conference, expressed the collective regrets and hopes of the 350,000 or more black people:

> It was the hope of the Negro membership of the Methodist Episcopal Church that his status would be improved in the new United Church and that no structural organization would set him apart and give him less dignity and recognition than he already had. . . . He, therefore, rejected the Plan of Union. . . . This was a stigma too humiliating to accept.[9]

It was a stigma that was to last from 1939 until 1968. The 1939 union was a compromise that established a black unit of the church that was to last until the last fragments of the nineteen black Annual Conferences were eliminated in 1974. William B. McClain was right when he reminded us anew that

> in setting up the Central Jurisdiction The Methodist Church capitulated to the counter currents of American racist proclivities and yielded to the prevailing morality of the society. Its ethic became those temporal pragmatic considerations of the world rather than the eternal claims of justice which its prophetic Lord had declared.[10]

197

The reality of the Central Jurisdiction came to the black members of the Methodist Church not in the Uniting Conference nor in the General Conference that followed the next year; rather, it came in the first Jurisdictional Conference in St. Louis in 1940. In the words of Bishop Robert E. Jones, "After the Negro had registered his opinion and had been outvoted by a majority in the three churches, he logically and loyally submitted to the outcome."[11]

However, from then on black people expressed their displeasure with their status within the church. Indeed, no compromise between Christianity and culture is ever completely acceptable, nor is it ever completely successful. The former contains elements that evaluate and judge human actions so that every human situation falls short of goals of the Commonwealth of God. No matter how hard one may try, it is not possible to make the message of the Gospel compatible with any plan that does not establish equality among the members of the human family under God. The people of the Central Jurisdiction accepted it as a mere temporary and expedient measure; they were never in complete harmony with the rest of The Methodist Church. They hoped, as Bishop Alexander P. Shaw expressed in his Episcopal Address in 1944 to the Central Jurisdiction, that "in the very near future our Methodism may become sufficiently Christian in character and maturity to find a more excellent way."[12]

POSITIVE AND NEGATIVE VIEWS OF MEMBERSHIP IN THE CENTRAL JURISDICTION

Positive Views

First of all, many people saw the Central Jurisdiction as an opportunity for black people to prove themselves worthy to the white people who had so long rejected them as being undesirable. One should recall that this was the period in the nation's history when black people dreamed of being at one with the rest of humanity, of a time when race and ethnicity would be forgotten and all personal differences would be submerged as black people proved themselves worthy of a total belonging.

There were those who also felt that the Central Jurisdiction would give black Methodists unlimited financial and administrative resources. However, many soon found that such would not be the case at either the local or the General Church level, and soon blacks realized that many of the general agencies of the church did not give equal support to the Central Jurisdiction churches, and that many of the resources given were restricted, limited, and unequal. When staff and other resources were extended, they were unable to meet many of the needs of the black Methodist churches simply because they had been trained or designed with white churches in mind.

In the third place, as William B. McClain pointed out, the first days of the Central Jurisdiction were hopeful days. Indeed, the Central Jurisdiction "hastened to take advantage of every advantage" of its separate existence and serve Black Methodists. Efforts were made to enrich worship experiences, upgrade church parsonages and church facilities, to recruit and train more clergy and lay leaders, increase and enliven the work of women's groups. And there was help from the National Church to support the efforts of the Black Methodists of the Central Jurisdiction.[13]

However, the efforts to revitalize the black constituency of the Methodist Church, set apart as they were, seemed to fall far short of the best efforts. It would seem that a part of the problem was that they were looking always to a better day for the church, when there would be no need for a Central Jurisdiction, and this made the Central Jurisdiction no more than a mere temporary roadblock in their path to a better future.

Negative Views

First of all, many people felt that black people made a grave mistake in not separating themselves from The Methodist Church in 1939. They felt that the 1940 Central Jurisdiction Conference should have marked the formation of a new black denomination or a merger with one of the other branches of the black Methodist tradition. A great majority felt that the Christian Methodist Episcopal Church would have been the logical black denomination with which to merge because of its historic relationship with the white Methodist Episcopal Church, South. (However, there was an opposing opinion that the Christian Methodist Episcopal Church had compromised itself too much by its continuing relations to the Methodist Episcopal Church, South, and that to merge or unite with them would be more like asking white Methodists, once again, to set blacks aside.)

Second, black Methodist Episcopal members were never able to forgive the white members for the humiliation of being set aside in the Central Jurisdiction. This deep disappointment affected their leadership, making it less than effective as a competing entity within the black community. A clean separation would have been their choice.

In the third place, in the face of advantages such as proportionate representation on all boards and agencies and even membership in its highest councils, and with the assertion, never fully implemented, that black people were eligible to hold the highest posts in the church without discrimination, there were many positions that black people did not dream that they would ever hold. Then, too, many white people, even of the most liberal mindset, thought of the Central Jurisdiction as if it were another denomination, separate and apart.

In the fourth place, beyond the intense efforts made by the leaders of the Central Jurisdiction, despite the accelerated efforts in education, evangelism, attempted upgraded worship, the improvement of property, and the establishment of a few new churches, the Central Jurisdiction had to struggle to hold its own. At best, we can say that the Central Jurisdiction started in 1940 with some 350,000 or more blacks and nineteen black Conferences; the membership count was about the same when the last of the seventeen then-fragmented black Conferences were merged with the regional white Jurisdictional Conferences in 1974. The fact that the total General Church never accepted the Central Jurisdiction was probably another contributing factor in its marginal success. Dr. John Graham points out that after the General Conference of 1940,

> for twelve years, the General Conference passed resolutions and appointed study committees. The 1944 General Conference declared: "We look to the ultimate elimination of racial discrimination in The Methodist Church." It also appointed its first study committee. Its function was to consider afresh the relationship of all races included in the membership of The Methodist Church and to report back to the 1948 General Conference.[14]

However, the 1948 General Conference, meeting in Boston, merely listened to the good report of the 1944 General Conference committee, expressed appreciation, and then referred it to the many boards and agencies of the General Church "for systematic use in their activities and publications." The 1948 General Conference also authorized another General Church study on social issues.

STEPS TOWARD THE ELIMINATION OF THE CENTRAL JURISDICTION

The more the General Church, speaking officially through its General Conference, conceded that racial separation within the structures of the church was not only wrong but also un-Christian, the stronger grew the deep opposition within the ranks of the Central Jurisdiction's black leadership. On August 28, 1951, Bishop Robert N. Brooks delivered an address to a group of black Methodists in which he said that racial segregation and discrimination were Methodism's twin evils: "It is the twin evils of discrimination and segregation that the Church has failed so lamentably. It has by its practices, sanctified racial prejudice which is rampant in the world today . . . but it cannot say a convincing word to society unless and until it eliminates these cancerous evils from its own Christian community."[15]

So pointed were these words of Bishop Brooks, and so pointed were their implications, and so pressed was the General Church to try to justify its inability to act, that it is no wonder that Bishop Paul Kern could have said no less in his Episcopal Address before the 1952 General Conference: "To discriminate against a person solely upon the basis of his race is both unfair and un-Christian. Every child of God is entitled to that place in society which he has won by his industry, his integrity and his character."[16] (We must take note, however, of what the bishop is really saying: that one is entitled to these places of equality only if one has been adjudged to be a good worker and to have acted acceptably, and only if he or she has been exceptional in conduct.)

It was only after the 1956 General Conference meeting in Minneapolis, Minnesota, passed the historic Amendment IX that the process of eliminating the Central Jurisdiction was seriously begun. It must be recalled, for the sake of history, that the Central Jurisdiction was never, as has been pointed out before, an acceptable solution to the problem of race within the church. The prior 1948 General Conference had passed a resolution to change the boundaries of the Central and the Western Jurisdictions under paragraph 532 of the *Discipline,* so that Negro churches in Arizona could become a part of the Southern California-Arizona Conference; also, the General Conference passed a resolution in 1952 making paragraph 532 more flexible and simple, so that Negro churches could transfer from the Central Jurisdiction to a regional jurisdiction. It must further be noted that every General Conference since 1940 had said something about the Central Jurisdiction, even if it had not taken any action. However, the 1956 General Conference under Amendment IX set in motion the process for the elimination of the Central Jurisdiction. The only question that remained was "When?" There were, in relation to this question, two views:

a) The first question for debate was whether the necessary elimination could be brought about by voluntary action, with the needed incentive provided by a moral sense of the right, and the inner urgency of the "ought." In other words, could it be done on a pure voluntary basis? b) The second question was: would it have to be achieved by forced legislation?[17]

There was always doubt in the minds of black people that the white people of The Methodist Church would ever press hard enough, motivated by a deep enough moral conviction that racial separation was evil and a sin, to achieve voluntary inclusiveness. Almost all of the black leadership felt that the process would be too slow.

Nevertheless, after many hours of debate, the General Conference of 1956 unanimously adopted Amendent IX to the constitution, which allowed for the voluntary transfer of Conferences, local churches, or parts of Annual Conferences from the Central Jurisdiction into the geographically situated regional jurisdictions. It fixed no timetable for the process to be completed.[18]

Just before it closed, in a climate of premature rejoicing, the General Conference of 1956 passed a statement of intent:

There must be no place in The Methodist Church for racial discrimination or enforced segregation. Recognizing that we have not attained this goal, yet rejoicing in the progress made, we recommend that discrimination or segregation, by any method or practice, whether in conference structure or otherwise, be abolished with reasonable speed.[19]

Dr. Graham reminded us all that in its school desegregation ruling, the United States Supreme Court used the phrase "with *deliberate* speed," while the 1956 General Conference used the phrase "with *reasonable* speed."

In 1960 Dr. Harold C. Case attempted to amend the report of the Interjurisdictional Commission to the 1960 General Conference to say that "it shall have in part as its expressed goal the abolition of the Central Jurisdiction by due constitutional process by 1968."[20] Dr. Charles F. Golden, in support of the Case Amendment, asserted that

certainly there will be a price to be paid for progress made, but this amendment will give us an opportunity to lift the level of performance in the conferences of the Central Jurisdiction, particularly in the area of leadership training, salaries, pension rates and other differences that increase the gap between conferences of the Central Jurisdiction and overlapping geographic jurisdictions.[21]

The Case Amendment lost, and the Golden statement stands as a reminder of the widespread differences that existed in the Central Jurisdiction and the other jurisdictions. After twenty years of effort (1940–1960), the Central Jurisdiction, as was pointed out above, did not have the comparable resources nor the incentive to compete with the other jurisdictions of the advantaged white people.

After losing the battle in the 1960 General Conference, the black leadership took note of the plight of black people within The Methodist Church and the need for more General Church direction from the black constituency of the church. The 1960 Central Jurisdictional Conference was alive with deep resentment that no timetable was set to end the Central Jurisdiction. However, so eager were the leaders to eliminate the Central Jurisdiction that not enough thought was given to the question of the price they were willing to pay. The 1960 Central Jurisdictional Conference appointed a Committee of Five whose mandate was to devise a plan for the elimination of the Central Jurisdiction:

1) First of all, it was to prepare a report indicating, in crystal clear language, what Black people expected of The Methodist Church and their White brothers and sisters; 2) it was to analyze the recommendations of the Interjurisdictional Relations Committee and make its recommendations to the annual conferences of the Central Jurisdiction; and 3) develop a plan of action for the Central Jurisdiction and devise strategies for implementing the plan of action.

The members of the Committee of Five were James S. Thomas, Atlantic Coast area; Richard Erwin, Baltimore area; John H. Graham, Nashville-Birmingham area; W. Astor Kirk, New Orleans area; and John J. Hicks, St. Louis area.[22]

To help them in the study and the writing of such a plan, the Committee of Five proposed a study conference, which was convened on March 26–28, 1961, in Cincinnati. Participants in the conference were the members of the College of Bishops, district superintendents, pastors, laymen and laywomen, youth, executive secretaries of Christian education, college presidents, and the black representatives of general boards and agencies of the General Church. Indeed, black Methodists came from a broad section of the church to help formulate strategies for the future of black people within the life of The Methodist Church. From that study conference came a collective voice of black Methodists, issuing forth in the form of a paper entitled "The Central Jurisdiction Speaks." It was an impressive statement, based on the following basic principles:

1. The fundamental objective in the dissolution of the Central Jurisdiction must be *de facto* inclusiveness in The Methodist Church.
2. The minimum requirements for *de facto* inclusiveness is the absence on all levels of church life of patterns and policies based on race or color.
3. Each step taken to dissolve the Central Jurisdiction must be an integral part of an overall plan or program to abolish all forms of racial segregation and discrimination from The Methodist Church.[23]

The one thing that the study conference did not do was write into the plan for the elimination of the Central Jurisdiction any safeguards for the future status of black people within the new inclusive future. Black people have not yet recovered much that they thereby lost. When the need for some safeguards was voiced by Major J. Jones at the study conference, the prevailing response was "We should trust our white brothers and sisters, and to suggest safeguards would convey to them a lack of trust."

However, shortly after the Cincinnati study conference, the 1960 General Conference–appointed Commission on Interjurisdictional Relations released its report number 1, in which it proposed that the Conferences of the Baltimore area should be transferred to the Northeastern Jurisdiction, the Conferences of the St. Louis area to the North Central Jurisdiction, the Conferences of the New Orleans to the South Central Jurisdiction, and the Conferences of the Atlantic Coast area and the Nashville-Birmingham area to the Southeastern Jurisdiction.

The Committee of Five of the Central Jurisdiction viewed these proposed transfers as totally unthinkable. They were at one in contending that such transfers would violate the basic principles set forth by the Cincinnati study conference, and that such transfers as were being suggested by the Interjurisdictional Relations Commission would have the effect of institutionalizing a system of racially segregated Annual Conferences in regional jurisdictions. It was the Committee of Five's contention that the plan overlooked the much deeper and more crucial problems of racial segregation and discrimination in the governmental structures of the General Church.

The elimination of the Central Jurisdiction was one of the central concerns of the 1964 General Conference when it convened in Pittsburgh, Pennsylvania, in April 1964. The Central Jurisdiction was still very much a segregated structure within the church, and Amendment IX had resulted in very few church transfers. There were pickets, there were calls for redress of many current social ills and glaring injustices, so rampant in American society in those times.

In his Episcopal Address Bishop Gerald Kennedy expressed the sentiments of many members of the 1964 General Conference when he said:

> We believe that this General Conference should insist upon the removal from its structures of any mark of racial segregation and do it without wasting time. . . . God Almighty is moving toward a world of interracial brotherhood so speedily and irresistibly that to hesitate is to fight against God and be crushed.[24]

The General Conference of 1964 decreed that

a) All local churches should be opened to all persons without regard to race, color, or national origin or economic condition. [This action put back in the *Discipline* of The Methodist Church a mandate which had been in the *Discipline* of The Methodist Episcopal Church since 1884.]

b) The General Conference adopted a detailed plan of action for the elimination of the Central Jurisdiction, which presupposed that the 1964 Central Jurisdictional Conference keep its commitment, made through its Committee of Five, that it would realign its conferences geographically so that no conference boundaries or Area would be located in any other regional jurisdiction.

c) In order to assume the burden of inadequate salaries and pensions in the Central Jurisdiction, the 1964 General Conference created a temporary general aid fund.

d) Probably the most far-reaching action taken was the creation of a Jurisdiction Advisory Council to work within each Jurisdiction and with other Jurisdictions to deal with matters related to the questions of transfers and mergers. This was the most direct action taken by any prior General Conference since the 1939 merger of the Methodist Episcopal Church, the Methodist Protestant Church and the Methodist Episcopal Church South. With this and other actions of the 1964 General Conference, the process had begun.[25]

The W. Astor Kirk Amendment to the 1964 report of the Interjurisdiction Commission's report to the 1964 General Conference, which was to report to a 1966 Special Session and to the 1968 General Conference on the final dissolution of the jurisdiction, was an attempt to accelerate the dissolution of the Central Jurisdiction. The amendment to the report was that the commission would recommend in its 1968 report that "no racial structures be carried over into the Constitution of the new United Church." However, after the amendment was interpreted "no structure," Dr. Kirk insisted that Dr. Charles Parlin, the chairperson of the commission, had intentionally dropped the *s* from the word "structures," so that the amendment only precluded the Central Jurisdictional structure and did not apply to Annual Conferences, districts, and local churches. Whether Mr. Parlin dropped the *s* intentionally or not, the fact still remains that the "structure" interpretation prevailed, and the amendment applied only to the Central Jurisdictional structure.

The 1964 General Conference, after considering the question of whether to dissolve the Central Jurisdiction by constitutional amendment, voted to continue the voluntary process by also continuing the Commission on Interjurisdictional Relations, which it had appointed in 1960. The General Conference further mandated the commission to continue working on abolishing the Central Jurisdiction, promoting interracial brotherhood through Christian love, and in general helping achieve a more inclusive church. By the Kirk Amendment, the church was also mandated not to continue any segregated structure of the Central Jurisdiction into the new church beyond the 1968 time of union. The commission also accepted an amendment by Major J. Jones that a progress report of the commission's work and progress be made at the proposed 1966 adjourned session of the 1964 General Conference in Chicago.

The 1964 Central Jurisdictional Conference, meeting in Daytona Beach, Florida, in keeping with the leadership's faith expressed to the 1964 General Conference by the Committee of Five, realigned the boundaries of its Annual Conferences so that each Conference fell within bounds of only one of the respective five regional jurisdictions. Soon thereafter, the Delaware and Washington Conferences, formerly both a part of the Central Jurisdiction, became, by merger, a part of the Northeastern Jurisdiction. The Lexington Conference, formerly of the Central Jurisdiction, became, by merger, a part of the North Central Jurisdiction.

By the time the 1966 special session of the General Conference met in Chicago, there was great unrest among the black leadership of the Methodist Church. They had, by this time, become aware of several facts:

1. The Central Jurisdiction was being fragmented by the transfer and merger of Annual Conferences into regional jurisdictions, without any prior agreements to protect the interests of black ministerial and lay members.

2. Many of the Conferences were agreeing to too few, if any, prior agreements.

3. There was always, without exception, a loss of black district and Annual Conference leadership.

4. The leadership within the merger agreements, where such agreements were being perfected, was majority white.

5. The black bishops in the transfers, without exception, were being removed from the black people's majority membership.

6. The Conferences were being fragmented so that little pockets of black people would be, without exception, located within majority white Annual Conferences, and that the black pastor would be among people—white United Methodists—who had heretofore been strangers.

7. Black people would be subjected to insensitive white majority rule.

Although the 1966 special session of the General Conference adopted many good-sounding resolutions, many had already been forgotten by the time of the 1968 Uniting Conference. The 1966 special session of the General Conference also authorized a special session of the Central Jurisdiction in 1967 to replace Bishop M. L. Harris, who had died in 1966, and to conclude the existence of the Central Jurisdiction. By 1972 all of the Conferences of the former Central Jurisdiction had been transferred and were in process of merger with the respective Conferences of the regional jurisdictions in which they were located geographically.

A POST–CENTRAL JURISDICTION QUESTION: I WONDER

One wonders whether, if the Central Jurisdiction had survived the 1960s, would black people have voted it out of existence in the 1970s, or even in our current times? Had the black leadership been able to foresee the future, they might not have pushed for the brand of integration that was then conceptualized. Racial and ethnic pluralism was not then the goal, but rather an integration that was conceived in terms of giving up much and being received by many—almost at any price. Black people now would probably vote against the Central Jurisdiction in favor of a caucus, such as Black Methodists for Church Renewal. Indeed, Black Methodists for Church Renewal was merely, at best, a quick and perhaps necessary attempt to recover a vantage point that black Methodists had lost when they pushed for the elimination of the Central Jurisdiction. And yet, though Black Methodists for Church Renewal has been an effective protest and pressure group, even a gadfly and monitor, it has suffered somewhat because it has not been a part of the official structure of the church. On the other hand, one has to wonder if the Central Jurisdiction leadership would not have been too conservative and too much a part of the structure to have pushed for and received some of the benefits that have been achieved because of the many implicit and explicit protests and demands that Black Methodists for Church Renewal and others who have been in support of the caucus made on the church at every level.

This uncertainty about giving up the Central Jurisdiction vantage point was alive as late as 1967. In spite of the fact that the Georgia Conference and the Tennessee-Kentucky Conference did not adopt the 1966 report of the Commission on Interjurisdiction's Merger Resolution, it was declared adopted by the Judicial Council on February 5, 1968, thus meeting all constitutional requirements for merger. On April 23, 1968, Union was declared adopted, and the Central Jurisdiction was no more—dissolved, obliterated.

Within The United Methodist Church, black people have seen newly elected and appointed black leadership at all levels of the church. It is indeed a *new* day for black United Methodists. However, there is no one opinion about whether it is a **better** day. It might well be more wise to say that for black people, the future is still "as we wish."

C H A P T E R 6

THE UNITED METHODIST CHURCH
New Church—Old Issues
1968–Present

Grant S. Shockley

Three monumental tasks confronted the new United Methodist Church at the close of the Uniting General Conference held in Dallas, Texas, in 1968: (1) the responsibility of combining two denominations into an organic whole; (2) the Christian moral obligation to unify the two races in the new church, which had previously been segregated by social custom and church constitutional law, making them an inclusive[1] fellowship; and (3) the practical necessity of understanding and responding to the new reality of the then recently emerged Black Consciousness movement and its demands for equality and empowerment. It is the purpose of this chapter to discuss these expectations, the role of black Methodists and other advocates in attaining them, and the achievements that resulted.

STRUCTURING THE NEW CHURCH

Black Methodists had a major concern in reference to the proposed organizational structure of The United Methodist Church. This concern was not so much with the design submitted by the Structure Study Commission (1972).[2] Rather, it was the feeling that the church was not quite as intentional about ridding United Methodism of its racism as it was interested in removing all semblance of the symbols of segregation and inequality.

It has been stated that United Methodism was more interested in eliminating segregation than in implementing inclusiveness. Black people were aware of this. The final message of the College of Bishops at the last session of the Central Jurisdictional Conference meeting in Nashville, Tennessee (August 1967), made their goals and objectives clear: structural and functional racial inclusiveness; enlarged support for black churches, colleges and other programs; and intentional effort and funding for community development to help alleviate black urban problems such as poor housing, poor education, unemployment, and social injustices. Black Methodists for Church Renewal, in their organizing national conference in Cincinnati, Ohio (February 1968), articulated an entirely new approach to race relations in the church with their demands for "self-definition," "self-determination," and "black solidarity."[3]

The remainder of this chapter will briefly reconstruct the response of the church to these expectations, which were generally endorsed and met. It will also relate some instances of miscommunication and reluctance.

The new situation of black Methodists in The United Methodist Church highlighted significant new advantages as well as continuing disadvantages in relation to Merger. An elevated sense of self-esteem in belonging to the whole United Methodist Church was sometimes negated by a practical insistence on assimilating into the white mainstream. Full participation in the whole church often meant a loss of one's place in the black community, and sometimes the development of what C. Eric Lincoln has referred to as a "middle-class mentality."[4] New and exciting perspectives on the mission of the black church were often blunted with the response of "not a priority" from the parent denomination. Leadership gains for black Methodists could not always be equated with gaining effective power to effect change in the highly bureaucratic United Methodist system. Improved physical facilities for worship and programming and economic benefits from standard salaries, pensions, and other rights were undoubtedly advantageous.

Leadership Gains

The most dramatic progress toward the goal of making The United Methodist Church an inclusive fellowship took place as black Methodists secured increased opportunities for black members (and other racial-group members) to share leadership in the denomination. Committed to the concept of racial equality and attempting to comply with the affirmative action principles found in the *Book of Discipline* (especially in ¶ 814.1), the general boards and agencies of the denomination made genuine efforts to "recruit, employ, utilize, recompense, and promote . . . professional staff and other personnel without regard to race, color, or sex." This same general principle was applied to the election of bishops, lay, and ministerial positions to General and Jurisdictional Conferences, board membership, and staff election.

This section will summarize the outcome of this movement to equitably diversify the selection of bishops, district superintendents, members of the Judicial Council, and other selected administrative and support boards, commissions, and committees. The significant leadership gains that were made in black voting membership power and executive-level staff positions will be

THE UNITED METHODIST CHURCH

discussed later and in relation to the programs and ministries to which they relate.

Episcopal Leadership

The selection of bishops at the Jurisdictional Conferences following the 1968 Uniting Conference in Dallas was noteworthy for two reasons. It witnessed the rise of a new type of episcopal election process for the selection of bishops. For the first time in the history of the denomination, election and assignment to episcopal areas was on a nonsegregated basis. This had not been the case in the Central Jurisdiction. Second, since it was no longer necessary to elect black bishops only to the Central Jurisdiction and only when specifically needed by the black constituency of the church, it had become possible to elect to the episcopacy persons suitable to the office in the mind of the church, color notwithstanding. The results of recent episcopal elections in each jurisdiction and in the denomination at large have tended to prove this more inclusive method of selecting episcopal leadership to be a highly positive approach. It possibly has resulted in the election of more black persons to the office as well.

Let us observe how the new system worked in practice. Prior to the election of any black bishop in any of the jurisdictions of the new United Methodist Church, the black bishops who had been elected in the former Central Jurisdiction were transferred and assigned to episcopal areas on a nonracial basis.

In 1964 Bishop Prince A. Taylor was transferred into the Northeastern Jurisdiction and assigned to the then newly created New Jersey area, and Bishop James S. Thomas, Jr., had been transferred to the North Central Jurisdiction and assigned to the Iowa area. Similarly, in 1968 Bishops L. Scott Allen, Charles F. Golden, and Noah W. Moore, Jr., had all been transferred to the Southeastern, Western, and South Central Jurisdictions, respectively. Retired bishops Willis J. King (1886–1976), Edgar A. Love (1891–1974), and Matthew W. Clair, Jr. (1890–1965) became members of the College of Bishops where they resided.

The first black bishop to be elected in the new United Methodist Church was Roy C. Nichols, elected by the Northeastern Jurisdiction in July 1968. Originally from the Eastern Shore of Maryland, Nichols grew up in Philadelphia and graduated from Lincoln University in Pennsylvania. He moved to the West Coast for his theological education at the Pacific School of Religion (Berkeley, California), became ordained, and pastored Downs Memorial Church in Oakland, California, for fifteen years. In 1964 he was transferred into the New York Conference and appointed to the pastorate of Harlem's renowned Salem Church, from which he was elevated to the episcopacy and assigned to the Pittsburgh area. He remained there until he was transferred to the New York area in 1980, from which he retired in 1984.

211

The Northeastern Jurisdiction elected four other black ministers to the episcopacy. In 1972 Edward G. Carroll emerged the victor in a close contest. Born in a parsonage home in Wheeling, West Virginia, Carroll received degrees from Morgan College, Yale Divinity School, and Union Theological Seminary (New York). Following teaching, a military chaplaincy, several Washington Conference pastorates (including Sharp Street Memorial), and a district superintendency, Carroll was elected to the episcopacy from the predominantly white Marvin Memorial Church (Silver Springs, Maryland). He was assigned to the Boston area where he remained until retirement in 1980.

The third black minister elected to the bishopric from the Northeastern Jurisdiction was F. Herbert Skeete. A native of New York City with degrees from Brooklyn College, Drew University, and New York Theological Seminary, Skeete served in the air force before entering the ministry. He held pastorates in New York City and was an executive in the City Mission Society before becoming the pastor of New York's Salem Church, from which he was elected a bishop in 1980. First assigned to the Philadelphia area (1980–1988), he now serves the Boston area.

In 1984 the Northeastern Jurisdiction elected two of its ministerial members to the episcopacy. These elections gave it the leadership in the denomination for the number (five) of blacks elected to the highest office in the church. Those elected in 1984 were Felton E. May and Forrest C. Stith. May, a Chicagoan, was active in the civil rights movement before and during his seminary days at Garrett and later at Wesley Theological Seminary, from which he graduated. Following several pastorates, a district superintendency, and directorship of the Peninsula Conference Council on Ministries, he was elected a bishop in 1984 and assigned to the Harrisburg (Pennsylvania) area. In January 1990 May was placed on special assignment by the Council of Bishops to represent and witness to the commitment the church has in confronting and combatting the drug problem. This first-ever appointment will be of one year's duration. Forrest C. Stith is a native of Marshall, Texas. He received his education at the University of Nebraska and the Theological School of Drew University. A member of the Baltimore Conference, Stith had been a pastor and Conference Council on Ministries executive before his appointment to the district superintendency of the Washington East District. He was assigned to the New York West area.

When the South Central Jurisdiction adjourned in July 1972, the record indicated that it had elected the first black bishop in their more than thirty-year history. A graduate of Samuel Huston College (magna cum laude), Austin, Texas, Ernest T. Dixon pursued theological study at Drew University. Upon completion of studies there he became director of Tuskegee University's Religious Extension Service. Later he taught at Gammon Theological Seminary. Subsequently he returned to the West Texas Conference to become its education executive before accepting a position with the former Board of Education. In 1965 Dixon was elected to the presidency of Philander Smith College. He remained there until he became the assistant general secretary of the then new Program Council, from which position he was elected a bishop in 1972. Bishop Dixon was assigned to the Kansas area for two quadrennia. In 1980 he was transferred to the San Antonio area, where he now serves. Dixon was president of the Council of Bishops during 1988.

The only other person elevated to the episcopacy by the South Central Jurisdiction was W. T. Handy, Jr., the son of W. T. Handy, Sr., of the former Louisiana Conference. A veteran of World War II (army), Handy graduated from Dillard University, Gammon Theological Seminary, and the Boston University School of Theology. His election to the episcopacy in 1980 climaxed an outstanding career as a pastor, district superintendent, and church publishing executive, including the positions of publishing representative and vice president for personnel for the United Methodist Publishing House. Handy was assigned to the Missouri area.

The first black person to win election to the episcopacy in the North Central Jurisdiction was Edsel A. Ammons. A Chicagoan by birth, Ammons holds degrees from Chicago's Roosevelt University, Garrett-Evangelical Theological Seminary, and Chicago Theological Seminary. Early in his ministry he transferred from the African Methodist Episcopal Church and held a pastorate in Chicago. In 1963 he became director of Urban Ministry for the Rockford District (Rock River Conference), and in 1966 a member of the Conference staff. Ammons was invited to teach at Garrett in 1968, where he remained until his election to the episcopacy in 1976. He was assigned to the Michigan area that same year, and in 1984 he was transferred to the West Ohio area. Ammons chaired the Board of Discipleship during the 1980–1984 quadrennium.

Woodie W. White, a native of New York City but long-time resident in the Detroit vicinity, was the second black ministerial member of the North Central Jurisdiction to become a bishop. A former member of the Christian Methodist Episcopal Church, White was a graduate of Paine College (Augusta, Georgia) and the Boston University School of Theology. He was ordained by the Detroit Conference in the 1960s. His ministerial career includes pastorates in Massachusetts and Michigan. A founding member of Black Methodists for Church Renewal and one of its prime movers, White was elected a bishop from a twelve-year tenure as General Secretary, Commission on Religion and Race. He was assigned to the Illinois area.

The Western Jurisdiction was the third region of the church to elect a black to the episcopacy. Louisianan Melvin G. Talbert, the first "person of color" to head a major program board in the denomination, is a graduate of Gammon Theological Seminary of the Interdenominational Theological Center. He had an illustrious career as a pastor in seven California churches in the Los Angeles area before being appointed to a Conference executive position and then to the district superintendency of the Long Beach District in 1968. In 1973 Talbert was elected to head the General Board of Discipleship, a position that he held until his elevation to the episcopacy in 1980. His assignment was to the Seattle area from 1980–1988, after which he was transferred to the San Francisco area.

The second person elected to the episcopacy by the Western Jurisdiction was Leontine T. C. Kelly, the first black woman bishop in a major religious denomination in the United States. The daughter of a Methodist pastor, Leontine Kelly was born in Washington, D.C., and baptized by Bishop Matthew W. Clair, Sr. (1865–1943). Trained as a public school teacher, Kelly received her call to the ministry following her minister-husband's death. A Wesley Theological Seminary education followed and then several extraordinarily effective years of ministry in local churches in the Virginia Conference. In 1983 she was elected assistant general secretary in the Section on Evangelism of the General Board of Discipleship. A surprise move to nominate her for bishop in the Western Jurisdiction resulted in her landmark election in July 1984. She served her one quadrennium before mandatory retirement in the San Francisco area.

History was made at the Southeastern Jurisdiction Conference in 1984 when on the eighth ballot Ernest W. Newman, the first black district superintendent of the DeLand District, Florida Conference, was elected a bishop. This significant action meant that finally each of the five jurisdictions had elected at least one black bishop. Newman, originally a South Carolinian, graduated from Claflin College and Gammon Theological Seminary. He pastored churches in the former South Carolina, Central Alabama, and Florida Conferences. Shortly after Merger he was appointed to the Melborne District in the Florida Conference. A pastorate at Plantation Church and a term as Associate Conference Council Director before returning to the district superintendency (DeLand District) climaxed his ministry prior to his election as bishop in 1984. Newman was assigned to the Nashville area.

Again in 1988 the Southeastern Jurisdiction elected one of its outstanding ministers to the episcopal office. Another South Carolinian (Dillon) and parsonage family offspring, Joseph B. Bethea, graduated from Claflin College, Gammon Theological Seminary, and did further academic study at Union Theological Seminary of Virginia at Richmond. His pastoral experience was gained in local churches in North and South Carolina. Three times a district superintendent, Bethea was the first director of Black Church Studies at the Duke University Divinity School and one of its early black faculty members. A delegate to every General and Jurisdictional Conference since Union and one-time administrative assistant to the bishop of the Raleigh area, he was elected to the episcopacy at the 1988 session of the Southeastern Jurisdictional Conference and assigned to the Columbia (South Carolina) area.

The District Superintendency

The adjournment of the 1964 Central Jurisdictional Conference marked the beginning of the process of dissolving the Central Jurisdiction. The Delaware, Lexington, and Washington Conferences were in various stages of transferring, merging, or otherwise reorganizing for imminent merger with jurisdictions, episcopal areas, Conferences, and districts. A major phase of this process was redistricting and appointing district superintendents to districts in the new entities on a nonracial basis. What follows here is a chronological summary of the first black appointments (by jurisdictions) to districts from 1964–1974. A concluding word will be said about the recent historic appointment of two black female district superintendents.

The first appointment of a full-term black district superintendent to a white district was made by Bishop Lloyd C. Wicke in the New York area in 1964. Charles L. Warren, pastor of St. Mark's Church, was placed in the newly created Metropolitan District. Warren remained in this district until 1967, at which time he resigned to accept the position of executive director of the Council of Churches of Greater Washington, D.C. He died in 1971. Other appointments of black superintendents from 1964 to 1974 were as follows: Boston area, Gilbert H. Caldwell; New Jersey area, Hooker D. Davis; New York area, John E. Carrington, Readus J. Watkins; Philadelphia area, Edwin L. Ellis, Walter R. Hazzard, William C. Strother; Washington area, William E. Bishop, James D. Foy, Harold G. Johnson, Levi B. Miller, Daniel L. Ridout, John R. Shockley; West Virginia area, Ramsey Bridges.

Harry B. Gibson was the first black district superintendent appointed in the North Central Jurisdiction. A former Lexington Conference cabinet member, he was made the district superintendent of the Western District, Rock River Conference, by Thomas M. Pryor, bishop of the Chicago area. This appointment was effected in 1964. At the expiration of his six-year term in 1970, Gibson accepted the position of black ombudsman at the board. Subsequent black appointments in North Central were as follows: Chicago area, Willie B. Clay; Michigan area, James D. Cochran; Ohio East area, J. Inman Dixon, Robert J. Talbot; Ohio West area, Sumpter M. Riley.

The Western Jurisdiction, though under no mandate to integrate its cabinet membership, chose to do so voluntarily. In 1966 Bishop Gerald H. Kennedy of the Los Angeles area appointed Robert D. Hill to the district superintendency of the Golden Gate District in the Southern California-Arizona Conference. Hill brought to this new position for a black minister the rich experience of a very effective pastorate at the historic Taylor Memorial Church in Oakland, California, and also more than twenty years of pastoral experience and community involvement. Over the decade of 1964–1974 other black ministers appointed to districts were as follows: Los Angeles area,

Melvin G. Talbert, Lanneau L. White; San Francisco area, Hamilton T. Boswell, Thomas P. Grissom, Jr.

A crucial understanding in the 1965 Plan of Union, implicit and explicit, was the disallowance of any semblance of segregation in policy, structure, or program in the new United Methodist Church. A major action in the implementation of this agreement, therefore, was the immediate, orderly transfer of the remaining Conferences of the former Central Jurisdiction into their regional counterparts in other jurisdictions. While compliance with the spirit and letter of the *Discipline* was never in question, the process proceeded somewhat more slowly in the southern jurisdictions than elsewhere in the church.

According to available records, the Southeastern Jurisdiction was the first one of the two southern regional bodies to appoint black district superintendents. Bishop Earl G. Hunt, Jr., of the Charlotte area named James C. Peters to the Western North Carolina cabinet. Peters was brought into the superintendency from the executive directorship of the Gulfside Assembly, Waveland, Mississippi. At the expiration of his term on the district, he went to the executive staff of the Conference Council on Ministries. The Southeastern Jurisdiction's subsequent numerous appointments of blacks to districts were as follows: Atlanta area, Adolphus S. Dickerson, A. C. Epps, Harold P. Gray; Birmingham area, M. C. Barrett; Columbia area, John W. Curry, Granville A. Hicks, Edward E. Jenkins, Omega F. Newman; Florida area, Ernest W. Newman, J. B. F. Williams; Holston area, Paul Y. Marchbanks, Raymon E. White; Jackson area, C. E. Appleberry, W. B. Crump, J. W. Moseley, S. L. Webb; Nashville area, John G. Cory, William W. Morris; Raleigh area, James H. McCallum; Richmond area, Godfrey L. Tate, Jr.

The South Central Jurisdiction was the last of the two southern jurisdictions in which black district superintendents were appointed. In 1969 Bishop W. Kenneth Pope of the Dallas-Ft. Worth area appointed Zan W. Holmes, Jr., to the Dallas Metropolitan District. At the close of his term on the district, he was appointed to a professorship in preaching in the Perkins School of Theology. Since that time, the following black district superintendents have been appointed: Houston area, Willie B. Randolph, Richard H. Robinson; Louisiana Conference, Robert F. Harrington, Alfred L. Norris; Missouri area, J. J. Johnson, C. Jarrett Gray; Nebraska area, Emmett T. Streeter; San Antonio–Northwest Texas area, J. Garfield Owens.

Black Women District Superintendents

In 1989–1990, new ground was broken with the announcement of the appointment of black women to district superintendencies. Their absence from this traditionally male office, long protested, gathered momentum with the increasing presence of black women ministers and the rise of the Black

Clergy Women's Caucus group in the 1980s. Bishop Joseph H. Yeakel of the Washington area announced the appointment of Charlotte A. Nichols, pastor of the Easton-Miles River Charge, to the Easton District of the Peninsula Conference. Several weeks later Bishop Yeakel also announced the appointment of Mary Brown Oliver, pastor of Northwood-Appold Church in Baltimore, to the Washington Central District of the Baltimore Conference. These appointments, effective in 1990, were significant breakthroughs.[5]

Summary

By the end of the transitional period for Conference and structural merger (1964–1974), an interracial district superintendency profile had emerged. Approximately fifty-four black superintendents had been appointed. In the 1974 Conference year, twenty-six districts were being served by black leadership. From 1974 to 1984 the average number of black district superintendents in a given year was twenty-two. This represented a substantial decline from the approximately seventy-five district superintendencies that had been available in any given year in the Central Jurisdiction. At the same time it represents a modest cumulative annual increase.

The Judicial Council

The 1968 Plan of Union introduced a provision in the constitution of the new church for the election of Judicial Council members that may be counted as a gain for black leadership. It will be recalled that in the establishment of the council in 1940 the General Conference made no reference to jurisdictional representation. The 1968 General Conference modified this at the nominating level with the following disciplinary provision: "Each of the jurisdictions and the overseas churches as a group shall be represented by at least one nominee, but it shall not be a requirement that each of the jurisdictions or the overseas churches be represented by an elected member."[6] Several black members were elected to this influential body, which was the final arbiter of the constitution of the church, *The Book of Discipline,* and episcopal and other rulings during 1968–1988. Theodore M. Berry, who had been elected in 1960, served on the council until 1976. Charles B. Copher, Ph.D., minister, dean, and professor of Old Testament at the Interdenominational Theological Center–Gammon Theological Seminary, was elected to the council in 1968 and served until 1984. Florence Lucas Edwards, an attorney at law, became the first black woman to become a member of the council in 1972. She was elected vice president in 1984 and served until her death in 1987. Attorney Willard H. Douglass, Jr., chief judge of the Juvenile and Domestic Relations Court of Richmond, Virginia, was elected to the Judicial Council in 1984.

BOARD AND AGENCY STRUCTURE

It is necessary to have a basic understanding of the overhead structure of the boards, agencies, commissions, and committees of the denomination at the general (national) church level to properly assess their degree of racial inclusiveness or evaluate their effectiveness in the enablement and empowerment of black missional objectives and strategies in the local church. The structure for The United Methodist Church proposed in the Plan of Union, authorized by the 1968 General Conference and approved by that body in 1972, had as its controlling purpose the accomplishment of the mission of the church through the local congregation. In keeping with this concept, the General Conference divided its work among about a dozen boards and agencies according to function: legislative, and supervisory, administrative, supportive, and programmatic. The supervisory aspect of the design, especially episcopal leadership and the district superintendency, has been reviewed. The Judicial Council has also been discussed. What follows are brief developmental sketches of the key administrative and support agencies. These agencies, in keeping with General Conference legislation in the *Discipline*, provide guidelines, oversight, technical assistance, and budgeted funding to churches and other units executing its mission. Advocacy commissions and programmatic boards, including black elected board and agency representatives and black elective staff, will be reviewed later in the chapter in the context of assigned program areas and organizational responsibilities.

General Council on Ministries

The 1972 General Conference renamed an originally designated "Program Council" (1965) as the General Council on Ministries (GCOM). An innovative structure, this critical and influential agency was to be "responsible, between the sessions of the General Conference, for the total program of The United Methodist Church,"[7] with the power to review and unify. Black members of this first General Council on Ministries were Charles F. Golden, bishop; Edward G. Carroll, minister; and Arvarh E. Strickland, layperson. Representing the Council of Secretaries were Theressa Hoover, Women's Division; Earnest A. Smith, General Board of Christian Social Concerns; and Woodie W. White, Commission on Religion and Race. Warren M. Jenkins, assistant secretary for Field Cultivation, was the council's first black staff member.

In subsequent quadrennia there were numerous elected black members on the council, including John E. Carrington, Abigail Cope, A. C. Epps, Mary H. Good, James C. Hardcastle, Charles W. Jordan, Richard V. Moore, Rodell Roberts, and Zan W. Holmes, Jr. Also John T. King served as president of the council (1972–1980), the first person of color to hold that position, as did

Bishop James S. Thomas (1984–1988). The council has been served by several black executives since its inception as the Program Council in 1968. Ernest T. Dixon, later elected to the episcopacy (1972), joined the General Council on Ministries staff in 1968 as assistant general secretary of coordination. Later Warren M. Jenkins went to the staff as assistant secretary for field cultivation. Around 1972 Mildred E. Wilkerson became an assistant general secretary. In 1976 C. Leonard Miller was named associate general secretary of the council. In the Advancement Department (around 1980) William T. Carter was appointed to direct the Advance program, United Methodism's support system for the missionary program of the church. In 1984 Trudie K. Preciphs joined the staff as associate general secretary.

General Council on Finance and Administration

The General Council on Finance and Administration was known as the General Council on World Service and Finance. The fiscal control body of the denomination, its major responsibility is the preparation, interpretation, and control of the massive national budget of The United Methodist Church.[8]

Black Methodists have had a long tradition of membership on its directing board. Since 1968 those who have served have been Lolita Bacon, Merlin D. Conway, John W. Curry, Helen Fannings, Mrs. William H. McCallum, Leon G. Netterville, Bishop James S. Thomas, and Zan W. Holmes, Jr. Also Helen Fannings was a member of the executive committee of the council (1976–1980). Bishop Thomas became its first black president in 1980. John F. Norwood has been a black staff executive at the council since 1972, when he was appointed assistant general secretary. In 1976 he became associate general secretary. Norwood retired from the council in 1988. In the fall of 1988, a second black executive and its first black woman professional came to the staff as assistant general secretary, Geneva Harton Dalton.

General Board of Pensions

The Board of Pensions has stewardship of one of the largest pension and benefit funds of its kind in the nation for ministers, their spouses, and dependent children.[9] It has been sensitive to its responsibility to adhere to the church's social principles and continuously monitors its investments and investors to ensure that they reflect these principles by not supporting apartheid in South Africa or nuclear weaponry, and by addressing the American rural farm crisis. Senior Associate General Secretary Allen M. Mayes has given strong leadership to this. He also afforded the board critical and astute guidance in assisting it to develop a strategy of pension and benefits equalization for former Central Jurisdiction ministers in transit to merging Annual Conferences.

Increased opportunity for membership and participation in Board of Pensions decision making has been provided through The United Methodist Church's structure in the presence and participation of the following black board members: Harry L. Burney, Jr.; Marie Copher; John C. Ferguson, Jr.; Robert W. Kelly; and Althea T. L. Simmons. Black professional staff leadership during this period has been provided chiefly by Allen M. Mayes, first appointed to the board in 1963. Quite recently others have been added: assistant general secretaries Vidette K. Bullock; Laurence E. Horton, Jr.; and Anne E. Wimberly; and Milton E. Jackson, controller.

General Commission on Archives and History

The Commission on Archives and History (CAH) was designated by the 1968 Uniting General Conference as "the official historical agency of the Church." Its main purpose was "to gather, preserve . . . and disseminate material on the history of the denomination."[10] Early in the commission's life, concerns about the omission or inadequate treatment of the contribution and heritage of the several racial groups in the history of the church were expressed. Black Methodists for Church Renewal were the first to do so, followed closely by other caucuses. During the Ethnic Minority Local Church Emphasis (1976–1980), consultations were held to focus on this issue. In response to these deliberations, the Commission on Archives and History created a subcommittee on Ethnic Minority Histories. Major J. Jones was selected to head this subcommittee. This book and its companion volumes on Asian-Pacific, Hispanic, and Native American contributions to the church represent the product of the subcommittee's effort.

Black elected members who have served terms on the commission since its organization have been Bishop L. Scott Allen, chairman (1980–1984); Warren M. Jenkins; Major J. Jones; Ralph H. Jones; C. Leonard Miller; and Grant S. Shockley. In 1988 C. Jarrett Gray, Jr., became a member of the staff.

Advocacy-Monitoring Commissions

Completing this survey of United Methodism's effort to desegregate itself and democratize its leadership in terms of race and gender at the national level is a review of two agencies whose mission it is to advocate and monitor United Methodism's inclusiveness: the Commission on Religion and Race and the Commission on the Status and Role of Women.

The Commission on Religion and Race (CRR) came into being through the action of the 1968 General Conference.[11] The purpose of the church in creating such a body was to "effect better relations" among the church's more than 500,000 ethnic minority persons, and to intentionally enable the denomination to become a more "inclusive" community. From 1968 to 1984, under the extremely able and skilled leadership of Woodie W. White and his staff associates, the Commission on Religion and Race had put in place an exemplary national program of multicultural education and race relations engineering.

The initial commission, one of the largest in the church, was ably headed by Bishop Kenneth G. Goodson. It was composed of Bishop Charles F. Golden, vice president; John L. Bryan; Gloster D. Current; Luther B. Felder; Dennis A. Fletcher; Warren M. Jenkins; Major J. Jones; Joseph E. Lowery; George E. Rice; Emmett T. Streeter; and Cecil Williams. Subsequent to 1968, bishops James S. Thomas, L. Scott Allen, and Melvin G. Talbert were either president or vice president of the commission. Black staff leadership has included Woodie W. White, executive secretary (1968–1980) and general secretary (1980–1984); Clayton E. Hammond, associate executive secretary (1968–1972); Albert H. Hammond, Jr., associate executive secretary (1976–1980); and Gilbert H. Caldwell, Jr., associate executive secretary and acting general secretary (1980–1985). Barbara R. Thompson became general secretary of the agency in 1985. The most recent black addition to the staff was the appointment of Warren C. Hill as assistant general secretary in 1986.

The ubiquitous presence and practice of sexism in the church and the general society stimulated the establishment of a Commission on the Status and Role of Women in 1972 "to monitor the progress of women's participation in the denomination."[12] In 1976 the General Conference made the commission permanent and charged it "to challenge The United Methodist Church . . . to a continuing commitment to the full and equal responsibility and participation of women in the total life and mission of the Church."[13] Barbara R. Thompson, an initiator in this movement, was the first president of the commission (1972–1978). Doris Handy, Mattie Henderson, and P. Harold Gray (1930–1987) were among the first commission members. Other black members have been Fred A. Allen, Ressie Bass, Euba Harris-Winton, Cornelius L. Henderson, Samuel E. NeSmith, Beverly J. Shamana, Chiquita J. Smith, Bishop Forrest C. Stith, Alfred E. Thompson, and H. Walter Willis. Black members of the General Secretariat staff have been Trudie K. Preciphs (1976–1985) and Geneva Harton-Dalton (1984–1988). Cecelia M. Long has since become a General Secretariat executive.

Annual Conference Inclusiveness

By 1972 the Conference merger process, begun in 1968 as a result of the dissolution of the Central Jurisdiction in 1967, had been completed. Its seventeen Conferences physically had become integral parts of fifty-three of a total of seventy-three Annual Conferences in five geographical jurisdictions. Opportunities for black involvement and leadership in these reconstituted

Conferences must be viewed on two levels: (1) elected board and agency membership and (2) appointments to Conference staff leadership. In reviewing black membership and officerships in Conference boards, agencies, and organizations including United Methodist Men (UMM), United Methodist Women (UMW), and the United Methodist Youth Fellowship (UMYF), the data from 1968–1972 indicate that much remains to be done if the church is to move beyond tokenism in this area. Black Methodists for Church Renewal in a 1969 "Resolution on Merger" acknowledged that while some progress had been made, the feeling in many merged Conferences is one of "severe disappointment, disillusionment, and frustration at the failures of the conferences to provide adequate and meaningful opportunities for Black leadership and participation at the conference, district and local church levels."[14]

The picture was somewhat improved in tabulating leadership gains in Annual Conference staff appointments. Even here, however, the indications were that less progress had been made, proportionately, in Conference-level appointments than in appointments to the district superintendency, elections by boards and agencies, or elections to the episcopacy.

There were black program council directors and other program staff executives in the merged Conferences at the time of Union in 1968. Many of these, however, had been transferred into these Conferences with these appointments. During a transitional period of about four years (1968–1972), most of the transfers continued to work primarily among their former black constituents until their positions could be merged. Among those who held these appointments were five former Annual Conference program directors: Cornelius L. Henderson, Matthew D. McCollum, W. S. P. Norris, H. Richard Robinson, and Prenza L. Woods. Former appointees as directors of Christian education were ten: Elmer C. Binford, Merlin D. Conoway, John W. Elliott, Laurence E. Hall, Cornelius L. Henderson, E. M. Johnson, Omega Newman, L. P. Norris, Charlamagne P. Payne, and H. R. Robinson.

First black appointees in white Annual Conferences to Conference council director (associate director or staff membership) began in 1966 with Edsel A. Ammons. Since then a number of appointments of this kind have been made: Melvin G. Talbert, 1967; R. Howard Robinson, 1970; Albert W. Hammond and Charles W. Jordan, around 1971. Between 1972 and 1984, more than two dozen black executives were appointed to such varied positions as executive secretaries for Conference boards of missions, associate and assistant Conference council directors, and regular staff positions. Probably the first full-time black Conference council director was Anthony J. Shipley, appointed by the Detroit Conference about 1971 or 1972. In 1988 the New York Conference became the first Conference to elect a black treasurer, Ernest L. Swiggett.

MEMBERSHIP, EVANGELISM, AND CHURCH GROWTH

The 1968 black Methodist membership statistic was derived from three sources: the former Central Jurisdiction membership, the non–Central Jurisdiction black membership, and the accession of members (and churches) from the former Evangelical United Brethren (EUB) denominations.

The membership strength of the Central Jurisdiction before the beginning of its dissolution in 1964 was estimated at 370,000 lay and preparatory members.[15] Distributed across seventeen (former) black Annual Conferences, the largest number were found in the South Carolina Conference (46,058). After South Carolina followed the Delaware Conference (43,375), the Washington Conference (41,397), and the Lexington Conference (40,455). The second source of the new black membership configuration was those black members of predominantly white United Methodist churches in the merged jurisdictions. It is interesting to note that those approximately 15,000 members came from churches generally larger than the former Central Jurisdiction churches and invariably located in the metropolitan areas of the Northeastern, North Central, and Western Jurisdictions. The black members of the former Evangelical United Brethren Church were the third source of the new United Methodist membership statistic. Two denominational traditions were represented by these churches: the Evangelical Church and the Church of the United Brethren in Christ. These bodies united in 1946 to form the Evangelical United Brethren Church. There was little growth or development among black people in the former Evangelical United Brethren Church after 1946. In 1968 only a few black members and possibly fewer than a dozen black congregations numbering several hundred people entered The United Methodist Church from the EUB Church (see Appendix I).

In summarizing the new black United Methodist statistics, the following profile emerges: black Methodists in 1968 numbering about 385,000 were about 4 percent of the United Methodist national membership. They were found in all five regional jurisdictions, in practically all forty-seven episcopal areas and seventy-three Annual Conferences (excepting in the states of the Dakotas, Idaho, Utah, Montana, and Wyoming), and in 85 percent of the church's more than five hundred districts. The inaccessibility of data precludes an estimation of the number of individual black members in white United Methodist churches.

Black Church Memberships

A review of black United Methodist membership records from 1964 to around 1984 again raises questions about a problematic declining membership, evangelism programs in black United Methodist churches, and why some black United Methodist churches are growing.

Membership

Black Methodist membership during 1968–1984, while not declining as much as its white counterpart in the same period, did fall off despite some episodic increases. In 1964, the last full-strength year of the Central Jurisdiction, it reported about 370,000 members. In late 1968, after factoring in the black membership from non-Central Jurisdiction churches and from the former Evangelical and United Brethren churches, the approximate total was 385,000. From 1968–1974 the black membership stabilized and slightly increased. Douglass W. Johnson, in a 1987 study, indicates that between 1974 and 1980 black membership in The United Methodist Church crested at an all-time high, but since that time "the percentage of membership decline of these churches has matched that of the total denomination."[16]

Evangelism

Black United Methodist churches during 1964–1974 became increasingly involved in the civil rights movement. Individually, their people and pastors contributed funds, time, and often leadership. Institutionally, churches lent their facilities, publicity networks, and power to release large sums of money from their Annual Conferences and General Church agencies. Membership increase records in this period, however, did not reflect this engagement. The record seems to indicate that most black United Methodists did not zealously evangelize among those for whose civil rights they labored. More specifically, during 1964–1974, the apex years of the Black Revolution, the black population, as a proportion of the total United States population, increased. But in that same period the black United Methodist membership, which may have slightly increased numerically, actually decreased as a proportion of the total membership of the church. George H. Outen (1931–1980), whose remarkable career as a pastor, prophetic preacher, evangelist, and church executive was cut short by death, spoke to this point when, in 1973, he said, "It is an indictment against our Church that the number of Blacks within our ranks shows a decrease since the abolition of the Central Jurisdiction."[17]

Church Growth and Innovative Churches

Black Methodist churches that have experienced significant membership and/or programmatic growth in recent years seem to have several characteristics or features in common: (1) commitment to ministry in black perspective, (2) an emphasis on recovering black spiritual roots, (3) a sense of community responsibility and accountability, and (4) commitment to pluralistic, inclusive community. It is interesting to note that with the exception of a few traditional churches that are on these cutting edges of ministry, the founding dates of most of them were in or near the Black Revolution period (1969–1974). Grouped by jurisdictions, the following churches are some among many that have been publicly acclaimed or cited by the media for having innovative programs based on one or more of the guidelines referred to above: North Central: Camphor, St. Paul, Minnesota; Cory, Cleveland, Ohio; Scott, Detroit; St. Mark, Chicago; Northeastern: Hoosier, Philadelphia; Metropolitan, Buffalo, New York; Metropolitan, New York; Salem, New York; Union Memorial, Boston; South Central: Hoover, Little Rock, Arkansas; St. James-Paseo, Kansas City; St. Luke, Dallas; Union Memorial, St. Louis; Windsor Village, Houston; Southeastern:[18] Ben Hill,[19] Atlanta; Cascade, Atlanta; Central, Atlanta; Clark, Nashville; St. Paul, Birmingham, Alabama; Western: Eastern Hills, Richmond, California; Glide Memorial, San Francisco; Holman, Los Angeles; Jones Memorial, San Francisco; and St. John's Watts Community Ministry, Los Angeles.[20]

Structure and Personnel

In an effort to relate all general church agencies concerned with the local church under one board, the 1972 restructuring placed evangelism, together with education and worship, in a General Board of Discipleship. Black elected board members and executive staff persons selected for these positions during 1968–1984 were as follows: board members: Bishops E. A. Ammons; N. W. Moore, Jr.; Roy C. Nichols; and W. W. White; ministers and laypersons: J. V. Booker; T. P. Grissom; L. L. Haynes, Jr.; C. Hutchinson; W. B. McClain; C. W. Selby; C. L. Warren; and D. White; elected staff members: C. L. Henderson; M. W. King; W. D. Lester; George H. Outen.

MISSION, WITNESS, AND OUTREACH

The Black Revolution, through the urging and inspiring of Black Methodists for Church Renewal (BMCR), challenged United Methodism in the 1970s to an unprecedented engagement in ministries of corrective social justice in the black community and Africa. Led by its black constituency and implemented through a national network of BMCR local caucuses in black communities, black and white churches were confronted with their missional responsibility to assist communities and churches in their effort to eliminate poverty, social and economic injustice, and racial discrimination. This new imperative dominated the goal setting and strategizing of the denomination for a quarter of a century following Merger (1968). Church racial integration, while continuing to be a desirable objective for the United Methodist fellowship, came to be viewed more realistically as a future possibility rather than as something that could or would take place in this generation. Signs of this changing perspective can be documented. Bishop Charles F. Golden, in the last episcopal message to the Central Jurisdictional Conference, cited five responsibilities that would need to be discharged cooperatively by black and white Methodists: "accountability for the plight of the urban community; increased financial support for Black colleges; alleviation of the problems of the disadvantaged; continuance of efforts to become 'structurally and functionally' inclusive; involvement in the total mission of the Church in the 'total world.' "[21]

BMCR's historic "Black Paper" stated, "We are . . . deeply disturbed about the crisis of racism in America . . . about the failure of . . . Black people, including Black Methodists . . . to respond appropriately to the roots and forces of racism and the current Black Revolution."[22]

Bishop W. Kenneth Goodson, when addressing the 1972 Southeastern Jurisdictional Conference, spoke for a then increasing number of United Methodists from that region when he said, "If the Church is to take seriously the need of the world in the present moment, it must embrace the ministry of liberation."[23]

The Commission on Religion and Race, in its 1972 report to the General Conference, said, "There is little realization and concerted programming directed to a ministry to the Black community."[24]

Barbara R. Thompson, general secretary of the Commission on Religion and Race, summarized the new mood of black (and other ethnic minority) churches as they viewed ministry: "Our vision must be expanded [to] increase outreach into the community to share the gifts and the talents God has shared with us."[25]

General Church Missional Response

The response of the church to the challenge to mission in the black community and black Africa resulted in actions that began specifically at the Uniting Conference in Dallas, Texas, in 1968 and continue today. They took place on four levels—legislation, policy, program, and personnel—and were implemented, essentially, through three channels: the national, women's, and world divisions of the General Board of Missions and its successor in 1972, the General Board of Global Ministries. Some of those actions were as follows:

1. The new constitution of The United Methodist Church legislated that inclusiveness was church policy and that discrimination in any form or of any kind was to be eliminated.
2. The General Conference established a Commission on Religion and Race whose particular responsibility it would be to develop, administer, and supervise all aspects of the desegregation and integration of the church in affirmation of its inclusive policy.
3. As part of the 1968–1972 quadrennial emphasis, "A New Church for a New World," the General Conference created the Fund for Reconciliation, with a goal of $20 million to enable the church to "move at once on

every level . . . to engage in constructive social change." (Black members of the Committee of Fifty on the quadrennial program were Bishop Charles F. Golden, Harry B. Gibson, J. D. Grier, Walter R. Hazzard, John T. King, and Randolph Nugent.)

4. In compliance with the 1968 *Book of Discipline,* the Council on World Service and Finance was required to "withhold approval of the entire budget of any agency or any church-related institution receiving general church funds" until and unless it met the requirements for nondiscriminatory employment established by the church.

5. In consideration of the exigencies related to salary and pension differentials consequent to Conference mergers, the 1970 General Conference extended the life of the Temporary General Aid Fund with minor rate and operational changes.

6. In approving a resolution condemning the use of church facilities for operating private schools, the 1970 General Conference made a policy statement clearly directed against certain local United Methodist churches that had allowed the use of their facilities "to preserve racially segregated education."

7. The Special Session of the General Conference (1970) approved five recommendations presented (as an unusual privilege) to the General Conference by BMCR. Following their approval, they became the initiating programs for twenty years of black liberation advance. Briefly, the recommendations were to reorder priorities to undergird black self-determination to redesignate pledged Fund for Reconciliation monies for black economic development, to guarantee $10 million to strengthen black colleges, to establish a black scholarship and loan fund for high school seniors, and to maintain a minimum of 30 percent black elected board and staff personnel.

The 1972 General Conference made two significant responses to BMCR's recommendations to the 1970 Special Session General Conference. It adopted a procedure authorizing Annual Conferences and local churches (guided by the *Book of Discipline*) larger measures of self-determination in "developing programs and concentrating on priorities for mission."[26] Second, in response to the request of the Commission on Black Colleges and the Council of Presidents of those colleges, it authorized the historic Black College Fund to assist United Methodism's financially needy schools. This six-million dollar annual fund became an apportioned general church obligation on a quadrennial review basis.

During the 1972–1976 quadrennium the General Commission on Religion and Race, as a result of extensive dialogue among black, Asian-Pacific, Hispanic, and Native American caucuses, sensed a need for a church-wide emphasis on the future of these racial groups within United Methodism. This concern, communicated to the General Council on Ministries, eventuated in its decision to make the Ethnic Minority Local Church Emphasis a missional priority for the 1976–1980 quadrennium. This missional priority, aimed at developing and strengthening black and other racial minority group churches for witness and mission, focused particularly on seven areas: witness, discipleship, liturgy, outreach, leadership, structures, and facilities. The church development, membership growth, and revitalization that this effort brought had a generally salutary effect in many churches, improving and better positioning them for missional ministries. It was continued for two quadrennia with minor changes in direction. The question of its having had more of a palliative than a prophetic impact was often raised.

In 1968 BMCR expressed concern that The Methodist Church had sought to have "Union" talks with the Evangelical United Brethren Church but made little effort to do the same with the African Methodist Episcopal, African Methodist Episcopal Zion, and Christian Methodist Episcopal churches, with whom historical ties were long and close.[27] The General Conferences made several efforts to amend this situation. In 1972 the General Conference was presented a resolution "to strengthen fellowship" within the Wesleyan tradition. For the first time in the history of all of these churches, representatives of their bishops met in 1979 in Atlanta. Their purpose was to discuss common concerns and to plan for future consultations. Following several joint celebrations of American Methodism's Bicentennial in 1984 and the formation of a Commission on Pan-Methodist Cooperation that same year, several subsequent meetings were held.

Board and Agency Missional Response

In addition to General Conference legislation, policy changes and resolutions in response to the crisis faced by black churches in the ghettos, the National Program Division responded to these situations in a variety of ways:

- Amid the turmoil of the civil rights struggle, burned and bombed black churches were rebuilt.
- Debt-ridden and dilapidated former Central Jurisdiction churches were aided and physically renovated upon merging with white Annual Conferences in the 1970s.
- Temporary general aid funds were administered by the Division to help equalize the salaries of black and white ministers from 1964 until about 1988.
- Program and staff participation in all National Program Division institutions were racially integrated as soon as feasible, including black and white deaconesses.

- Under the inspired and creative leadership of Negail Riley (1930–1987), the Community Developers Program was conceived, administered, and supervised. A complementary program, Community Economic Development, was also initiated about this same time.
- Congregational Development and Black Church Growth programs to rejuvenate sagging black congregations and arrest membership decline were put in place through the division in the late 1970s and 1980s.
- Finally, leadership development strategies were developed and modeled as important features of education for self-determination.

National Program Division black staff from 1968–1988 were Clyde Anderson, Charles E. Frost, Cathy P. Fulwood, Lulu M. Garrett, Mary H. Good, Ruby D. Hill, Marian Jones, Ruth Lawson, Brenda J. Norwood, William T. Robinson, Sandra Swans, Jean S. Turner, Errol Tyrell, and Joyce D. Wilkerson.

Women's Program Division Response

The basic objective of the Women's Program Division is to be "actively engaged in fulfilling the mission of Christ and the Church [and to] interpret the purpose of United Methodist Women . . . with continuing awareness of the concerns and responsibilities of the Church in today's world."[28] Another facet of this objective is equally important and quite pertinent as background in reviewing United Methodist developments between 1968 and 1984, "to advocate for the oppressed and dispossessed with special attention to the needs of women and children."[29] In the light of this objective, it is instructive to briefly review the involvement of black women in "witness, mission and outreach" given Merger and the challenge of liberation confronting the church.

In working toward the accomplishment of the mission just stated, black United Methodist women have had to be aware of several things: their worth and value as black women, the condition of black people in the black community, and the essential mission of the church.

Prior to Merger, black United Methodist women participated in jurisdictional and national meetings where they helped to develop strategies for the equalization of representation in the new structure. Based on their preceding charters of racial policy, the first of their kind in the denomination, the Women's Division led the way in demonstrating commitment to nonracial employment practices. In 1968 Theressa Hoover, then secretary of Christian Social Relations, was elected to the highest executive position in the Women's Division, and the second highest in the then Board of Missions. In the early 1970s the new Board of Global Ministries requested all of its divisions "to consider ways to add more ethnic minority staff persons."[30] This request led to a Women's Division study of the situation and improvement. By the close of the 1984 quadrennium, the number of black women on the staff of the division had risen from three in 1968 to almost a dozen. During this same period, black women, including board members and staff, persistently monitored compliance with division nonracial employment practices in institutions related to it, including community centers, schools, dormitories and residential homes, and hospitals.

The Women's Division and the jurisdictional constituency showed a growing willingness to elect members to top positions on a nonracial basis during this period. By 1984 United Methodist Women had elected a national president who was black, Mai H. Gray (1976–1980); four of the five jurisdictions had elected black United Methodist Women presidents: Southeastern Jurisdiction, Nettie Alice Green (1972–1976); Northeastern Jurisdiction, Jessie B. Pratt (1976–1980); South Central Jurisdiction, Zenobia P. Waters (1984–1988); and Southeastern Jurisdiction, Effie E. Miller (1988–1992). Numerous black women were elected to membership on the Women's Division board of directors between 1968 and 1984. Elected staff during the period were as follows: 1968–1972—Dorothy Barnette, Ruth Gilbert, Theressa Hoover, Cornelia L. Smith, Mae Frances Spencer, and Minnie F. Stein; 1972–1976—Mary L. Harvey, Annette Hutchins-Felder, and Bernadette Sanders; 1976–1988—S. Helen Daniels, Mary Kercherval-Short, Edna Rouse, Andris Salter, Chiquita G. Smith, and Maxine West.

World Program Division Response

World Division response to black United Methodist missional and liberation issues came as a result of three forces: a generally awakened new world consciousness, a remembered challenge from Bishop Charles F. Golden's valedictory message for the College of Bishops to the Central Jurisdiction, and the James Forman Riverside Church confrontation.

Following the trauma associated with the assassination of Martin Luther King, Jr., on April 4, 1968, the black community, the black church, and the nation came to a new resolve. They were more determined than ever to work toward actualizing King's vision of a society in which different races and faiths could live harmoniously and in peace. Many black and white people and their leaders also became more critically aware of the necessity to remove the impediments to attaining that vision—namely, poverty, discrimination, and racism. Bishop Golden's message urged black United Methodists to become involved in the total mission of the church in the total world.[31] Third, James Forman's confrontation quickened the response of the Board of Missions to United Methodism's black demands. His presentation of the "Black Manifesto," interrupting the Sunday worship of New York City's Riverside Church on May 4, 1969, demanding $500 million in reparations from the religious establishment for historic and cumulative injustices, was one of the most dramatic events of the decade. A brief account of the developments that followed the Forman confrontation and the response of the Board of Missions, later (1972) the Board of Global Ministries, is now in order.

During the week following the Riverside Church event, several black Board of Missions staff members called an informal meeting to discuss the Forman demands and what, if anything, could or should be done about them. It was the unanimous opinion of the group present that the Forman demands were valid and should be met, but within the context of the racism within the Board of Missions and The United Methodist Church. At that point it was decided to meet on a regular basis to do two things: develop a missional agenda from a black perspective and outline a strategy that would gain approval and funding from the Board of Missions. By the middle of May (1969) the group that had been meeting for informal conversation became an Ad Hoc Black Staff Task Force. Dennis R. Fletcher, then senior black staff member (National Division), was unanimously elected chairperson, and Grant S. Shockley (World Division) was chosen as secretary. (By the end of 1970 black staff groups had been organized at most of the other Methodist centers: Dayton, Ohio; Evanston, Illinois; Nashville, Tennessee; and Washington, D.C. They named themselves the Black Staff Forums.)

The position paper written by the Black Staff Task Force outlined its purposes as "prophetic, catalytic, supportive and interpretive." It saw its task to be one of convincing the Board of Missions of the need for more black involvement in decision making and more control in helping the board respond to the current racial crisis. Specifically, it requested the board to change policies, reorder priorities, and reprogram for greater self-determination and more black economic and community development projects.[32] Initially, the board staff was quite willing to discuss these issues, and at some points it even seemed willing to make some changes. A period of nonproductive conversation followed; however, BMCR appeared on the scene, under the charismatic leadership of their newly elected executive director, Cain H. Felder. Nonnegotiable demands were made, which at that time could not be met by board staff. The end result was the occupation of the offices of the Board of Missions late in May. The occupation was terminated when the Board of Missions agreed to call a special meeting of its Board of Managers. Following a day-long meeting in New York, the board made some significant reallocations of funds for black empowerment projects and authorized their executive committee to meet in June 1969 to work out the details.

Another programmatic outgrowth of the Black Staff Task Force was the creation of the African Affairs Office in the World Division. The initial concept and design of this office was the work of Isaac H. Bivens, then a staff member of the Joint Commission on Missionary Personnel. The purpose of the office was to deal with the mission of the church in Africa and "to adequately focus attention on policy direction of the World Division."[33] The position was actually created in 1971 and filled by Isaac Bivens. It sponsored several consultations on African affairs throughout the 1970s. The 1979 Africa Consultation held in Nairobi, Kenya, designed the Africa Growth and Development Program, which became a missional priority by General Conference action in 1980 and again in 1984.

A third outgrowth of the work of the original Black Staff Task Force was the passage of General Conference legislation (1970) creating a fund "to support self-determination of minority people." This programmatic piece was designed, advocated, and lobbied for by BMCR.

Black Missionary Presence

There has been cause for deep concern in the World Program Division of the Board of Global Ministries about its miniscule black missionary presence for a number of years. Blacks were never more than 4 percent of the total missionary force. Their numbers slightly increased in the 1950s but declined in the 1960s. While there was a hopeful sign in a small increase of black missionaries during the 1970s, it was hardly substantial enough to have established a trend. Other concerns were the geopolitical shift of world balances of power from West to East, the changing pattern of world population dominance from white to non-white, and the probability that Africa could "become the homeland of the largest number of Christians in the world."[34] These and other trends reported in a study, ordered by the board and published in 1978, indicate that major efforts must be continued in the cultivation and recruitment of blacks for missionary service.[35]

The black Methodist missionary statistic follows: Since 1968 about a dozen new or continuing black missionaries have served United Methodism in Japan, Korea, the Philippines, and Sierra Leone. Among them are Alford W. Alphonse, Percy Brown, Veronica Jackson, Mabel Johnson, Douglass A. McArthur, Ronald G. Mitchell (and wife), Barbara C. Pessoa, and Melvin G. Williams.

World Program Division black elected staff during this period have included Albert J. D. Aymer, Isaac H. Bivens, Elizabeth Colvin, Rose M. Catchings, G. Loraine Harriott, Julius Jefferson, Dennis Lewis, James V. Lyles, Keith D. Rae, Grant S. Shockley, Doreen Tilghman, and Brenda Wilkinson.

PREACHING, WORSHIP, AND THE NEW HYMNALS

Reconciling the perceived staid, white-oriented, middle-class preaching, worship, and hymnody of The United Methodist Church with the emerging new-style black church of the early 1970s posed a formidable and critical task for black Methodists. It involved recovering a fervent preaching style, a more expressive worship experience, and more evangelistic singing. What follows is a brief record of some efforts on the part of the church to work on the problem.

Major changes in the late 1960s and the early 1970s radically altered the image of the black United Methodist minister in both the black church and the black community. Prior to the Black Revolution, black United Methodists were generally accepted in the black church as colleagues in ministry. After the revolution (1968), they were expected to be in total solidarity with the black struggle for liberation in the black community. It was expected that this solidarity would be expressed by ministers in fervent "social crisis" preaching and by lay members in a "classless" church community. Many of the churches in the black community that thrived in the 1970s seemed to experience this kind of preaching and offered this kind of fellowship. Many that did not declined in membership. The other fact that remains is the coincidence of church growth in black United Methodist churches of the 1970s that were community-involved and those that were not. A third observable fact is about preaching, worship, and music and the black church in relation to the Black Consciousness movement. Black churches that intentionally encouraged and emphasized black heritage through the use of cultural symbols, songs, spirituals, and gospel music also seemed to evidence healthy and often extraordinary growth. This was applicable to black Methodist churches as well.

Beyond the local church there were other movements in the area of worship designed to deepen the spiritual life of black Methodists. Three programs accenting spiritual formation in the black church were instituted in the late 1980s by Eugene A. Blair, dean of the Upper Room Chapel and director of Church Cultivation for the Board of Evangelism. The Southeastern Jurisdiction developed "A Closer Walk with God—A Focus on Black Spirituality." The goal of this three-year-long program comprising three three-day sessions at Lake Junaluska was "to foster responsiveness to God" through experiential learning. In cooperation with the Board of Discipleship's Academy for Preaching, a second program was initiated, the Upper Room Preaching Series. In this program, selected pastors covenanted to attend and hear outstanding black preachers in a context of worship and dialogue. The inaugural preacher for the series was William B. McClain, professor of homiletics, Wesley Theological Seminary. A weekend event introducing ways to develop and enrich personal and corporate prayer life was a third program.

Black elected members who served with the Board of Discipleship or its predecessors were as follows: Commission on Worship (1968–1972)—J. DeKoven Killingsworth; Division of Evangelism, Worship, and Steward-ship—L. L. Haynes, Jr.; William B. McClain; Betty Henderson; A. C. Epps; Maceo D. Pembroke; Lorrine Smith; Benjamin Ward; Luther Henry; and

Gloster B. Current. In 1972 W. Maurice King became the first black dean of the Upper Room Chapel.

The New Hymnals

One of the major advances in United Methodism's march toward its goal of inclusive community occurred when it published *Songs of Zion* (1981) and *The United Methodist Hymnal* (1989). These advances did not happen in a vacuum but within the context of circumstances and events consequent to the process of structuring the new denomination. The racial caucuses—Asian, black, Hispanic, and Native American—were firmly insistent that not only must racism be eliminated, but "the gifts which particular ethnic histories and cultures bring to our total life"[36] must be recognized.

Songs of Zion

The hymnal created for use in The Methodist Church (1939) patently ignored the presence of black people. They were not a part of the planning, development, or editorial process. Black representation in the 1964 edition of *The Methodist Hymnal* was limited to one hymn by Charles A. Tindley and six Negro spirituals, all erroneously referred to as American folk hymns. In 1973 the landmark Consultation on the Black Church (Atlanta, 1973) urgently requested the development of a "songbook" that would reflect the black religious experience. This recommendation was effectively lobbied by the black staff concerned (William J. Washington and Willard A. Williams), approved by the Board of Discipleship, and sent to the 1976 General Conference. Simultaneously, other caucuses were promoting ethnic song-books. The issue climaxed at the General Conference (1976), which approved a recommendation to publish a "supplemental contemporary hymnal" reflecting the contemporary religious climate and diversity in the church.[37]

Meanwhile, black advocates for a separate songbook, while cooperating with the Supplemental Resource Project, persisted in their efforts to produce a resource in the 1976–1980 quadrennium. Fletcher J. Bryant gave strong leadership to this project, lodged in the new section on the Ethnic Minority Church. William B. McClain was elected to chair a national advisory task force to produce the hymnal, to which Dorothy Turner-Lacy was a consultant. Other professional leadership for the project came from editors J. Jefferson Cleveland (b. 1932), the acknowledged "Crown Prince of Gospel," and Verolga Nix. Other members of the task force were Fletcher J. Bryant; Cynthia Felder; Douglass E. Fitch; Donald Gilmore; Howard M. Ham; Hoyt L. Hickman; Zan W. Holmes, Jr.; Charlotte A. Meade; Maceo D. Pembroke; Israel Rucker; Forrest C. Stith; Ethel Lou Talbert; and Melvin G. Talbert.

Songs of Zion, whose primary objective was to "bring under one cover a collection of the best hymns and tunes [and] spirituals . . . to be used . . . in the Black worship experience" became a significant publication from its inception in 1981,[38] gaining wide use across Methodism and beyond. *The Supplement to the Book of Hymns,* containing Asian, Hispanic, and Native American selections, including the 1964 black material (and some additional spirituals), was published in 1982.[39]

The United Methodist Hymnal

Black involvement in the planning, content, and editing of *The United Methodist Hymnal* was more intentional than that for any previous work of its kind. The 1968 General Conference named a " 'Commission on Worship' to make recommendations to the 1972 General Conference concerning future editions of *The United Methodist Hymnal.*" J. DeKoven Killingsworth, a distinguished musician and veteran Clark College faculty member, was named to that commission. In the process of restructuring the boards and agencies in 1972, the worship and music functions were assigned to the Division of Evangelism, Worship, and Stewardship of the Board of Discipleship. L. L. Haynes, Jr., minister of historic Wesley Church, Baton Rouge, Louisiana, was a member of that board. During 1976–1980, when extensive research was being done on the "services of public worship" to be used in the new church, culminating in the publication of *We Gather Together,* black representation on the board was well placed in William B. McClain, then minister at Union Memorial in Boston. In the 1980–1984 quadrennium, further restructuring of the Board of Discipleship yielded additional black representation: Bishop Edsel A. Ammons, president; Betty Henderson; A. C. Epps; Maceo D. Pembroke; Lorrine Smith; Benjamin Ward; Luther Henry, Jr.; and Charles Hutchinson. In 1984 Gloster B. Current, a musician by avocation, became a member of the Board of Discipleship's new Section on Worship. The central and controlling Hymnal Revision Committee (HRC) included a significant number of black members: Bishop W. T. Handy, Jr.; J. Edward Hoy, Tindley Temple, Philadelphia, organist and minister of music; and J. LaVon Wilson, noted Springfield, Illinois, public school musician. In addition to this representation, William B. McClain, Wesley Theological Seminary and William Farley Smith, St. Marks, New York, served as consultants, and Betty Henderson made a special presentation for BMCR. Reader consultants were black bishops, black board and agency executives, black United Methodist Men's and United Methodist Women's leadership, and other prominent black ministers and laypersons.

Beyond representation and participation at the committee, board, and staff levels, the most historic feature of *The United Methodist Hymnal* is its black hymnic content. The new edition contains forty hymns and songs from the black church tradition, carefully integrated under the various "doctrine and experience" pattern headings of the hymnbook: "The Glory of the Triune God" (four), "The Grace of Jesus Christ" (five), "The Power of the Holy

Spirit" (twenty-four), "The Community of Faith" (two), and "A New Heaven and a New Earth" (five). Welcome additions to the growing corpus of black Methodist hymnody are C. Eric Lincoln's trendsetting words toward real inclusiveness in the hymn "How Like a Gentle Spirit." Also of more than passing interest in this collection are numerous black gospel selections.[40]

CHRISTIAN EDUCATION, YOUTH, AND CURRICULUM RESOURCES

The Black Revolution shook the foundations of every institution in the black community, including the church. Its strident cries and insistent demands for self-definition, self-expression, and self-determination became the battle cry for the remainder of the 1960s, the 1970s, and beyond. The implications of these new realities for Christian education in black United Methodist churches were many and far-reaching. The basic challenge was stated well in Philip A. Harley's proposal for a contextual approach to local church education: "to underscore the pressing need for the construction of an educational philosophy, methodology and curricula . . . for Black people . . . sensitive to the kinds of goals and purposes that speak to the Black condition and are consistent with Black understanding of the gospel."[41] This revolutionary proposal meant radical adjustments from within the black United Methodist community as well as from within the denomination. The following paragraphs briefly trace those developments.

Christian education programs and leaders in the merging black Conferences found themselves in a generally precarious situation. Church schools, youth and family ministry programs, and leadership development enterprises and personnel, previously related in cohesive black interconference networks of relationships, were now dispersed in unfamiliar environments among more than fifty white Conferences. Equally serious and distressing was the widely held assumption in those Conferences that Merger meant assimilation. Little if any effort was made to understand or accommodate the then recent insights of black theologies of liberation and their missional priorities, despite the fact that many, if not most, black people, including thousands of black Methodists, were more than sympathetic to those points of view. This miscommunication or noncommunication and its perceived insensitivity to black aspirations led to protests climaxing in an August 1969 BMCR-led confrontation at the headquarters of the General Board of Education (Nashville). There it was made unmistakably clear that United Methodism must rethink its rationale, goals, objectives, strategies, and designs and renovate them in the light of the new realities of the black struggle for justice and equality.

Following almost a year of dialogue and negotiation, the Board of Education responded positively to the demands of its black constituents led by the Black Staff Forum and BMCR. In 1970 it appointed Willard A. Williams, a black pastor from Buffalo, New York, assistant general secretary of the new department, Developing Educational Ministries with Ethnic Constituencies. At that same time the United Methodist Publishing House brought Ernestine A. Calhoun to its staff as a children's editor. Willard Williams joined William J. Washington in the Division of the Local Church as the only other black staff member. Likewise, Calhoun, later (1972) to become a full editor, joined James S. Gadsden and H. Walter Willis as staff members of the Editorial Division.

Recognizing the need for children to identify with characters in their church school materials and thus learn their concepts more easily, a Black Task Force from the Southern California-Arizona Conference investigated the availability of such materials. Finding none, with the expert help of Jean and Nathaniel Lacy, the task force produced a series of Old Testament illustrative drawings from a black perspective (1971). The series was approved as supplementary material and was subsequently produced by the United Methodist Publishing House. Barbara J. Smith, a member of Holman Church in Los Angeles, was director of the project for the Conference.

The first printed statement by Willard Williams was *Foundations for Christian Education in Black Churches* (1972). Produced as a study guide for use with *Foundations for Teaching and Learning in The Methodist Church* (1979), it "summarizes our biblical and theological beliefs . . . and is so written that Blacks and other ethnic minority persons can use it as a base for educational ministry."[42]

The years immediately following Merger (1968–1972) witnessed two shifts in black Methodist emphases: from general to local church concerns and from exclusively black church concerns to black community needs. This transition was also compatible with the restructuring of United Methodism in 1972, which viewed discipleship as the objective and the local church as the focus of the church's ministry. Willard Williams articulates this change in two Board of Discipleship publications. In 1972 he observed, "The more I have consulted with Black and White churches, the more I am convinced of the need for ministry in the Black community."[43] In 1974 he further clarified this and put it in a theological context in saying, "The emerging concept of Black theology is not an opposing view in the understanding of the Christian faith. [It] appropriates the gospel to the Black experience."[44]

The programmatic response to the black theology-black community approach was made in two ways: training events and curriculum resources. Workshops were held to identify relevant needs in black churches and communities. Pilot projects were initiated to test and design pertinent programs. Human relations seminars were held to explore some of the personal, social, and church implications of racism. In the curriculum resources area, the Section on Curriculum Resources generated two types of materials: age-level materials and leader development materials. Age-level resources included *Can Blacks Be Christian?* (1973) by George M. Daniels, *The Black Church and the Black Experience* (1974) by John A. Blackwell and George H. Outen, and *Gifted and Black* (1975) by William M. Morris.

From 1976 to 1984 Christian education was advanced through the Board of Discipleship's Division of Education and the Curriculum Resources Committee with the timely, assisting momentum of the denomination's quadrennial Ethnic Minority Local Church missional priority. Designed to be United Methodism's response to critical needs, this emphasis also gave needed support to black Methodist efforts in evangelistic outreach, missional program development, and curriculum resources. More specifically, the Curriculum Resources Committee sponsored curriculum consultations with black (and other minority) local church and Conference leaders to discover curriculum resource needs. These led to the production of the following resources: *Ethnic Minorities in The United Methodist Church* (1976), *Children We Are Free* and *Jesus as Liberator* by Elsie and Cornish Rogers, and the Faith Journey Series (1983), a Christian Education: Shared Approaches publication.

The work of the Board of Discipleship and the Curriculum Resources Committee was greatly strengthened during this period by six black staff additions: Fletcher J. Bryant, assistant general secretary, Division of Education; Karen Y. Collier, coordinator of interpretation; Lina H. McCord, director of services in Family Ministries; Dorothy Turner-Lacy, assistant general secretary, Ethnic Minority Local Church Coordination; David L. White, assistant general secretary, Ethnic Minority Local Church Coordination; and H. Walter Willis, director, Ethnic Minority Local Church Coordination.

The final phase of the Ethnic Minority Local Church missional priority, continued by a close vote of the 1984 General Conference, was designed to work toward several goals. The discipleship objective, however, lent itself more closely to black educational concerns and became the focal point of a joint endeavor between the black staff of the Board of Discipleship and the resources of the Ethnic Minority Local Church priority. Several things were accomplished in Christian education with black churches in the middle 1980s. Noteworthy was the New Models in Christian Education Project developed by Joseph V. Crockett, appointed to the Section on Christian Education, Board of Discipleship, as director of Ethnic Minority Local Church Education in 1986. Crockett's strategy—a cooperative effort with selected black churches in all jurisdictions, black seminary teachers, and the General Council on Ministries staff—was "to identify models of Christian Education for Afro-American congregations in various . . . settings . . . and to enable local churches to develop teams of lay and clergy persons [to] acquire the skills . . . for executing [these] models."[45] A second effort to enhance Christian education was BMCR's "Black Youth Meet Across the Nation," which took place in each jurisdiction during the summer of 1986. In 1987

BMCR sponsored a National Youth Ministry Conference at Rust College, Holly Springs, Mississippi. In 1988, the New Orleans bi-district undertook a Christian education project to develop educational programs there.

New resources for use primarily in black congregations that were produced in the 1984–1988 quadrennium include *Black Americans in The United Methodist Church, Touched by Grace, The Many Faces of United Methodists,* and *Creating a New Community.*

Black appointees to Board of Discipleship and Church School Publications (formerly Curriculum Resources) positions since 1984 were Joseph V. Crockett, Ethnic Minority Local Church; Janice L. Frederick, editor; Juanita Ivie, Ethnic Minority Resourcing; Marilyn W. Magee, assistant general secretary, Ministry of the Laity; Marlu P. Scott, director, Education in Large Membership Churches; and Jessy E. Thomas, director, Development of Family Life Ministries.

Several separate boards or parts of boards, agencies, commissions, and organizations were consolidated in 1972 to form the Board of Discipleship: the Division of the Local Church and the Division of Curriculum Resources, Board of Education; the Board of Evangelism; and the Board of Lay Activities, including the Methodist Men's organization and the Commission on Worship. There were numerous black representatives to these boards and agencies from 1972 to 1984.

HIGHER EDUCATION, THEOLOGICAL EDUCATION, AND MINISTRY

The Methodist–Evangelical United Brethren merger in education posed two fundamental problems for the newly restructured Board of Higher Education and Ministry's Division of Higher Education; first, providing culturally inclusive academic programs in racially affirming campus environments for what would become an increasing number of black students; second, maintaining a historic network of accredited, church-related, academically creditable schools.

Prior to national court rulings outlawing segregation in public higher education and later in all federally assisted school programs, black students generally attended black schools and colleges. Between 1954 and 1964 some few black students attended white private and church-related colleges. That number increased in the 1970s, and by the middle 1980s more black students were in white colleges and universities than in all black schools combined. United Methodism met this new racial pattern emerging in its own schools with a clearly inclusive policy. The 1968 and 1972 editions of the *Discipline* state, "In establishing and maintaining educational institutions and in ministering to students without respect to racial or national origin, the Church continues its historic work of uniting knowledge and vital piety" (1972 *Discipline,* ¶ 1026). While not more important than developing racism-free learning environments for black students entering the often hostile world of white academe, the problems of integrating the black colleges of the former Central Jurisdiction claimed most of the attention, time, and thought of United Methodism for more than the next decade. White schools and colleges of The United Methodist Church were church-related in a variety of ways. The predominant pattern was a quasi-legal relation to the Annual Conference. Like their sister institutions, black schools and colleges were also related to Annual Conferences. Unlike their counterparts, however, they were also related, often legally, to the Division of Higher Education. This is understandable in historical perspective and even today. Financially, the responsibility of operating these schools alone was too costly, despite sacrificial and creditable giving. The future, mission, and support of these colleges, a medical school, and a theological seminary became a paramount issue in the early years of the first quadrennium of the new denomination. Should the church continue them? If so, all of them? If the church withdraws its support, what happens to its mission? How shall the church more adequately do whatever it is that it decides to do about these schools? These and other questions were raised and resolved by the General Conferences from 1968 to 1976. BMCR commissioned studies and legislation.

In 1968 the General Conference appointed a church-wide biracial Commission on Black Colleges. Headed by W. Astor Kirk, it was requested to report "the educational and financial resources that must be mobilized for the future development of the Black colleges of the church."[46] Black sociologist Daniel C. Thompson (1912–1988) of Dillard University directed the study and wrote the report. In 1967 a BMCR antidiscrimination protest was staged at the Board of Education in Nashville, Tennessee, making the following demands:

- $8 million to meet the immediate needs of the black colleges
- an interagency church council to channel these funds to the black colleges
- larger Annual Conference giving by white Conferences to black colleges
- the creation of a $1 million non-cosigner black college student loan fund
- black membership on the Black College Study Commission
- monitored racially inclusive admissions policy at all church-related schools

There were tangible results from the Nashville episode. First, the Special Session of the General Conference in 1970 authorized the Division of Higher Education to coordinate a Negro Colleges Advance program to seek $8 million for general aid to these schools and $2 million in scholarship and loan money by December 31, 1972. This effort was directed by E. Clayton Calhoun and Dennis R. Fletcher, Fletcher taking a leave from his Board of Missions position to do this. (Prior to the Negro Colleges Advance program, the black colleges had been funded partially through the annual February Race Relations Sunday offerings. This offering peaked at $625,000 in 1970 and was phased out at that time.)

The 1972 General Conference further responded to the urgent need to assist the shamefully underfunded black colleges. In answering a request from the Commission on the Black Colleges and the Council of Presidents of the Black Colleges, it created the Black College Fund. This General Church–apportioned fund, with an annual goal for the 1972–1976 quadrennium of $6 million, represented the largest investment made by any Protestant church in black colleges in the country. The Black College Fund has since raised more than $80 million for United Methodism's twelve black colleges since 1972.

At this same General Conference, it was recommended that the Commission on Black Colleges be reappointed for the 1972–1976 quadrennium "to study problems examined in the 1972 report . . . with recommendations to . . . the 1976 General Conference."[47] Apart from the Black College Fund, the Conference had made some other important decisions: It reaffirmed a racially inclusive policy for all of its institutions and asserted that "black colleges are necessary for stable black progress [and] must become first rate in every respect."[48] Bishop Ernest T. Dixon, Jr., a former president of Philander Smith College (1965–1969), chaired the Continuing Commission on Black Colleges, which reported to the 1976 General Conference. It recommended the continuation of all twelve of the colleges, renewal of the Black College Fund at $6 million a year in the 1976–1980 quadrennium, and the establishment of guidelines to qualify for the receiving of black college funds. The Black College Fund Office also directed four ancillary programs related to its primary responsibility to administer and promote the fund. A Lina H. McCord Fund was created honoring McCord's ten-year tenure (1976–1985). The fund provided expenses for a student itinerate program enabling the chosen itinerate Black College Fund student to itinerate for ten summer weeks. Since about 1985, Black College Fund students also involved themselves in the Minority in Service Training (MIST) program. Under supervision, they served in churches on campuses or in communities. Similarly, Ethnic Minority Local Church programs were available for Black College Fund students. These allowed students to serve in local churches, working on Ethnic Minority projects. Finally, a new recruitment program involving Black College Fund school graduates was unveiled. This program involved contacting black teenagers in high schools, community centers, and churches "to acquaint [them] with the opportunities offered by United Methodist-related historically Black colleges."[49] Past executive directors of the Black College Fund have been DePriest Whye (1972–1980) and Lina H. McCord (1980–1988). The present executive director, Shirley W. Lewis, has been in the position since

1986. Shirley W. Lewis holds bachelor and master's degrees from the University of California, Berkeley, and a doctorate from Stanford University. Before accepting the position with the Black College Fund, Dr. Lewis was the associate dean for academic affairs at Meharry Medical College.

Institutional and Personnel Changes

A number of institutional and personnel changes took place in the life of United Methodism's twelve black schools and colleges in the twenty-year period 1968–1988. Each of these institutions celebrated their centennial anniversaries and entered into their second century of service with black youth under the auspices of The United Methodist Church. Strategically located at choice sites in nine southern states and educating approximately ten thousand students from a variety of backgrounds, this largest group of black colleges related to any Protestant denomination has provided higher education for thousands for whom this experience could have been "a dream deferred."

Two major institutional changes occurred and two significant proposals were made among these institutions in the 1980s. Clark College and Atlanta University, the latter a renowned black graduate school of arts and sciences located adjacent to Clark in Atlanta, consolidated in 1988 to form Clark Atlanta University. Morristown College, Morristown, Tennessee, founded in 1881 after more than a century of significant service as a junior college in Appalachia, decided to merge with Knoxville College, a historically black four-year institution affiliated with the Presbyterian Church (USA). Also in the 1980s, Huston-Tillotson and Wiley colleges were urged by the General Board of Higher Education and Ministry to merge with Texas College, a four-year institution of the Christian Methodist Episcopal Church in Tyler, Texas. After two or three years of negotiating, these historically black schools decided against merger. In the early stages of these merger conversations, Philander Smith College in Little Rock, Arkansas, had been invited to consider a "merged" or consortial relationship with Wiley, Huston-Tillotson, and Texas College. Philander Smith, the only fully accredited, private, black, four-year college in Arkansas and in the contiguous state of Missouri, was disinclined to become involved in talks that could remove it from the Arkansas-Missouri area.

A number of deaths and retirements brought many new faces to the presidential offices of the black colleges between 1968 and 1988. Among the deceased were James P. Brawley, Matthew S. Davage, Albert W. Dent, Henry L. Dickason, John W. Haywood, Vivian W. Henderson, Lucius H. Pitts, John J. Seabrook, and Julius S. Scott, Sr. (Thomas W. Cole, Sr., succeeded Julius S. Scott, Sr., after Scott's retirement in 1958. He is the father of Thomas W. Cole, Jr., president of Clark Atlanta University.) Several retirements from the ranks of presidencies of black United Methodist colleges further changed the campus scene: Harry V. Richardson, founding president of the Interdenominational Theological Center (1968); Richard V. Moore, president of Bethune-Cookman College for twenty-seven years (1974); Hubert V. Manning, Claflin's president for twenty-eight years (1984); Major J. Jones, Gammon Theological Seminary's president-dean for eighteen years (1985); Robert E. Hayes, president of Wiley College for fifteen years (1986); John T. King, Huston-Tillotson's president for twenty-two years (1987); and Isaac Miller, Bennett College's president for twenty-one years (1987).

New Presidents

Each of the schools and colleges except Rust College elected new presidents during 1968–1988. Several institutions elected two or more. Meharry Medical College elected its dean, Lloyd C. Elam, M.D., to the presidency in 1968. When Elam became chancellor in 1982, David Satcher, M.D., became president. Dillard University selected Broadus N. Butler, a Wayne State University (Detroit) administrator as president in 1969. Upon accepting an American Council on Education post, Duke University political scientist Samuel D. Cook succeeded him in 1975. The pastor of Tindley Temple Church (Philadelphia), Walter R. Hazzard, was elected to the presidency of Philander Smith College in 1969. Following his resignation to return to the pastorate in 1979, he was succeeded by Grant S. Shockley (1979) and Hazo D. Carter (1983). Myer T. Titus, former chief instruction officer for the Board of Community Colleges in Denver, became president in 1987. Robert E. Hayes was Wiley's selection for president in 1971. Following a term as president of the Council of Black College Presidents (1974–1975) he retired in 1986. Hayes was followed in the presidency at Wiley by the director of development at Rust College, David L. Beckley (1987).

The presidential succession at Paine is interesting. Lucius H. Pitts became its first black president in 1971. Following his death (1977), Julius S. Scott, Jr. (the son of Julius S. Scott, Sr., president of Wiley College 1948–1958) became the first United Methodist president of this historically Christian Methodist Episcopal college. Upon Scott's resignation to become the associate general secretary of the Board of Higher Education and Ministry in 1982, William H. Harris became president. In 1988, Scott returned to the Paine presidency. Bethune-Cookman College selected one of its illustrious graduates, Oswald P. Bronson, then president of the Interdenominational Theological Center in Atlanta, to follow the twenty-seven-year presidential tenure of Richard V. Moore. Bronson, one-time president of the Religious Education Association of the United States and Canada, has remained at Bethune-Cookman since his election in 1974.

In 1977 Clark College elected educator and research consultant Elias Blake, Jr., to the presidency. Upon resigning to pursue research and teaching at

Howard University in 1987, he was succeeded by Thomas W. Cole, Jr., in 1988. Cole came to Clark Atlanta University from the Chancellorship of the West Virginia Board of Regents. Claflin College selected Allan Rogers, Jr., to be its seventh president in 1984. The former dean of the graduate school at Jackson State University (Mississippi) was an ordained United Methodist minister. In 1987 Bennett chose Gloria Dean Randle Scott, a Clark College vice president, to head its unique women's institution. The third woman to head a black United Methodist college, Scott brought an impressive national and international profile in higher education to her task. Gammon Theological Seminary called Alfred L. Norris, an alumnus, pastor, former district superintendent and one-time Gammon administrator, to head its institution following the retirement of Major J. Jones. A distinguished churchman and a Louisiana native, Norris was elected in 1985. Huston-Tillotson's 1988 replacement for John T. King's more than two decades of leadership of the college and in the church was Joseph T. McMillan, a higher education executive for the United Church of Christ. The only black United Methodist college to retain its presidential leadership for the entire period under discussion, 1968–1988, was Rust. W. A. McMillan continues to serve there with distinction as dean of the presidents.

Program Developments

In addition to the pace-setting Black College Fund, a scholarship program and the appointment of a black trustee to an overseas university highlighted the work of the Division of Higher Education since Merger. Through United Methodism's several loan and scholarship programs earmarked for black students (and other racial groups), hundreds of black American students have been assisted in their efforts to secure a college and/or a graduate degree in United States schools. These opportunities have included

- loans and scholarships through the United Methodist Student Day Offering
- scholarships funded through the World Communion Sunday Offering or the Ethnic Minority Scholarship Program
- the Myron F. Wicke Scholarship at Dillard University
- the United Methodist Publishing House Merit Scholarship for ethnic persons
- the Crusade Scholarship awards given since the 1940s to ethnic minority persons "who have a commitment to mission and will stay in it after graduation"
- the Bicentennial Scholars Program, which encourages ethnic minority high school graduating seniors to continue their education.

This expanded program of loans and scholarships for all students in United Methodism became the particular responsibility of Angella Current in 1988, when she became the first black American to hold the position of Associate General Secretary in the Office of Loans and Scholarships in the Board of Higher Education and Ministry. A second significant development in the Board of Higher Education's effort to establish, from the outset, a peer relationship with the new African University project was the appointment of Gloria R. Scott, Bennett College's new president, to the founding Board of Trustees of the forthcoming Methodist university in Zimbabwe.

Higher Education and Ministry Elected Members and Staff

The restructuring of the General Board of Higher Education and Ministry following Merger took place in two phases. The General Conference put in place an interim structure in 1968–1972 to care for the immediate work of the higher education and ministry units. These units and their black elected members were Department of Educational Institutions, T. W. Cole, Sr., and Richard V. Moore; Department of Campus Ministry, Hubert V. Manning; and Department of the Ministry, Richard V. Moore and Bishop J. Thomas, Jr. (Advisory Committee). Daniel W. Wynn, who had succeeded Bishop Thomas as associate director of the Department of Educational Institutions of the Division of Higher Education in 1965, remained in that position until 1975. In this same quadrennium, Luther B. Felder II served as a member of the National Council of the new United Methodist Student Movement, and Major J. Jones became a member of the Association of United Methodist Theological Schools. Members of the University Senate for the 1968–1972 period were Ernest T. Dixon and Vivian W. Henderson.

The reconstituted General Board of Higher Education and Ministry that resulted from the 1972 restructuring process (and further changes in 1976) presented the most racially inclusive picture American Methodism had ever had in this area. By 1984 every unit of this major program board had elected at least one of its black members as chairperson or vice chairperson. (A new unit, the Division of Chaplains and Related Ministries, became a part of the redesigned Board of Higher Education and Ministry program. John W. Heyward, Jr., was a director on this staff from 1972–1975.) In 1972 Bishop Ernest T. Dixon was elected to the presidency of the Board of Higher Education and Ministry, and Vivian W. Henderson chaired the University Senate. In 1984 Major J. Jones and Isaac H. Miller, Jr., were presidents of the Association of United Methodist Theological Schools and the National Association of Schools and Colleges of The United Methodist Church, respectively. During 1976–1980, Bishop Dixon chaired the Continuing Commission on Black Colleges.

Vice presidents of units within the Board of Higher Education and Ministry

245

from 1972–1984 included Charles Fuget, Division of Higher Education (1984–1988); Bishop W. T. Handy, Jr., Division of Ordained Ministry (1980–1984); John W. Heyward, Jr., chairperson, Division of Chaplains and Related Ministries (1980–1984); Ethel R. Johnson, chairperson, Division of Lay Ministries (1972–1976); Julius S. Scott, Jr., National Association of Schools and Colleges of The United Methodist Church (1980–1984); Bishop F. Herbert Skeete, president, Division of Higher Education (1980–1984); and Bishop Prince A. Taylor, chairperson, Division of Chaplains and Related Ministries (1972–1976).

Black members at the policy-making levels of the units cited above almost tripled following Merger and the church-avowed inclusive position. From 1972–1984 the following persons served the Division of Chaplains and Related Ministries: G. Wayne Cuff and Bishop Prince A. Taylor (1972–1976) and John W. Heyward, Jr. (1976–1984). Heyward chaired the division from 1976–1980. Black members of the Division of Higher Education during this period were Helen M. Fannings (1984–1988); Charles Fuget, secretary and vice chairperson, (1980–1988); Bishop Charles F. Golden (1972–1976); James C. Hardcastle (1984–1988); Isaac H. Miller, Jr. (1972–1980, 1984–1988); Richard V. Moore (1980–1988); and Bishop F. Herbert Skeete (1980–1988). Bishop Skeete headed the division during the 1980–1984 quadrennium. Members of the Division of Lay Ministries, renamed the Division of Diaconal Ministry in 1976, were Bishop Ernest T. Dixon, Jr., (1972–1976); Alexina Hazzard (1972–1980); Ethel R. Johnson (1972–1980, chairperson of the division, 1972–1976); Russell F. McReynolds (1980–1988), Anthony J. Shipley (1972–1976); and Arvarh E. Strickland (1976–1980). Black members of the Division of the Ordained Ministry from 1972–1988 included Jerome K. Del Pino (1984–1988); Bishop Charles F. Golden (1972–1980); Bishop W. T. Handy, Jr. (1980–1988); William M. James (1976–1984); and Hubert V. Manning (1972–1976).

A total of fifteen black persons engaged in higher education have been members of United Methodism's University Senate since Merger: Elias Blake (1984–1988); Oswald P. Bronson (1976–1984); Samuel D. Cook (1984–present); Bishop Ernest T. Dixon, Jr. (1968–1972); Charles Fuget (1984); Vivian W. Henderson (1968–1976; Henderson was the first black member of the University Senate to become its president [1972–1976]); Carolyn E. Johnson (1988–present); Ethel R. Johnson (1984–1988); John T. King (1980–1984); William A. McMillan (1972–1980); Isaac H. Miller (1971–1972); Willa B. Player (1964–1968, 1976–1984); Gloria R. Scott (1988–present); Julius S. Scott, Jr. (1980–1984, 1988–present); and Grant S. Shockley (1984–present). Several persons of color have been members and officers of three adjunct national United Methodist higher education organizations since their inception: Major J. Jones, president-dean of Gammon Theological Seminary, was a member of the Association of United

Methodist Theological Schools from 1968. In 1976 he was elected to its executive committee, and in 1985 he became its first black president. Julius S. Scott, Jr., president of Paine College, was elected a vice president of the National Association of Schools and Colleges of The United Methodist Church in 1980. In 1984 Isaac H. Miller, Jr., president of Bennett College, became the first black head of this association. Another landmark was achieved in 1984 when Julius S. Scott, Jr., became the first black trustee of the National Methodist Foundation for Christian Higher Education.

In concluding this section detailing black participation in the work of the Division of Higher Education and Ministry, the names of the members of the influential Continuing Commission on the Black Colleges (1976–1980) should be mentioned: Bishop Ernest T. Dixon, Jr., chairperson; Robert E. Hayes, Sr., president of Wiley College; John T. King, president of Huston-Tillotson College; William A. McMillan, President of Rust College; and Willa B. Player, then director of the Division of Institutional Development of the federal Department of Health, Education, and Welfare.

Campus Ministry

In seeking to provide ministry to and with black students, faculty, and staff in various United Methodist campus and campus-related settings, black and white campus ministers encountered crises and challenges. On predominantly white campuses the crises were three: the presence of covert and increasingly overt instances of racism, especially as the numbers of black students increased; the demand for full black participation on an equal basis with white participation at all levels of college life; and the tensions resulting from the polarization and mutual interpersonal and intergroup isolation syndrome. The challenges included—and still include—meeting the special needs of black and other minority students and developing a comprehensive strategy with policies, programs, and resources to promote a demonstrably witnessing Christian and intentionally caring Christian community.

The black campus and campus-related situations presented other kinds of crises and challenges. As a consequence of the Black Consciousness movement of the 1960s, the black campus—including its religious program—was revolutionized.

Student-centered religious work of the 1940s and 1950s, under the impact of the civil rights movement, was completely refocused and began to define and implement radical social action objectives involving nonviolent direct action for black liberation. The Black Theology movement of the late 1960s and the Black Studies movement of the early 1960s combined to demand an authentic curriculum on black religion as an aspect of claiming self-identity and self-esteem.

The resurgence of the black spirituality,[50] with its indigenous religious

247

expressions, the phenomenal impact of black Pentecostalism in the 1960s and 1970s, together with the rise of the Black Gospel Choir movement, ushered in a new era in spirituality, music, and worship on the black (and white) campuses of America. A profile of campus ministry centers across the nation will give some idea of the extent of black United Methodism's thrust in this area.

United Methodist Campus Ministry Settings

There are several campus ministry settings in higher education among black colleges and universities: United Methodist campus ministries, Wesley Foundations, college church programs, and ecumenical campus ministries. What follows are vignettes of these approximately fifty programs that serve hundreds of black United Methodist students (and students of many other denominations and faiths) annually.

United Methodist Campus Ministries

A primary source of campus ministry to black United Methodist students are the twelve campuses of our United Methodist–related colleges and universities. Programs in these settings prior to Merger were largely in the hands of volunteer faculty, students, and local church persons. After Merger most, if not all, of these schools employed college ministers, directors of religious life, or chaplains. These persons, many of whom rose to prominence in the denomination, were also faculty members and taught courses in Bible, religion, and philosophy.[51]

Wesley Foundations

A second significant campus ministry development has been the Wesley Foundation Movement. Founded in the 1920s, these programs operate on the campuses of non–United Methodist institutions (state or private) as a church presence. This type of ministry has expanded from the two original exemplars at Morgan Christian Center (1938), Morgan State University, Maryland, and the Wesley Foundation (1953) at Lincoln University, Missouri, to more than fifteen Wesley Foundations in twenty states including the District of Columbia.

Ecumenical Campus Ministries

Black United Methodists have been engaged ecumenically in campus ministry efforts since the 1940s. They functioned only marginally, however, within the then developing network of interracial, ecumenical student structures such as the United Student Christian Council (1944), the National Student Christian Federation (1959), United Ministries in Higher Education (1964), and the University Christian Movement (1966). Since 1969 they have worked cooperatively with whites through an all-black ecumenical coalition, Ministry to Blacks in Higher Education. Conceived and founded by Harold L.

Bell (1934–1973), a former Methodist director of the Wesley Foundation at Howard University in Washington, D.C., and the first executive director of the coalition, this intentionally black organization of campus ministers "for self-definition and self-determination" perceived its mission to be one of shaping the black higher educational experience around the black struggle for liberation. Including the work of the Wesley Foundations, the campus ministries on United Methodist campuses, and situational ministries on several more campuses, Ministry to Blacks in Higher Education represented as impressive and exciting an adventure in campus ministries as could be found anywhere in the Protestant field.

Campus ministry staff in the Division of Higher Education since the 1970s have been Frank L. Horton, director of Campus Ministries (1970–1976); Joe L. Gipson, assistant general secretary, Campus Ministry (1976–1984); and Richard R. Hicks, director of Campus Ministry (1987–present).

Ministry to Blacks in Higher Education staff have included founding executive director Harold L. Bell (1969–1973) and Richard R. Hicks, executive director from 1975–1976. United Ministries in Higher Education employed Richard R. Hicks as its southeastern regional secretary from 1974–1976.

Campus Church Pastoral Ministry

A unique ministry has developed in the past and persists in the present among black United Methodist colleges and black colleges and universities of various origins that happen to be in a given community. In numerous instances, local churches and schools have developed close relationships to these colleges and "adopted" them as "their" schools. Volunteer participation and leadership from college to church and from church to college often provided (and provides) helpful opportunities for witness, fellowship, and service. In some cases, these situations have been made the adjunct responsibilities of the local pastor, and skills in this area of ministry are considered in appointments to these churches.

THEOLOGICAL EDUCATION AND SEMINARIES

The black rebellion against social, economic, and political oppression in the black community in the 1950s and 1960s created a crisis of meaning and mission in the black church in the 1970s. A new-found pride and a fearless determination to be self-defining, self-determining, and self-governing and to work in solidarity for the liberation of the oppressed and the upbuilding of depressed black urban communities had profound implications for the education of black ministers and the seminaries that they attended. Biblical, historical, theological, ethical, and practical studies required contextual reorientation to meet the challenges of this unprecedented and novel situation.

In relation to United Methodism, two sets of institutions were affected: Gammon/Interdenominational Theological Center and other accredited black seminaries that trained black ministers and United Methodism's white seminaries (and other seminaries training black United Methodists). The task in the black schools was essentially one of rediscovering, redefining, and reappropriating the Christian faith in relation to the black religious experience. The task of the white seminaries was reaffirming this new black awareness and reinforcing it in terms of an inclusive environment, a contextual curriculum, and an adequate support system, including field education and financial aid.

Merger was a second factor. The Methodist–Evangelical United Brethren union had been consummated on the assumption of an inclusive and nonsegregated denomination. At that same time, however, many black Methodists questioned integration as white assimilation. However, at the same time as they questioned absorption, separatism in any definitive sense was deemed equally unacceptable.

Gammon/Interdenominational Theological Center

Under the able and astute leadership of Oswald P. Bronson, who assumed the presidency of the Interdenominational Theological Center (ITC) in 1968 following the retirement of the founding president of ITC, Harry V. Richardson—Gammon and ITC moved toward the resolution of their new dilemma by adopting a contextual black liberation theology position. This stance grew out of and centered around the publication of James H. Cone's landmark work, *Black Theology and Black Power* (1969). Cone defined the task of black theology thus: "to analyze the black man's [sic] condition in the light of God's revelation in Jesus Christ with the purpose of creating a new understanding of black dignity among black people, and providing the necessary soul in that people to destroy racism."[52] Later in 1969, Charles Shelby Rooks, then executive director of The Fund for Theological Education, delivered a provocative lecture at ITC entitled "Should ITC be a Seminary Devoted to an Emphatic Understanding, Study of, and Service to the Black Religious Experience?" In giving a resounding yes to his question, Rooks emphasized that in his opinion the survival and uniqueness of ITC rested on this point. Early in 1970, at a first conference on curriculum and the black religious experience in theological education at Howard University, Washington, D.C., Charles B. Copher, professor of Old Testament and dean at ITC, outlined five requisites for a black seminary curriculum that takes the study of the black experience seriously: reclamation of black heritage, development of black pride, knowledge of liberation skills, liberation of whites from their ignorance of blacks, and an analysis of the black religious experience to discern its total liberating potential for black and white. This conference was followed by the key Consultation on Black Studies in Theological Education, held at ITC in November 1970. At this conference ITC discussed a document written by Gayraud S. Wilmore, entitled "Experimental Program of Black Studies in Theological Education." This important document became the basis for the ITC program of the 1970s and 1980s. (Gayraud S. Wilmore, professor of church history and Afro-American religious studies at ITC, was a major mover in the development of the black theology movement and one of its most prolific writer-scholars.)

Affirmation and support from the denomination paralleled the efforts of ITC to align itself with the spirit and method of black liberation theology and its consequent new black church style. In 1968 United Methodism developed a new strategy for recruiting and supporting its ministry through a Ministerial Education Fund. Made available to Gammon as one of the thirteen seminaries of the church, the fund has played a crucial role in enlarging the resources of the seminary for recruitment, financial aid, curriculum improvement, and continuing education.

Beyond the curriculum and financial support issues at Gammon during this period was a more fundamental issue, namely, the question of the future of Gammon itself. An important action of the Uniting Conference of 1968 was the establishment of a commission to study "the best utilization and deployment of theological schools"[53] in the new denomination, with a requested report to the 1972 General Conference. The 1972 report concluded that "The United Methodist Church could provide theological education of high quality with fewer than fourteen seminaries."[54] (Merger added Evangelical Theological Seminary, Naperville, Illinois, and United Theological Seminary, Dayton, Ohio.) The General Conference accepted this recommendation and appointed a commission to explore what this would mean for the five clusters of seminaries in the East, the Greater Atlanta region, the Greater Chicago region, the Ohio region, and the West. The Greater Atlanta Region Task Force, chaired by W. T. Handy, was assigned a fourfold task: exploring ways of cooperation, developing common programs and ministries, justifying Candler and Gammon in Atlanta, and suggesting ways in which Gammon and Candler could mutually enrich each other. The Task Force, meeting periodically from 1973 to 1975, made the following recommendations to the commission: (1) no merger of Candler and Gammon at that time, (2) continued effort to extend and increase cooperation, and (3) the long-term study of ways in which there eventually could be a merger.

Black Faculty and Administrators

Gammon Theological Seminary had not had its own faculty since its incorporation into ITC (1958–1959). The faculties of the first constituent institutions—Gammon Theological Seminary, Turner Theological Seminary,

Morehouse School of Religion, and Phillips School of Theology—were the ITC faculty. Black and white United Methodists, therefore, have been members of the ITC faculty since its inception and continue to serve and be appointed. J. DeKoven Killingsworth, Ma. Mus. Ed., Chicago Conservatory of Music, taught under a joint appointment at both Clark College and Gammon until retirement. Charles B. Copher, Ph.D., Boston University, professor of Old Testament, was appointed to the Gammon faculty in 1948 and served as dean from 1953–1959. In 1959 Copher was elected professor of Old Testament and academic dean of the new ITC. He retired in 1978 after a distinguished career in the classroom and a pioneering role in developing black biblical perspectives research. The three other black United Methodist appointments to ITC between 1968 and 1972 have been Jonathan Jackson, Th.D., Boston University, professor of Christian education (1969–present); Edward P. Wimberly, Ph.D., Boston University, professor of pastoral care (1974–1983); and Michael I. N. Dash, D.Min., Boston University, assistant professor of field education (1986–present). Several non-black United Methodists also served on the Gammon faculty between 1968 and 1984: Justo L. Gonzalez, J. Edward Lantz, Stephen C. Rasor, and Edward O. Trimmer.

Black United Methodist administrators have figured prominently in the conception, development, and administration of ITC for more than two decades of its three-decade history. United Methodist Oswald P. Bronson succeeded Harry V. Richardson in 1968. He had served as his vice president from 1966 to 1968. Bronson's firm and fruitful leadership from 1968 to 1975 guided ITC through its proactive participation in the turbulent years of the Black Revolution. Following Bronson's resignation to accept the presidency of Bethune-Cookman College, Emeritus President Harry V. Richardson was recalled to the interim presidency prior to the assumption of office by president-elect Grant S. Shockley (January 1, 1976–December 31, 1979). Shockley resigned the presidency to accept a similar position at United Methodist Philander Smith College. United Methodist Edith D. Thomas was appointed dean of students and student life during the Shockley administration.

President/Deans of Gammon Theological Seminary since 1968 have been Major J. Jones, author, black theological studies scholar, and prominent churchman (1967–1985); and Alfred L. Norris (1985), a well-known Louisiana Conference minister, administrator, and ecumenical leader.

Black Presence in United Methodist and Other Seminaries

A second phase of the Black Revolution in theological education unfolded in white United Methodist (and other theological schools). In 1959 there were only 327 black students in all of the Association of Theological Schools (ATS) institutions. Harry V. Richardson reported that 117 of that number were found in seven historically black theological schools. This left only 210 in the more than 100 other Protestant theological seminaries. The situation was similar in reference to faculty and administrators. In 1959 there were only six black faculty in all ATS schools and no black administrators. Two decades later (1982), these situations were greatly improved. The Selantic Fund, Inc., established the Fund for Theological Education (1960). Within the fund's program, major attention was focused on recruiting and financing black students. Charles Shelby Rooks became the director of this Protestant Fellowship Program, later renamed the Benjamin E. Mays Fellowship Program. Rooks was remarkably effective during his tenure as director (1960–1972) in assisting the ATS schools in enrolling 2,576 black students—627 in the then five major black theological schools. It should be noted at this point that during the period 1960–1980, the balance of numerical strength in the enrollment of black students noticeably shifted from the black to the white seminaries.

The situation in United Methodist seminaries from 1968–1984 generally replicated that of the ATS schools. Black United Methodist enrollment at ITC has generally increased annually since Merger. In that same time period, however, collectively more black United Methodist students attended white United Methodist theological schools. Conversely, however, few white students attended Gammon at ITC.

Assessment and Critique

American theological schools gave scant attention to the pleas of the black theology movement for serious attention to the academic study of the black religious experience until the late 1960s. Probably the earliest recognition of this need came from the Seabury Consultation on the Training of Negro Ministers held at Greenwich, Connecticut, March 6–8, 1959. Black United Methodists who were consultants to the Seabury Consultation were Bishop Matthew W. Clair; John H. Graham, professor, Gammon Theological Seminary; and Harry V. Richardson, the then newly elected president of ITC. This important consultation pointed to the need among white seminaries "to revise their courses of study in order to prepare students for other than middle class pastorates [and] devote more attention to the history and tradition of the Negro churches."[55] The American Association of Theological Schools provided significant leadership in this area in 1968 when its executive committee appointed a special committee of black theological educators "to formulate what needed to be said to theological schools about the significance of black religious experience."[56] During the middle and late 1960s fledgling black theological studies programs were launched in centers such as Berkeley, Boston, Chicago, New York City, and Rochester, New York. In 1973 the

Steering Committee of the Ecumenical Workshop on Education for Ministry in the Black Church and Community was launched in the Los Angeles area "to meet the needs of Black Church Leadership . . . for professional skills."[57] Leadership for this program was provided by Henry H. Mitchell. In the early stages of its planning, United Methodist Douglass E. Fitch sought funds for this project through BMCR.

In summary, during a two-decade period (1960–1980), black theological studies in white theological schools were less than spectacularly introduced. In the words of Charles Shelby Rooks, "It would not be accurate to say that theological schools have been totally unresponsive . . . but it is true that such responses . . . have been minimal."[58]

Program Development

Aware of the fact that most United Methodist seminaries rarely understood and often did not cope with or adequately support the needs of their increasingly larger black student constituencies, BMCR and the Commission on Religion and Race advocated, recommended, and monitored programs and personnel appointments at their twelve seminaries to enhance the cultural relevance of their curricula and the professional skills of their black theological students. During 1968–1972, BMCR and the commission sought to persuade the theological schools to affirm the black religious experience as a legitimate aspect of theological education and an integral component of the curriculum. This goal was moderately achieved despite the lack of black staff in the division and the reluctance of some seminary administrators to make a fundamentally needed shift in thinking about their task from a then absolute assimilationist position to a radically pluralist one.

Events and studies in the 1972–1976 quadrennium further reinforced the need for a contextual theological education, namely, the black religious experience in United Methodist seminaries. The National United Methodist Convocation on the Black Church held in Atlanta on December 10–13, 1973, felt strongly that it was crucial "to enable, strengthen, and radicalize the local Black United Methodist Church so that it may minister to the Black community."[59] Philip A. Harley in a 1973 article in the *Christian Advocate*, "Being Practical in Preparing Black Youth for Ministry," states, "There are skills and understandings not available . . . in current theological education that will prepare black youth for leadership in the black community."[60] In a 1976 survey of the black church by G. S. Shockley, E. D. C. Brewer, and M. Townsend, it was predicted that "unless successful recruitment and educational programs for future Black pastors are launched immediately, the future of Black churches in United Methodism is not bright."[61]

Ethnic Minority Local Church Programs and Theological Education

Two major theological education programs for black United Methodists grew out of the 1976–1984 Ethnic Minority Local Church missional priority. The 1972 General Conference directed the Division of the Ordained Ministry (DOM) to develop a high-priority plan to recruit ethnic minorities for the ordained ministry in cooperation with the seminaries of the church and the Annual Conferences. In developing the required plan, jurisdictional consultations were held with Annual Conference boards of ministry and district superintendents during 1972–1976. By the 1976 General Conference, with the guidance of Douglass E. Fitch and the aggressive concern of the late Vivian W. Henderson, representing the Council of Black College Presidents, three important steps had been taken toward empowering black youth in their preparation for entering the ministry: (1) the church-wide Ethnic Minority Scholarship Fund was established, (2) five jurisdictional scholarship programs were initiated, and (3) a black minority recruiter, Jesse H. Walker, was employed.[62]

The second program to grow out of the 1976–1980 Ethnic Minority missional priority thrust was the Multi-Ethnic Center for Ministry concept. Beginning in 1976, centers were established on the campuses of four strategically located United Methodist seminaries to provide enlistment programs for the ministry, continuing education, contextual teaching and resources, and models for creative ministries. These centers were the Mexican American one (1976) at Perkins School of Theology, Dallas, the Asian American one (1977) at the School of Theology at Claremont, California, and the Native American one (1983) at Oklahoma City, Oklahoma. William B. McClain was the founding director of the Multi-Ethnic Center for Ministry at Drew University (1978), serving the special needs of black and other racial groups attending the three Northeastern Jurisdiction seminaries—Boston, Drew, and Wesley. McClain directed the center until 1981, resigning to accept a professorship at Wesley Theological Seminary. He was succeeded by Willard A. Williams, who retired in 1984. William M. Jones, veteran pastor of New York City's Metropolitan Church, is the present director of the program.

Review of Theological Schools

The function of monitoring the progress of United Methodist seminaries in achieving announced racially inclusive goals in recruitment, curriculum, faculty employment, campus environment, financial aid, and decision making became the task of theological school review teams of the Commission on Religion and Race. In 1982–1983, when the first review visits were made, several weaknesses and causes for concern were found. Black student enrollments were low, especially for United Methodists. Black faculty were scarce, and few appointments were in process. Seminary curriculum committees were less than enthusiastic about major revisions of courses toward a multicultural approach. Black representation on boards of directors was sparse. Clearly problematic was the paucity of black United Methodists receiving theological education in our thirteen seminaries.

The 1985–1986 cycle of revisits revealed commitment and effort but little positive change and some declining situations in the thirteen schools. Recruitment efforts focusing on black preministerial students had resulted in very small increases since 1982–1983. Black enrollments still averaged 9–10 percent of the total of black students in all of our schools except Gammon, and still between 5 and 10 percent in the individual schools. Where curriculum improvement occurred in reference to the black religious experience, it was additive and elective rather than comprehensive and required. During the 1980s the scarcity of black faculty and competition for them became a cause of alarm at the seminaries. While the seminary campuses were externally in situations of relatively harmonious coexistence, covert and overt racist actions and incidents were detectable. Another concern of the 1980s was increasing campus racial polarization in worship and community life. Finally, little progress beyond tokenism seems to have been made in involving blacks in the decision-making process of the seminaries.[63]

Black Faculty and White Methodist Seminaries

Several major white theological schools made full-time black appointments to their faculties prior to 1968. Garrett Theological Seminary's appointment of Grant S. Shockley as professor of Christian education (1959) was a first for Methodists. Since that time, each of the remaining eleven white United Methodist seminaries have made black appointments. The list that follows identifies the full-time black faculty appointees, their academic field and/or position, and the appointing seminary.

1. Garrett-Evangelical Theological Seminary
   - Edsel A. Ammons (1968), urban ministry
   - John H. Cartwright (1970), social ethics
   - Philip A. Harley (1971), church administration
   - Henry J. Young (1980), systematic theology
   - Edward P. Wimberly (1985), psychology and pastoral care

2. Candler School of Theology, Emory University
   - Grant S. Shockley (1970), Christian education

3. Perkins School of Theology, Southern Methodist University
   - Nathaniel L. Lacy, Jr. (1970), practical theology and coordinator of black studies
   - Zan W. Holmes, Jr., (1969), practical theology

4. Methodist Theological School in Ohio
   - Ethel R. Johnson (1971), church administration
   - Ervin H. Smith (1981), applied Christianity

5. Saint Paul School of Theology
   - Julius E. Del Pino (1978), pastoral theology and church administration

6. Boston University School of Theology
   - John H. Cartwright (1980), social ethics

7. School of Theology at Claremont
   - Cornish R. Rogers (1980), pastoral theology and urban ministries

8. Wesley Theological Seminary
   - James M. Shopshire (1980), sociology of religion and associate dean
   - William B. McClain (1980), preaching and worship

9. The Theological School, Drew University
   - Albert J. D. Aymer (1981), social ethics and associate dean

10. The Divinity School, Duke University
    - Joseph B. Bethea (1972), director of black church studies
    - Karen Y. Collier (1977), director of black church studies
    - Grant S. Shockley (1983), Christian education

11. United Theological Seminary
    - William J. Augman (part time, 1988), sociology of religion

12. Iliff School of Theology
    - Vincent Harding (non–United Methodist), historian

Full-time black administrators in United Methodist seminaries (1968–1988) have included the following:

1. The Divinity School, Duke University
   - Laurence E. Johnson, director of black church affairs

2. Garrett-Evangelical Theological Seminary
   - Helen M. Fannings, assistant director of student affairs

3. Methodist Theological School in Ohio
   - Henry C. Stringer, dean of admissions

4. Wesley Theological Seminary
   - Linda E. Thomas, dean of students

United Methodist Black Faculty at Non-Methodist Seminaries and University Religion Departments

Black United Methodist scholars have held full-time faculty positions in theological schools and departments of religion other than those related to The United Methodist Church. A partial listing of such persons and their appointments since 1968 follows:

1. Vanderbilt University
   - Lewis V. Baldwin, department of religious studies

2. New York Theological Seminary
   - Gilbert H. Caldwell, dean for black students

3. Howard University School of Divinity
   - Evans E. Crawford, dean of the chapel and professor of social ethics
   - Calvin S. Morris, professor of social ethics
   - Cain Hope Felder, professor of New Testament

4. Union Theological Seminary and Fisk University
   - C. Eric Lincoln, professor of sociology of religion

5. Duke University
   - C. Eric Lincoln, department of religion

6. Temple University
   - Donald Matthews, department of religion

7. Universities of Virginia and Pennsylvania
   - Joseph R. Washington, department of religion

Ordained Black Women Increase

Since Sallie A. Crenshaw (1900–1986) and Emma P. H. Burrell (d. 1989) were ordained as elders and admitted into full connection in Annual Conferences (1958 and 1959, respectively), black women have annually entered the United Methodist ministry in increasing numbers. By the end of the 1980s about 200, or almost 9 percent, of all clergywomen in the denomination were black.[64] While this numerical growth of black clergy women in United Methodism has not been as spectacular as that of white United Methodist clergywomen, it has been noticeably steady and enhancing for the church and ministry generally and for black Methodism particularly. It is interesting to trace this growth from the scant data available.

Prior to 1968, there were barely two dozen fully ordained black women in the traveling ministry. Practically all of these were serving small stations or circuit charges. Their training for the ministry had come mainly from the Ministerial Course of Study School. Only two or three had attended or graduated from a theological seminary. Since 1968 there seems to have been an unprecedented and surprising response to the low-profile recruitment efforts among black women of the BMCR, the Commission on the Status and Role of Women, and community women's liberation movements, producing a current presence of more than two hundred black ordained women, essentially new since the 1970s and basically (75 percent) engaged in the pastoral ministry. They are about equally distributed across the five jurisdictions of the church. Those women who do not serve as pastors are under "special appointment" as seminary instructors, college teachers of religion, campus ministers, missionaries, church board and agency executives, curriculum editors, and chaplains of several kinds. Three black women pastors were recently appointed to the district superintendency: Charlotte Ann Nichols, Peninsula Conference; Joethel J. Cooper, West Ohio Conference; and Mary Brown Oliver, Baltimore Conference. Leontine T. C. Kelly became in 1984 the first black clergywoman ever to be elected to the episcopacy. Recently organized (1989) into a national group for fellowship, support, and networking, the Black United Methodist Clergywomen's Association has sought to internalize their group. Karen Y. Collier, the first black United Methodist clergywoman to earn the doctor of philosophy degree (Duke University, American Christianity) and Sadie D. Reynolds, Rust Church minister, Oberlin, Ohio, were elected co-conveners of the group.

Division of Ordained Ministry: Elected Members and Staff

From 1968 to 1988 the following persons were elected by the denomination to serve on the Division of Ordained Ministry: Jerome K. Del Pino (1984–1988), Bishop Charles F. Golden (1972–1980), Bishop W. T. Handy (1984–1988), William M. James (1980–1984), and Hubert V. Manning (1972–1976). Three black executive staff members have served the Division of Ordained Ministry since 1968. In 1974 Douglass E. Fitch was appointed a director in the Division of Ordained Ministry. While there, he successfully engineered a plan for the utilization of Ethnic Minority Local Church funds for higher education and ministry programming purposes. In 1980 Fitch became an associate general secretary of the Board of Higher Education and Ministry for program. In 1980 Hector J. Grant became a director in the division with responsibility for enlistment and ethnic concerns, remaining there until 1984. Lynn Scott went to the Division of Ordained Ministry as director of Support Systems and Spiritual Formation in 1989.

LAY LIFE AND WORK

Emphases, programs, and structures designed to implement United Methodism's mission with laity expanded and differentiated following Merger. Historically, laypersons had played relatively passive roles in the life, thought, and work of the churches. (The exception to this fact was [and is] the ongoing proactive United Methodist Women's organization, which programmatically functions in a fairly autonomous way but at the same time represents United Methodism and exercises its considerable strength and influence in a connectional way toward the empowerment of women, children, and oppressed people.) The challenge of the "church as laity" movement of the 1960s brought more involved participation in the total life and ministry of the churches. Evidence of this new expression was to be found among the laity of black United Methodist congregations. For an example, since the 1970s a small but growing number of black laity have been attracted to the diaconal ministry. This lay office, without ordination or episcopal appointment, provides women and men with opportunities to serve as ministers in churches or in church-related settings. Working full-time or part-time as directors of Christian education, music, parish associates, community developers, campus ministers, church board/agency staff executives, Annual Conferences, staff members, or in other approved positions allows diaconal ministers "to be in ministry" as an ongoing part of what they perceive to be their calling as Christians. They are now located in all of the five jurisdictions, with the possible exception of the Western Jurisdiction.

Another sign of lay renewal in black United Methodist churches and among black members of predominantly white churches is the new interest in and modest growth of United Methodist Men's organizations. These groups, whose purpose is to "be a creative support fellowship of men who seek to know Jesus Christ, to grow spiritually and to seek daily his will,"[65] have probably grown to at least a thousand units since the demise of the Central Jurisdiction. This increase represents approximately a 20 percent advance.

In recent years, several black Methodist men have served as district and Conference presidents of United Methodist Men. Leonard W. Thompson serves as president of its Northeastern Jurisdiction. In 1985 Harold E. Batiste, Jr., of the Southwest Texas Conference, a retired army officer and currently (1988–1992) a member of the General Council on Ministries, was elected president of the National Association of Annual Conference Presidents of United Methodist Men.

Division of Laity Elected Members and Staff

Black elected members of the Board of Discipleship's Division of the Ministry of the Laity since 1968 have been Bishop L. Scott Allen (1968–1972); Bishop Edsel A. Ammons (1976–1984; president of the Board of Discipleship, 1980–1984); J. Vernita Booker (1976–1980); Allen L. Brown (1972–1976); Bishop Edward G. Carroll (1972–1976); Henry C. Clay, Jr. (1976–1980); Merlin Conoway (1976–1980); A. C. Epps (1980–1984); L. L. Haynes (1968–1972); Bettye Henderson (1980–1984); Luther Henry, Jr. (1980–1984); Charles Hutchinson (1980–1984); Maceo Pembroke (1980–1981; served one year of a four-year term before his death on July 13, 1981); Cora N. Selby (1972–1976); Lorrine Smith (1980–1984); Benjamin Ward (1980–1984); and Clarence Winchester (1968–1972).

Black elected staff with specific responsibilities for lay life and work prior to and following restructuring (1972) included Charles P. Kellogg, assistant general secretary (1968–1972); Allen L. Brown, director, Section of United Methodist Men (since 1980); and Dorothy Turner-Lacy, assistant general secretary, Ethnic Minority Local Church Coordination (1980–1984). Marilyn W. Magee was elected assistant general secretary of the Board of Discipleship in 1986 with responsibility for lay leadership development and planning and age-level ministries. The first black woman to hold such a position, she headed this unit until her election in 1989 as assistant general secretary for the Section on Christian Education and Age-Level Ministries. Other black members of the Board of Discipleship staff with responsibilities for the development of laity were J. LaVon Kincaid, director for Stewardship (1980–1984), and Earl Wilson, director for Evangelism (1980–1984).

Division of Lay Ministries of the Board of Higher Education and Ministry: Elected Members

In the course of restructuring the boards and agencies of the church (1968–1972), it was recommended that provision be made for an agency to study, standardize, and monitor unordained career (lay) workers' diaconal ministry consecration. In 1972 this responsibility was placed in the newly created Division of Lay Ministries of the Board of Higher Education and Ministry. In 1976 the division was renamed the Division of Diaconal Ministry. Elected members who served this division have been Bishop Ernest T. Dixon, Jr. (1972–1976); Alexina Hazzard (1972–1980); Ethel R. Johnson (1972–1980); Russell F. Reynolds (1980–1988), Anthony J. Shipley (1972–1976), and Arvarh E. Strickland (1976–1980). Ethel Johnson chaired this division during her tenure.

CHRISTIAN UNITY AND INTERRELIGIOUS CONCERNS

Denominational Relations

Black United Methodist ministers and laypersons were involved in ecumenical work during 1966–1988 in a variety of contexts and at several levels. Locally and at the state level, scores participated in city councils of churches, ministerial associations, and interdenominational and interfaith ministries and projects. Some notable examples were Charles L. Warren (1911–1971), first black executive director of the Council of Churches of Greater Washington, D.C. (1965–1971); Sumpter M. Riley, president, Interdenominational Ministers Alliance of Cleveland, Ohio; L. L. White, president, Los Angeles Council of Churches; James W. Ferree, president, North Carolina Council of Churches; Bishop Ernest T. Dixon, president, Texas Conference of Churches.

Two black United Methodists were selected for membership on the historic Joint Commissions on Church Union (Methodist/Evangelical United Brethren): Theressa Hoover and Sumpter M. Riley.

Pan-Methodist Developments

Just prior to 1968, BMCR expressed grave concern that the Methodist Church had sought union with the Evangelical United Brethren Church but had made little, if any, effort to do the same with the African Methodist Episcopal (AME), African Methodist Episcopal Zion (AMEZ), and Christian Methodist Episcopal (CME) churches, which had equally close and historic ties with Wesleyan Methodism.[66] This concern was forcefully presented to the Uniting Conference in Dallas and resulted in an invitation to the black denominations to explore possible closer relations. In 1972 a General Conference Resolution was passed to "strengthen fellowship" within the Wesleyan tradition. This marked the first time in American Methodist history that representatives of the AME, AMEZ, and CME churches had considered meeting together to discuss their mutual concerns. The Pan-Methodist initiative was again strengthened by the 1976 General Conference, which shifted the leadership for further involvement to the bishops of the various Methodist denominations. In March 1979 the bishops of the four Methodist denominations met in Atlanta. It was decided at this exploratory meeting that "some formal arrangement [should] be developed for the regular consulting together by these four churches that have so much in common."[67]

Plans for the celebration of the bicentennial of American Methodism (1784–1984) were inclusive of the black Methodist denominations. It was recommended by the Bicentennial Committee (1980–1984) that celebrations of the bicentennial be planned and held with the black Methodist groups participating.

The Bicentennial General Conference (1984) took additional action regarding Pan-Methodist cooperation. It established a Commission on Pan-Methodist Cooperation in cooperation with the three other black Methodist General Conferences. This commission had its first meeting May 27–28, 1985, in Arlington, Virginia, focusing on four areas of possible cooperation: higher education, mission outreach, social witness, and evangelism. A subsequent organizational meeting of the commission (May 1985) was held, at which other areas of possible cooperation, such as a common hymnal and curriculum resources use, were discussed. The fourth consultation of episcopal representatives of the four denominations also met in Arlington, Virginia. Its agenda was mainly to prepare its "Statement to the Churches and the Nation" and to discuss future consultations. Mary A. Love, editor of church school literature of the AMEZ Church, was elected administrative secretary for the commission at this meeting.

Participation in World Methodist Work

Two additional satellite international Methodist organizations will now be discussed before concluding this section with a review of the development of black United Methodist participation in the World Methodist Council.

In 1956 a World Federation of Methodist Women was organized at Lake Junaluska, North Carolina, "to exchange ideas, program materials, and to deepen spiritual life." By 1968 the federation embraced sixty units in fifty countries. An intentional leadership development program for women, "especially in developing countries," was established. An affiliate of the World Methodist Council, the federation is at work on four continents. Black United Methodist Women periodically has been represented in the United Methodist Women's delegations to these quinquennial sessions. Doris M. Handy of Pittsburgh, Pennsylvania, is a member of the World Executive Committee of the World Methodist Council, the Executive Committee, and the American Section of the Council, and during 1976–1981 she was president of the North American area of the World Federation of American Women.[68]

The World Methodist Historical Society was organized in 1947 as the International Methodist Historical Society. During 1968–1972 Bishop Willis J. King was an elected member of the group. Restructuring in 1972 renamed the body World Methodist Historical Society. This group has not had black representation from The United Methodist Church since that time. Grant S. Shockley, while professor of Christian education at the Candler School of Theology, was selected in 1973 to lecture at the first regional conference of the society at Wesley College, Bristol, England (July 17–21, 1973). The lecture he presented was entitled "Methodism, Society, and Black Evangelism in America: Retrospect and Prospect."

World Methodist Council

The World Methodist Council, composed of more than sixty Methodist or Methodist-related bodies in approximately ninety countries, provided an international framework for fellowship, communication, witness, and mission. Referred to as the Ecumenical Methodist Conference until 1951, it has met at five-year intervals since 1947. The work of the council is carried on through ten or more committees and two affiliated organizations, the World Federation of Methodist Women and the World Methodist Historical Society.

Black Methodists have been fairly prominent in attending and participating in the quinquennial conferences, especially since 1966, by which time Third World concerns were being forcefully articulated: executive committee— Bishop Noah W. Moore, Jr. (1966–1972); Bishop Prince A. Taylor, Jr. (1966–1991); Bishop L. Scott Allen (1971–1976); Bishop James S. Thomas, Jr. (1971–1981); Bishop Ernest T. Dixon, Jr. (1976–1986); Bishop Roy C. Nichols (1976–1986); Bishop Melvin G. Talbert (1981–1991); Bishop F. Herbert Skeete (1981–1991); and Bishop Joseph B. Bethea (1986–1991). Ministerial members of the World Methodist Council were Joseph B. Bethea (1981–1986) and Gregory V. Palmer (1971–1976). Lay members of the council were Claire C. Harvey (1971–1981), Brenda Walker (1971–1976), Kathryn M. Brown (1976–1981), Doris M. Handy (1976–1986), Mai H. Gray (1986–1991), and Louis M. Smith (1986–1991).

Interdenominational Relations

Interdenominational contact between black Christians and within black churches and black church organizations since 1968 has been practically synonymous with civil rights and black liberation advocacy activity. In keeping with this, black United Methodists were among the earliest supporters and leaders of these groups, and innumerable black United Methodist local churches gave much to them in time, effort, paid memberships, and assistance.

Space allows the mentioning of only a few of the more widely known black racial justice and community development activists who worked through interdenominational church and community organizations during this period. The Southern Christian Leadership Conference (SCLC) was inspired and initiated by Martin Luther King, Jr. (1929–1968). A black, church-based, protest-oriented network of southern civil rights groups organized in 1957, it became and remained the strategy center of the civil rights movement for almost two decades. Foremost in the leadership of SCLC from the beginning was Joseph E. Lowery, then (1952–1961) the pastor of Warren Street

Church, Mobile, Alabama. Lowery, early a vice president of the group, was a fearless and articulate spokesperson throughout the civil rights period and especially during the bitter confrontations with Governor George Wallace in Alabama. Ruby Hurley, southeastern regional director of the National Association for the Advancement of Colored People (NAACP) and an active United Methodist woman (Warren Church, Atlanta), also worked with SCLC.

Black Methodists, including three bishops, were signatories to the landmark statement on Black Power developed by the National Committee of Negro Churchmen (NCNC). This statement, in the form of a full-page advertisement in the *New York Times* (July 31, 1966), further signaled the acceptance of at least this cadre of black Methodist leaders of a proactive equalitarian approach to merger issues on a quid pro quo basis. The signatories to this historic statement were Bishop Charles F. Golden (1912–1984); Anna Arnold Hedgeman, member, St. Mark's Church (New York City); Bishop Noah W. Moore, Jr.; Bishop James S. Thomas, Jr.; and Frank L. Williams, minister, Metropolitan Church (Baltimore). Following publication of this statement, the National Committee of Negro Churchmen was renamed the National Committee of Black Churchmen. The new organization had its first formal meeting in November 1967 in New York City. The National Committee of Black Churchmen (NCBC) became a national ecumenical organization of black clergy and laity dedicated to uniting black church members in the task of effecting strategies of empowerment for a disempowered people in depressed communities. Members of NCBC, in addition to the signatories to the Black Power statement, included the following: North Central Jurisdiction—Edsel O. Ammons (later elected a bishop); Gerald H. Brantford; Harry A. Gibson; Philip O. Harley; Richard Lawrence; Maceo D. Pembroke; James M. Shopshire; C. Jarrett Gray, Sr.; Archie Rich; Northeastern Jurisdiction—Gilbert H. Caldwell; John W. Coleman; Harry B. Gibson; Joe L. Gipson; Clayton E. Hammond; Frank L. Horton; William C. Jason, Jr.; Ethel R. Johnson; Joshua E. Licorish; Felton E. May (later elected a bishop); Charles L. Warren; Willard O. Williams; Negail R. Riley; Calvin O. Pressley; South Central Jurisdiction—Earl Allen; Philip Lawson; Southeastern Jurisdiction—Thelma P. Barnes; William C. Dobbins; Cain H. Felder; C. Jasper Smith; and Joseph E. Lowery; Western Jurisdiction—Charles A. Belcher; Hamilton T. Boswell; Odis Fentry; Thomas P. Grissom; A. Cecil Williams.

Further Developments

Black United Methodists were not only involved in the founding of NCBC but also participated as pioneers in every phase of its development. They participated in the organizing work of the NCBC's Theological Project, which produced the (1969) NCBC Black Theology Statement. They were charter members of the Society for the Study of Black Religion (1970), the first professional society in the country devoted exclusively to the comprehensive study of the black religious experience. Finally, black United Methodists were full participants in the initiation of the 1975 Detroit Conference on Theology in the Americas, which opened a new phase of black theological study through dialogical discussions among blacks, Latin Americans, and citizens of Third World countries.

The Congress of National Black Churches

Changing issues, priorities, circumstances, and leadership in the middle 1970s caused a decline in the appeal and the effectiveness of SCLC and NCBC. The focus of need shifted from protest to community development. Diminished funding by white church sources required serious fundraising in the black community and its churches. The loss of charismatic leaders signaled the need for an intentional, collegial, and coalitional style of leadership. The Congress of National Black Churches arose to meet this challenge. In 1975 seven black denominations, inspired and led by AME bishop John H. Adams, developed an imaginative and viable program to meet the needs of the black community, as the community and churches perceived them. This collective approach identified six objectives: "theological education, employment, economic development, media, evangelism, and human development."[69] While not formally a part of the Congress of National Black Churches, black United Methodist churches and their pastors were de facto participants in it in a number of communities.

Other Interdenominational Relations

Black United Methodists maintained a presence in the American Bible Society and the National Council of the Churches of Christ in the USA. Bishop F. Herbert Skeete and Jessie B. Pratt, Eastern Pennsylvania Conference, represented United Methodism on the board of managers of the American Bible Society. Fred A. Allen, New York Conference, was appointed to the executive staff of the society as director of Church Relations.

Black United Methodist representation in the National Council of Churches since Merger has been strong and diverse. During 1968–1972 our representatives were Vivian W. Henderson, Theressa Hoover, John T. King, Allen M. Mayes, and John F. Norwood. Following a major restructuring of the National Council of Churches, the governing board took the place of the general assembly. The following black United Methodists were named governors: Henry C. Harper (1976–1980), Dorothy Height (1972–1980; vice president, 1976–1980), Cleo Henry (1972–1976), Randolph Nugent (1972–1976, 1984–1988), George H. Outen (1972–1976), Negail Riley

(1980–1984), Melvin G. Talbert (1972–1988), William J. Washington (1984–1988).

David W. Briddell of the Eastern Pennsylvania Conference has been director of the Intermedia Department, Division of Mission of the National Council of Churches, since 1984. Prior to that time he held various positions in the same field in the Board of Global Ministries. Randolph W. Nugent, Jr., of the New York Conference was associate general secretary, Division of Overseas Ministries of the National Council of Churches, from 1970–1972.

ECUMENICAL RELATIONS

Ecumenical work and interdenominational work are distinguishable by their differing objective strategies and programs. The basic thrust of interdenominational work is cooperation around common goals to accomplish what can best be done in unity. Ecumenical ministry by its nature means encounter, involvement, engagement, and communion on all levels of a denominational, interdenominational, or other relationship, with the hope of renewal and unity. There have been two continuing invitations to continue the search for the "sacrament of unity" offered through the Consultation on Church Union (COCU) and the World Council of Churches (WCC). What has been the depth and impact of black United Methodist involvement in these ventures?

The ecumenical question has been an issue-laden one for black Methodists. The question of church unity has never been more problematic for them than for other Christians. The issue at point is not separation or unity in or through a church body but separation and hence the impossibility of unity because of color or race. Given the initial reason that black members separated from white churches in this country, namely, discrimination, the black church, including most black Methodists, is frankly ambivalent about church union. Probably for this reason, most black United Methodists have only been marginally involved in ecumenical activity. Furthermore, it was a fact that as the civil rights movement became more insistent on full social equality, the Protestant establishment opted out of the civil rights movement.

A fairly serious problem that black United Methodists have had with COCU is communication. As a racial group within a predominantly white denomination, the real interface on the issue of race has not been so much between black United Methodists and COCU as it has been between the black member denominations and COCU.

Despite this background, however, there have been some intentional efforts toward church union without regard to race, color, or class, and some black Methodist involvement. During the 1960s and 1970s COCU assembled several functional task groups from its member-denominations to explore cooperative and union possibilities. The United Methodist representatives named several black clergy and laypersons to these responsibilities. In the late 1970s and 1980s the Ecumenical and Interreligious Concerns Division of the Board of Global Ministry cooperated with COCU in beginning the publication of *Liberation and Unity,* a Lenten meditations publication initiated by the AME, AMEZ, and CME churches. Several United Methodist black clergy wrote for this booklet. In 1984 Ethel R. Johnson, professor of Church Administration at the Methodist Theological School in Ohio, was elected a voting delegate to the 1984 Consultation on Church Union Plenary.

Church Women United

Barbara E. Campbell, in her book *United Methodist Women in the Middle of Tomorrow,* notes the fact that "women have been leaders in ecumenical concerns and members of United Methodist Women are the largest segment of the membership of Church Women United."[70] In keeping with Campbell's observation, it may also be noted that black United Methodist women have had a continuing concern for Christian unity issues and have participated in its ecumenical services and action projects across the years and in several relationships.

Since its founding in the early 1940s, black Methodist women have been involved in Church Women United (CWU) activities through their local Women's Society of Christian Service units (1940–1968) and following Merger through United Methodist Women's groups. (Theressa Hoover, deputy general secretary, Board of Global Ministries, officially relates the Women's Division to CWU through her office.) They have participated in CWU local observances of World Day of Prayer (March), May Fellowship Day (May), and World Community Day (November); met in small groups for Scripture study and prayer; and been active in community service programs such as Women in Community Service (WICS), Adult Basic Education, Women in Prison, and health care volunteering. United Methodists took pride in the election of one of their outstanding members as national president of CWU in 1971, Claire Collins Harvey of Jackson, Mississippi. An active United Methodist layperson, she is a leader in the human rights field. She was founder of Womanpower Unlimited, an interracial human relations group of Protestant, Jewish, and Catholic women who provided aid to civil rights workers in the 1960s. She has also been a member of the Mississippi Advisory Committee to the United States Civil Rights Commission.[71]

World Council of Churches

United Methodists have been actively related to the World Council of Churches during all of its more than four decades of existence. A worldwide Christian fellowship organized in Amsterdam, the Netherlands, in 1948 "for study, witness, service, and the advancement of unity," it is one of the most prominent groups of Christians in the world, "pledged to search together with other churches for ways to express visible unity and obedience."[72] It has been noted that Bishop Alexander P. Shaw was an alternate delegate to Amsterdam (1948) and that Harry V. Richardson was a delegate to Evanston (1954) and New Delhi (1961). In the United Methodist period, several have been participants and made significant contributions. Theressa Hoover, deputy general secretary, Women's Division, Board of Global Ministries, has been a delegate to all World Council assemblies since the 1968 Uniting Conference: Uppsala (1986), Nairobi (1975), and Vancouver (1983). She has been a member of the council's Commission on Churches' Participation in Development since its establishment in 1976 and was elected its vice moderator in 1983. Hoover was elected to the Central Committee of the council for the 1983–1990 term. Bishop Roy C. Nichols was elected to the Executive and Central Committees of the council in 1968 and served until 1975. Barbara R. Thompson, general secretary, Commission on Religion and Race, was a member of the Central Committee (1975–1983). Randolph W. Nugent, general secretary, Board of Global Ministries, is currently a member of the Church and Society Committee, Faith and Witness Program Unit. Bishop Woodie W. White was a member of a World Council of Churches task force to examine racism and race relations in Australia and New Zealand for the council's Commission to Combat Racism.

Interreligious Cooperation

Late in 1966 a group of blacks, Chicanos, Native Americans, and poor whites in some of the nation's most depressed communities were assembled by Catholic, Jewish, and Protestant agency representatives. The purpose of the gathering was to form a coalition of community group and funding agencies for self-help community development and other projects that had merit but were difficult to fund. The project, which soon became a unit of the National Council of Churches, took the name Interreligious Foundation for Community Organization (IFCO). By 1973 IFCO had fourteen foundation and special fund sources and had been widely acclaimed as an exemplary ecumenical model for liberating the oppressed.

Black United Methodists associated with IFCO were Thelma P. Barnes, BMCR; Gilbert H. Caldwell, National Committee of Black Churchmen; Anna A. Hedgeman, Office of the Mayor, City of New York; Negail R. Riley, Board of Global Ministries; and Earnest A. Smith, Board of Church and Society. In addition to these official representatives to IFCO, other support came from the National Council of United Methodist Youth and from some individual United Methodist Women's organizations.[73]

Project Equality

The Board of Christian Social Concerns made the following explanatory statement to the 1968 General Conference, seeking its endorsement:

> In recognition of The United Methodist Church's responsibility to make ethical use of its own financial resources . . . in the conviction that "Project Equality," a voluntary cooperative interdenominational enterprise of churches, synagogues, and related institutions . . . provides a responsible, consistent, ethical, practical, effective, and positive means whereby The United Methodist Church . . . can support fair employment practices in the United States, The United Methodist Church endorses "Project Equality" and recommends cooperation . . . on the part of all United Methodist Annual Conferences, local churches, local or national institutions, agencies, and organizations.[74]

Woodie W. White, then General Secretary of the Commission on Religion and Race, was elected to the national board of Project Equality in 1974. He was elected to the episcopacy in 1984.[75]

In concluding this section on interreligious affairs, attention should be called to the fact that in 1974 the Louisiana Conference took a significant step in an ecumenical direction in appointing Robert F. Harrington, a black district superintendent, to the full-time executive directorship of the Louisiana Interchurch Conference. The Interchurch Conference is "one of the oldest and largest statewide ecumenical bodies in the South . . . with full Roman Catholic participation."[76]

Elected Members and Staff of the General Commission on Christian Unity and Interreligious Concerns

Prior to the 1972 restructuring of the boards and agencies of the denomination, the cultivation of responsibility to proclaim and work for the "unity of the whole of Christ's church" was lodged in the Commission on Christian Unity and Interreligious Concerns. The 1972 General Conference reconstituted the Commission as the Ecumenical and Interreligious Concerns Division in the Board of Global Ministries. In 1980 it again became a General Commission on Christian Unity and Interreligious Concerns. The following black persons were elected to membership on these directing units since 1968: Thelma P. Barnes (1980–1984); Oswald P. Bronson (1968–1972); Bishop Edward G. Carroll (1976–1980); Mai H. Gray (1972–1976); Doris M. Handy (1968–1972); Theressa Hoover (1968–1972); Sumpter M. Riley, Jr. (1968–1972); Vivian W. Robinson, a member of the CME Church (1988–1992); Grant S. Shockley (1976–1980); Bishop Melvin G. Talbert

(1984–1992); Dorothy Mae Taylor (1988–1992); Barbara R. Thompson, vice president (1980–1985); and Robert J. Tolbert (1988–1992). Janice L. Frederick, a member of the South Carolina Conference, was executive secretary of the General Commission for a brief period in the early 1980s.

CHRISTIAN SOCIAL ACTION

Seldom has Methodism failed to relate the gospel to the society in which its people lived. The Methodist Episcopal Church (1784–1939) confronted the institution of slavery with its earliest and strongest church indictment. From the 1870s to the 1930s, Methodism thundered against liquor abuse and gave the temperance movement some of its most powerful voices. Workers in the 1890s and early 1900s acknowledged with gratitude Methodist support in their effort to unionize. The peace movement between the two world wars applauded Methodism's support for conscientious objectors.

The Methodist Church era (1940–1968) found Methodists providing exemplary support for a "just and durable peace" and making a massive contribution to the rehabilitation of a war-torn world. The early support of the Women's Division of Christian Service for the Supreme Court's desegregation decision (1954), closely followed by a similar affirmation by the Council of Bishops, caught the attention of the nation in a very positive way. Finally, the pioneering efforts of the World Division of the Board of Missions in ecumenically promoting development projects in the Third World in the 1960s was salutory.

The Black Revolution of the late 1960s, however, clearly presented Methodist social justice advocates with their most difficult challenge. Could The United Methodist Church become a truly inclusive fellowship? When viewed in relation to the changes that took place in the lives of black Americans as a direct result of the Black Revolution, this question presented a troublesome dilemma. On the one hand, it was evident that there was a new sense of black identity, black consciousness, and black pride in African Americans. It was also quite clear that they had a reawakened sense of accountability to the truly disadvantaged in their black communities. On the other hand, in response to demands to end all forms and appearances of segregation in the new denomination, The United Methodist Church was constituted and structured (on the associative level at least) as inclusive. Ironically, the problem was precisely in the meaning of the term "inclusive." From a black perspective it meant not only the end of exclusion but also the presence of full equality or inclusive pluralism—social, cultural, and religious. As events began to unfold, however, it was all too apparent that for many white Methodists "inclusive" meant little more than inclusive assimilation based on standardized white norms and structures, derived from a white ethos. In this section the record, events, and activities of the 1968–1984 period in regard to this problem will be reviewed.

Social Action and United Methodism

Despite the past sterling efforts and achievements of United Methodists in the social action arena, the church had generally not been either radical or crisis oriented.[77] Further, as a matter of record and fact, it usually has not been movement oriented. Essentially, United Methodists have considered social transformation to be a by-product of personal transformation. Much of this changed with the coming of BMCR. This ad hoc group of generally younger black United Methodists, restive and apprehensive that inclusiveness in the new church would not be total or relevant, called the now historic 1968 meeting at Cincinnati (February 6–9). Three crucial things happened at this gathering: (1) Leadership in the areas of equal rights and inclusiveness in United Methodism was transferred from whites to blacks, (2) Negro (later "Black") Methodists for Church Renewal was founded "to explore strategies for helping The United Methodist Church to really become effective"[78] as a multiracial church, and (3) a document, "Findings," was produced that assessed what the denomination needed to do to become truly inclusive in mission and ministry. What follows here will briefly detail how BMCR, with support and assistance from and through the General Conference, United Methodist women and youth, and numberless white laypersons, implemented their vision of social renewal and enacted their "agitating conscience."

Led by the dynamic James M. Lawson, Thelma P. Barnes, Cain H. Felder, Woodie W. White, Gilbert H. Caldwell, and others, BMCR orchestrated a dramatic, peaceful witness-protest at the 1968 General Conference in Dallas, demonstrating their determination to achieve inclusive participation in the total life of The United Methodist Church and exhibiting their own newly found "life of power and unity." This show of pride and strength, together with the cooperation of many white advocates of inclusiveness, prepared the church for an essentially revolutionary General Conference in the areas of racial and other justice issues. Almost a dozen far-reaching changes were made and actions taken:

- The racism issue was lifted from a place of polite visibility and symbolic restructuring to the level of an urgent priority.
- The high posturing and low product-achievement on desegregation of former General Conferences (1940–1964) was rejected, and unequivocal statements legislating equality into the constitution of Methodism were made.
- Directives about the inclusiveness of church attendance, church participation, and church membership, once unobtrusively found in the

"Social Creed," *The Book of Resolutions,* or public pronouncements, were made paragraphs in *The Book of Discipline.*

Other substantial advances made toward inclusiveness were

- the launching of a full-scale investigation of alleged unfair employment practices at the United Methodist Publishing House and the "recommended participation by all boards and agencies in Project Equality"
- the provision of means for funds to be withheld from "any agency or institution receiving general church funds until [it] has complied"[79] with the church's policy of nondiscrimination
- the appointment of a Social Principles Study Commission to develop a "United Methodist Statement of Social Principles" (Black members of the Social Principles Study Commission were Bishop James S. Thomas, Jr., chairperson; James M. Lawson, Jr.; and Melvin G. Talbert.)
- the approval of the creation of an ad hoc Commission on Religion and Race (to succeed the Commission on Interjurisdictional Relations) to be a liaison between the denomination and its boards and agencies for the purpose of implementing and monitoring progress in the elimination of racial discrimination
- the adoption of a $20 million quadrennial Fund for Reconciliation to enable United Methodism to respond to escalating racism, poverty, and oppression in the nation's cities, including the initial funding of the Black Community Developers Program (This program grew out of Negail R. Riley's doctoral research at Boston University.)
- the facilitation of open itinerancy or cross-racial appointments—namely, making appointments without regard to race, ethnic origin, sex, color, or age, by General Conference affirmation, which had been forthrightly stated in the *Book of Discipline* since 1964 (¶ 432)

The 1970 Special Session of the General Conference was similar to the 1968 meeting and almost equally as effective. Again led by James M. Lawson, Jr., with allies from across the church, the black church, and the national community, still further demands for inclusiveness and recognition were made. Following a stirring and compelling presentation by Lawson on behalf of BMCR and others, the General Conference voted in three things:

- a two-year $2 million annual grant for minority group economic empowerment, to be administered by the Commission on Religion and Race
- a new annual goal of $4 million to benefit the denomination's twelve black colleges and to be received through the Race Relations Day Offering

- an effort to increase "racial minority" membership on all boards and agencies at the General, Jurisdictional, and Annual Conference levels as well as in the local churches

Social Action Activity, 1972–1984

General Conference legislation, BMCR lobbying, Commission on Religion and Race monitoring, the advent of the Ethnic Minority Local Church Emphasis, convocations, and pronouncements climaxed two decades (1964–1984) of a united black and white struggle to liberate United Methodism for social and racial justice ministries and witness.

Gilbert H. Caldwell, national president of BMCR, assisted by Cain H. Felder, executive secretary, made an eloquent presentation to the 1972 General Conference in Atlanta, urging it not to retreat from the high ground it had taken in the 1968–1972 quadrennium. Partially as a consequence of this, the Commission on Religion and Race was instituted as a permanent agency, the Minority Group Self-Determination Fund was financed for the next four years, and Annual Conferences and local churches were allowed to develop indigenous programming in response to missional priorities in their communities. A memorable event of the General Conference was the cogent and impassioned statement by J. E. Lowery (Central Church, Atlanta), a member of the Conference, demanding a cut-off date for the transfer and merger of former Central Jurisdiction Conferences into the South Central and Southeastern Jurisdictions. The apex of accomplishment for the forces of social and racial justice came in 1976. For the first time in its social concerns history, Methodism went beyond encouraging "Christian lines of action which assist humankind to move toward a world where peace and justice are achieved" (*Book of Discipline*, 1972, ¶ 955) and embraced the role of social change agent. The 1976 *Discipline* states that in implementing the Social Principles, the Board of Church and Society "shall give special attention to nurturing the active constituency of the board by encouraging an exchange of ideas on strategy and methodology for social change" (*Book of Discipline*, 1976, ¶ 1220).

Elected Members and Staff of the Board of Christian Social Concerns and the Board of Church and Society

Black elected members of the Board of Christian Social Concerns (1968–1972) and its successor, the Board of Church and Society (since 1972), frequently found themselves at the storm-center of controversy. Seldom if ever have they refused to move the church toward the cutting edge of its social responsibility. Serving the boards and their divisions and departments have been Joseph B. Bethea (1968–1972); James Campbell (1972–1976); Sarah Clardy (1972–1976); Henry C. Clay (1980–1988); Merlin D. Conoway

274

(1980–1984); Hooker D. Davis (1968–1976); Claude A. Edmonds (1988–1992); James W. Ferree (1980–1988); Vivienne N. Gray (1984–1988); Bishop Charles F. Golden (1968–1972); Vivian W. Henderson (1968–1972); Mary L. Hudson (vice president, 1972–1980); Charles L. Hutchinson (1976–1980); Bishop Leontine T. C. Kelly (1984–1988); John T. King (1968–1972); W. Astor Kirk (treasurer, 1980–1988); Ernest S. Lyght (1984–1988); Bishop Roy C. Nichols (1972–1976); Bishop James S. Thomas, Jr. (vice president, 1968–1972); David L. White (1980–1984); and LaVon Wilson (vice president, 1972–1980).

Black elected staff who have guided Christian Social Concerns and Church and Society activities have included Earnest O. Smith, associate general secretary (1968–1976); George H. Outen, general secretary (1976–1980); Beverly R. Johnson, director, Department of Human Welfare (1980–1986); W. Astor Kirk, interim general secretary (1987–1988); Fred Allen, associate general secretary (1984–1988); Mary Council Austin, associate general secretary (1986–1989); and Claudia T. Williamson, director of Administration (since 1989).

PUBLICATIONS AND COMMUNICATIONS

In preparation for the 1968 Uniting Conference of the Methodist and Evangelical United Brethren churches, the Central Jurisdiction College of Bishops called a special session of its Jurisdictional Conference in August 1967. The specific purposes for this meeting were to fill a vacancy in episcopal leadership, to assign bishops to the jurisdictions of their prospective residences, and to bring the affairs of the Central Jurisdiction "to an orderly close."[80] This historic Conference also marked the cessation of the publication of the *Central Christian Advocate* since the Plan of Union merged the remaining black Conferences and dispersed them across the five regional jurisdictions of the new denomination. Despite this fact, however, the purposes of the *Central Christian Advocate* remained valid—namely, gathering and disseminating of news about black Methodists and ensuring a continued presence of African Americans in executive roles at the decision-making levels of the journalistic enterprise of the church.

The former editorship was immediately replaced with the position "publishing representative" for the United Methodist Publishing House. A young Baton Rouge pastor, W. T. Handy, Jr. (St. Mark Church), was appointed to the post, becoming the first person of color to occupy an executive seat on the Board of Publication. In 1972 Handy became a vice president of the Publishing House, and in 1980 he was elected to the episcopacy. The Cokesbury bookstore system employed its first black bookstore manager in 1972, James J. DeBerry (Boston).

Communications

It became quite apparent in the communications field after Merger that there was no intentional strategy or concerted approach for the continuance of the kind of networking that the *Central Christian Advocate* had provided. Isolation threatened the destruction of the fragile sense of community that black members had brought with them into their new jurisdictional settings. Often little recognition was given to their contributions and achievements. More important, however, was the danger of the loss of a church-wide public forum for discussing and interpreting black issues, concerns, and opinions. The Joint Committee on Communications (1972–1976), United Methodist Communications (1976–1980), and (since 1980) the Commission on Communication have attempted to address this precarious situation. In restructuring the boards and agencies in 1972, the General Conference recommended that black and other racial minority groups be represented on the newly created Joint Committee on Communications (1972 *Discipline,* ¶ 899).

During that ensuing quadrennium (1972–1976), the Television, Radio, and Film Commission (TRAFCO) produced "Making a Difference," a film describing the critically important role of the black pastor in the community. (William B. McClain had a major role in this film.) In 1976 the General Conference emphasized that one of the functions of United Methodist Communications was the promotion of Human Relations Day and the Black College Fund (1976 *Discipline,* ¶ III.II). A further responsibility was given to the Commission on Communication in 1980 by the General Conference, namely, "consultation with and assistance to . . . racial and ethnic groups, in the training of local church persons" in communication skills.[81] In the 1984–1988 quadrennium, "Catch the Spirit," United Methodism's weekly cable television ministry program relating how Christians live out their commitment, aired on several major national networks including Black Entertainment Network (BET), reaching millions of viewers. Co-hosts for this unique and increasingly popular television series are Hilly Hicks (black) and Anisa Mehdi.

United Methodist Communications has given support to black Methodists in two other ways. Throughout the period of the Ethnic Minority Local Church Emphasis *The Interpreter,* United Methodism's program journal, has highlighted its activities and events. It also provided critically needed technical assistance and consultation to BMCR and its newspaper, *NOW.*

Black United Methodist Periodical Editors

Several black United Methodist journalists rose to assistant, associate, and executive editor positions in the United Methodist communications system in the 1970s and 1980s. While in these roles they made significant contributions in writing, policy making, administration, and public relations.

George M. Daniels, the senior tenured black journalist-executive in United Methodism and formerly news editor for the *Chicago Defender* newspaper, became associate director, Department of News Services, Board of Missions, in 1961. He rose through the ranks, becoming director of Interpretive Services and in the 1980s executive editor and associate editorial director of *New World Outlook*. In this position, Daniels became a nationally and internationally known church journalist. In 1989 he announced his early retirement to pursue writing and research. For a brief period during 1968–1972, Betty Burns was an assistant editor in the Office of Information and Publicity, Division of Higher Education, Board of Education. It was mentioned earlier in this chapter that James S. Gadsden, H. Walter Willis, and Ernestine A. Calhoun were the first black age-level editors in the Division of Curriculum Resources during the early 1970s. James F. Campbell and Newtonia V. Harris were associate editors of *United Methodists Today,* the short-lived successor periodical to *Together* magazine. During his tenure as dean of the Upper Room Chapel (1976–1984), W. Maurice King served as one of the associate editors of *The Upper Room,* a widely used devotional guide. M. Garlinda Burton, trainer of regional and national church communicators in media relations and racial and cultural sensitivity training, was the first full-time black writer on the editorial staff of *The United Methodist Reporter.* She is now the first black news director (Nashville office) for the United Methodist News Service. Other editors and writers have been Allen Brown, a national director of United Methodist Men who began editing *Mennews,* a bimonthly newsletter, in the early 1980s; Pamela J. Watkins, an assistant editor of the innovative *Alive Now!* magazine in the 1980s; and Janice L. Frederick, editor of *Invitation Resources* for ages 3–4 from 1984–1988.

Black Editors Beyond United Methodism

From 1968 to the present, several black United Methodists, while retaining their United Methodist identity and relationship, have occupied editorial positions that are non–United Methodist related or ecumenical. John L. Bryan (1913–1982) was the first black editor of *The Methodist Churchman* (1971–1977), a periodical that sought to continue the independent Methodist social crusading of the famed *Zion's Herald.* In 1975 it reclaimed its former name. George L. Daniels was the editor-in-chief of *Renewal,* the quarterly publication of the National Committee of Black Churchmen, from its inception in 1973. Cornish R. Rogers was the first black journalist appointed associate editor of *The Christian Century* (1970).

Elected Members and Staff of the Board of Publications and the Commission on Communication

Black elected members and staff appointments to the Board of Publications and Commission on Communication from 1968 to 1988 are noted below.

Board of Publication members were Henry H. Nichols (1968–1980); Prenza L. Woods (1968–1980); Joseph Echols Lowery (1968–1972); Bishop L. Scott Allen (1972–1976, 1980–1984); John R. Shockley (1972–1980); Clarence M. Winchester (1976–1984); Harold E. Batiste (1980–1992); Alfred L Norris (1980–1992); Cornelius L. Henderson, member and secretary since election (1980); Bishop W. T. Handy, Jr.; James S. Gadsden; Beverly J. Shamana; and Diane P. Kinsey (1988).

Staff members were W. T. Handy, Jr. (1968, until election as bishop in 1980); James D. DeBerry (1972); Ernestine Calhoun, editor (1970–1985); James F. Campbell, associate editor (1972–1976); James C. Peters, vice president (1980–1988); Cedric Foley, Special Services (1980); and Walter H. McKelvey (1988).

Commission on Communication members were Bishop Charles F. Golden (1968–1972), Mrs. W. A. Henry (1968–1972), C. Jasper Smith (1968–1972), John E. Carrington (1972–1980), Zan W. Holmes (1972–1976), Lawrence Peterson (1972–1976), Bishop Ernest T. Dixon (1976–1984), Cornish R. Rogers (1976–1984), Newtonia Harris-Coleman (1980–1984), and Bishop Ernest W. Newman (1984–1988).

Staff members are George M. Daniels; David W. Briddell, assistant general secretary (1968–1980); Charlotte O'Neal, administrative assistant (1968, 1976); Warren M. Jenkins, executive staff, Joint Committee on Communication (1972–1976); J. Readus Watkins, associate general secretary (1980–1988); Newtonia Harris-Coleman, assistant general secretary (1984–1988) and associate general secretary since 1988; M. Garlinda Burton; John W. Coleman, Jr., account executive since 1984; and Jeneane Jones, director of the Audio-Visual Department (since 1988).

NOTABLE PERSONS

A number of individual black United Methodists were recognized in the 1970s and 1980s for outstanding contributions to the arts, religion, civil rights, human welfare, sports, and government. These women and men were inspirational not only to their local communities but also to the nation and in some cases to the world.

On the local and state levels the following persons were among those elected or appointed to public offices: United Methodist Ann Knight, after participating in a Women's Division political skills workshop, sought and won election to the city council in Fort Myers, Florida. She became its first black member and the first woman in the council.[82] Marguerite Justice (St. Mark's Church, Los Angeles) became the first black woman in the nation and the first in Los Angeles history to become a police commissioner. Doris Davis, elected mayor in Compton, California, in the 1970s, was a member of Wesley Church, Los Angeles. In 1972 Attorney Theodore M. Berry (Mt. Zion Church), a Judicial Council member (1960–1976), was elected mayor of Cincinnati, Ohio.[83]

At the state level, Zan W. Holmes, a West Texas Conference District Superintendent, was elected to the Texas House of Representatives in 1968. A Louisiana legislative district elected Dorothy Mae Taylor as its legislator in 1972. State Representative Willie Brown became the first black Speaker of the California Assembly in the 1980s. I. DeQuincy Newman (brother of Bishop Ernest W. Newman), a Methodist minister, became South Carolina's first black state senator since 1888 when elected in 1983. Judge Ernest Finney, another South Carolina black Methodist, was appointed associate justice of the South Carolina Supreme Court in 1985. Aaron E. Henry, an active layperson in The United Methodist Church, was president of the Mississippi State Conference of the NAACP for ten years. Henry, who represented the Board of Christian Social Concerns in testimony before the United States Senate Judiciary Subcommittee (1970), was also one of the leaders of the Mississippi Freedom Democratic Party.[84]

The forty-two-minute ovation that Leontyne Price received in 1961 when she debuted at the New York Metropolitan Opera House as Leonora in Verdi's *Il Travatore* was a prelude to a star-studded twenty-five-year career that bestowed many honors upon her: the title "prima donna absoluta," six Grammy awards, the NAACP's Spingarn Medal, and the President's Medal of Freedom. National and international fame notwithstanding, she fondly remembers and visits her home church (St. Paul, Laurel, Mississippi) and supports Rust College.[85]

The spectacular growth of Ben Hill Church, Atlanta, designated by the Board of Discipleship as one of the denomination's ten fastest growing churches in the country, was due to a remarkable response of people to the call of the gospel. Led by Cornelius L. Henderson,[86] an unusually gifted pastor and preacher, Ben Hill grew from a modest 400 members in 1975 to almost 5,000 in 1986. The comprehensive community-oriented ministry of Ben Hill has been a critical factor in its continuing growth and effectiveness under the vigorous and dynamic leadership of Walter L. Kimbrough, who succeeded Henderson in 1986. Kimbrough came to Ben Hill from a remarkably effective pastorate at Cascade Church, also in Atlanta.

Theressa Hoover occupies a singular place in two domains within the religious structure of the United States. She holds the highest staff position a black woman has ever held, or that any woman could ever hold, in The United

Methodist Church, and she is the chief executive officer of the largest denominational segment of Protestant women in the country. In her position she gives executive leadership to a large national staff, 28,000 local organizational units, and more than 1.2 million United Methodist women across the nation. Long an advocate for the liberation of the oppressed, racial minorities, and women, she has voiced and enacted these concerns in her writing, speaking, and leadership style. A keen observer of and participant of world Christian affairs, she has played leadership roles in the World Federation of Methodist Women and the World Council of Churches. By her admission, she acknowledges that some of her strengths to fulfill these roles comes from her Arkansas Methodist roots and her active Salem Church (New York City) membership.[87]

It can truthfully be said, in response to Leontine T. C. Kelly's belief that her election to the episcopacy "was a miracle," that she herself was the miracle. The first black woman bishop in The United Methodist Church and the first black woman bishop of a major denomination in the United States, Leontine Kelly has also been the first woman to preach on the National Radio Pulpit, the first woman assistant general secretary of the Board of Discipleship's Evangelism unit, and the only woman bishop to participate and be arrested in the 1985 Good Friday Protest at the Livermore Weapons Laboratory in California. The daughter, sister, and widow of United Methodist ministers, Kelly was called to the ordained ministry shortly after her husband's death. Educated for a teaching career, she retooled for the ministry, obtained a theological degree, and served her late husband's church. After a pastorate at Asbury Church Hill (Richmond, Virginia), she began a meteoric rise in United Methodism to climax in her surprising election by a jurisdiction (Western) other than her own (Southeastern). Bishop Kelly presided over the San Francisco area's nearly 400 churches and 100,000 members for a four-year term before retirement to become visiting professor at Pacific School of Religion and president of the AIDS National Interfaith Network.[88]

Widely known among United Methodists but often unrecognized as one is C. Eric Lincoln, the distinguished professor of religion and culture at Duke University. One of the nation's foremost sociologists of religion, Lincoln is the author of nineteen books, including the classic *Black Muslims in America* (1961), said by the late Gordon W. Allport of Harvard University to have been "one of the best technical case studies in the whole literature of social science."[89] Equally notable in the 1980s was his *Race, Religion, and the Continuing American Dilemma*, a landmark study in race relations. Lincoln has lectured and taught at the principal educational institutions in the country. He has been cited by Pope John Paul II for scholarly work in religion. His long-awaited *Black Church in the African American Experience* was published in 1990. The "Singing Methodists" will further be able to identify the multitalented Lincoln with the words of a hymn he wrote for *The United Methodist Hymnal*—"Many Gifts, One Spirit."

Administering the program of mainstream Protestantism's largest mission agency with work and relationships in more than one hundred countries on six continents is Randolph W. Nugent, Jr., general secretary of the Board of Global Ministries of The United Methodist Church. Formerly a New York Conference pastor, Nugent held similar high-level positions in missions before coming to his present post. He was the organizing executive director of Metropolitan Urban Service Training, United Methodism's innovative response to the national urban crisis of the late 1960s. Following five years with that agency, Nugent was selected to head the National Council of Churches' Division of Overseas Ministries, which included Church World Service, one of the world's largest Protestant relief programs. He returned for service in United Methodism to lead the National Division of the Board of Global Ministries in the late 1970s. In 1982 he became General Secretary of the board. Fluent in several languages, he is widely known in national and world missions and ecumenical circles, having traveled widely and represented United Methodism at National and World Council meetings as well as on numerous boards and agencies.[90]

For more than a quarter century, Joseph E. Lowery has been a tower of strength in black Methodist circles and at the same time a leader of prominence in the civil rights movement. A fearless, courageous, and articulate spokesperson for human and civil rights causes, he has been in the forefront of liberation struggles since the earliest years of the SCLC, which he has headed since 1977. Lowery was Martin Luther King's representative to meet with Governor George C. Wallace following the "Bloody Sunday" march from Selma to Montgomery, Alabama, in 1965. (This meeting was facilitated by Bishop W. Kenneth Goodson, then resident bishop of the Birmingham area.) In United Methodism, he was an uncompromising advocate of full equality for black Methodists during the 1966–1968 Merger conversations. He attracted international attention as SCLC's representative in a delegation of black American leaders to conversations with Middle East leaders. Cited by *Ebony* as one of "America's fifteen greatest preachers" and as one of the one hundred most influential black Americans for several successive years, Lowery's latest accolade was the 1990 Martin Luther King, Jr., Nonviolent Peace Prize. What Bishop Francis J. McConnell (1871–1953) often said about the Methodist Federation for Social Action may be said of Joseph E. Lowery—his role was "to raise the critical issues ahead of their time and to help their time to come."[91]

United Methodist Althea T. L. Simmons was the quiet, unassuming chief congressional lobbyist of the NAACP and director of its Washington, D.C., bureau. On Capitol Hill she was considered to be an extremely effective lobbyist. In her position she instigated, negotiated, and brokered legislation affecting the civil rights of black people. In her more than twenty-five years of

281

experience, including field work and various executive roles in the NAACP, she enabled and empowered black people to avail themselves of the benefits of the many laws that have been enacted to secure their civil rights. She was highly instrumental in the passage of bills for the extension of the 1982 Voting Rights Act, sanctions against South Africa, and a national holiday for Martin Luther King, Jr. Also Simmons, a lawyer, once chaired the Asbury Church (Washington, D.C.) administrative board. She was a member of the Missional Priorities Committee of the Baltimore Conference and an elected member of the Board of Pensions.[92]

The *Washington Post,* in eulogizing Vivian Wilson Henderson, Ph.D. (1924–1976), referred to him as "the traveling economist of the [Civil Rights] movement." One of the nation's few black economists and a manpower economics specialist, Henderson had been president of United Methodism's Clark College for a decade at the time of his death. A Bristol, Tennessee, native, he was a member and church school teacher in John Wesley Church. He was a member of the General Board of Christian Social Concerns, the first black president of the University Senate (1972–1976), and a United Methodist representative to the General Assembly, National Council of Churches. A scholar, teacher, researcher, and writer on economic affairs, Dr. Henderson also masterminded bank recapitalizations, South African involvement plans, black college development programs, and black economic boycotts. His public service affiliations included the Ford Foundation (trustee), Southern Regional Council (president), Southern National Bank (director), President's Committee on Race/Rural Poverty, National Bureau of Economic Research, and United States National Commission to UNESCO.[93]

Aptly described as a modestly proud United Methodist woman who has "broken barriers and built bridges," Dorothy Irene Height has played a major role in the American human and civil rights struggles. As president of the four-million member National Council of Negro Women (NCNW), the nation's foremost advocacy group for black women, she gives brilliant and exceptional leadership to a coalition of thirty black women's organizations that mobilize women to combat hunger, malnutrition, illiteracy, inferior education, and health services. She was also an original member of the "Big Six" civil rights team, which included James L. Farmer; Martin Luther King, Jr. (1929–1968); John R. Lewis; Roy Wilkins (1901–1981); and Whitney M. Young, Jr. (1921–1971). Among her affiliations are African affairs consultant, United States Secretary of State; President's Commission on the Status of Women; President's Committee for Equal Opportunity; United States Information Agency; United States Delegate, United Nations Mid-Decade Conference on Women (1970s); and founding organizer of NCNW's National Black Family Reunion Celebration. Recognized continually in *Ebony* magazine's annual article, "The 100 Most Influential Black Americans," and recently sketched in Brian Lanker's *I Dream a World: Portraits of Black Women Who Have Changed America*, Dorothy Height holds her church membership at St. Mark's in New York City.[94]

Classically educated Willa Beatrice Player (Ohio Wesleyan University, Oberlin College, Columbia University [Ed.D.], and Grenoble, France) holds the distinction of being the first woman to head a United Methodist college (Bennett, Greensboro, North Carolina, 1955) and the first woman to be elected to the University Senate (1964). During her presidential tenure at Bennett (1955–1966), it became one of the first black senior colleges to be admitted to membership in the Southern Association of Colleges and Schools (SACS). A North Carolina state consultant for the 1950 White House Conference on Education, Dr. Player was appointed (1966) to direct the Division of College Support, United States Office of Education. In 1972 she was appointed executive administrator in the Office of Education, United States Department of Health, Education, and Welfare. She received the prestigious Distinguished Service Award from the department in 1973. Willa Player was a key figure in implementing the landmark Higher Education Act (1965).[95]

The recent appointment of Benjamin J. Primm, M.D., as assistant administrator for Treatment Improvement in the Department of Health and Human Services' Alcohol, Drug Abuse, and Mental Health Administration by Louis W. Sullivan, M.D., Secretary of Human Health and Services, recognized a life-long black United Methodist (St. Mark' New York City) who was a pioneer in the treatment of hard-core drug addicts in New York City. Primm, the executive director of the Addiction, Research, and Treatment Corporation (ARTC), a New York-based network of drug diagnosis and treatment facilities, had been the founder-director of Narcotics Control Hospital Orientation Center, Harlem Hospital Center, New York; medical director of Los Angeles Clinics of the Bay Area Addiction Research Treatment Corporation in California; and president of the Urban Resources Institute before going to ARTC. College educated in the United States and medically trained as an anesthesiologist in French and Swiss universities, Primm soon became concerned with substance abuse treatment programs and intentionally redirected his career to concentrate in this area. The distinguishing characteristic of the ARTC program was its broad treatment approach, including social and psychological counseling as well as medical prescriptions.[96]

Shirley A. Chisholm was the first black woman in American history to be elected to the Congress (1968) and the first black woman to make a bid for the presidential nomination (1972). Her name has become practically synonymous with the words "integrity" and "new breed" politics. Refusing to be defined by ally or adversary, she has risen to the highest level of responsibility in the House of Representatives, the Congressional Black Caucus, and the Democratic party on the principle so well stated in the title of her forceful autobiography, *Unbought and Unbossed* (1970). Born in Brooklyn, New York's, Bedford-Stuyvesant, Chisholm was educated at Girls High School and graduated from Brooklyn College (cum laude) and Columbia University. As an educator, she has been a teacher, Child Care Center director, and New York City consultant. In politics she was elected to the New York State Assembly (1964) and the Congress (1968). Well organized, gregarious, and positively aggressive, she developed a formidable support group of women, minorities and students. Not so well known is her relation to Janes Memorial United Methodist Church in her neighborhood, where she joined in the middle 1950s, taught in the church school, and assumed responsibility in the educational program.[97]

Samuel R. Pierce, Jr., the second black appointee to a full cabinet-level position by an American president, presents an impressive career profile in law, government, and politics. A Phi Beta Kappa graduate of Cornell University and its law school, with a second specialty law degree in taxation from New York University, Pierce was admitted to the practice of law in New York State in 1949. He served terms as an assistant United States attorney and as assistant to the undersecretary of state for Labor, and Counsel to a House of Representatives anti-trust subcommittee. After this first circuit of positions in Washington, D.C., he practiced law in New York City again and taught at the New York University Law School. Pierce was appointed to a judgeship in the New York Court of General Sessions in 1959. Following a term there, he returned to law practice for a second time, remaining there until his appointment to President Reagan's cabinet in 1980 as secretary of Housing and Urban Development. Pierce is an active layperson in St. Mark's Church (New York City). He was also a member of the 1964–1968 Commission on Interjurisdictional Relations.[98]

In 1991 two United Methodists made interesting headlines. Evander Holyfield, Windsor Village Church, Houston, Texas, became the heavyweight boxing champion of the world. Kansas City, Missouri, elected Emmanuel Cleaver as its first black mayor. Cleaver is pastor of St. James Church, Kansas City.

C H A P T E R   7

RECLAIMING OUR HERITAGE

William B. McClain

Black people in United Methodism and its antecedent bodies, from the very beginning, have faced a never-ending struggle to be a part of a simple fellowship of believers in Jesus Christ where the grace of God removes all barriers and stains and distinctions. When the black slave, Anne, of the Sweitzer family heard the white Methodist preacher in the back country of Maryland declare divine grace as prevenient, justifying, and sanctifying, she believed it to be good news to her soul. When black Betty of the Barbara Heck household heard that same message proclaimed at the little John Street Society in New York City, she responded enthusiastically to a message that was different from any she had ever heard in a cruel world where significant truths and values were compromised and the worth of persons so frequently racially determined.

These black women's faith and the faith of many thousands gone and thousands still here, now moving into the third century of Methodism in America, is that the church to which they belong can be a truly inclusive fellowship where people who are black, white, brown, red, and yellow can sit together at the Welcome Table as brothers and sisters. They expected, as thousands after them have, that Methodism would witness to the whole world that the God of grace and glory is no respecter of persons and expects and commands the household of faith to exemplify the wholeness of the grace that entails justice, mercy, and forgiveness. That is why they answered yes to the invitation to Christian discipleship and why so many black people have remained Methodist, both inside and outside of what came to be known in 1968 as The United Methodist Church.

A FRAGILE FAITH IN INCLUSIVENESS

Even though the church to which they belonged had so many times compromised its nobly inclusive and radically Christian beginnings and stance on racial issues to mirror the dominant attitudes of the nation under the pressures of social reality, black Methodists held on to a fragile faith that the church would do right on the issue of race. After all, the Methodists had not been alone in being divided over the issue of slavery; most all major denominations had split as America became a broken nation with broken churches. And even throughout the existence of separate black Annual Conferences and structural segregation, and enduring the racially constituted Central Jurisdiction from 1940 to 1967, these black Methodists who remained in the church clung to a tattered remnant of hope that Methodism would become a truly inclusive fellowship.

This hope was probably based more on pride than reason, more on eager expectations than anything reality suggested, but it was nevertheless a hope, a faith, a gossamer anticipation that sometime, somewhere, somehow, their presence in the church would cease to be the great anomaly that it was.

1968: A PIVOTAL YEAR

The year 1968 became a pivotal year, a trying year, for a faith in inclusiveness—and perhaps a watershed year for all that was to follow. The events of that year were to have continuing effects on what black Methodists were to think and feel, and how they were to define their faith, themselves, and how they would live out their lives as United Methodists.

But there is little wonder that 1968 became a pivotal year for Methodism regarding inclusiveness. The events of the decade or so had set the stage for transformation of many social realities: the discovery and the use of atomic power, the mounting of liberation movements throughout the world, the birth of independent and self-governing African nations, the shrinking of the world as air travel permitted people to commute swiftly from one remote place to another. In addition to these massive social changes, there had been successful legal assaults upon de jure segregation, the civil rights movements of the 1950s and 1960s, the rise of the Black Power and Black Pride movements, and the registration of black people to vote in great numbers.

AMERICA'S CONTINUING DILEMMA

Gunnar Myrdal, the Swedish sociologist, in 1944 had pointed out the American dilemma—the conflict of racism, morality, culture, and religion. What he wrote surprised some Americans: that the American dilemma derived from the conflict between the profession of high-sounding Christian concepts as embodied in the American creed and the fact that self-acknowledged Christians acted consistently in ways that contradicted their teachings.[1] The dilemma, Myrdal wrote, that America, a nation profoundly committed to the freedom of all people, had not risen above deep divisions based on race, rigidly enforced segregation by law and the powerful institutions of silent and thereby more lethal discrimination, and therefore suffered a widening gap between the fortunes of the black and white races. Of course many black writers and thinkers had already made that discovery. W. E. B. DuBois, for instance, had written more than forty years before that "Christianity is contrary to the spirit of caste—spiritual kinship transcends all other relations." He added further that "the problem will be solved when Christianity gains control of the innate wickedness of the human heart, and men learn to apply in dealing with their fellows the simple principles of the Golden Rule and the Sermon on the Mount."[2] The more serious offense, of course, was that the nation became so accustomed to such a system that it somehow seemed right. And therein lay the tragic dilemma for the church and the black people in it.

THE BLACK METHODIST DILEMMA

As 1968 dawned, black people in the predominantly white Methodist Church found themselves members of a church approaching merger with another predominantly white body, the Evangelical United Brethren, with the question of inclusiveness unsolved. To put it more sharply, they were faced with defending their presence in a church that had unsuccessfully incorporated them into full fellowship as equally important souls. Although millions of black Methodists had lived, suffered, struggled, fought, sung, cried, preached, pleaded, walked out, knelt in, passed resolutions, hoped, prayed, made demands, organized committees, written books, dreamed, and died faithful to their church, as the General Conference of 1968 approached black Methodists were still neither *in* nor *out*.

Despite the efforts of many tortured strategies and well-intentioned actions on the part of those fine Methodists whose consciences were agonizing but whose well-being and life-style remained rooted firmly in the status quo, and despite the consciousness-raising program of the Women's Society of Christian Service and the organizational efforts of Methodists for Church Renewal, the Board of Christian Social Relations, and other such socially aware groups and individuals in the church, the issue of color still polluted the environment of 1968 American Methodism and strained the parameters of credibility in the arena of power and pride and respect. The overwhelming question of Methodism's *will* to solve the problem, or its ability "to gain control of the innate wickedness of the human heart," was fresh in the minds of black Methodists. The racially constituted Central Jurisdiction had been Methodism's compromised solution in 1939; black Methodists had opposed it but also had made the most of it, while defending its existence to other black

287

Methodists and the other black denominations. The romantic notions that flourished about the Central Jurisdiction after its demise notwithstanding, at least it gave black Methodists a chance to gather in one place, elect their own bishops, sing their own songs along with those of the Methodist hymnal (which carried no songs of the black tradition), hear good black preaching, and speak in one voice to the national church. It offered an opportunity to promote black colleges and support black institutions, and it provided that unique fellowship of a "church within a church."[3]

But by 1968 the homey if confining Central Jurisdiction was gone. In the streets the shouts were for "black power" and "black identity," and any self-respecting black person was wearing an African hairstyle and an African dashiki and the liberation colors of red, black, and green. The black community was bursting with black pride and slogans and African sayings. A black theology was being developed by such thinkers as James H. Cone, De Otis Roberts, Gayraud Wilmore, C. Eric Lincoln, and Major Jones. The National Committee of Black Churchmen had been organized and was active and vocal, with outstanding leadership in its statements about Black Power and black theology. Black study programs and centers and institutes were being formed on college and university campuses, and a hundred other black identity efforts were launched.

The dilemma had to be faced by blacks in predominantly white churches: Do we join the movement? What about the struggle for integration? What about the faith, the sacrifices and hopes of the fathers and mothers who brought us thus far? But what about the church to which we belong, and whose contributions to human betterment we have made sacrifices to contribute to and defend? The mood of the black community was one of enhanced self-esteem, self-respect, and self-determination, of black identity and a new realization that black is beautiful, and full of grace and truth and worth. It was a time of decision, and each black Methodist had to decide for himself or herself. For some it was clearly a question of whether or not one had to give up the essentials of the faith, the integrity of the gospel, and a long-time faith in integration and the "progress" the church was making toward becoming an "inclusive" church. For others it was a time when dreams were shattered and illusions destroyed. For all, it was a time to decide what was illusion and what was fact, what was dream and what was reality. The decision could not wait!

THE FOUNDING OF BLACK METHODISTS FOR CHURCH RENEWAL

A clearly defined group of black Methodists were sure that "from this forward our time under God is now."[4] Time had caught up with us; decisions had been too slow and tentative; racism and its insidious tentacles had reached too deep into too many aspects of the life of the church and the nation to tolerate any longer qualified stances, conditional statements, and precarious agreements held together loosely by weak alliances and shifting commitments. Concrete actions, bold expressions, and specific changes were required. It was this group who formed the nucleus of Black Methodists for Church Renewal (BMCR) in Cincinnati, Ohio, February 6–9, 1968. Their motto became "Our time under God is now." It was 1968, and that was to be a year of change—radical change. The new group was to attempt to forge a way to be black and United Methodist and to stay in the church with dignity, respect, power, and integrity.[5]

This meeting of black Methodists in Cincinnati had been called by an ad hoc committee of more than one hundred members who issued an invitation to all black Methodists to participate in developing a "life of power and unity in the United Methodist Church."

A total of 259 black Methodist delegates officially registered from every geographical jurisdiction in Methodism, and others came to

> explore strategies for helping the United Methodist Church to really become effective on the local level, through annual conference, boards and agencies, jurisdictional conferences, and the General Conference; to consider the recruitment and itinerancy of Negro pastors; to live up to the distinctive mission that the black church must carry into the "new" church; to propose urgent priority missions for the cities where we live; to suggest new forms for the life of local congregations; and to precipitate creative motives for the kind of unity among Negro Methodists that can mean a vigorous faithful Methodism.[6]

This group of Negro Methodists met for four days, struggling with the very heart of their lives and identity, which were, in their own words, "judged by the scandal of our separateness."[7] These four days spent in speech making; passing resolutions; worship; long, heated, free, and open debates in plenary sessions; hard-hitting and hard-working small groups; intense and dramatic and sometimes tearful confessions and soul-searching assessment; and probing of history and identity produced several results and recommendations, among which were (1) the publication of their findings, later issued as "The Black Paper;"[8] (2) specific legislation to be proposed to the 1968 General Conference relating to issues growing out of speeches, discussions, and research papers; (3) a blueprint for urban ministries; (4) a clear call for the national church to more adequately and intentionally support the traditionally predominantly black Methodist colleges; (5) a carefully worded but affirmative statement of support for Black Power; (6) a call and plan for local black Methodist churches to become more actively involved in the local black community; and (7) a plan for the permanent organization of this group and others into an official caucus to be called Black Methodists for Church Renewal. Perhaps the most accurate summary of this overwhelmingly productive conference is as follows: An *ad hoc* group of *Negro* Methodists gathered at Cincinnati to review their past, assess their present, and ponder their future, and left there an *organized black* Methodist caucus, committed "to exert the necessary influence and/or pressure upon the power structures of the United Methodist Church on all levels to bring about change and renewal in order that it might unconditionally include all Methodists in its total life."[9]

This sensitizing, reconciling force was determined that the 1968 General Conference would be, in their words a "prophetic" one. The very presence of black people in The United Methodist Church and the changes in the church in general are a direct result of this Cincinnati gathering.

THE DEATH OF MARTIN LUTHER KING, JR.

Before the 1968 General Conference could convene in Dallas, Texas, another signally important event occurred in Memphis, Tennessee, on April 4: the death of Martin Luther King, Jr., the undisputed leader of the civil rights movement and the prophet to the nation. Not only had King helped to tear away the mask of white superiority and uncover the feculence and filth of a foul and fetid racism, he was the voice of the nation's conscience, articulating perfectly the central and clarion message of the Christian faith. His voice had been silenced by an assassin's bullet—a shot that was heard around the world—and his death essentially signaled the end of an era of mass-led, ecumenical, nonviolent protest.

As black Methodists traveled to the 1968 quadrennial meeting of their church, they were painfully aware and grievously determined that the General Conference and the Methodist Church would no longer act as if they did not know what King had meant to all the world, nor what the gospel required. Fresh in their hearts and minds were the haunting words of the ancient scripture, "Judgment begins with the household of faith."

Prompted by these several events of early 1968 and motivated by a determination that their church must change, these black Methodists gathered at the General Conference as delegates and lobbyists and crusaders for justice. Weary at heart but undauntedly committed to confront the church, their time of self-delusion and humiliation was over. This was no time for playing games and accepting compromise. The church had to act decisively, and act now.

A PROPHETIC GENERAL CONFERENCE

The 1968 General Conference did not simply approve the merger of the two predominantly white church bodies, the Methodist Church and the

290

Evangelical United Brethren. Through effective lobbying and "gadfly" activities, black Methodists prompted the Conference delegates to

- establish the Commission on Religion and Race
- order an investigation of employment practices of the Methodist Publishing House
- provide a $20 million quadrennial fund (the Fund for Reconciliation) to finance community action projects in the inner cities of America

These black Methodists who banded together to create BMCR were attempting to seize control of their future. Their caucus was to become a means of communicating the new self-image and mood of the black community to the church. It was designed to serve as an arena for black Methodists to express collectively common concerns, to critically evaluate both themselves and their church, and to plan new ways for the church to implement programs of social justice and empowerment for the poor, alienated, and oppressed. They were determined to remain in the church in the belief that "a so-called Christian structure could move beyond its racism."[10]

HOW CAN SO FEW TRANSFORM SO MANY?

Despite consistent efforts by white Methodists and others to delegitimize the organization by accusing BMCR of being "separatist," and in the face of some who felt there would be or *should* be a massive black exodus from the church, the group persisted in its goal "to transform the Church utilizing its resources for a new sense of mission to black people."[11] The resulting dilemma was still there: How can so few transform so many? But that was not new; that was the central riddle of the New Testament Church from the beginning—a minority movement of a few people dedicated to following a Leader who believed the world could be changed and thereby saved, in part with a change of priorities.

The new organization elected James M. Lawson, long-time civil rights leader and an associate of Martin Luther King, Jr., nonviolence strategist, and pastor of Centenary United Methodist Church of Memphis, Tennessee, as its first national chairman. Soon afterward, Cain H. Felder, a native of Boston and a young, recent graduate of Union Theological Seminary of New York City, was hired as executive director of the new organization. The forty-three–member board of directors was a veritable "Who's Who in Black Methodism," representing all sections of the United States:

James Lawson, *Chairman*

Frederick Arnold	Harold L. Bell
Thelma Barnes	Gilbert Caldwell

Ernestine Cofield	Roy Neal
George Daniels	Randolph Nugent
Fannie Dorsey	Robert J. Palmer
Douglass Fitch	Archie Rich
T. F. Frierson	Negail Riley
Joseph Gipson	Anthony Shipley
Mary Good	C. Jasper Smith
Clayton Hammond	Cornelia L. Smith
Richard Hicks	Howard Spencer
Kenneth Holley	Marion Spencer
Zan Holmes, Jr.	Minnie Stein
Frank Horton	Melvin Talbert
William Jason	William J. Washington
Charles Kellogg	Woodie White
Merrill Lindsey	A. Cecil Williams
Joseph Lowery	Frank Williams
William B. McClain	Willard Williams
Marie McFarland	W. Earle Wilson
James McRee	Samuel Wright
E. A. Mayes	

Spurred by the battle cry "Black is beautiful" and urged on by the political impetus of Black Power, but also undergirded by the Wesleyan legacy of a warm-hearted Methodist zeal for social change and faith in organizational structure, this new band of crusaders for justice moved into uncharted and sometimes troubled waters. Although at times guilty of being overly influenced by the excesses of enthusiastic black cultural nationalists, whose atavistic conceits led to racial litmus tests that occasionally bordered on nostalgic paeans to tribalism in disguise, BMCR aggressively pursued its course to encourage and involve black Methodists in the black revolution, to expose obvious and latent racism in The United Methodist Church, and to bring about renewal in the church at all levels of its existence. They were, as they said, "determined to serve God by redeeming our brothers [*sic*], which in turn redeems us."

At the Special Session of the General Conference in 1970 at St. Louis, BMCR made a presentation emphasizing the need for the church to take specific actions in the area of education and economic development. Gathering support from a cross-section of community groups and organizations as well as members of other races and ethnic minorities, the General Conference adopted several resolutions in response to BMCR's demands:

- allocation of $2 million annually for 1971 and 1972 to the Commission on Religion and Race for Minority Group Economic Empowerment

- establishment of an annual goal of a $4 million donation to twelve United Methodist black colleges
- the establishment of a $1 million scholarship fund for minority college students, to be administered by the General Board of Education

The few had done much to transform many. In response to some three hundred BMCR members' surrounding the delegates in Kiel Auditorium in St. Louis calmly and courteously, in what BMCR president James M. Lawson called "a demonstration in love and in witness," the General Conference took decisive action to reorder the denomination's World Service budget for the next two years. It may well be that it was the mood black Methodists created that led the Conference to respond to the presence of a large number of youth, offering ten nonvoting seats for young people on the Conference floor, opening up study commissions to youth representatives, acting on two constitutional amendments that would lead to eliminating the requirement that Annual Conference members be twenty-one years of age, and giving each district two youth members in Annual Conferences. As the 1970 General Conference sputtered to a stop when the departure of so many delegates forced the Conference to adjourn early for lack of a quorum (the first time in 102 years), the newly elected president of the Council of Bishops, John Wesley Lord, boldly proclaimed to those remaining, "The conference that no one wanted has become the conference in which God has spoken to his people."

THE FUND FOR RECONCILIATION

The watershed year 1968 also gave birth to a new approach to reconciliation in United Methodism that was to have far-reaching effects. Championed at the General Conference by Bishop James K. Mathews, then resident bishop of Boston, the quadrennial emphasis was established as the Fund for Reconciliation, a $20 million program to finance community action projects in the inner cities of America. More than 1,300 such projects were funded. Administered by a broadly representative Quadrennial Emphasis Committee, its design was that half of the funds were retained by local Annual Conferences for their own programs to combat racism and to aid those long locked out of the American dream to find full opportunity and enfranchisement.

Following publication of the blue ribbon Kerner Commission Report on white racism clearly documenting America to be two nations, "one black, one white," The United Methodist Church sought to dedicate itself to committing a portion of its vast resources, both spiritual and material, toward the mobilization of a holy crusade against the insidious evil of racism, which was tearing the nation apart. The prescription for cure was reconciliation. The method was the empowerment of the powerless to participate more fully in the determination of their economic and political destiny. It is interesting to note the comment of Whitney Young, then national executive director of the Urban League: "No other church has done as much to combat racism in America." Roman Catholics were soon to copy this program and establish the Campaign for Human Development. The Conference of Catholic Bishops sent a representative to the United Methodists' Quadrennial Emphasis Committee meeting to express its thanks for offering the momentum and the model, according to Bishop Mathews, who chaired the committee.

THE BLACK COMMUNITY DEVELOPERS PROGRAM: AN EXPERIMENT IN RELEVANCE

One of the programs initiated under the Fund for Reconciliation was the Black Community Developers Program, the brainchild of Negail Riley, a founder of BMCR and the Black United Fund. As Randolph Nugent, general secretary of the General Board of Global Ministries and a close associate of Riley's put it at the time of Riley's untimely death September 25, 1987, "His personal experience of the Christ gave him incredible power and energy. . . . The Community Developers Program was initiated and nurtured by him out of his strong belief that the church should be leaven in the community."

In conceiving the program, Riley was critical of the "affluent white conferences" spending most of their money and energies in "white situations affected by racial change, paying little attention to the already existing black institutions struggling to be in mission in the community."[12] What Riley advocated was that a program for the procurement, training, and ministry of seventy-five developers be funded from the national funds of the Fund for Reconciliation to meet the challenge of the new mood in the ghetto. Such developers would be recruited locally by the pastors, many of whom were carrying a heavy load of community involvement in addition to their full-time positions as pastors of traditionally black churches. The persons chosen as developers would typically be laypersons, and in many instances younger men and women who might use this experience to test the vocational possibilities of a professional church leadership career. The degree of success in achieving this auxiliary goal was not envisioned at its conception. The number of pastors, superintendents, and full-time lay church workers throughout the United States who made definite vocational commitments as a result of their involvement in this program is nothing short of astounding. These came from a vast and untapped reservoir of potential leaders whose response came because the church challenged them to act out their faith in the world. During this period it became the single most important and prolific source of persons entering the ministry in The United Methodist Church.[13] The program demonstrated what can happen when social action and evangelism are not separated and the black church recovers its deep-rooted heritage of the whole gospel for the whole person. The Black Community Developers Program was indeed an experiment in relevance.

Riley as coordinator of the Policy Committee was joined by the enthusiastic former pastor of Ezion Church in Wilmington, Delaware, John Wesley Coleman, as field representative. Coleman brought considerable energy and experience from the liberation struggle in the streets and urban pastorates and a deep commitment to helping black United Methodist churches become involved in the black community and, in his words, "become a force for the abolition of the enslavement of a people kept in bondage by the systemic evil and institutionalized oppression of a nation motivated by economic greed and dominated by policies oft-times akin to savagery."[14]

While the program was designed to enable the local group (a policy committee composed of the supervising pastor, local church leaders including youth and young adults, and broad and ecumenical representation of black community leaders/activists, with consultation with the bishop, district superintendent and Annual Conference leaders) to determine the specific problems the local program would address, there were clear guiding principles and objectives set forth by the national office to which each individual project was to adhere. Through intensive training and consultation, these goals and guidelines were spelled out, and skills to accomplish them were learned. A regularly scheduled evaluation procedure was built into the process. A succinct listing of these "goals and guidelines"[15] will hint at the philosophy that informed this vital undertaking:

1. to effect social change through church involvement
2. to strengthen the church by developing stronger black leadership and to provide training for lay involvement in community change
3. to plan and push for social, political, and economic justice in black communities, and to gain control of those communities by gaining power through a process of development
4. to participate with national and local organizations striving for black empowerment, self-determination, and economic, social, and political development across the country
5. to "plug in" or relate to community developer programs across the country to help create a network of Black Community Developer programs and black church and secular agencies
6. to develop models of change for members of the black middle class, black youth, and black young adults and to develop planning and strategy components and communication networks among black churches
7. to organize an active policy committee that is representative of church and community, with adequate youth and young adult involvement

The Black Community Developer Program can be seen as a bold vision for justice, a new chapter in church/community organization, and an experiment in relevance. It has enabled many black churches, particularly in the city, to give a ring of reality to the church's glowing rhetoric about equality. Whether its attempts to utilize the social hermeneutics of the gospel to interpret the whole message of salvation to the whole community eventuates in a renewed church and a new world is left to be determined by those who come after us. But it is certainly a bold effort and a creative commitment to community.

THE COMMISSION ON RELIGION AND RACE: A BRIDGE OVER TROUBLED WATER

The year 1968 also produced the Commission on Religion and Race (CORR). While it may have appeared to be born on the floor of the 1968 General Conference, the motion Roy Nichols, then pastor of Salem Church in Harlem, made to establish the commission was actually forged in the blistering fires of BMCR's attempt to force the church to act out its call to inclusiveness. Many feel that the savvy and astute political role Nichols played in this critical decision enabled him to become the first black bishop elected outside of the Central Jurisdiction. In any case, the motion was to establish a new type of agency that would deal with the nature and needs of *all* the church's ethnic minorities. Moreover, it became a new concept in allowing ethnic minorities to become the majority in this one agency. Needless to say, this did not occur without maneuvered legislative challenge. But the Judicial Council ruled that jurisdictions did not have to elect minorities to fill most of the CORR membership slots. Thus it became a bridge over troubled water, with ethnic minorities essentially in control of its policies and operation as well as its day-to-day functioning.

The commission's tasks were soon set forth: to help merge the racially separate Annual Conferences (since the 1968 General Conference had agreed to "do everything possible to eliminate any structural organization based on race by 1972"), to counsel local churches seeking inclusiveness, to cooperate with other black denominations, to coordinate support for justice, and to supervise funds and other efforts aimed at more equal opportunities within the church. The commission saw its mission as helping the church "to understand the pervasive nature of racism and to move . . . to lessen its impact and to finally eliminate it."[16]

A person who brought a bridge-building perspective and experience was needed and quickly chosen: Woodie W. White, now a bishop of The United Methodist Church. White's educational background included studies at Paine College in Georgia and at Boston University under the tutelage of Dean Walter G. Muelder and L. Harold DeWolf, Martin Luther King's teachers, as well as Allan Knight Chalmers (a white professor/activist and then national treasurer of the National Association for the Advancement of Colored People who had almost singlehandedly raised defense funds for the Scottsboro Boys case in Alabama), and Harrell Beck, an Old Testament Professor and teacher/leader for prophetic preaching in the church. White had also grown up in the 1950s black Harlem's gentler side while exposed to its toughness, and had gone South to learn of segregation in its nastiest and rawest reality, as a college student and leader in the Georgia Student Christian Association. He had also served as an inner city pastor and religious leader in Detroit in one of those so-called "transitional churches." It is perhaps because of his leadership as executive director and the staff he acquired that led Winston Taylor to observe about CORR in 1987, "Out of it came a community—a 'family' relationship which this writer saw nowhere else among United Methodist boards and agencies."[17]

Through efforts of confrontation, reconciliation, enablement, and initiation, the commission seeks to move the church from separateness to inclusiveness. The Minority Group Self-Determination Fund administered by CORR has worked with all racial caucuses, taking BMCR as its leader and model, to bring about an awareness on the part of these groups and the church as a whole of the real diversity in United Methodism and the continuing presence of racism in the church and the society.

Some have felt that the commission watered down the initial message of black Methodists. By including the concerns of other ethnic minorities, whom they feel do not have the longevity, numbers, pain, or experience that blacks have with Methodism in North American society, their case and cause has been weakened. They argue that an "ethnic minority" emphasis was a way to cut the thin slice of the pie even thinner and have to spread it around to more. They further insist that for Orientals, Hispanics, and Native Americans, *language* is more often the issue, whereas with blacks it is simply and purely a matter of *color*. Perhaps all of this can be boiled down to seeing the *real* problem: the failure of the church, at this tick of the watch, to be truly inclusive—a church that follows God obediently in a winding path of faithfulness to be the church and "to help establish a world in which every person can have bread with dignity, peace with justice, liberation with power, and life with wholeness."[18] After all, that is what those responding black women thought grace offered when they accepted the Gift in a Wesleyan revival. And many after them have come because they heard and believed the promise that the love of God in a crucified and risen Lord welcomes, pardons, cleanses, and relieves, and that such divine love "hast broken every barrier down."[19] Or is that a song without meaning, simply sweet and soothing? The commission was established as a justice arm of God's love.

Well, whatever may be the assessment of its work, or whatever else may have been the expectations of such an agency, in the last two short decades of the existence of CORR, the road to inclusiveness has been made clearer, even if not smoother. As for inclusiveness, it is surely history in the making and not an accomplishment to be reported. Acts of history are never without their consequences.

One of the earliest leaders for merger and a consistent and clarion voice for inclusiveness has been Bishop James S. Thomas, now retired. He was among the last bishops elected by the Central Jurisdiction, and the first black assigned to the all-white Iowa area. Thomas credits CORR for being a real force for change, for being "helpful, not negative," for "careful" achievements in monitoring, training, and funding for empowerment.

In 1981 Woodie White thoughtfully spoke of the racial situation of the church. He said it was the "first time I [felt] the health of the church in matters of race [was] in better condition than that of the nation." Well, at least part of that has to be credited to the kind of bridge that he helped to build in CORR. But he is realistic in seeing that it has been much more successful, or as he put it, "done remarkably well," in the realm of structural inclusiveness, and has not succeeded in developing attitudinal changes that have occurred at the top to reach fully to the local church, where most United Methodists have their only experience with the Lord's church.

The Endless Lines of Splendor: Black Women of Methodism

Outside of CORR, whose mandate was specific, there is probably no segment of the church that has worked harder and longer than the Women's Division and its predecessor bodies for true inclusiveness at every level of the church. Black women have been joined very often by their white sisters in insisting on racial justice, human rights, and lived-out Christian mutuality.

We are forced to recall Dorothy Tilly, a white Methodist woman of Atlanta, Georgia, long-time secretary of Christian Social Relations and Local Church Activities of the Southeastern Jurisdiction. Mrs. Tilly annually assembled black and white women to work together on issues of public concern and especially racial justice and inclusiveness. Her Fellowship of Concern was seen as so controversial that she was required to have police protection for years, as Thelma Stevens, herself another of those women, reports in her *Legacy for the Future*. It is to these women's everlasting credit that they seriously mounted the steps by the path of the cross to a higher glory and joined the march of endless lines of splendor. What a different church and world we would have if their number became a number that no man can number! Perhaps then we could resolve our dilemma of separateness and inclusiveness. Perhaps we will yet. But we will need to quicken our pace, for time has a roguish quality about it that steals our breath away. History is as cynical as it is inexorable. Our dilemma could be resolved if we could rediscover the ancient Galilean's intent, hear the sound of his voice above the noisy cries of race and clan, and catch a vision of his tears.

C H A P T E R 8

A VISION OF HOPE

William B. McClain

HERITAGE AND HOPE

As Bishop James S. Thomas, a highly respected and beloved black general superintendent, closed the bicentennial United Methodist General Conference at 12:32 A.M. on May 12, 1984, in Baltimore, Maryland, he prayed, "Lead us now to make new history." He was making new history that very moment. He was praying as president of the Council of Bishops in the very same seaport city where the Methodist movement became a church two hundred years earlier, where two black ministers, Harry Hosier and Richard Allen, had gathered with their white brothers at the organizing Christmas Conference. Heritage and hope were blended together at both meetings. Neither of the black preachers who were there in 1784 could have ever imagined this moment. But the basis for that hope had been meticulously placed there by the message of Methodism and its answer to Wesley's question, "What can we reasonably expect of Methodist preachers?" They heard the answer, "To reform the nation, and especially the church, and to spread scriptural holiness over the land."

In many ways Methodism has done much in the course of its two centuries to reform the nation and the church, even though it has had a checkered career of compromises and broken promises as it has dealt with the presence of black people within its membership. Much rich history, which this book covers, took place between that first General Conference and the General Conference that opened the door to Methodism's third century. Whether Bishop Thomas's prayer will be fulfilled ultimately must await the verdict of the future.

The continuing American dilemma nags at the faith and cries out to the faithful for a resolution: to become a truly inclusive church—the people of God, reflecting the colors of the rainbow as they gather in whatever place—and not simply at national meetings; to be a pluralistic church that recognizes our God-given uniqueness, but that embraces our Christ-given oneness; to be a church able to achieve internally, and model internationally, racial empowerment, justice, and inclusiveness. In becoming that rehearsing church, we are preparing to live in the kingdom. But in the process of solving a problem of such magnitude, black and white Methodists and those of all the hues in between these colors may well rediscover that larger community of interest they knew when there was neither Jew nor Greek, neither white nor black, but just a simple fellowship of believers in Jesus Christ who could gather around a common meal to say or sing, "Christ has died, Christ is risen, Christ will come again."

TETHERED BY ONE SOLITARY LINE: METHODISM AND RACE

C. Eric Lincoln, a professor of religion and culture at Duke University and a Black United Methodist himself, has penned the lines:

> Look back if you would plot the course ahead
> For past and future in life's design
> Are tethered by one solitary line
> And what will be is anchored in what was
> For nothing is except it finds its cause
> In what has gone before.[1]

The people called Methodists were from the very beginning able from time to time to evidence unusual solicitude toward black people. That was why Betty and Aunt Annie Switzer and Richard Allen and Black Harry Hosier joined them. That is why Richard Allen offered his passionate confession that he preferred Methodism, even after having had to depart from St. George's Church to found the African Methodist Church. James Varick, Peter Williams, and other blacks who left John Street in New York also remained Methodists, although African Zionists. Perhaps even more revealing and dramatic was Gabriel Prosser's order to his comrades in the slave revolt he led that Methodists be spared in his anticipated slaughter of the slavemasters who held and tormented his people in bondage.

There is even another group of black Methodists—black *United* Methodists now. This is the group of black people who joined the Methodist movement from the very start, who found their spiritual home in the Methodist Episcopal Church, who have remained a part of this body throughout its social metamorphosis, its changing structure, and its checkered history and about whose experiences this book is written. It is this group of black Methodists who have been what I have called elsewhere a remnant in the grand community of United Methodism.[2] It is they who have defended their presence and prodded the church for reform, renewal, and change. It is they who have fought for justice and inclusiveness and who have insisted that they have as much claim on The United Methodist Church as any other United Methodists. They stayed through the compromises on slavery, structural separation, and the committees to end segregation and discriminatory hiring practices at all levels of the church. They have pushed for and prodded the church for renewal and change. And they have been at the center and the leaders for programs to be correctives to be in witness and service—the "Crusade for Christ," the Fund for Reconciliation, and (the most recent) the Ethnic Minority Local Church initiative. They have persisted through a past "tethered by one solitary line." And they have witnessed change.

STEPS OF CHANGE

C. Eric Lincoln's assessment of Methodism is that The United Methodist Church, since 1964, has been the leading example of churches that have gone beyond tokenism in their efforts to undo the American dilemma. He points out that black bishops have been routinely elected and assigned without much regard to the racial composition of their jurisdictions. In his words, "No other denomination has gone so far in depth and determination as the Methodists."[3] And, indeed, he is correct. As Bishop Thomas documents, "In 1986, black bishops serve in eleven areas and each is strategically located for some high program purpose." He goes on to list the bishops and their areas and to observe, "However one looks at these figures, it is significant to move from two bishops in a structurally inclusive church to eleven."[4]

There are other significant ways in which The United Methodist Church has changed as it relates to blacks. The all-black Central Jurisdiction was abolished in 1968. One can see changes in such areas as leadership and jobs, funds, church growth, and racial attitudes. In 1965 there were eight newly appointed black superintendents of districts whose churches were mostly white. That was big news in 1965 and a real surprise to most black United Methodists. By 1978 the number had climbed to 39, and in 1988 it was more than 60.

In the area of General Conference delegates there was dramatic change. In 1964 the number elected from newly merged Conferences was 14. A quadrennium later the figure rose to 24. At the last General Conference the number was higher than it was in the days of the all-black Central Jurisdiction. Black general board leadership at the top level dramatically increased after 1968 and concerted efforts of black Methodists for church renewal. From 1969 to 1984 executive posts held by blacks went from 50 to 110. Major boards and agencies were headed by competent black leaders such as Randolph Nugent at the Board of Global Ministries. The late George H. Outen, evangelist, scholar, social activist, and preacher par excellence, headed the

Board of Church and Society. Melvin G. Talbert, the first secretary of the national office of Black Methodists for Church Renewal, headed the Board of Discipleship before being elected a bishop in the Western Jurisdiction. In 1968 Theressa Hoover went to head the Women's Division. Barbara Thompson was elected to replace another black, Woodie White, at the Commission on Religion and Race when White was elected a bishop by the North Central Jurisdiction. A comparable increase was seen in elected membership on these boards. Winston Taylor points out that ethnic membership changed from 14 percent in 1968 to 30 percent in the span of time from 1969 to 1984. These are not merely token changes. These are very significant strides unparalleled by any denomination. It is reported by the San Francisco District that nearly all congregations have minority members, "significant in that most have small memberships."[5]

Surprisingly, in the Alabama-West Florida Annual Conference in 1988, forty of the largest churches report ethnic members. And even in the South, not only do Negroes refer to themselves as black, indicating a resolution of an identity search, but so do most speakers (at least in public) and most writers. This is a major shift in a short time, since the black social revolution.

These changes are significant and must be applauded. They are the results of a lot of praying, preaching, marching, protesting, strategizing, politicizing, and boycotting, a lot of group relations sessions, education, and books and pamphlets written and read. Many icons have been defaced, a lot of brass idols have been toppled, a whole lot of myths have been decoded, and a lot of change has taken place. But the millennium is not yet, and the kingdom has not come.

PARALYZED MOTION

No, the millennium is not yet. Racism is still very much alive and well. To make a funeral announcement would be premature. In fact, many feel that it has gone underground, become more subtle and thereby much more dangerous and difficult to identify and extirpate. And, the Ku Klux Klan still marches and recruits. For the inner city poor (which is most often people of color) life has gotten harder. Illiteracy is increasing. Homelessness and hunger grow daily with society becoming more conservative, callous, and cold. The overall income gap between blacks and whites continues to widen. The percentage of black young people attending college is lower year after year. Programs for urban ministry have been largely phased out or operate on shoestring budgets as the suburbs become the focus of ministry and church growth. Welfare programs are ever more dehumanizing, with few creative solutions being proposed. Apathy stalks the legislative halls, government chambers, and the parlors of the church meetings. Economic egoism has become an acceptable and even an expected philosophical stance. Racial incidents on prestigious white college campuses are more frequent and even supported by columnists, white alumni, and the rich. Drugs threaten to rip apart every major city in the nation as international relations, government officials, and the upper class become intertwined in a strange network of profit, politics, and parties. The accompanying violence is destroying our young, and they each other, as drugs cost more and life gets cheaper. Our schools suffer desperately for lack of competent and committed teachers and concrete curricula. Family life is suffering as economics and values become enemies, and conservative rhetoric and pseudo-religious language masquerade as genuine wrestling with the deeper issues of life and death. Style substitutes for substance. Vogueness on the outside belies the vagueness on the inside.

No, the millennium is not yet. Not for blacks. Not for whites. Not for young people. Not for women. And not for the church, either—not even for United Methodism, in spite of some strides toward inclusiveness and justice. There is still an American dilemma that persists in most every neighborhood and in our local churches. As Lincoln aptly observes, "to endorse carefully selected blacks for unusual appointments, or even to elect a few blacks to high national office is one thing; it is quite another to bring about inclusiveness at the level of the local church. Here, even *the Methodists are no exception*. It is the American dilemma all over again: High ideas with low-grade implementation. Form without substance. *Paralyzed motion.*"[6]

NEW AGENDA FOR AN OLD PROBLEM AND A NEW CHURCH

Gilbert H. Caldwell has made some very helpful suggestions to United Methodism in his recent article in *Circuit Rider,* "Courage, Confession, and Creativity Are Essential for a Racially Inclusive UMC."[7] He argues that the affirmation of our uniqueness as racial/cultural beings has been an important phase for us to experience. It has been extremely important for people of color and whites to challenge and reverse the lack of appreciation of variety and diversity, but in the process of affirming our groups and ourselves, "we have put on a back burner our understanding of, and commitment to, the oneness in Christ that makes the church the Church."[8] He applauds our most recent missional priority as necessary to direct resources to long-neglected needs, but he suggests "it never attracted and commanded the undivided attention, commitment and support of *all* of the leadership of the denomination . . . because we identified our uniqueness without embracing our oneness."[9]

To become a truly inclusive church, he suggests we shall need courage, confession, and creativity. While not denying there is much to be celebrated in the gains we have made (and surely we have), he states that "even those who claim to be enlightened and liberated . . . acquiesce to the traditions of racial separatism." He cites housing patterns, church attendance, attitudes toward interracial marriage, and the choice of schools, doctors, dentists, and friends as being "reflective of how captive we are of our negative racial history." He suggests we need courage to acknowledge and transcend this racial/cultural captivity—the courage to live as brothers and sisters, as colleagues, as a church faithful to God and our mission.

Our courage ought to express itself in trusting Christ enough "to confess our racial sins of omission and commission." Caldwell quotes Bonhoeffer approvingly: "The pious fellowship permits no one to be a sinner. . . . It is the grace of the gospel, which is so hard for the pious to understand." Caldwell calls us to confess those things (e.g., our negative racial attitudes) that violate our expressed belief in God as Creator and Jesus as Lord.

If we would be a *new* church, creativity is required. And if we would be creative there are some decisions we must make:

- to be intentional in affirming and experiencing our diversity in unity
- to avoid "cheap inclusiveness," which has no substance
- to receive the gifts of those who have been shut out
- to provide every United Methodist the opportunity to study the history of those whose histories are different, and to experience work and worship with them
- to experience the same rainbow of humanity in the church that we see in entertainment and spots
- to be truthful and candid with one another

Then Caldwell adds the clearest and most helpful suggestion that can be imagined: *"learn to say in the presence of one another what we say in the absence of one another."* Now that would surely make for a new church. That would be unlike anything we have ever seriously done or been before. That could surely occupy a whole lot of meetings, but if it were done in love and the spirit in which Dr. Caldwell suggests, we could seriously become a new church. We could in fact build a new world—not in competition or hostility or for *our* group, but in a common effort to truly become an inclusive fellowship. Perhaps then we would become what those early blacks expected the church to be when they joined in the first place.

As we move into a third century of Methodism, black United Methodists must be intentionally black, with all of their heritage a part of who they are—sons and daughters of Africa with all of the gifts that come from that background—but also Methodists who have received a gospel of prevenient, justifying, sanctifying grace. We must drink from the springs from which our forebears drank. Somehow the cool waters gave them a refreshed soul that helped them to survive with an inner dignity, a spirituality that celebrated life and the people around them, a grace that created ethical concerns for all of God's creation, that issued forth in a Christlike dignity. They perceived the divine intent that no matter how nefarious the strategies of others, the faith could not be rendered destitute and the righteousness of God would not be left without a witness. Throughout its winding development, it has been a voice crying in the wilderness. Their spirituality was a mirror of the American dilemma—surely a tragedy, but also a vision of hope that the dilemma can be resolved and that all flesh can see it together. Such a faith was not anti-intellectual but rather put the mind to work in service of the spirit. It sought some bright tomorrow where all of God's children would sit down at the Welcome Table. It is that faith they received, practiced, and transmitted to us. That faith and that hope can "lead us now to make new history"[10] that can be even more glorious than our gracious illustrious past. God grant that it shall be so!

APPENDIX A
Landmark Sites

Adam's Chapel, Fairfax County, Va.: Harry Hosier (d. 1806), known as "Black Harry," preached the historic sermon "The Barren Fig Tree" (Mark 11:12-25) on May 13, 1781, on the stump of a tree outside Adams Chapel. It is reputed to have been the first recorded Methodist sermon preached by a black person in America (Harmon, *Encyclopedia of World Methodism*, p. 651).

Zoar Church, Philadelphia, Pa.: The oldest (1794) black Methodist congregation in the denomination. It was dedicated by Francis Asbury in 1796 and became a "station church" in 1836. Incorporated in 1837, its first black pastor was Perry Tilghman, who served from 1835–1844 (Clark, *The Journals and Letters of Francis Asbury,* vol. 2, p. 93).

Sharp Street Memorial Church, Baltimore, Md.: Organized by 1802, it was built by free Negroes to house a congregation that had existed since about 1786. It was constituted a station in 1831 with a membership of 1,191. It housed one of the early day-schools for black people in Baltimore (Clair, "Methodism and the Negro," in Anderson, *Methodism,* p. 243).

Henry Evans' Chapel, Fayetteville, N.C.: About 1790 Henry Evans (d. 1810), a black itinerant preacher-evangelist, initiated Methodism in Fayetteville. A building was erected to house the congregation he started there composed of blacks and whites. Visited by Francis Asbury in 1805, Evans' Chapel is the present-day Evans Metropolitan African Methodist Episcopal Zion Church (Harmon, *Encyclopedia of World Methodism,* p. 814).

Wyandotte Indian Mission Church, Upper Sandusky, Ohio: One of United Methodism's official historic shrines is the Wyandotte Indian Mission Church. Buried in the church yard is the mission's founder-missionary, John Stewart, a black convert to Methodism, a self-appointed missionary to the Wyandottes, and one of the denomination's most effective "ambassadors of the gospel" (Harmon, *Encyclopedia of World Methodism,* pp. 2251–52).

Mt. Zion Church, Lawnside, N.J.: This history-laden church, the oldest on the old White Horse Pike, dates back to 1828. Famous as an Underground Railroad station in the 1840s and 1850s, it was incorporated in the denomination in 1892. The first black presiding elder of the Delaware Annual Conference (1864) was a member of this church (Philip T. Drotning, *A Guide to Negro History in America,* p. 127).

Tindley Temple Church, Philadelphia, Pa.: Made famous by the preaching and ministry of Charles A. Tindley (1851–1933), Tindley Temple was organized as John Wesley Church in 1839 by a group of Zoar members. The seat of the organizing session of the Delaware Annual Conference, it has successively been known as Bainbridge Street Church (1881–1906) and East Calvary Church (1906–1924). Tindley Temple (1924–present) was one of the twelve largest churches in the denomination, with its membership in excess of 5,000 (Graham, *Black United Methodists,* p. 62).

Wesley Chapel, New Orleans, La.: In almost continuous existence since its founding in 1838, Wesley Chapel, referred to as "Mother Wesley," has a rich heritage. In 1863 the Emancipation Proclamation was first heard in Louisiana from its pulpit. The organizing sessions of two black Annual Conferences were held there—the Mississippi Mission Conference (1865) and the Louisiana Mission Conference (1869). The first public school for Negroes in Louisiana started there, and the organization that led to the formation of the Woman's Home Missionary Society was begun in "Mother Wesley" (W. Scott Chinn, compiler, *Wesley Methodist Church, 1838–1951*, pp. 3-22). Wesley Chapel was relocated in New Orleans in 1951.

Bishop Matthew W. Clair, Sr., Birth Marker, Union, W. V.: The following words are on the Clair birth marker:

BISHOP MATTHEW W. CLAIR, SR.

Born at Union, 1865. Converted at 15 at Simpson M. E. Church, Charleston. Licensed to preach; his first parish was Harpers Ferry, 1889. His most distinguished pastoral work was the rebuilding of Asbury Church, Washington, with a seating capacity of 1800. He was one of the first two Negroes in Methodism to achieve the office of bishop. He died in Covington, KY, in 1943, and was buried in Washington, D.C. (WV Department of Archives and History, 1970)

Mary McLeod Bethune Monument, Washington, D.C.: The first memorial erected to either a black person or a woman on public land in the District of Columbia, it honors Methodist Mary McLeod Bethune. The daughter of freed slaves and advisor to United States Presidents, Bethune was generally acknowledged as one of the most influential leaders of her day (Harmon, *Encyclopedia of World Methodism,* pp. 260-61).

308

APPENDIX B
Historic Churches

REGION/STATE	CHURCH	LOCATION	DATE
Northeast			
Pennsylvania	Zoar	Philadelphia	1794
New Jersey	Mt. Hope	Salem	1801
Maryland[a]	Sharp Street	Baltimore	1802
Delaware	Ezion	Wilmington	1805
Washington, D.C.	Mt. Zion	Washington, D.C.	1814
Massachusetts	Union	New England	1823
Southeast			
North Carolina	Evans Chapel	Fayetteville	ca. 1800
Georgia	Newnan Station	Newnan	ca. 1840
Kentucky	Asbury	Lexington	ca. 1844
Midwest			
Ohio	Calvary	Cincinnati	ca. 1824
Southwest			
Louisiana	Wesley Chapel	New Orleans	1838
Missouri	Union Memorial	St. Louis	1846
Arkansas	Wesley	Little Rock	1863
West			
California	First Colored Methodist[b]	Sacramento	1850

[a]William B. McClain rehearses a 1791 claim of St. Paul Church, Oxon Hill, Md. (McClain, *Black People in the Methodist Church*, 42n.)
[b]This church mission failed. In 1851 it became an African Methodist Episcopal Church.

APPENDIX C

Annual Conference Organizations, 1864–1939

No.	Conference	Year Organized	Place	Divided	Merged	Terminated	Continued
1.	Delaware	1864	Philadelphia				1939
2.	Washington	1864	Baltimore				1939
3.	Mississippi Mission	1865	New Orleans	1867 1869			
4.	South Carolina	1866	Charleston				1939
5.	Tennessee	1866	Murfreesboro	1880 E. Tenn.			1939
6.	Tex.	1867	Houston	1874 W. Texas			1939
7.	Central Alabama	1867	Talladega	1900 Mobile			1939
8.	Mississippi	1869	Holly Springs	1891 Upper Miss.			1939
9.	Louisiana	1869	New Orleans				1939
10.	North Carolina	1869	Alexander Co.				1939
11.	Lexington	1869	Harrodsburg, Ky				1939
12.	Florida	1873	Jacksonville	1925 South Fla.			1939
13.	West Texas	1874	Austin				1939
14.	Savannah	1876	Augusta	1896 Atlanta			1939
15.	Little Rock	1879	Van Buren		1902	1928	
16.	East Tennessee	1880	Greenville				1939
17.	Central Missouri	1887	Sedalia			1928	
18.	Upper Miss.	1891	Holly Springs				1939
19.	Atlanta	1896	Atlanta				1939

No.	Conference	Year Organized	Place	Divided	Merged	Terminated	Continued
20.	Mobile	1900	Mobile		1908		
21.	Okaneb	1902	?		1903		
22.	Lincoln	1903	?		1927		
23.	So. Florida	1925	Bradenton				1939
24.	Southwest	1928	McGhee, Ark.				1939
25.	Central West	1929	Kansas City Mo.				1939

Source: Albea Godbold, "Table of Methodist Annual Conferences (USA)," *Methodist History* 8 (January 1969): 25-64.

APPENDIX D

Central Christian Advocate Editors, 1884–1968[a]

EDITOR	TERM	CONFERENCE
Marshall W. Taylor	1884–1887	Lexington
A.E.P. Albert	1888–1892	Louisiana
E.W.S. Hammond	1892–1896	Lexington
Isaiah B. Scott	1896–1904	Texas
Robert E. Jones	1904–1920	North Carolina
Lorenzo H. King	1920–1931	Atlanta
Alexander P. Shaw	1931–1936	Southern California
Robert N. Brooks	1936–1944	North Carolina
J.W.E. Bowen, Jr.	1944–1948	Louisiana
Prince A. Taylor, Jr.	1948–1956	North Carolina
L. Scott Allen	1956–1967	Georgia

[a]The *Central Christian Advocate* discontinued publication January 1, 1968.

APPENDIX E

First College Presidents

INSTITUTION	LOCATION	FOUNDED	FIRST BLACK PRESIDENT	ELECTED	CURRENT PRESIDENT
Rust College	Holly Springs, Miss.	1866	M.S. Davage	1920	W. A. McMillan
Morgan College[a]	Baltimore, Md.	1867	D. O. W. Holmes	1938	(see note below)
Philander Smith College	Little Rock, Ark.	1877	J. M. Cox	1899	M. L. Titus
Claflin College	Orangeburg, S.C.	1869	J. B. Randolph	1922	O. A. Rogers
Clark Atlanta University	Atlanta, Ga.	1869	W. H. Crogman	1903	T. W. Cole, Jr.
Dillard University	New Orleans, La.	1869	W. S. Nelson	1936	S. D. Cook
Bethune-Cookman College	Daytona Beach, Fla.	1872	Mary McLeod Bethune	1923	O. P. Bronson
Bennett College	Greensboro, N.C.	1873	C. N. Grandison[b]	1926	G. R. Scott
Wiley College	Marshall, Tex.	1873	I. B. Scott	1893	D. L. Beckley
Huston-Tillotson	Austin, Tex.	1878	R. S. Lovingood	1900	J. T. McMillan, Jr.
Meharry (Medical School)	Nashville, Tenn.	1876	Harold D. West	1952	D. Satcher
Gammon Theological, ITC	Atlanta, Ga.	1883	J. W. E. Bowen, Sr.	1906	A. L. Norris

[a]Morgan College began as a Methodist Episcopal school (Centenary Biblical Institute). It became Morgan College in 1890, Morgan State College in 1938, and Morgan State University in 1975. Morgan Christian Center continues a United Methodist presence on the campus.

[b]Charles N. Grandison was the first black president of any Freedmen's Aid Society institution (Brawley, *Two Centuries of Methodist Concern*, p. 157).

APPENDIX F

Gammon Theological Seminary Presidents, 1888–1988

NAME	TERM	PREVIOUS POSITION
Wilbur P. Thirkield	1883–1899	Dean of the Seminary
L. G. Adkinson	1901–1906	Pres., New Orleans Univ.
J.W.E. Bowen, Sr.	1906–1910	Prof. Historical Theology
S. E. Idleman	1910–1914	Dist. Supt., N. Ohio Conf.
Philip M. Watters	1914–1925	Pastor, New York City
George H. Trevor	1926–1928	Prof. New Testament
Franklin H. Clapp	1928–1932	Minister, Michigan Conf.
Willis J. King	1932–1944	Prof., Old Testament
John W. Haywood	1944–1948	Pres. Morristown Jr. College
Harry V. Richardson[a]	1948–1958	Chaplain, Tuskegee Inst.
M. J. Wynn[b]	1958–1967	Prof. Practical Theology
Major J. Jones	1968–1984	Dist. Supt., Tenn-Ky. Conf.
Alfred L. Norris	1984–present	Dist. Supt., La. Conference

Source: Brawley, *Two Centuries of Methodist Concern*, pp. 315-46.

[a]Richardson became the founder-president of the Interdenominational Theological Center in 1958 and remained in that position until retirement in 1968.

[b]The presidents (or deans) of the cooperating institutions in the Interdenominational Theological Center were originally entitled "Director." Legal necessity required the Gammon director to keep the term "President" in its corporate title. Gammon, therefore, employs the term, President-Director (Brawley, *Two Centuries of Methodist Concern*, p. 341).

APPENDIX G

Black Bishops

I. Methodist Episcopal Missionary Bishops, 1858–1920

Name	Born	Consecrated	Annual Conference	Retired	Death
Francis Burns	1809	1858	Liberia		1863
John W. Roberts	1812	1866	Liberia		1875
Isaiah B. Scott	1854	1904	Texas	1916	1931
Alexander P. Camphor	1865	1916	Cent. Ala.		1919

II. The Methodist Church

Name	Born	Consecrated	Annual Conference	Retired	Death
Robert E. Jones	1872	1920	No. Car.	1936	1960
Matthew W. Clair, Sr.	1865	1920	Washington	1936	1943
Alexander P. Shaw	1879	1936	So. Calif.	1952	1966
W. A. C. Hughes	1877	1940	Washington		1940
Lorenzo H. King	1878	1940	New York		1946
Willis J. King	1886	1944	Texas	1960	1976
Robert N. Brooks	1888	1944	No. Car.		1953
Edward W. Kelly	1880	1944	Cent. West	1952	1964
J.W.E. Bowen, Jr.	1889	1948	Louisiana	1960	1962
Edgar A. Love	1891	1952	Washington	1964	1974
Matthew W. Clair, Jr.	1890	1952	Lexington	1964	1968
Prince A. Taylor, Jr.	1907	1956	No. Car.	1976	
Charles F. Golden	1912	1960	Lexington	1980	1984
Noah W. Moore, Jr.	1902	1960	Delaware	1972	
N. Lafayette Harris	1907	1960	Lexington		1966
James S. Thomas, Jr.	1919	1964	So. Car.	1988	
L. Scott Allen	1918	1967	Georgia	1986	

III. The United Methodist Church

Name	Born	Consecrated	Annual Conference	Retired	Death
Roy C. Nichols	1918	1968	New York	1984	
Edward G. Carroll	1910	1972	Baltimore	1980	
Ernest T. Dixon	1922	1972	S.W. Texas		
Edsel A. Ammons	1924	1976	No. Ill.		
W. T. Handy, Jr.	1924	1980	Louisiana		
F. Herbert Skeete	1920	1980	New York		
Melvin G. Talbert	1934	1980	Pac./S.W.		
Leontine T. C. Kelly	1920	1984	Virginia	1988	
Felton E. May	1935	1984	Peninsula		
Ernest W. Newman	1928	1984	Florida		
Forrest C. Stith	1934	1984	Baltimore		
Woodie W. White	1935	1984	Detroit		
Joseph B. Bethea	1932	1988	No. Car.		

APPENDIX H

Black United Methodist Chaplains, United States Armed Forces[a]

World War I
(1914–1918)

J.W.E. Bowen (bishop)
Andrew D. Brown
Frank W. Brown
Robert W. Jefferson
Edgar A. Love (bishop)

Reuben N. McCallister
Robert G. Morris
George C. Parker
Charles Y. Trigg
Elkin O. Woolfolk

World War II
(1941–1945)

Name	Conference
Theodore R. Albert	Louisiana
John C. Bain	Central West
Frank A. Blackwell	Upper Mississippi
Harry C. Booze	Texas
Emmanuel L. Briggs	Lexington
James C. Calvin	Louisiana
Edward G. Carroll	Washington
William M. Conyers	South Carolina
Alfonso W. Crump	Central West
Theodore R. Frierson	South Carolina
Elmer P. Gibson	Delaware
Charles F. Golden	bishop
Junius E. Hall	Lexington
John W. Handy, Jr.	Delaware
David S. Harkness	Savannah
Robert F. Harrington	Savannah
Ellsworth G. Harris	Upper Mississippi
Ernest L. Harrison	Upper Mississippi
Arthur R. Howard, Jr.	Lexington
Pliny W. Jenkins	North Carolina
Hubert C. Jones	East Tennessee
James L. Jones	Texas
John J. Lewis	Savannah
Norman G. Long	Lexington
Argalius E. Martin	Delaware
Ernest N. Mattison	North Carolina
Alphonse Maxwell	Central West

Joseph R. Middleton	Mississippi
Cyrus W. Perry	East Tennessee
Cato H. Pierson	Texas
Ira A. Pointer	Southwest
Isaac B. Points, Jr.	Central Alabama
Douglas M. Ray	Mississippi
Warren W. Sater	Louisiana
Robert E. Skelton	Lexington
Augustus G. Spears	Louisiana
Carey D. Stemley	Lexington
William C. Strother, Jr.	Delaware
Ennis L. Taylor	Texas
Lee A. Thigpen, Jr.	Texas
Phylemon Titus	Texas
Fore C. Whary	Central West
Arthur D. Williams	Lexington
Carson J. Williams	Delaware
George W. Williams	South Carolina
Alpheus T. Wilson	Savannah

[a]Data from R. R. Wright, Jr., "The Church and Religious Work Among Negroes," *Negro Yearbook, 1941–1946* (Tuskegee, Ala.: Department of Records and Research, Tuskegee Institute, 1947), pp. 130-33; *Chaplains of The Methodist Church in World War II: A Pictorial Record of Their Work* (Washington, D.C.: Methodist Commission on Chaplains, 1948), pp. 36-157.

APPENDIX I

The Evangelical United Brethren Black Presence[1]

The Evangelical Church and the Church of the United Brethren in Christ brought to the 1968 Union with the Methodist Church somewhat limited experience in racial matters. They did bring, however, many decades of missionary work in Africa, especially Sierra Leone and Nigeria. In the Evangelical Church John Sybert attempted to start a "Negro Mission" in the home of a Negro, David Wilson, in Orwigsburg, Pennsylvania, about 1823, in connection with a revival that was taking place.[2] From 1896–1913 the United Brethren sponsored a mission among blacks, but in retrospect it seems to have been given to the Methodist Episcopal Church.[3] The Evangelical United Brethren (EUB) organized a Third EUB church in Dayton, Ohio, early in the nineteenth century. It was from this congregation that the Joseph Gomers, a black couple, went out to Sierra Leone to serve as missionaries in the 1850s.[4] In the Deep South (Vicksburg, Mississippi) there was a mission to the then recently freed slaves in the 1860s. It seems not to have lasted for more than a few years. Sarah Dickey, a well-known United Brethren missionary, seems to have been active in the Vicksburg work. When she left Mississippi she established Mt. Herman Seminary for "Negro" girls.[5] K. James Stein, an EUB historian, gives the negative side of this story. He reports that the United Evangelical General Conference of 1898 felt compelled to refuse the offer of a black congregation in Alexandria, Virginia, to join their denomination because it "had insufficient funds to support . . . a . . . Normal School attached to this congregation."[6] In short, by 1968 only a few black members and possibly fewer than a dozen congregations numbering several hundred people ever actually entered the United Methodist Church.

---

1. K. James Stein, "With Parallel Steps: The Evangelical United Brethren and the American Scene," *Methodist History* (Vol. XII, No. 4, April, 1974), pp. 27-29.
2. K. James Stein cites Raymond W. Albright, *A History of the Evangelical Church* (Harrisburgh, PA: The Evangelical Press, 1925), p. 156.
3. K. James Stein, p. 29
4. Ibid. p. 29
5. K. James Stein cites Leonard Barrett, "The Negro and the Evangelical United Brethren Church," *The Telescope Messenger,* August 3, 1963, pp. 5-6.
6. K. James Stein, p. 29

N O T E S

CHAPTER ONE

1. Lewis V. Baldwin, "New Directions for the Study of Blacks in Methodism," in *Rethinking Methodist History: A Bicentennial Consultation,* ed. Russell E. Richey and Kenneth E. Rowe (Nashville: The United Methodist Publishing House, 1985), p. 185.

2. Ibid.; Frederick A. Norwood, *The Story of American Methodism: A History of the United Methodists and Their Relations* (Nashville: Abingdon Press, 1974), p. 164.

3. Lewis V. Baldwin, *"Invisible" Strands in African Methodism: A History of the African Union Methodist Protestant and Union American Methodist Episcopal Churches, 1805–1980* (Metuchen, N. J.: The Scarecrow Press, Inc., 1983), pp. 62-65; and Lewis V. Baldwin, "Languishing in the Backwaters of African Methodism: Small Black Methodist Denominations, 1805–1985." Unpublished paper, Vanderbilt University, 1985.

4. Norwood, *The Story of American Methodism,* 65-69; J. H. Graham, *Black United Methodists: Retrospect and Prospect* (New York: Vantage Press, 1979), p. 11; William B. McClain, *Black People in the Methodist Church: Whither Thou Goest?* (Cambridge, Mass.: Schenkman Publishing Co., 1984), p. 16.

5. Norwood, *The Story of American Methodism,* p. 166; Harry V. Richardson, *Dark Salvation: The Story of Methodism as It Developed Among Blacks in America* (New York: Doubleday, 1976), 35.

6. Norwood, *The Story of American Methodism,* p. 166; Richardson, *Dark Salvation,* p. 35; Graham, *Black United Methodists,* p. 11; McClain, *Black People in the Methodist Church,* p. 17.

7. Richardson, *Dark Salvation,* p. 63; Baldwin, *"Invisible" Strands,* pp. 25-30.

8. See Frederick E. Maser et al., ed., *The Journal of Joseph Pilmore, Methodist Itinerant* (Philadelphia: The Historical Society of the Philadelphia Annual Conference of the United Methodist Church, 1969), pp. 26ff.; "Richard Boardman's Letter to John Wesley" in *History of the Methodist Episcopal Church in the United States of America,* vol. 1, ed. Abel Stevens (New York: Carlton & Porter, 1866), pp. 53-57; *The Journals and Letters of Francis Asbury,* vol. 2, ed. Elmer T. Clark, (Nashville: Abingdon Press, 1958), pp. 4ff.; Richard Whatcoat, "Journal," TMs, pp. 10ff, The Collection of Garrett-Evangelical Theological Seminary, Evanston, Ill. The diaries of Thomas Coke, Thomas Rankin, Freeborn Garrettson, George Whitefield, William Colbert, and others are also fruitful sources for treating this subject.

9. Richardson, *Dark Salvation,* p. 168; Baldwin, *"Invisible" Strands,* pp. 24-25.

10. Richardson, *Dark Salvation,* chap. 10; Baldwin, *"Invisible" Strands,* pp. 24-25; McClain, *Black People in the Methodist Church,* chap. 5.

11. Baldwin, *"Invisible" Strands,* pp. 24-25.

12. Warren T. Smith, *Harry Hosier: Circuit Rider* (Nashville: The Upper Room, 1981), pp. 13ff.; McClain, *Black People in the Methodist Church,* pp. 41-46.

13. Grant S. Shockley, "Negro Leaders in Early Methodism," in *Forever Beginning, 1766-1966:*

Methodist Bicentennial Historical Papers (Lake Junaluska, N.C.: Commission on Archives and History, The United Methodist Church, 1968), pp. 45-46.

14. Smith, *Harry Hosier,* pp. 13ff.; Baldwin, *"Invisible" Strands,* pp. 24-25.

15. M. S. Davage, "Methodism: Our Heritage and Hope," *The Daily Christian Advocate,* May 11, 1939, p. 474.

16. Richardson, *Dark Salvation,* p. 170; Baldwin, *"Invisible" Strands,* pp. 24-25.

17. Richard Allen, *The Life, Experience and Gospel Labors of the Rt. Rev. Richard Allen* (Philadelphia, 1793; reprint, New York: Abingdon Press, 1960), pp. 19-23 (page references are to reprint edition).

18. Richardson, *Dark Salvation,* p. 170; Baldwin, *"Invisible" Strands,* pp. 24-25.

19. Quoted in Nathan Bangs, *A History of the Methodist Episcopal Church,* vol. 1 (New York: T. Mason & G. Lane, 1838), pp. 63ff.; Albert J. Raboteau, *Slave Religion: The "Invisible" Institution in the Antebellum South* (New York: Oxford University Press, 1978), pp. 131; Marcus Jernegan, "Slavery and Conversion in the American Colonies," *American Historical Review* 21 (Apr. 1916): 504-27.

20. Norwood, *The Story of American Methodism,* p. 74; Raboteau, *Slave Religion,* p. 131.

21. Maser et al., ed., *The Journal of Joseph Pilmore,* pp. 26ff.

22. William V. Davis et al., comp., *George Whitefield's Journals, 1737–1741* (Gainesville, Fla.: Scholars Facsimiles and Reprints, 1969), p. 420; quoted in Bangs, *The Methodist Episcopal Church,* vol. 1, p. 11.

23. Allen, *The Life, Experience and Gospel Labors,* p. 29.

24. Albert J. Raboteau, "The Slave Church in the Era of the American Revolution," in *Slavery and Freedom in the Age of the American Revolution,* ed. Ira Berlin and Ronald Hoffman (Urbana, Ill.: The University of Illinois Press, 1983), p. 197.

25. Norwood, *The Story of American Methodism,* ch. 17; Richardson, *Dark Salvation,* pp. 53-58.

26. Clark, *The Journals and Letters of Asbury,* vol. 1, p. 293.

27. Thomas Rankin, *The Diary of the Rev. Thomas Rankin, One of the Helpers of John Wesley* (1790), pp. 149ff. The Collection of Garrett-Evangelical Theological Seminary, Evanston, Ill.

28. Freeborn Garrettson, *The Experience and Travels of Mr. Freeborn Garrettson* (Philadelphia: Parry Hill, 1791), pp. 76ff.; Thomas Coke, *A Journal of the Rev. Dr. Coke's Fourth Tour on the Continent of North America,* vol. 1 (London: 1792), pp. 15ff.

29. Clark, *The Journals and Letters of Asbury,* vol. 2, pp. 151, 284, 591.

30. Quoted in Lars P. Qualben, *A History of the Christian Church* (New York: Thomas Nelson, 1942), p. 541, note 13.

31. Quoted in Norwood, *The Story of American Methodism,* pp. 167-68.

32. Davage, "Methodism: Our Heritage and Hope," p. 474.

33. Robert Emory, *History of the Discipline of the Methodist Episcopal Church* (New York: G. Land & P. P. Sanford, 1844), pp. 42-43; Mason Crum, *The Negro in the Methodist Church* (New York: n.p., 1951), p. 11.

34. Quoted in L. M. Hagood, *The Colored Man in the Methodist Episcopal Church* (Cincinnati: Cranston & Stowe, 1890), p. 29.

35. J. Beverly F. Shaw, *The Negro in the History of Methodism* (Nashville: Parthenon Press, 1954), p. 15.

36. Donald G. Mathews, *Slavery and Methodism: A Chapter in American Morality, 1780-1845* (Princeton: n.p., 1965), pp. 293-99.

37. Richardson, *Dark Salvation,* p. 157.

38. Dwight W. Culver, *Negro Segregation in the Methodist Church* (New Haven, Conn.: Yale University Press, 1953), p. 43.

39. Baldwin, *"Invisible" Strands,* pp. 27-30.

40. Raboteau, *Slave Religion,* p. 131.

41. Allen, *The Life, Experience and Gospel Labors,* p. 14.

42. Gayraud S. Wilmore, *Black Religion and Black Radicalism: An Interpretation of the Religious History of Afro-American People* (Maryknoll, N.Y.: Orbis Books, 1983), pp. 81-84.

43. Ibid., p. 83; Baldwin, *"Invisible" Strands,* pp. 3-4.

44. Wilmore, *Black Religion and Black Radicalism,* pp. 80-89.

45. *Colored American,* October 21, 1837, p. 2.

46. William J. Walls, *The African Methodist Episcopal Zion Church: Reality of the Black Church* (Charlotte, N.C.: AME Zion Publishing House, 1974), chap. 6.
47. Norwood, *The Story of American Methodism*, pp. 172-73; Carter G. Woodson, *The History of the Negro Church* (Washington, D.C.: The Associated Publishers, 1921), pp. 68-71.
48. Ibid.; *Colored American*, May 20, 1837, p. 2.
49. Will B. Gravely, "African Methodisms and the Rise of Black Denominationalism," in *Rethinking Methodist History*, ed. Russell E. Richey and Kenneth E. Rowe (Nashville: The United Methodist Publishing House, 1985), pp. 118-19.
50. Ibid.
51. Quoted in Baldwin, *"Invisible" Strands*, pp. 49, 74.
52. Ibid., pp. 46, 62-63; Lewis V. Baldwin, *The Mark of a Man: Peter Spencer and the African Union Methodist Tradition* (Lanham, Md.: University of America Press, Inc., 1987), pp. 16-17.
53. Baldwin, *"Invisible" Strands*, p. 46; Gravely, "African Methodisms," p. 118; Norwood, *The Story of American Methodism*, p. 279.
54. Baldwin, "Languishing in the Backwaters," pp. 12-13; Sterling Stuckey, *Slave Culture: Nationalist Theory and the Foundations of Black America* (New York: Oxford University Press, 1987), pp. 92-93.
55. Stuckey, *Slave Culture*, p. viii.
56. *The Delaware State Journal*, Aug. 30, 1883, p. 1.
57. James H. Cone, *Liberation: A Black Theology* (Philadelphia: J. B. Lippincott, 1970), p. 59.
58. Will B. Gravely, "The Rise of African Churches in America (1786–1822): Re-examining the Contexts," *The Journal of Religious Thought* 41 (Spring-Summer 1984): 64, 72-73.
59. Norwood, *The Story of American Methodism*, p. 177; McClain, *Black People in the Methodist Church*, pp. 46-51. Stewart has not been given the recognition he deserves by scholars of American church history, even in major works on Protestant missions among Native Americans. Only fleeting references are made to his work in studies like Robert F. Berkhofer, Jr., *Salvation and the Savage: An Analysis of Protestant Missions and American Indian Response, 1787–1862* (New York: Atheneum, 1972), p. 116.
60. Hagood, *The Colored Man in the Methodist Episcopal Church*, p. 29; *Minutes of the Annual Conferences of the Methodist Episcopal Church, 1773–1828* (New York: Mason & Lane, 1840), pp. 1ff.
61. W. D. Weatherford, *American Churches and the Negro* (Boston: The Christopher Publishing House, 1957), pp. 85ff.
62. Milton C. Sernett, *Black Religion and American Evangelicalism: White Protestants, Plantation Missions, and the Flowering of Negro Christianity, 1787–1865* (Metuchen, N.J.: The Scarecrow Press, Inc., 1975), pp. 37-45.
63. Norwood, *The Story of American Methodism*, pp. 195-96; Baldwin, *"Invisible" Strands*, pp. 21-22.
64. Norwood, *The Story of American Methodism*, p. 279; Clarence E. Walker, *A Rock in a Weary Land: The African Methodist Episcopal Church During the Civil War and Reconstruction* (Baton Rouge: Louisiana State University Press, 1982), pp. 124, 132.
65. Norwood, *The Story of American Methodism*, pp. 198-99; Richardson, *Dark Salvation*, pp. 59-60.
66. Norwood, *The Story of American Methodism*, pp. 206-7.
67. Sernett, *Black Religion*, p. 55; Eugene P. Southall, "The Attitude of the Methodist Episcopal Church, South Toward the Negro from 1844 to 1870," *The Journal of Negro History* 16 (Oct. 1931): 368.
68. Sernett, *Black Religion*, pp. 54-55.
69. Walker, *A Rock in a Weary Land*, pp. 30-31.

CHAPTER 2

1. Wade Crawford Barclay, *History of Methodist Missions: Early American Methodism, 1769–1844*, vol. 2 (New York: The Board of Missions and Church Extension of The Methodist Church, 1950), pp. 1-2.
2. Edwin S. Gaustad, *Historical Atlas of Religion in America* (New York: Harper & Row, 1962), p. 149.

3. J. Jefferson Cleveland, "A Historical Account of the Hymn in the Black Worship Experience," in *Songs of Zion* (Nashville: Abingdon Press, 1981), p. 1.

4. Wendell P. Whalum, "Black Hymnody," *Review and Expositor* 70 (1973): 347-48.

5. Quoted in C. Eric Lincoln, *The Black Church Since Frazier* (New York: Schocken, 1974), p. 55.

6. Ralph H. Jones, *Charles A. Tindley: Prince of Preachers* (Nashville: Abingdon Press, 1982), ch. 15.

7. Elmer T. Clark, *The Journals and Letters of Francis Asbury*, vol. 2 (Nashville: Abingdon Press, 1958), pp. 92-93; *The Journal of Zoar: Centennial of the Delaware Annual Conference, The Methodist Church, 1864–1964* and *The One Hundred and Seventieth Anniversary of Zoar Methodist Church, 1794–1964*, p. 10.

8. C. W. Derrickson, "Mt. Hope Methodist Church, Salem, New Jersey," *The Historical Society of the Southern New Jersey Annual Conference of The Methodist Church* 2 (1968): 10.

9. Bettye C. Thomas, "History of Sharp Street Memorial Methodist Episcopal Church," in *The One Hundred Seventy-Fifth Anniversary Journal of Sharp Street Memorial United Methodist Church, 1977*, p. 3.

10. Elmer T. Clark, *The Journals and Letters of Francis Asbury*, Vol. 2 (Nashville: Abingdon Press, 1958), p. 501.

11. William B. McClain, *Come Sunday: The Liturgy of Zion* (Nashville: Abingdon Press, 1990), p. 166

12. Joshua Hutchins, Jr., "Celebrating Our One Hundred Fiftieth Year," *The Asburyan* (July 20, 1986): 1; Winston H. Taylor, "Congregations in Mission: Washington's Asbury," *New World Outlook* (Nov.-Dec. 1986): 21-24.

13. Clark, *The Journal and Letters of Francis Asbury*, vol. 2, p. 456; Nolan B. Harmon, ed., *Encyclopedia of World Methodism*, vol. 1 (Nashville: United Methodist Publishing House), pp. 814, 834-35.

14. Linda D. Addo and James H. McCallum, *To Be Faithful to Our Heritage: A History of Black United Methodism in North Carolina* (Winston-Salem, N.C.: Hunter Publishing Co., 1980), p. 27.

15. Tradition and some evidence suggest that the oldest black Methodist Episcopal church in Georgia is probably Newnan Chapel in Newnan, Georgia, reputedly organized about 1840.

16. James P. Brawley, *Two Centuries of Methodist Concern: Bondage, Freedom and Education of Black People* (New York: Vantage Press, 1974), pp. 228-29.

17. Cf. David M. Jordan, Sr., *The Lexington Conference and the Negro Migration* (Evanston, Ill.: n.p., 1957), p. 5.

18. *Journal of the Fourth (Final) Session of the North Carolina-Virginia Annual Conference of The Methodist Church*, Bennett College, (Greensboro, N.C., Mar. 26-28, 1968, p. 48.

19. Gene Ramsey Miller, *A History of North Mississippi Methodism, 1820–1900* (Nashville: Parthenon Press, 1966), p. 70.

20. Warren M. Jenkins, *Steps Along the Way: The Origin and Development of the South Carolina Conference of the Central Jurisdiction of The Methodist Church* (Columbia: Socamead Press, 1967), pp. 6-7; "Two South Carolina Churches Observe Their 100th Anniversary," *The Voice of the Nashville-Carolina Area* (May-June 1966).

21. *Souvenir Journal of the Eighth Session of the Central Jurisdictional Conference of the Methodist Church*, Nashville, Tenn., Aug. 17-19, 1967, p. 25.

22. *Program and Ninety-Seventh Anniversary of the Saint Paul Methodist Church*, Birmingham, Ala., May 1-8, 1966, p. 1.

23. William E. Brooks, *From Saddlebags to Satellites: A History of Florida Methodism* (Nashville: Parthenon Press, 1969), p. 113.

24. W. E. B. DuBois, ed., "The Negro Church," in *Atlanta University Publications*, no. 3 (Atlanta: Atlanta University Press, 1903), pp. 92-93; Matthew Simpson, *Cyclopedia of Methodism* (Philadelphia: Everts/Stewart, 1878), p. 216; D. E. Skelton, *History of Lexington Conference* (n.p., 1950), p. 72.

25. Simpson, *Cyclopedia of Methodism*, pp. 293, 480.

26. Ibid., p. 478.

27. "Short History of St. Mark Methodist Episcopal Church (Chicago, IL)," in *Souvenir Program* Booklet. July 18, 1915.

28. W. Scott Chinn, ed., *Wesley Methodist Church (New Orleans, LA: A History, 1838–1951)*.

29. "History of Union Memorial Methodist Church," in *Souvenir Journal: To Serve the Present Age, 1846–1963*, St. Louis, Nov. 8-23, 1963.

30. Woodie D. Lester, *The History of the Negro and Methodism in Arkansas and Oklahoma: The Little Rock-Southwest Conference, 1838–1972* (Little Rock, Ark.: The United Methodist Church, 1979), p. 13.

31. John H. Graham, *Black United Methodists: Retrospect and Prospect* (New York: Vantage Press, 1979), pp. 63-64.

32. Theodore L. Agnew, ed., *The Bicentennial; America and Oklahoma, 1776–1976: A Study Booklet* (Oklahoma City: Oklahoma Annual Conference, The United Methodist Church, 1976) p. 8.

33. Don W. Holter, *Fire on the Prairie: Methodism in the History of Kansas* (Nashville: The United Methodist Publishing House, 1969), p. 152.

34. Leon L. Looflourow, *Cross in the Sunset,* vol. 2, (San Francisco: Historical Society of the California-Nevada Annual Conference of the Methodist Church, 1961), pp. 222-24; Graham, *Black United Methodists,* p. 71.

35. Grant S. Shockley, "Methodism, Society and Black Evangelism in America," *AME Zion Quarterly Review/Methodist History News Bulletin* (July 1974): 160-63; "Negro Leaders in Early American Methodism," in *Forever Beginning, 1766–1966* (Lake Junaluska, N.C.: Association of Methodist Historical Societies, 1966), p. 42.

36. Frank C. Tucker, *The Methodist Church in Missouri, 1798–1939* (Nashville: Parthenon Press, 1966), p. 246.

37. *Journals of the General Conference,* 1800, vol. 1, p. 44.

38. Barclay, *History of Methodist Missions,* vol. 2, p. 56.

39. W. Thomas Smith, *Harry Hosier: Circuit Rider* (Nashville: The Upper Room, 1981), p. 55.

40. Clark, *The Journals and Letters of Francis Asbury,* vol. 2, p. 506.

41. Ibid., p. 694.

42. Ibid., p. 568.

43. *Journal of the General Conference,* 1832, p. 915.

44. Graham, *Black United Methodists,* pp. 34-35.

45. Frank C. Tucker, *The Methodist Church in Missouri, 1798–1939* (Nashville: Parthenon Press, 1966), p. 247.

46. Archie Vernon Huff, Jr., *United Methodist Ministers in South Carolina* (Columbia: South Carolina Conference of The United Methodist Church, 1984), pp. 399-400.

47. Frederick J. Handy, *History of the Delaware Conference of The Methodist Church,* ca. 1952, p. 12. Unpublished manuscript.

48. *Journal of the General Conference,* 1920, p. 430.

49. Graham, *Black United Methodists,* p. 83.

50. D. E. Skelton, *History of Lexington Conference* (n.p., 1950), p. 79.

51. Sylvia M. Jacobs, "Francis Burns, First Missionary Baptist of the Methodist Episcopal Church, North," in *Black Apostles at Home and Abroad,* ed. David W. Wills and Richard Newman (Boston: G. K. Hall Co., 1982), pp. 256-57.

52. *Minutes of the Delaware Annual Conference of the Methodist Episcopal Church,* Philadelphia, 1864, p. 11.

53. Edward G. Carroll, "The Washington Conference: Early Period, 1864–1915," in *Those Incredible Methodists: A History of the Baltimore Conference of The United Methodist Church* (Baltimore: Commission on Archives and History, The Baltimore Conference, 1972), p. 289.

54. John H. Graham, *Mississippi Circuit Riders* (Nashville: Parthenon Press, 1967), p. 56.

55. Jenkins, *Steps Along the Way,* p. 11.

56. W. H. Riley, *Forty Years in the Lap of Methodism, 1869–1909: History of the Lexington Conference* (Louisville: Mazes Printing Co., 1915), p. 51.

57. Barclay, *History of Methodist Missions,* vol. 3, p. 303.

58. Ibid.

59. Ibid.

60. Ibid.

61. William C. Jason, Sr., *A History of the Delaware Annual Conference of the Methodist Episcopal Church from 1864 to 1924,* n.d. unpublished manuscript.

62. See Carroll, "The Washington Conference: Early Period, 1865–1915," pp. 284-313.

63. See Graham, *Mississippi Circuit Riders,* esp. pp. 1-116.

64. See Graham, *Black United Methodists,* pp. 39, 42-43.

65. Barclay, *History of Methodist Missions,* vol. 3, p. 309; Harmon, *Encyclopedia of World Methodism,* vol. 2, p. 1456; Graham, *Black United Methodists,* p. 41.

66. Jenkins, *Steps Along the Way,* pp. 9-46.

67. Graham, *Black United Methodists,* pp. 38-39, 41, 43, 44, 45.

68. Simpson, *Cyclopedia of Methodism,* p. 664; Barclay, *History of Methodist Missions,* vol. 3, p. 308.

69. Graham, *Black United Methodists,* pp. 39, 43, 45.

70. Graham, *Black United Methodists,* pp. 42, 46; Brooks, *From Saddlebags to Satellites,* pp. 80, 115-16.

71. David M. Jordan, Sr., *The Lexington Conference and the Negro Migration* (Evanston, Ill.: David M. Jordan, 1957); Riley, *Forty Years;* Skelton, *History of the Lexington Conference.*

72. Harmon, *Encyclopedia of World Methodism,* vol. 1, p. 439; *Final Journal, Central West Conference of The Methodist Church,* 1965–1966, p. 109.

73. Barclay, *History of Methodist Missions,* vol. 3, p. 207.

74. Lester, *History of the Negro and Methodism in Arkansas and Oklahoma.*

75. Matthew W. Clair, Jr., "Methodism and the Negro," in *Methodism,* ed. William K. Anderson (Nashville: The Methodist Publishing House, 1947), p. 242.

76. Barclay, *History of Methodist Missions,* vol. 3, pp. 117-18, 424.

77. Barclay, *History of Methodist Missions,* vol. 3, pp. 321-24; 148-53; Graham, *Black United Methodists,* pp. 48-49; Riley, *Forty Years in the Lap of Methodism,* pp. 140-53; *Journal of Zoar Celebrating the Centennial of the Delaware Annual Conference,* p. 11; Emory S. Bucke, ed., *History of American Methodism,* vol. 3 (Nashville: Abingdon Press, 1964), p. 494.

78. Clair, "Methodism and the Negro," p. 243; Barclay, *History of Methodist Missions,* vol. 1, p. 336; Frederick D. Leete, *Methodist Bishops: Personal Notes and Bibliography* (Nashville: Parthenon Press, 1948), pp. 36, 37, 158; *To a Higher Glory: The Growth and Development of Black Women Organized for Mission in The Methodist Church, 1940–1968* (New York: Women's Division of the Board of Global Ministries, The United Methodist Church, n.d.), pp. 36-40; *Board of Global Ministries Report: Missionary Personnel,* 1978, p. 8.

79. Harmon, *Encyclopedia of World Methodism,* vol. 1, pp. 361, 384-85; vol. 2, 2031, 2111.

80. Addie G. Wardle, *History of the Sunday School Movement in the Methodist Episcopal Church* (New York: The Methodist Book Concern, 1918), pp. 46, 47, 52; William P. Harrison, *The Gospel Among Slaves* (Nashville: Publishing House of the Methodist Episcopal Church, South, 1893).

81. I. L. Thomas, *Methodism and the Negro* (New York: Eaton/Mains, 1910), pp. 240-42; Graham, *Mississippi Circuit Riders,* pp. 202-3.

82. Timothy B. Echols, *Pioneering in Religious Education: Four Decades in The Methodist Church* (New York: Exposition Press, 1964).

83. Brawley, *Two Centuries of Methodist Concern,* pp. 55-57.

84. Willis J. King, "The Central Jurisdiction," in *The History of Methodism,* vol. 3, Emory Stevens Bucke, gen. ed. (Nashville: Abingdon Press, 1964), p. 487.

85. Brawley, *Two Centuries of Methodist Concern,* pp. 501-8.

86. Ibid., pp. 445-68.

87. Ibid., pp. 487-91.

88. Ibid., pp. 201-21.

89. Ibid., pp. 223-65.

90. Ibid., pp. 177-200.

91. Ibid., pp. 267-314, 303-10.

92. Ibid., pp. 155-75.

93. Ibid., pp. 469-86.

94. Ibid., pp. 433-44.

95. Ibid., pp. 347-81.

96. Ibid., pp. 399-410, 134-36.

97. Ibid., pp. 315-46, 383-97.

98. Ibid., pp. 542-43.

99. Louis Charles Harvey, "William H. Crogman," in *Something More Than Human: Biographies of Leaders in American Methodist Higher Education,* ed. Charles E. Cole (Nashville: United Methodist Board of Higher Education, 1986), pp. 41-50; see Brawley, *Two Centuries of Methodist Concern,* pp. 2, 325, 334, 438, 490, 491.

100. Brawley, *Two Centuries of Methodist Concern*, pp. 544-48.

101. Brawley, *Two Centuries of Methodist Concern*, pp. 225-342, 347-48; Gerald O. McCulloh, *Ministerial Education in the American Methodist Movement* (Nashville: United Methodist Board of Higher Education and Ministry, 1980), p. 151.

102. Brawley, *Two Centuries of Methodist Concern*, p. 319.

103. John R. Mott, *Methodists United for Action* (Nashville: Department of Education and Promotion, Board of Missions, the Methodist Church, 1939), p. 170. In 1894 William F. Stewart established a Missions Department at Gammon known as the Stewart Missionary Foundation for Africa. He had hoped that the foundation would "become a center for the diffusion of missionary intelligence [and] enthusiasm"; Brawley, *Two Centuries of Methodist Concern*, pp. 326-28.

104. Ralph E. Morrow, *Northern Methodism and Reconstruction* (East Lansing, Mich.: Michigan State University Press, 1956), p. 192.

105. See Harmon, *Encyclopedia of World Methodism*, vol. 1, p. 56, for a wider discussion of the *Southwestern Christian Advocate*.

106. Henry N. Oakes, Jr., "The Struggle for Racial Equality in The Methodist Episcopal Church: The Career of Robert E. Jones, 1904–1944" (Ph.D. diss., University of Iowa, 1973), p. 229.

107. Ibid., pp. 230-37.

108. Ibid., p. 230.

109. Graham, *Black United Methodists*, pp. 80-81.

110. See Appendix G for a chronological list of Negro Methodist bishops.

111. William J. Walls, *The African Methodist Episcopal Zion Church* (Charlotte, N.C.: AME Zion Publishing House, 1974), p. 490.

112. Joshua E. Licorish, *Harry Hosier; African Pioneer Preacher* (Philadelphia: Afro-Methodist Associates, 1967) pp. 1-6.

113. W. A. Low and V. A. Clift, eds., *Encyclopedia of Black America* (New York: Da Capo Press, 1981), pp. 412-13.

114. Harmon, *Encyclopedia of World Methodism*, vol. 2, pp. 2251-52.

115. Harvey, *Something More Than Human*, pp. 41-50.

116. John R. Van Pelt, "John Wesley Edward Bowen," *Journal of Negro History* (Apr. 1934): 217-21.

117. William B. Gravely, "A Black Methodist on Reconstruction in Mississippi: Three Letters by James Lynch in 1868–1869," *Methodist History* (July 1973): 3-18.

118. Harmon, *Encyclopedia of World Methodism*, vol. 2, pp. 2005-6.

119. Low and Clift, *Encyclopedia of Black America*, p. 748.

120. *Centennial Anniversary Journal, 1871–1971* (New York: St. Mark's United Methodist Church, 1971), p. 24.

121. An interesting and detailed account of the life and minisry of F. A. Cullen is available in his autobiography, *Frederick Asbury Cullen; From Barefoot Town to Jerusalem* (New York: F. A. Cullen, 1944).

122. *Those Incredible Methodists*, p. 37.

123. Jones, *Charles A. Tindley*.

124. Harmon, *Encyclopedia of World Methodism*, vol. 1, p. 1337.

125. Ibid., p. 1171.

126. John T. King and Marcet H. King, *Mary McLeod Bethune: A Woman of Vision and Distinction* (Lake Junaluska, N.C.: Commission on Archives and History, The United Methodist Church, 1977).

CHAPTER 3

1. C. Eric Lincoln, *The Black Church Since Frazier* (New York: Schocken, 1974), p. 112.

2. H. Richard Neibuhr, *The Social Sources of Denominationalism* (New York: Henry Hold & Co., 1924; New York: New American Library, Inc., Meridian, 1975), p. 270.

3. *Joint Commission on Unification of the Methodist Episcopal Church and the Methodist Episcopal Church, South Proceedings,* 3 vols. (Nashville: Publishing House of the Methodist Episcopal Church, South), vol. 2, p. 373.

4. Ibid., vol. 2, pp. 374-75.

5. *Minutes of Several Conversations Between the Reverend Thomas Coke, the Reverend Francis Asbury and others, at a Conference, Begun in Baltimore, in the State of Maryland, on Monday, the 27th of December, in the year 1784* (Philadelphia: Charles Cist, 1985), p. 15.

6. Gayraud Wilmore, *Black Religion and Black Radicalism* (Garden City, N.Y.: Doubleday, 1973), pp. 103-4.

7. John M. Moore, *The Long Road to Methodist Union* (New York: Abingdon-Cokesbury Press, 1943), p. 19.

8. Ibid., p. 69.

9. Carter G. Woodson, *The History of the Negro Church,* 2nd ed. (Washington, D.C.: The Associated Publishers, 1972), p. 170.

10. Hunter Farish, *The Circuit Rider Dismounts* (Richmond, Va.: The Dietz Press, 1938), pp. 48-49, 53-60.

11. Paul Neff Garber, *The Methodists Are One* (Nashville: Cokesbury Press, 1939), p. 47. According to Bishop Garber, "The basic issue was whether a General Conference had the constitutional right to depose a bishop because he held slaves."

12. Ibid., pp. 115-16.

13. Moore, *Long Road to Methodist Union,* p. 43. The decision of the Supreme Court was rendered in favor of the Methodist Episcopal Church, in that the General Conference was considered to be the final authority.

14. Edwin Holt Hughes, *I Was Made a Minister: An Autobiography* (New York: Abingdon, 1943), p. 272. For the text of the Cape May declaration, see Moore, *Long Road to Methodist Union,* p. 65.

15. Although Negro Methodists had been the center of many discussions on unification, they did not formally participate in the deliberations until 1916.

16. Moore, *Long Road to Methodist Union,* p. 77.

17. Erastus O. Haven, a cousin of Bishop Gilbert Haven, devised a plan Oct. 2, 1875, that proposed that Negroes in the Methodist Episcopal Church merge with the colored, now Christian Methodist Episcopal Church. Morrow, *Northern Methodism and Reconstruction* (East Lansing, Mich.: Michigan State University Press, 1956), p. 196. The plan was not adopted.

18. Thomas Lewis, "Address to the General Conference of the Methodist Episcopal Church, South," *Methodist Union in Its Initial Stages,* ed. James H. Straugh (Methodist Protestant Church, 1908–1912), p. 5.

19. Garber, *The Methodists Are One,* p. 90.

20. Moore, *Long Road to Methodist Union,* pp. 96-97.

21. Ibid., p. 91.

22. Ibid., p. 93.

23. Ibid.

24. Ibid., p. 110.

25. Ibid., p. 116.

26. Lewis, "Address to the General Conference," pp. 3-7.

27. *Joint Commission on Unification,* vol. 1, p. 44.

28. Moore, *Long Road to Methodist Union,* p. 136. See also *Joint Commission on Unification,* vol. 2, pp. 25-98.

29. *Joint Commission on Unification,* vol. 2, p. 100. The meeting began Jan. 23.

30. Ibid., vol. 1, p. 464.

31. Ibid., vol. 2, p. 109.

32. Ibid., vol. 2, p. 138.

33. Moore, *Long Road to Methodist Union,* p. 137.

34. Neither of the two Negro commissioners, Robert E. Jones or I. Garland Penn, supported this report. *Joint Commission on Unification,* vol. 1, pp. 466-67.

35. Ibid., vol. 1, p. 447.

36. Ibid., vol. 2, p. 100.

37. Ibid., vol. 2, p. 102.

38. Moore, *Long Road to Methodist Union,* p. 143.

39. *Joint Commission on Unification,* vol. 3, p. 281.

40. Moore, *Long Road to Methodist Union,* p. 147.

41. The subcommittee, which included fourteen of the Commission members (none of whom were Negro), convened in Richmond, Virginia, Nov. 7, 1919.

42. The full text of the proposed Constitution is found at the end of the proceedings of the *Joint Commission on Unification,* vol. 3, pp. 561-67.

43. Ibid., vol. 3, p. 561.

44. Ibid., vol. 3, p. 564.

45. Ibid., vol. 3, p. 562.

46. Central Conferences were a part of Methodist Episcopal Church structure beginning in 1920.

47. Lud H. Estes et al., eds., *Journal of the Uniting Conference of the Methodist Episcopal Church, Methodist Episcopal Church, South, Methodist Protestant Church* (New York: The Methodist Publishing House, 1939), pp. 23-24.

48. Ibid., pp. 25-26.

49. James P. Brawley, "The Uniting Conference," *Journal of the 8th Session of the Central Jurisdiction Conference* 8 (1967): 123.

50. Dean John Haywood presents a representative opinion of the plan from the perspective of a majority of black people in an article entitled "This Damnable Unification Plan," *Southwestern Christian Advocate* 57 (Apr. 23, 1936): 261.

51. James P. Brawley, "The Plan of Union Rejected by Negroes," *Journal of the 8th Session of the Central Jurisdictional Conference* 8 (1967): 122.

52. "An Epochal Meeting," *Southwestern Christian Advocate* 45 (Feb. 24, 1916): 38. In his editorial about the meeting, Bishop Jones notes, "while many have been seeking a basis for union, no one claims to have found the basis. It was very clear [at the Evanston meeting] that there would be something like jurisdictional conferences which would care for the local interests with a General Conference overall in which would be considered all legislative and connectional questions."

53. "The Joint Meeting of Methodist Commissions," *Southwestern Christian Advocate* 44 (July 8, 1915): 1.

54. "A Correction on Negro Church Union," *Nashville Christian Advocate* 99 (Mar. 25, 1938): 368.

CHAPTER 4

1. *Journal of the Central Jurisdictional Conference of The Methodist Church,* St. Louis, June 18-23, 1940.

2. J. Beverly and F. Shaw, *The Negro in the History of Methodism* (Nashville: The Parthenon Press, 1954), p. 189.

3. The Uniting Conference passed certain compensatory legislation in reference to the Central Jurisdiction beyond that which would ordinarily have prevailed. This included authorization for the election of two additional bishops (one for Liberia) and provision for the election of Board-and/or agency-elected representatives and staff positions to create a situation of relative parity with the other jurisdictions.

4. Negro members of the Survey Commission that reported to the 1952 General Conference were John W. Curry, V. E. Daniel, T. R. W. Harris, and Mary J. Todd McKenzie. Subsequent Negro members of the Program Council (1968) and the General Council on Ministries (1972) were Mrs. E. J. Badgett, Bishop Robert N. Brooks, John W. Curry, V. E. Daniel, Mary M. Drake, Richard C. Erwin, Sr., Joe D. Grier, T. W. R. Harris, Hally P. Johns, Bishop Willis J. King, Bishop Edgar O. Love, and Mary J. Todd McKenzie.

5. *Journal of the Eighth Session of the Central Jurisdictional Conference of The Methodist Church: Special Session,* Nashville, Aug. 17-19, 1967, p. 74.

6. The only other Negros elected to the Judicial Council between 1945 and 1968 were Theodore M. Berry, lawyer and one-time vice mayor of Cincinnati, Ohio, elected in 1960; and Charles B. Copher and Richard C. Erwin, elected alternate members of the council in 1964.

7. Ibid.

8. Ibid.

9. Much of this work was created due to the arduous efforts of Methodist Protestant missionaries among Negroes before the Civil War. Especially notable was the outstanding work of Francis Brown (c. 1830–c.1890), a Negro Methodist Protestant in South Carolina.

10. Earl H. Crampton, "Is the Central Jurisdiction Necessary?" Speech delivered at Easton District Preacher's Meeting, Delaware Conference, The Methodist Church, Easton, Md., Oct. 12, 1954.

11. Robert L. Wilson and Alan K. Waltz, *The Methodist Church in Urban America* (New York: Division of National Missions, Board of Missions, 1962), p. 75.

12. Robert L. Wilson, James H. Davis, and Joseph D. Kipfer, *Horizons in Home Missions* (New York, N.Y.: Department of Research and Survey, National Division, Board of Missions, The Methodist Church, 1964), pp. 11-12.

13. Wilson and Waltz, *The Methodist Church in Urban America*, p. 83.

14. *The Book of Discipline, 1985* (Nashville: The United Methodist Publishing House, 1988), p. 15.

15. C. Eric Lincoln, *The Black Church Since Frazier* (New York: Schocken, 1974), p. 37.

16. *The Image of The Methodist Church in the Negro Community,* vol. 1 (New York: National Division of the Board of Missions of The Methodist Church, 1965), p. 39.

17. C. Eric Lincoln, "Black Methodists and the Middle Class Mentality," in *Experiences, Struggles and Hopes of the Black Church,* ed. James S. Gadsden (Nashville: Tidings, 1975), ch. 5.

18. Cf. St. Clair Drake and Horace Clayton, *Black Metropolis: A Study of Negro Life in a Northern City* (New York: Harcourt and Brace, 1945), pp. 537-40.

19. M. O. Williams, *The Involvement of Ethnic Minority Persons in Overseas Missions in The United Methodist Church and Its Predecessors, 1942–1977* (New York: World Division of the Board of Global Ministries, 1978), p. 9.

20. Ibid., p. 10.

21. Ibid.

22. David M. Jordan, Sr., *The Lexington Conference and the Negro Migration* (Evanston, Ill.: n.p., 1957), pp. 10-27; cf. E. Franklin Frazier, *The Negro Church in America* (New York: Schocken 1963), ch. 4.

23. Harry V. Richardson, *Dark Glory: A Picture of the Church Among Negroes in the Rural South* (New York: Friendship Press, 1947), ch. 4.

24. Jinx C. Broussard, "Gulfside's New Day," *The Interpreter* (Jan. 1981): 12-15.

25. Emory S. Bucke, gen. ed., *The History of American Methodism,* vol. 3 (Nashville: Abingdon Press, 1964), p. 542.

26. *To a Higher Glory: The Growth and Development of Black Women Organized for Mission in The Methodist Church, 1940–1968* (New York: Women's Division of the Board of Global Ministries, The United Methodist Church), pp. 21-22.

27. Ibid., pp. 23-27.

28. Ibid., p. 48.

29. Ibid., pp. 60-61.

30. Ibid., p. 113.

31. Ibid., p. 112.

32. Ibid., p. 75.

33. Ibid., p. 78.

34. Ibid., pp. 73-74.

35. Ibid., p. 72.

36. Thelma Stevens, *Legacy for the Future: The History of Christian Social Relations in the Women's Division of Christian Service, 1940–1968* (New York: Women's Division, Board of Global Ministries, The United Methodist Church, 1978), pp. 28-53.

37. *To a Higher Glory,* pp. 103-11.

38. Ibid., p. 31.

39. *Journal of the Central Jurisdictional Conference,* 1940, p. 110.

40. Ibid., p. 111.

41. *Journal of the Central Jurisdictional Conference,* 1944, p. 58.

42. *Journal of the Second Session of the Central Jurisdictional Conference of The Methodist Church,* Bennett College, Greensboro, N.C., June 8-11, 1944, pp. 95-96.

43. *Journal of the Fourth Session of the Central Jurisdictional Conference of The Methodist Church,* Tindley Temple Methodist Church, Philadelphia, June 18-22, 1952, p. 127.

44. *Journal of the Sixth Session of the Central Jurisdictional Conference of The Methodist Church,* Cory Methodist Church, Cleveland, Ohio, July 13-17, 1960, p. 132.

45. Ibid.

46. Historically, Timothy B. Echols was the first full-time executive secretary of Christian education in any of the black Annual Conferences. Echols was appointed in 1934 as director of religious education for the New Orleans area. The second such appointment was Fredrick J. Handy, appointed executive secretary of Christian education for the Delaware Conference in 1937. By 1960–1964 each of the seventeen black Annual Conferences had executive secretaries.

47. James P. Brawley, *Two Centuries of Methodist Concern: Bondage, Freedom and Education of Black People* (New York: Vantage Press, 1974), p. 150.

48. Ibid., p. 145.

49. *Journal of the Central Jurisdictional Conferences of The Methodist Church*, 1940, p. 110.

50. Ibid.

51. Ibid., p. 111.

52. Walter N. Vernon, Alfredo Nanez, and John H. Graham, eds., *One in the Lord: A History of Ethnic Minorities in the South Central Jurisdiction, The United Methodist Church* (Oklahoma City, Okla.: Commission on Archives and History, South Central Jurisdiction, 1977), p. 119.

53. Brawley, *Two Centuries of Methodist Concern*, pp. 146-47.

54. *Crusade Scholarships: A Week of Dedication Project*, 1952, p. 12.

55. Brawley, *Two Centuries of Methodist Concern*, p. 524.

56. Ibid., pp. 147-49.

57. *Doctrines and Discipline of The Methodist Church* (New York: The Methodist Publishing House, 1940), ¶ 1050.

58. Timothy B. Echols, *Pioneering in Religious Education: Four Decades in The Methodist Church* (New York: Exposition Press, 1964), p. 136.

59. Ibid.

60. Wade Crawford Barclay, *History of Methodist Missions: Early American Methodism, 1769–1844*, vol. 2 (New York: The Board of Missions and Church Extension of The Methodist Church, 1950), pp. 1-2.

61. H. Richard Niebuhr, *The Social Sources of Denominationalism* (New York: Living Age Books, 1957), p. 66.

62. William B. Gravely, *Gilbert Haven: Methodist Abolitionist* (Nashville: Abingdon Press, 1973). This is an excellent account of Gilbert Haven and his time.

63. *Discipline of the Methodist Episcopal Church*, 1908.

64. *Journal of the 1944 General Conference of The Methodist Church* (Nashville: The Methodist Publishing House, 1944), p. 729.

65. *Journal of the 1948 General Conference of The Methodist Church* (Nashville: The Methodist Publishing House, 1948), p. 739.

66. *Journal of the Southeastern Jurisdictional Conference of The Methodist Church*, Lake Junaluska, N.C., July 8-12, 1964, p. 92.

67. *Journal of the Central Jurisdictional Conference*, 1940, p. 119.

68. L. Scott Allen, "Editorial," *Central Christian Advocate* 131, no. 11 (June 1, 1956).

69. James P. Pilkington, *The Methodist Publishing House: A History* (Nashville: Abingdon Press, 1968), p. 360.

70. Roy H. Short, *United Methodism in Theory and Practice* (Nashville: Abingdon Press, 1974), p. 98.

71. *Journal of the Central Jurisdictional Conference*, 1940, p. 60.

72. J. H. Touchstone's exemplary church involvement had marked him as a logical choice for the position from the inception of the selection process.

73. *Journal of the Seventh Jurisdictional Conference of The Methodist Church*, Bethune-Cookman College, Daytona Beach, Fla., 1964, p. 115.

74. Murray H. Leiffer, *The Methodist Ministry in 1948: Its Composition and Training and the Recruitment Needs of the Church* (Nashville: The Commission on Ministerial Training, 1948), pp. 21-22.

75. Murray H. Leiffer, *The Methodist Ministry in 1952 and the Recruitment Needs of the Church* (Nashville: The Commission on Ministerial Training, 1952), pp. 20-21.

76. *Journal of the Third Central Jurisdictional Conference of The Methodist Church*, Clark College, Atlanta, Ga., June 9-13, 1948, p. 142.

77. Leiffer, *The Methodist Ministry in 1952*, pp. 20-21.

78. *Journal of the Central Jurisdictional Conference,* 1940, pp. 117-18; *Journal of the Fourth Central Jurisdictional Conference,* 1952, p. 121; Timothy B. Echols, "Adventure with the General Board of Pensions," in *Pioneering in Religious Education: Four Decades in The Methodist Church* (New York: Exposition Press, 1964), pp. 148-49.

79. Echols, "Adventure with the General Board of Pensions," pp. 149-50.

80. *Journal of the Seventh Central Jurisdictional Conference,* 1964, p. 115.

81. The data for this section on black women in the ministry in the Methodist Church was found in the General Minutes (1956–1967).

82. Gerald O. McCulloh, *Ministerial Education in the American Methodist Movement* (Nashville: United Methodist Board of Higher Education and Ministry, Division of Ordained Ministry, 1980), p. 59.

83. *Journal of the New York Annual Conference of The Methodist Church,* New York, May 7-12, 1963, p. 305.

84. *Conference Journal and Yearbook,* New York Conference of The Methodist Church, Drew University, Madison, N.J., June 9-14, 1964, p. 170.

85. Nolan B. Harmon, *The Organization of The Methodist Church* (New York: n.p., 1948), p. 70.

86. Nolan B. Harmon, ed., *Encyclopedia of World Methodism* (Nashville: United Methodist Publishing House), p. 1320.

87. *Quadrennial Reports of the Boards and Commissions of The Methodist Church to the General Conference* (Nashville: The Methodist Publishing House, 1952), p. 626.

88. The Detroit example was one of many Northern/Western examples of what the Southern Christian Leadership Conference had been doing ecumenically in the South since its organization by Martin Luther King and others in 1957.

89. Bruce Hilton, *The Delta Ministry* (London: The Macmillan Co., 1969), pp. 28, 29-30.

90. McCulloh, *Ministerial Education in the American Methodist Movement,* p. 60.

91. John H. Graham, *Black United Methodists* (New York: Vantage Press, 1979), p. 133.

92. *The Methodist Fact Book* (Evanston, Ill.: The Statistical Office of The Methodist Church, n.d.), pp. 132-33.

93. *The Methodist Directory, 1965,* p. 99.

94. *The Methodist Fact Book, 1960,* p. 145.

95. *Journal of the Eighth Session of the Central Jurisdictional Conference of The Methodist Church,* Nashville, Aug. 17-19, 1967, p. 74.

96. *Journal of the Central Jurisdictional Conference of The Methodist Church,* St. Louis, June 18-23, 1940, p. 59.

97. Peter Paris, *The Social Teaching of the Black Churches* (Philadelphia: Fortress Press, 1985), pp. 47-49.

98. William J. Walls, *The African Methodist Episcopal Zion Church: Reality of the Black Church* (Charlotte, N.C.: AME Zion Publishing House, 1974), pp. 490-91.

99. Virgil E. Lowder, "Negro Methodists Consider Union," *The Christian Century* (February 19, 1964): 251-52.

100. The documentation for this commonly acknowledged petition cannot be verified in the *Journal of the Eighth Session of the Central Jurisdictional Conference.* There is, however, a supporting reference for this action in the *Quadrennial Reports of the Boards and Commissions of The Methodist Church to the General Conference,* 1952, p. 586, beginning with the sentence "The last General Conference (1948) suggested . . . Ecumenical Council."

CHAPTER 5

1. C. Eric Lincoln, *The Black Experience in Religion* (Garden City, N.Y.: Doubleday, 1974), pp. 1-2.

2. Gayraud S. Wilmore, *Black Religion and Black Radicalism* (Garden City, N.Y.: Doubleday, 1972), p. 14.

3. Cited in W. W. Sweet, *Virginia Methodism* (Richmond, Va.: Whittet & Shepperson, 1950), pp. 295ff.

4. Richard Allen, *The Life, Experience and Gospel Labor of the Rt. Reverend Richard Allen* (New York: Abingdon Press, 1960), p. 30. Reprint.

5. Daniel A. Payne, *History of the African Methodist Episcopal Church,* p. 20.

6. Daniel W. Shaw, "Should the Negro of the Methodist Episcopal Church Be Set Apart in a Church by Themselves?" quoted in *Methodism and the Negro,* ed. William K. Anderson (Nashville: The Methodist Publishing House, 1950), p. 245.

7. Dwight Culver, *Negro Segregation in the Methodist Church* (New Haven, Conn.: Yale University Press, 1953), p. 72.

8. Willis J. King, "The History of the Negro in the Methodist Church Prior to 1939," *Journal of the Central Jurisdictional Conferences* (1967): 110.

9. James P. Brawley, "The Central Jurisdiction in the Methodist Church, 1939–1967," *Journal of the Central Jurisdictional Conferences* (1967): 122.

10. William B. McClain, *Black People in the Methodist Church: Whither Thou Goest?* (Nashville: Abingdon Press, 1984), p 85.

11. Robert E. Jones, "On The Central Jurisdiction," *The Daily Christian Advocate,* Central Jurisdictional Conference, 1940, p. 8.

12. Alexander P. Shaw, "The Episcopal Address," *The Daily Christian Advocate,* Central Jurisdiction, 1944, pp. 91-92.

13. McClain, *Black People in the Methodist Church,* p. 89.

14. Graham, *Black United Methodists,* p. 94.

15. Robert N. Brooks, "Fishing in Troubled Waters, 1951, p. 22.

16. Paul Kern, "The Episcopal Address," *Journal of the 1952 General Conference,* p. 167.

17. *Journal of the General Conference of 1956,* p. 1693.

18. Ibid.

19. Ibid.

20. Harold C. Case, *Journal of the General Conference of 1960,* p. 365.

21. Charles F. Golden, *Journal of the General Conference of 1960,* p. 323.

22. Graham, *Black United Methodists,* p. 98.

23. Ibid., pp. 98-99.

24. Gerald Kennedy, "The Episcopal Address," *Journal of the 1964 General Conference* 1 (1964): 205.

25. The Book of Discipline, 1964, Par. 1824.5; 1813.2; 1685; 1813.6.

CHAPTER 6

1. For the definition of "inclusive" used in this chapter, see Alan K. Waltz, *A United Methodist Dictionary* (Nashville: Abingdon Press, 1991), p. 108; *The Book of Discipline,* ¶ 4 (since 1968).

2. There were two explicitly positive things about the report of the Structure Study Commission that validated its effort to rid the church of structured racism: (1) a nominating process that practically ensured racial group representation on all program boards (1972 *Discipline,* ¶ 803.2) and the presence of four black members on the commission itself: W. Astor Kirk (vice chairperson); Richard C. Erwin, Sr.; Claire C. Harvey; and Bishop Prince A. Taylor.

3. Cf. *Findings of Black Methodists for Church Renewal* (New York: Black Methodists for Church Renewal, 1968), passim.

4. C. Eric Lincoln, "Black Methodists and the Middle Class Mentality," in *Experiences, Struggles and Hopes of the Black Church* (Nashville: Tidings, 1975), ch. 5. (Nashville, TN: The United Methodist Publishing House): Dec. 15, 1989, p. 4; Jan. 26, 1990, p. 4; *West Ohio News/United Methodist Reporter* (Columbus, OH: West Ohio Conference, Mar. 16, 1990, p. 1).

5. *Newscope: The National Weekly Newsletter for United Methodist Leaders.*

6. *The Book of Discipline,* 1968, ¶ 814.1, 815.4.

7. Jack M. Tuell, *The Organization of The United Methodist Church,* rev. ed. (Nashville: Abingdon Press, 1989), p. 130.

8. Ibid., p. 131.

9. Cf. ibid., pp. 133-34.

10. *The Book of Discipline,* 1972, ¶ 1266.

11. This estimated figure (500,000) includes Asian, black, Hispanic, and Native American members of the United Methodist Church.

12. Earl D. C. Brewer, *Continuation or Transformation* (Nashville: Abingdon Press, 1982), p. 57.

13. Tuell, *Organization of The United Methodist Church,* p. 142.

14. Cf. "Black Methodists Speak on Conference Mergers," *Methodists Make News,* March 28, 1969, pp. 1-2.

15. *The Methodist Fact Book, 1962,* pp. 156-65.

16. Douglass W. Johnson, *A Study of Former Central Jurisdiction Church Data, 1974–1984* (New York: National Program Division, General Board of Global Ministries, The United Methodist Church, 1987), p. 11.

17. George H. Outen, "Trusting Our Evangelists in the Black Community" *Christian Advocate* (January 4, 1973): 7.

18. Special mention should be made of the exciting example of church growth in the North Mississippi Conference. There, with the leadership of Merlin Conoway, more than thirty-five new churches were constructed and twenty-five ministers were recruited during the 1976–1980 quadrennium.

19. Ralph and Nell Mohney, *Parable Churches: Stories of United Methodism's Ten Fastest Growing Churches* (Nashville: General Board of Discipleship of The United Methodist Church, n.d.), p. 5.

20. A somewhat different example of innovative church growth is found in the North Mississippi Conference. With the leadership of Merlin Conoway, more than thirty-five new churches were constructed and twenty-five ministers were recruited during the 1976–1980 quadrennium.

21. *Journal of the Eighth Session of the Central Jurisdictional Conference,* Nashville, Aug. 17–19, 1967, p. 77.

22. "The Black Paper," *Findings of Black Methodists for Church Renewal,* p. 3.

23. *Daily Christian Advocate,* Proceedings of the Southeastern Jurisdictional Conference, The United Methodist Church, Lake Junaluska, N.C., July 12, 1972, p. 1.

24. *Report of the Commission on Religion and Race to the General Conference of The United Methodist Church* (Atlanta: The Commission on Religion and Race, 1972), p. 46.

25. *Diaconal Report* (Nashville: Division of Diaconal Ministry, Board of Higher Education and Ministry, The United Methodist Church, 1988), p. 5.

26. Cf. Thelma P. Barnes, "Black Methodists for Church Renewal: A Sensitizing, Reconciling Force," *Response,* June 1972, p. 8.

27. *Findings of Black Methodists for Church Renewal,* p. 18.

28. *The Book of Discipline of The United Methodist Church, 1988,* ¶ 1421a.

29. Ibid., ¶ 1421b.

30. *To a Higher Glory: The Growth and Development of Black Women Organized for Mission in The Methodist Church, 1940–1968* (New York: Women's Division of the Board of Global Ministries, The United Methodist Church, 1978); p. 97.

31. *Journal of the Eighth Session of the Central Jurisdictional Conference,* Nashville, Aug. 17-19, 1967, p. 77.

32. *A General Critique of the Black Manifesto and Some Qualifications for the Board of Mission* (New York: Black Staff Task Force, Board of Missions, The United Methodist Church, 1969), p. 1.

33. *Daily Christian Advocate: Proceedings of the General Conference of The United Methodist Church* (Baltimore: May 1-12, 1984): E44-45.

34. David B. Barrett, ed., *World Christian Encyclopedia* (New York: Oxford University Press, 1982).

35. M. O. Williams, *The Involvement of Ethnic Minority Persons in Overseas Missions in The United Methodist Church and Its Predecessors, 1942–1977* (New York: World Division of the Board of Global Ministries, 1978), p. 6.

36. *The Book of Discipline of The United Methodist Church, 1972,* ¶ 730.

37. Diana Sanchez, *The Hymns of The United Methodist Hymnal* (Nashville: Abingdon Press, 1989), p. 10.

38. Quotation from a speech by Maceo D. Pembroke (1919–1981), prominent pastor of St. Mark Church, given in 1981 in Chicago at the publication event of *Songs of Zion.*

39. Sanchez, *The Hymns of the United Methodist Hymnal,* p. 11.

40. *The United Methodist Hymnal: Book of United Methodist Worship* (Nashville: The United Methodist Publishing House, 1989).

41. Philip A. Harley, "Being Practical in Preparing Black Youth for Ministry," *The Christian Advocate* (Sept. 13, 1973): 12.

42. Willard A. Williams, *Foundations for Christian Education in Black Churches: A Study Guide* (Nashville: Discipleship Resources, 1979), p. 1.

43. Willard A. Williams, *Educational Ministry in the Black Community: Resource Booklet* (Nashville: Board of Education, The United Methodist Church, 1972), p. 1.

44. Willard A. Williams, *Educational Ministries with Blacks: Position Paper* (Nashville: Board of Discipleship of The United Methodist Church, 1974), p. 7.

45. Joseph V. Crockett, *New Models in Christian Education for the Black Church: A Cooperative Project* (Nashville: Section on Christian Education of The General Board of Discipleship, The United Methodist Church, 1988), p. 3.

46. Cf. *Higher Education Project* (Nashville: Division of Higher Education, Board of Education, The United Methodist Church, 1970), p. 4.

47. The General Conference of The United Methodist Church, Portland, Ore., (Apr. 27, 1976): H-8.

48. Cf. *The Black College Fund Story* (Nashville: The Black College Fund, Division of Higher Education, General Board of Higher Education and Ministry, n.d.).

49. "College Recruitment," *The Interpreter* (Jan. 1990): 45.

50. Frank L. Horton, *Black Spirituality and the Black College Campus* (Nashville: Department of Campus Ministry, Division of Higher Education, General Board of Education, The United Methodist Church, n.d.).

51. Richard R. Hicks, letter to Grant S. Shockley, "Memorandum: A Brief Historical Sketch of Campus Ministry Among Black United Methodists, 1938–1988." 1990.

52. James H. Cone, *Black Theology and Black Power* (New York: Seabury Press, 1969), p. 117.

53. *Daily Christian Advocate* (Atlanta, Georgia, Apr. 19, 1972):226.

54. Ibid., p. 228.

55. *One Ministry: A Report of the National Consultation on the Negro in the Christian Ministry* (Greenwich, CT: The Department of the Ministry Commission on Higher Education, National Council of the Churches of Christ in the USA, 1959,) pp. 10-11.

56. *Manual for the Committee on the Black Religious Experience and Theological Education* (Dayton, Ohio: Association of Theological Schools, 1968), p. 87.

57. *A Proposal for an Ecumenical Center for Black Church Studies* (Los Angeles: Steering Committee of the Ecumenical Workshop on Education for Ministry in the Black Church and Community, 1973).

58. Cf. Charles S. Rooks, "Vision Reality and Challenge: Black Americans and North American Theological Education, 1959–1983," *Theological Education* (Autumn 1983): 37-52.

59. Quoted from *Experiences, Struggles and Hopes of the Black Church,* ed. James S. Gadsden (Nashville: Tidings, 1975), p. viii.

60. Philip A. Harley, "Being Practical in Preparing Black Youth for Ministry," *The Christian Advocate* (Sept. 13, 1973): 11.

61. Grant S. Shockley, Earl D. C. Brewer, and Marie Townsend, *Black Pastors and Black Churches in United Methodism* (Atlanta: Center for Research in Social Change, Emory University, 1976), p. 8.

62. Douglass E. Fitch, *The Crisis in Ministry Among Ethnic Minority Clergy in The United Methodist Church* (Nashville: Division of the Ordained Ministry, General Board of Higher Education and Ministry, 1976.) Unpublished manuscript.

63. St. Louis, *Daily Christian Advocate* (*Advance Edition*) (Apr. 26-May 6, 1988): F124-F130.

64. Geneva Harton Dalton, "Black American Women: Ministry in the 80s," *Response* (Jan. 1989): 10-11.

65. *Guidelines for Leading Your Church: United Methodist Men, 1984–1988* (Nashville: Discipleship Resources, n.d.), p. 4.

66. *Findings of Black Methodists for Church Renewal,* p. 18.

67. *Proceedings of the Consultation of Methodist Bishops of the A.M.E., A.M.E. Zion, C.M.E. and United Methodist Churches,* Atlanta, Ga., Mar. 15-16, 1979.

68. *Encyclopedia of World Methodism,* vol. 2, pp. 2599-600; *World Methodist Council Handbook of Information,* 1976–1981, p. 29.
69. C. Eric Lincoln, *Race, Religion and the Continuing American Dilemma* (New York: Hill & Wang, 1984), pp. 118-22.
70. Barbara E. Campbell, *United Methodist Women in the Middle of Tomorrow* (New York: Women's Division, Board of Global Ministries, 1975), p. 58.
71. The Women's Division of the Board of Global Ministries officially relates to Church Women United through the head of the Women's Division, who is also Deputy General Secretary of the Board of Global Ministries.
72. *The World Council of Churches* (Geneva, Switzerland: World Council of Churches Publications Office, n.d.), p. 3.
73. Interreligious Foundation for Community Organization, *IFCO: Annual Report* (New York: IFCO Foundation, 1974), p. 21.
74. Uniting Conference, Dallas, *Daily Christian Advocate* (Apr. 29, 1968): p. 325.
75. Barbara R. Thompson was elected chairperson of the National Board of Project Equality in 1989. *New World Outlook* (Sept./Oct. 1989): 208.
76. *Newscope* (June 7, 1974): 4.
77. Herbert E. Stotts and Paul Deats, Jr., *Methodism and Society: Guidelines for Strategy* (Nashville: Abingdon Press, 1962), p. 257.
78. *Findings of Black Methodists for Church Renewal,* p. 1.
79. *The Book of Discipline of The United Methodist Church, 1972,* ¶ 846.
80. *Journal of the Eighth Session of the Central Jurisdictional Conference,* Nashville, Aug. 17-19, 1967, p. 7.
81. *The Book of Discipline of The United Methodist Church, 1980,* ¶ 1106.10.
82. Rosalie Whelan, "Political Empowerment," *Response* (July 1989): 18-19.
83. *Together* (Jan. 1972): 52-53; Graham, *Black United Methodists,* p. 139; "People," *Together* (Mar. 1972): "United Methodists in the News," 22.
84. "United Methodists in the News," *Together* (Feb. 1969): 16; Graham, *Black United Methodists,* p. 139; "Annual Meeting," *NOW,* Dec. 1988, p. 5; *New York Times,* Oct. 27, 1985 see. 1, p. 17, "Black Judge Elected," *Jet* (Apr. 22, 1985): 5; William C. Matney, ed., *Who's Who Among Black Americans* (Northbrook, Ill.: Who's Who Among Black Americans, Inc., Publishing Co., 1976), p. 286.
85. W. A. Low and V. A. Clift, ed., *Encyclopedia of Black America* (New York: Da Capo Press, 1981), p. 707.
86. Ralph and Nell Mohney, *Parable Churches,* pp. 5-7.
87. *To a Higher Glory,* p. 33.
88. Brian Lanker, *I Dream a World* (New York: Stewart, Tabori/Chang, 1989), p. 112.
89. "Foreword," in C. Eric Lincoln, *The Black Muslims in America* (Boston: Beacon Press, 1961).
90. Biographical sketch prepared for the editor.
91. Biographical sketch prepared for the editor.
92. Lanker, *I Dream a World,* p. 34.
93. Low and Clift, *Encyclopedia of Black America,* p. 435.
94. Lanker, *I Dream a World,* p. 132.
95. Low and Clift, *Encyclopedia of Black America,* p. 678.
96. Biographical sketch prepared for the editor.
97. Lanker, *I Dream a World,* p. 106.
98. Low and Clift, *Encyclopedia of Black America,* p. 677.

CHAPTER 7

1. Gunnar Myrdal, *The American Dilemma* (New York: Harper, 1944).
2. W. E. B. DuBois, *The Negro Church* (Atlanta: Atlanta University Press, 1903), p. 208.
3. William B. McClain, *Black People in the Methodist Church: Whither Thou Goest?* (Cambridge, Mass.: Schenkman Publishing Co., 1984), pp. 83-99, for a more detailed discussion.

4. From a statement from the keynote address at the first national meeting of what was initially called National Conference of Negro Methodists, later to be changed to Black Methodists for Church Renewal. Dr. Ernest A. Smith gave the address. The fuller statement was "From this day forward our dedication must be deep, our commitment sure and our action certain. God's work and way are contemporary in every age. There is no waiting for tomorrow—it is blasphemous to shunt the expectations from our time to another—it is cowardly and without faith to cry that the situation will adjust itself. Our time under God is now!"

5. See Gilbert H. Caldwell's article "Black Folks in White Churches," reprinted in *The Black Experience in Religion,* C. Eric Lincoln (Garden City, N.Y.: Anchor Books, 1974), pp. 29ff.

6. *Findings of Black Methodists for Church Renewal* (New York: Black Methodists for Church Renewal, 1968), p. 1.

7. Ibid., p. 2.

8. Published as *Findings of Black Methodists for Church Renewal.*

9. Ibid., p. 6.

10. See Black Methodists for Church Renewal, *Black Methodists for Church Renewal at the General Conference of the United Methodist Church* (Atlanta: Black Methodists for Church Renewal), pp. 1-3.

11. Ibid.

12. Negail R. Riley, *A Proposal for the Black Community Developers Program* (New York: Board of Global Ministries,) mimeographed, p. 2.

13. See McClain, *Black People in the Methodist Church,* p. 153.

14. John W. Coleman, "Black Community Developers: An Experiment in Relevance," (a report of the Black Community Developers Program to the 1972 General Conference, p. 5.

15. Ibid.

16. See Winston H. Taylor, "Religion and Race in the UMC," *New World Outlook,* vol. LXXVII, no. 7, July-August, 1987 (New York: Board of Global Ministries, UMC), pp. 10ff.

17. Ibid., p. 16.

18. See William B. McClain, *Traveling Light* (New York: Friendship Press, 1981), p. x.

19. The hymn, "Just As I Am, Without One Plea" by Charlotte Elliot.

CHAPTER 8

1. C. Eric Lincoln, "Retrospection", *This Road Since Freedom,* unpublished anthology. Quoted in his book, Race, Religion and the Continuing American Dilemma. (New York: Hill and Wang, 1984), p. 170.

2. See William B. McClain, *Black People in the Methodist Church* . . . for a fuller discussion of Blacks in Methodism from the First Methodist Society at Sam's Creek, Frederick County, Maryland through the 1984 General Conference. Also see William B. McClain, "Black People in United Methodism: Remnant or Residue?" *Quarterly Review* Vol. 4, no. 1 (Spring 1984): pp. 96-100.

3. C. Eric Lincoln, *Race, Religion, and the Continuing American Dilemma* (New York: Hill & Wang, 1984), p. 170 p. 189.

4. James S. Thomas, "From This Day Forward", (unpublished paper), 1987, pp. 2-3

5. Winston H. Taylor, "Religion and Race in UMC", *New World Outlook* (July-August, 1987): pp. 10-19.

6. Lincoln, Race, Religion, p. 189.

7. Gilbert H. Caldwell, "Courage, Confession, Creativity," *Circuit Rider* (May, 1988).

8. Ibid.

9. Ibid.

10. "Daily Christian Advocate": Proceedings of the General Conference of The United Methodist Church (Baltimore, May 12, 1984), Roundup Edition, No. 14, p. 1

BIBLIOGRAPHY

Addo, Linda D., and James H. McCallum. *To Be Faithful to Our Heritage: A History of Black United Methodism in North Carolina.* Raleigh, N.C.: Western North Carolina Annual Conference, The United Methodist Church, 1980.

Allen, Richard. *The Life Experiences and Gospel Labors of the Rt. Rev. Richard Allen.* Nashville: Abingdon Press, 1983. Reprint.

Baldwin, Lewis V. *"Invisible" Strands in African Methodism: A History of the African Union Methodist Protestant and Union American Methodist Episcopal Churches, 1805–1980.* Metuchen, N.J.: Scarecrow Press, 1983.

Barclay, Wade C. *History of Methodist Missions.* 4 vols. New York: Board of Missions, The Methodist Church, 1949–1973.

Beheney, J. Bruce, and Paul H. Eller. *The History of The Evangelical United Brethren Church.* Ed. by Kenneth W. Krueger. Nashville: Abingdon Press, 1979.

Bethea, Joseph H. "Black Methodists in North Carolina." In *Methodism Alive in North Carolina: A Volume Commemorating the Bicentennial of the Carolina Circuit.* Edited by Kelly O. Ingram. Durham, N.C.: Duke University Divinity School and the North Carolina and Western North Carolina Conference, The United Methodist Church, 1976.

Brawley, James P. *Two Centuries of Methodist Concern: Bondage, Freedom and Education of Black People.* New York: Vantage Press, 1974.

Bronson, Oswald P. "The Origin and Significance of the Interdenominational Theological Center." Ph.D. dissertation, Northwestern University, 1965.

Brooks, William E., ed. *From Saddlebags to Satellites: A History of Florida Methodism.* Nashville: Florida Annual Conference, The United Methodist Church, 1969.

Bucke, Emory S., ed. *History of American Methodism.* 3 vols. Nashville: Abingdon Press, 1964.

Case, Riley B. *Understanding Our New United Methodist Hymnal.* Wilmore, Ky.: Bristol Books, 1989.

Clair, Matthew W. "Methodism and the Negro." In *Methodism.* Edited by William K. Anderson. Nashville: The Methodist Publishing House, 1947.

Clark, Elmer T., ed. *The Journals and Letters of Francis Asbury.* 3 vols. Nashville: Abingdon Press, 1958.

Cranston, Earl. *Breaking Down the Walls.* New York: The Methodist Book Concern, 1915.

Crum, Mason. *The Negro in The Methodist Church.* New York: Division of Education and Cultivation, Board of Missions and Church Extension, The Methodist Church, 1951.

Culver, Dwight W. *Negro Segregation in The Methodist Church*. New Haven, Conn.: Yale University Press, 1953.

Daniel, W. Harrison. "The Methodist Episcopal Church and the Negro in the Early National Period." *Methodist History* 11 (January 1973): 40-53.

Del Pino, Julius E. "Black Leadership in The United Methodist Church: An Historical Review and Empirical Study." Ph.D. dissertation, Northwestern University, 1976.

Diffendorfer, Ralph E., ed. *The World Service of the Methodist Episcopal Church*. New York: Council of Boards of Benevolence, The Methodist Episcopal Church, 1923.

Echols, Timothy B. *Pioneering in Religious Education: Four Decades in The Methodist Church*. New York: Exposition Press, 1964.

Farish, Hunter D. *The Circuit Rider Dismounts: A Social History of Southern Methodism*. Richmond, Va.: The Dietz Press, 1938.

Felton, Ralph A. *The Ministry of the Central Jurisdiction of The Methodist Church*. Madison, N.J.: Drew Theological Seminary, 1951.

Freedmen's Aid Society of the Methodist Episcopal Church. *Annual Reports*, 1868–1912.

Gadsden, James S., ed. *Experiences, Struggles and Hopes of the Black Church*. Nashville: Tidings, 1974.

Graham, John H. "Black Methodists in the South Central Jurisdiction." In *One in the Lord: A History of Ethnic Minorities in the South Central Jurisdiction, The United Methodist Church*. Ed. Walter N. Vernon. Oklahoma City, Okla.: Commission on Archives and History, South Central Jurisdiction, The United Methodist Church, 1977.

———. *Black United Methodists: Retrospect and Prospect*. New York: Vantage Press, 1979.

———. *Mississippi Circuit Riders, 1865–1965*. Nashville: Parthenon Press, 1967.

Gravely, William B. *Gilbert Haven: Methodist Abolitionist*. Nashville: Abingdon Press, 1972.

Hagood, Lewis M. *The Colored Man in the Methodist Episcopal Church*. Cincinnati: Cranston & Stowe; New York: Hunt & Eaton, 1890.

Handy, Frederick J. "History of The Delaware (Annual) Conference of The Methodist Church." Unpublished mimeographed document.

Harmon, Nolan B., ed. *Encyclopedia of World Methodism*. Nashville: United Methodist Publishing House, 1974.

To a Higher Glory: The Growth and Development of Black Women Organized for Mission in The Methodist Church, 1940–1968. Cincinnati: Women's Division, Board of Global Ministries, The United Methodist Church, 1978.

Hoover, Theressa. *With Unveiled Face: Centennial Reflections on Men and Women in the Community of the Church*. New York: Women's Division, General Board of Global Ministries, The United Methodist Church, 1983.

Jason, William C., Sr. "A History of the Delaware Annual Conference of the Methodist Episcopal Church from 1864 to 1924." Unpublished mimeographed document.

Jenkins, Warren M. *Steps Along the Way: The Origin and Development of The South Carolina Conference of the Central Jurisdiction of The Methodist Church*. Columbia: State Printing Co. for Socamead Press, 1967.

Johnson, Douglas W. *A Study of Former Central Jurisdiction Church Data, 1974–1984*. New York: National Program Division, General Board of Global Ministries, The United Methodist Church, 1987.

Joint Commission on Unification of the Methodist Episcopal Church and the Methodist Episcopal Church South Proceedings. 3 vols. Nashville and New York: Publishing

House of the Methodist Episcopal Church, South, and the Methodist Book Concern, 1920.

Jones, Ralph H. *Charles Albert Tindley: Prince of Preachers*. Nashville: Abingdon Press, 1982.

King, Willis J. "The Negro Membership of the Former Methodist Church in the New United Methodist Church." *Methodist History* 7 (April 1969): 32-43.

Lester, Woodie D. *The History of the Negro and Methodism in Arkansas and Oklahoma: The Little Rock-Southwest Conference, 1838-1972*. Little Rock, Ark.: Little Rock Conference, The United Methodist Church, 1979.

Licorish, Joshua E. *Harry Hosier, African Pioneer/Preacher, Including Brief History of African Zoar Methodist Church, Founded 1794, Philadelphia, Pennsylvania*. Philadelphia: Afro-Methodist Associates, 1967.

Lincoln, C. Eric. *The Black Church Since Frazier*. New York: Schocken, 1974.

Loud, Ira B. "Methodism and the Negroes." In *History of Texas Methodism*. Edited by Olin W. Nail. Austin: Capital Printing Co., 1961.

McClain, William B. *Black People in The Methodist Church: Whither Thou Goest?* Cambridge, Mass.: Schenkman Publishing Co., 1984.

Moore, John M. *The Long Road to Methodist Union*. New York/Nashville: Abingdon/Cokesbury, 1943.

Morrow, Ralph E. *Northern Methodism and Reconstruction*. Ann Arbor: Michigan State University Press, 1956.

Murray, Peter C. "Christ and Caste in Conflict: Creating a Racially Inclusive Methodist Church." Ph.D. dissertation, Indiana University, 1985.

Norwood, Frederick A. *The Story of American Methodism*. Nashville: Abingdon Press, 1974.

———. *Sourcebook of American Methodism*. Nashville: Abingdon Press, 1982.

Oakes, Henry N., Jr. "The Struggle for Racial Equality in the Methodist Episcopal Church: The Career of Robert E. Jones." Ph.D. dissertation, University of Iowa, 1973.

Richardson, Harry V. *Dark Salvation: The Story of Methodism as It Developed Among Blacks in America*. Garden City, N.Y.: Doubleday, 1976.

———. *Walk Together Children: The Story of the Birth and Growth of the Interdenominational Theological Center*. Atlanta: The ITC Press, 1981.

Riley, Walter H. *Forty Years in the Lap of Methodism, 1869-1909: History of Lexington Conference*. Louisville, Ky.: Mayes Printing Co., 1915.

Shaw, J. Beverly F. *The Negro in the History of Methodism*. Nashville: Parthenon Press, 1954.

Shockley, Grant S., Earl D. C. Brewer, and Marie Townsend. *Black Pastors and Churches in United Methodism*. Atlanta: Center for Research in Social Change, Emory University, 1976.

Simpson, Matthew. *Cyclopedia of Methodism*. Philadelphia: Everts/Stewart, 1878.

Skelton, David E. *History of Lexington Conference*. Published by the author, 1950.

Sledge, Robert Watson. *Hands on the Ark: The Struggle for Change in the M. E. Church, South, 1914-1939*. Lake Junaluska, N.C.: General Commission on Archives and History, The United Methodist Church, 1975.

Smith, Warren T. *Harry Hosier, Circuit Rider*. Nashville: Discipleship Resources, 1981.

Straughn, James H. *Inside Methodist Union*. Nashville/New York: The Methodist Publishing House, 1958.

Taylor, Prince A., Jr. "A History of Gammon Theological Seminary." Ed.D. dissertation, New York University, 1948.

Thomas, I. L., ed. *Methodism and the Negro*. New York: Eaton/Mains, 1910.

Thomas, James S. "The Central Jurisdiction: Dilemma and Opportunity." *Drew Gateway* 34 (Spring 1964):119-27.

Wesley, John. *The Works of John Wesley.* Grand Rapids, Mich.: Zondervan Publishing House, 1958–1959.

Williams, M. O., Jr. *The Involvement of Ethnic Minority Persons in Overseas Missions in The United Methodist Church and Its Predecessors, 1942–1977.* New York: World Division, Board of Global Ministries, The United Methodist Church, 1978.

Wogaman, J. Philip. *Methodism's Challenge in Race Relations: A Study of Strategy.* Boston: Boston University Press, 1960.

Woolever, Harry E. *The High Road of Methodism.* Washington, D.C.: Commission on Methodist Union, ca. 1939.

Black Community Developers Program, 294-96
Black Consciousness Movement, 209, 233, 247
Black Methodists for Church Renewal (BMCR) 206-7, 210, 220, 222, 225-28, 236-37, 254, 272-74, 288-92
Black missionaries, 232
Black Power, 265, 286-92
Black Remnant, 18-19, 43
Black Revolution, 128, 224-26, 233, 236, 271
Black Staff Forums, 231
Black Staff Task Force (GBGM) 231
Black Student Revolution, 141
Black Studies movement, 247
Black Theology, 237-38, 247, 250-51, 253-54, 265-66, 288
Black United Methodist Clergywomen's Association, 259
Blackwell, John A., 238
Blair, Eugene A., 233
Blake, Elias, 243
Board of Church and Society, 274-75
Board of Christian Social Concerns, 145, 148, 274-75
Board of Publications, 277
Board of Missions and Church Extension, 72, 125
Board of Pensions, 155-56
Board of Social and Economic Relations, 145-46
Boston University School of Theology, 257
Boswell, Hamilton T., 216
Bowen, John Wesley Edward, Sr. (photo), 70, 82, 83, 85, 87, 91-92, 143
Bowen, John Wesley Edward, Jr., 149, 1559, 160-61
Bowen, Margaret Davis, 133, 161
Boylan Home, 79
Brawley, James P., 126, 143, 170, 197, 242, 337
Briddell, David W., 151, 267, 278
Bridges, Ramsey M., 158, 215
Bronson, Oswald P., 243, 250, 252
Brooks, Robert Nathaniel, 61, 70, 86, 143, 149, 152, 159, 164, 200
Brooks, Walter H., 43, 93-94
Brown, Allen L., 261, 277
Brown, Benjamin, 57
Brown, Dorothy L., 170
Brown, Morris, 31
Brown, Willie, 279
Browning Home/Mather Academy, 79
Brumbry, Grace, 169
Bryan, John L., 148, 151, 277
Bryant, Fletcher J., 234, 238
Bureau of Negro Work, 66

Burney, Harry L., Jr., 220
Burns, Betty, 277
Burns, Francis, 46, 54, 67
Burrell, Emma P. H., 155, 258
Burton, M. Garlinda, 277
Butler, F. H., 70
Bynum, Alvin, S., 150

Cabean, Daisy M., 134
Caldwell, Charles W., 124, 152
Caldwell, Gilbert H., 215, 221, 258, 303-4
Calhoun, Ernestine A., 237, 278
California, 78
Campbell, James F., 277, 278
Camphor, Alexander P., 66, 67
Campus ministry, 247-49
Candler School of Theology, 251, 256
Cape May (NJ) meeting, 103
Capers, William, 37, 65, 68
Carrington, John E., 215, 218
Carroll, Edward G., 158, 212, 218
Carter, Hazo D., 243
Carter, William T., 219
Cartwright, John H., 256, 257
Cary, Pauline, 155
Catchings, Rose M., 127
Cartwright, Solomon, 66
Centenary Church, Charleston, SC, 45
Centenary Biblical Institute, 73
Central Alabama Annual Conference, 60
Central Alabama College, 72
Central Christian Advocate, 67, 86, 126, 148-49, 275, 311
Central Church, Atlanta, 44
Central Jurisdiction, 20, 99, 114-15, 117-18, 145, 147, 189-207, 286-88, 301
Central Jurisdiction Conference, 1940 (photo), 159
Central Jurisdiction Conference, 1952 (photo)
Central Jurisdiction Conference, 1960, 139
Central Jurisdiction Daily Christian Advocate, 149-50
Central Jurisdiction Study Committee (photo)
Central Mission Conference, 63
Central Missouri Annual Conference, 62, 64
Central Tennessee College, 72-73, 83
Central West Annual Conference, 63
Champion, James, 51
Chaplains, Armed Forces, 316-17
Charleston, John, 50, 68
Charter of Racial Policies, 136
Childress, R. C., 89
Chisholm, Shirley, 283-84
Christentery, Inez, 150
Christian education, 67-70, 137-40, 235-39
Christian Endeavor Movement, 68
Christian Methodist Episcopal Church (CME), 131, 262